Revolutions Thwarted: Poland, South Africa, Iran, Brazil, and the Legacies of Communism

John Rose

Edited by Alex Callinicos and George Paizis

Revolutions Thwarted: Poland, South Africa, Iran, Brazil, and the Legacies of Communism
by John Rose

Edited by Alex Callinicos and George Paizis

Published 2025 by Bookmarks Publications
c/o 1 Bloomsbury Street, London WC1B 3QE

Cover design by Simon Assaf
Typeset by Simon Assaf

Printed by Halstan, Amersham HP6 6HJ

ISBN paperback 978-1-917020-41-1
Kindle 978-1-917020-42-8
ePub 978-1-917020-43-5
PDF 978-1-917020-44-2

Cover Image: First Quds Day, 17 August 1979 Tehran, Iran.

CONTENTS

ACKNOWLEDGEMENTS

This book is based on a PhD Thesis, "Workers' Power and the Failure of Communism", awarded by King's College London in 2020. I would like to thank my supervisor, Stathis Kouvelakis, for his tremendous support, intellectual stimulation and patience; my partner, the Iranian academic and writer Elaheh Rostami-Povey, for her support, intellectual stimulation and patience; Alex Callinicos, ex-editor of the journal *International Socialism* for encouraging me to start my PhD; Andrzej Zebrowski of *Pracownicza Demokracja* (*Workers Democracy*) in Warsaw, Poland for guidance on locating professional Polish language translators and our intensive discussions about the politics and history of the Solidarity period; Professor Kate Alexander, retired Research Chair in Social Change, University of Johannesburg, for appointing me Research Associate for the period of the PhD and helping me locate vital primary and secondary sources; my friend Peyman Jafari, Iranian scholar and expert on the role of the Iranian oil workers in the 1979 Revolution, again for helping me locate vital primary and secondary sources; and Dr Stephanie Cronin, Iran specialist, for reading and commenting on the Iran chapter. Thanks also to Palestinian Professor Nur Masalha and Iraqi scholar Sami Ramadani for their professional support for my original PhD application. Last, but not least, I'd like to express my gratitude to those who agreed to be interviewed by me—activists in different political traditions in the four countries studied in this book.[1]

John Rose

EDITORS' PREFACE

John Rose fell ill while working on the publication of this book, and so was unable to complete this task. So the two of us, old friends and comrades of John's, took over getting his book ready for publication. Alas, John died on 30 October 2024. So he didn't live to see the book published, though he knew it was coming out. It remains very much John's own work; we have concentrated primarily on editing his text. It is a very original book, which not only compares the trajectory of four mass workers' movements in the late 20th century, in Poland, South Africa, Iran, and Brazil, but draws on a very rich group of interviews John conducted with leading activists involved in these movements. This in itself makes the book a very valuable historical document, exploring the destabilising and radicalising effects of rapid industrialisation beyond the "centre" of the global capitalist system (other examples of this pattern might be Greece, Portugal, and South Korea). But the book and interviews also show John relentlessly pursuing the political lessons of what all proved to be missed opportunities for the Marxist left. This makes it of great relevance to the revolutionary movements unfolding in the 21st century.

John's original PhD thesis covered Poland, South Africa, and Iran. The thesis examiners—Steve Smith and Marcel van der Linden—suggested that when revising it for publication John add a fourth case study on Brazil. With characteristic energy, John took up their advice. His research was the basis of an article, "Year Zero 1989: two Trotskyisms and the workers' movement in Brazil", published in *International Socialism*, 2.172, in October 2021. We would like to thank the editor, Joseph Choonara, for allowing us to include a revised version as Chapter 5 of this book.

We are also grateful for the help of Elaheh Rostami-Povey, Valerio Arcary, Claire Ceruti, and Andrzej Zebrowski, not to mention the encouragement of Mark Thomas of Bookmarks.

Alex Callinicos and George Paizis

FOREWORD

The reader should not be deceived by appearances: this book is a highly unusual object. It originates in a doctoral thesis, which I supervised at King's College London. From a purely academic perspective, this work met all the standard requirements, that is a combination of scholarship and research bringing new material to the study of its object. And yet, the profile of its author couldn't contrast more sharply with that of an average PhD candidate: not a young researcher orienting herself toward academia but a lifelong militant, John Rose, who, after a long journey, came to the "conclusion that a fundamental re-think was required on [his] part" about what has been the aim of his entire political life: the possibility of a socialist revolution. Or, more precisely, he decided exploring the reasons for its failure could show, by contrast, alternative possibilities that might lead to a different outcome in the future.

To be productive, this questioning needed to be properly, that is historically, situated in such a way that made empirical research meaningful. The perspective adopted was a comparative one: studying three moments—to which a fourth was eventually added—during which a rising workers' movement had reached a point where a radical break with the existing social order appeared as a concrete possibility: Iran in 1979, Poland in 1980, South Africa and Brazil in the late 1980s. To these case studies John applied a research question formulated as follows: "How and why did independent workers' movements that played a decisive role in removing tyrannies in these countries but then lose the political initiative. But a further question is buried in the phrase 'lose the political initiative'. What does that mean? The implicit implication is that workers could have carried forward the political struggle in their own interests. But that would have required self-belief in such an audacious challenge to the new post-revolutionary status quo which, in different forms, emerged in all four countries, and in different forms capitulated to neoliberalism."

The project of a monograph dealing with this issue from such a comparative standpoint was in itself quite an original endeavour. But also a promising one since it allowed a proper historicisation of the object of study and facilitated the collection of fresh material, which took the form of interviews with a significant sample of protagonists of these movements, fortunately close enough chronologically to us for many of them to be still alive. There is another important implication deriving from this apparently trivial observation: these four cases are all situated in the last decade of what Eric Hobsbawm called the "short twentieth century". This is a period relatively neglected from the perspective of its revolutionary possibilities, since it is usually assimilated to the rise into power of neoliberalism—with Thatcher and Reagan's victories in 1979-80 acting as the decisive landmarks.

This rise paved unquestionably the ground for neoliberalism's global triumph in the decades following the collapse of the Soviet bloc. But this is only the retrospective judgment of history. And, as Daniel Bensaïd strongly emphasized, there are good reasons to be sceptical about this kind of judgment: "the temptation is strong to appeal to the old capital fetishes of History or Humanity, [and] to slip from the historical judgment that is always under appeal to the definitive tribunal of History".[2] This study takes the side of a such a "historical judgment" contradicting "the definitive tribunal" of History understood as the inert sum of accomplished facts in demonstrating, with solid empirical evidence, that this course of events is itself based on repressed possibilities that have to be patiently uncovered. To be accomplished, this task needed to go beyond the boundaries of standard academic research while meeting its requirements for theoretical rigour and empirical validation. It needed the combination of partisanship, intellectual honesty and a critical distance. That was the challenge which John took seriously, as he did with everything else he undertook, and which brought him to a result that deserves to be taken equally seriously by everyone interested not just in the history, but, above all, in the future of revolutionary politics.

The horizon for this sort of praxis looks presently rather bleak. To reemerge as a credible perspective a radical rethinking of past experience is indispensable, albeit not sufficient in itself. Seen from that angle, the missed opportunities of the 1980s, which constitute the object of the following inquiry, might give some crucial missing keys. As John writes in the above cited passage, these peaks of the self-activity of the working class encountered defeat, as did most previous revolutionary moments, but this defeat took a particular form: it was a "capitulation to neoliberalism", a capitulation coming *from within* these movements. The root of such a regressive dialectic is strongly underlined in the chapters devoted to each of these cases: it was the search of a "compromise" that proved illusory, or, at the very least, synonymous with the abandonment of the emancipatory possibilities emerging from these mass movements. In Poland, the idea of a "self-limiting revolution" ultimately brought the reconstituted Solidarność leading the "transition" from "socialism" to neoliberal capitalism; in South Africa, the great compromise put an end to apartheid while perpetuating one of the most unequal capitalist societies of the planet; in Brazil, the rightwards drift of Lula's PT (Workers' Party) delivered a modestly "social" management of the neoliberal order. Only in Iran did a proper revolution happen, which, without abolishing capitalism, amounted to some significant gains for the dominated classes. But, in this case, on top of lacking an independent leadership, the workers' movement was only a component of a broader popular insurrection which overthrew a dictatorial regime subjected to Western imperialism.

As appears clearly throughout these case studies (with the exception of Brazil), the gap between the transformative potential of these movements and the results they achieved is not an accidental outcome. It is inscribed in the very form taken by these movements, more precisely in its internal limitations. The notion of "revolutionary syndicalism" seems appropriate for such a discussion. John adopts the definition of this term proposed by the Iranian sociologist Asef Bayat as "workers' action confined to the industrial workplace, assuming in principle that social relations at the point of production were the determining factor in the social structure". When theorised, as with Georges Sorel and the early 20th century French radical unionism, a further implication should be added: the organised form of this action. The trade union, the factory council or committee, or a combination of both, is seen not only as the "determining factor" but also as the central, if not the sole legitimate actor, of social change. As John emphasizes, this conception "raises the crucial question: can workers seize control of the means of production without confronting the state?". As experience indicates, the answer can only be negative, but the reasons need to be clarified. It does indeed appear that the trade union, even of an insurgent type such as Solidarność, or the workers' councils, or any other form of self-organisation at the workplace, is inadequate to confront the issue of state power in its own terms. But this issue is nevertheless raised by the very dynamic of intense class struggle that inevitably transcends the limitations of pure economic or local demands and acquires a political dimension. Hence what can be described as the aporia of the political, a blockage that led these movements to a dead end, and ultimately to capitulation and defeat.

This aporia is twofold: as organisations aiming to regroup and unify the entirety of a class, they are the site of contradictory political options, which makes it difficult, if not impossible, to raise by themselves to the level of strategic initiative that is necessary to articulate an alternative to the established state power. But they also appear insufficient to constitute as such an alternative institutional framework able to manage both the economy and the overall social activity at the scale of a country. The objections to the project of an "active strike", which, if successful, would inevitably have led to the overthrow of the Polish government, formulated by Karol Modzelewski, a key figure of the left of Solidarność, as quoted in these pages, appear in that respect quite convincing: "Modzelewski thought the project of an active strike unrealistic. An active strike in a national economy means taking over economic power. The union lacked the apparatus to do that. 'Let's imagine that now; our union has—on the scale of national economy—to divide resources and supplies. On the scale of national economy. Who will do this? Factory councils? The Presidium of the National Commission?'" In South Africa, the "workerist" wing of the trade-union movement missed the properly political level of the strategy and alliances that could successfully overthrow the apartheid regime. It thus left the field clear for the "two-stages" approach of the Communist Party, which postponed social revolution to an indeterminate future. In Iran, the weakness of the Marxist left, combined with the mass appeal of political Islam in broader society, led to the shoras being quickly dominated by a centralised organisation linked to the Islamic movement, and, eventually, to the state institutions, under Khomeini's authority.

In all cases, the decisive political mediation, ie the political party, proved missing. Of course, it is not of any political party we are talking about here, but of a party able to provide leadership and propose a strategy that would allow a revolution to take place, in other terms of a "revolutionary party", however it is understood. In some cases, the failure of the workers' movement can be attributed to the negative role played by existing parties, that is, by the Communist parties of these countries. John puts strong emphasis on this aspect: "I argue that Soviet Communism, manifest in different forms, is a conservative factor in the revolutionary processes unleashed in Poland, South Africa, Iran, and Brazil. This is not a counterfactual, since I claim to provide empirical evidence to prove it. It follows that without the malign influence of Soviet Communism, different outcomes might have been possible." As far as oppositional Communist parties are concerned, this appears to have been the case in South Africa and, to a certain extent, in Iran. In Poland, the state itself was ruled by a Communist Party making it impossible for an independent mass workers' movement to reclaim an explicitly socialist agenda, despite the radical demands for self-management of production. In the two cases at the end of the decade

(South Africa and Brazil), the collapse of the Soviet system had profoundly disorienting consequences for the mass organisations of the left.

However, the trajectory of the Brazilian PT, a party entirely alien to Communist orthodoxy emerging out of the rise of radical trade-unionism in the late 1970s, indicates that the problem might be broader, and deeper, than the conservatism of Soviet Communism. And in all cases, one might wonder why in all these situations no revolutionary alternative seemed to have been able to play a noticeable political role. In one of his interviews quoted in the pages that follow, Zbigniew Kowalewski, a Solidarność leader in Łódź in 1980, suggests if not an answer, at least a possible direction of research: "The level of Marxist theoretical knowledge of the Soviet bloc as social formation was pitiful. There was not even a Marxist knowledge of the forms and particularities of the exploitation of the working class in the societies of the Soviet bloc. There was not a serious Marxist knowledge of the functioning of their economies and societies. There was not a serious theory of workers' democracy. Marxism was in crisis, but Marxists, with some rare exceptions, were not aware of it." In a famous text dated 1977, Louis Althusser diagnosed the "crisis of Marxism"[3], meaning both its inability to come to terms with the consequences of Stalinism and the blocking of revolutionary possibilities in the post-1968 conjuncture in Europe and beyond. As John writes, "The absence of a non-Stalinist Marxist theory and organisation proved decisive."

A further obstacle to the emergence of such a combination of theory and organisation is the fact that in the two cases at the crossroads of the 1970s and the 1980s, Iran and Poland, the place of socialism as a mass ideology was taken by another worldview, which, once again, proved unbeatable in terms of its capacity for mobilising the masses: religion. In the Arab-Muslim world, the failure of secular nationalism, tainted with some sort of socialist reference, led to the rise of political Islam as the focal point of movements contesting the post-colonial order and imperialist domination. In Poland, the powerful Catholic

Church, an institution embedded in the national identity of the country, provided an alternative space to a public sphere subjected to the total control of a party that claimed to be "Communist". True, the mass influence of religious ideologies didn't prevent the outbreak of radical workers' action in both countries, as abundantly demonstrated in the pages that follow. But it certainly acted as an impediment to the spread of socialist, and even more so of Marxist ideas and forms of organisation. In South Africa and Brazil, the socialist and Marxist left had no such competitor—in Brazil it was even the case that a strong left-radical current within Catholicism made a decisive contribution to the formation of the trade-union movement and of the PT. But, in the most crucial moment of the political developments in these countries, the left had to endure the consequences of the collapse of the Soviet bloc.

In all cases, a revolutionary alternative, in John's words "an internationalist and socialist counter claim on that legacy—as [Józef] Pinior [a figure of the left of Solidarność] put it: 'a real alternative not only to the Stalinist regime but to global capitalism', proved missing". John added: "Unfortunately, demonstrable proof that Marxism has been liberated from its Stalinist straitjacket is a precondition for achieving this, and it is a marker of the continuing failure of the remnant of the internationalist Marxist left, that this remains elusive a generation later." But, as suggested above, this absence should not be understood as the "final Judgment of History" but as a call for future work, for the reinvention of a theoretical and political praxis that remains faithful to the emancipatory tradition of Marxism and of the workers' movement.

Unfortunately, John didn't live long enough to see his effort taking the form of what the reader now has at hand. But he substantially won his wager. And this is not a minor achievement.

Stathis Kouvelakis

ANC Veterans' League

Condolences on the passing of Comrade John Rose

Dear Elaheh Rostami-Povey,

It is with heartfelt sorrow that we of the African National Congress Veterans League extend our condolences to you and your family, comrades and friends, on the passing of an outstanding internationalist, John Rose.

As a young student John was one of the celebrated band of London Recruits that assisted the South African liberation movement, in the darkest of periods in our struggle against Apartheid. On two occasions in 1969 and 1970 he carried out an extremely dangerous mission, with other comrades, in distributing the leaflets of the outlawed ANC in a daring operation, which is celebrated in the book and documentary film, The London Recruits.

John showed great determination and resolve in carrying out these missions and on one occasion would have been caught but for the revolutionary audacity and courage he displayed. Although the likes of comrade Rose, and other remarkable internationalists like him, have been extremely modest about the role they played, it was deeds like his that contributed to the overthrow of the heinous Apartheid system in our country. They were part of a glorious global solidarity movement that reinforced the struggle of our people.

We raise our flag in salutation to comrade John Rose, who we are well aware, remained a principled revolutionary all his life, and among other significant commitments, loyally served the working class of Britain, and was outstanding in his support for the freedom of the Palestinian people, as he was for all people fighting imperialism and colonialism.

Our world is poorer for the loss of John Rose, but richer for his outstanding contribution. His was a life well lived. He has an honoured place in the annals of South Africa's liberation history. Hamba Kahle Comrade John Rose.[4]

Sincerely,
Dr Snuki Zikalala
ANC VL President

INTRODUCTION

"What's Left?" asked the headline on a discussion of centenary books in 2017 on the October 1917 Russian Revolution.[5] Not much, concluded reviewer Sheila Fitzpatrick, also a historian of the revolution. The agonising of Eric Hobsbawm, arguably one of the last century's greatest historians, served as Fitzpatrick's guide. The Russian Revolution had been the central event of the 20th century for Hobsbawm, "far more profound and global" than the French Revolution a century earlier. Fitzpatrick argued that before 1991, this was a fairly standard view, even among historians who, unlike Hobsbawm, were neither Marxists nor Communists. But finishing his book *Age of Extremes*, on the "short" 20th century, running from 1914 to 1991, and the world the Russian Revolution had shaped, Hobsbawm noted it was now a "world that went to pieces at the end of the 1980s". It was a lost world—now being replaced by a post-20th-century world whose outlines could not yet be discerned. Today we might conclude that the outlines are now signalling something rather ominous.

Fitzpatrick quipped that nothing fails like failure, and for historians approaching the revolution's centenary the disappearance of the Soviet Union casts a pall: "The revolution, stripped of the old Marxist grandeur of historical necessity, turns out to look more or less like an accident. Workers—remember when people used to argue passionately about whether it was a workers' revolution? ... Socialism is so much of a mirage that it seems kinder not to mention it." She reports wanting to distance herself from this consensus even though she admits to being part of it, identifying herself as a contrarian. She warms to the one possible contrarian in the pack, science fiction novelist and former member of the Socialist Workers Party, turned, at least for this October "moment", popular historian, China Miéville. Yet we find even Miéville is a little half hearted. The world's first socialist revolution deserves celebration, he writes, because "things changed once, and they might do so again". "Liberty's dim light" shone briefly, even if "what might have been a sunrise [turned out to be] a sunset." In any case, Miéville is uneasy with the revolution's leader, Lenin, unable to deny his centrality but still keen to identify his mistakes and leaving a lingering sense of Lenin's possible undemocratic instincts. Now in 2017 was anyone ready to defend, uncompromisingly, not just the Russian Revolution but its acknowledged leader, Lenin? Well, yes, there was, Tariq Ali. And it is a great pity that Sheila Fitzpatrick didn't include Tariq Ali's book, *The Dilemmas of Lenin*, in her review.

Tariq Ali is the great survivor. Forever identified with the 1968 "revolution" in Britain, he has stayed the course, standing by its principles, not least still ready to defend "October 1917" as a faltering step forward for humanity, whatever its defects. In his book, he was determined to restore this humanity both to the revolution and its principal leader, Lenin, as well as offering plausible explanations for its failure. The book's unlikely title signals this intention, its contents resisting both Lenin's monstering in the west, as well as Stalin's sanctification of him in the east: cynical selections of his words given quasi-theological significance, providing a shroud concealing Stalin's counter revolution. Both the *Guardian* newspaper and the *New York Times* recognised the book's originality, each allowing the author a full page for a selected extract from the book. I reviewed it for *International Socialism* (Rose, 2017b). I am a 1968 contemporary of Tariq Ali. My first memory of him is sharing a platform appealing for opposition to the US war in Vietnam. I was a student at the London School of Economics (LSE), increasingly drawn to IS, the International Socialists, led by Tony Cliff, forerunners of today's Socialist Workers Party. Tariq was a member of a "rival" organisation, the International Marxist Group (IMG), part of the Fourth International, led by Ernest Mandel. IS and the IMG were the backbone of the Vietnam Solidarity Campaign in the UK, which led huge student demonstrations against the Vietnam war, most famously in battles with the police in Grosvenor Square, in front of the US embassy in 1968.

IS and the IMG had differing interpretations about what had gone wrong with the Russian Revolution. But both began their criticisms with Leon Trotsky's *The Revolution Betrayed* and the IMG was not unsympathetic to the IS 1968 slogan: Neither Washington nor Moscow but International Socialism. I was particularly interested in how Tariq Ali would frame these criticisms in his new book after all these years. International isolation and the civil war that followed the revolution devastated the post-revolutionary economy. We have Lenin warning at his 50th birthday party celebrations in 1920 (which he did not want) that the gloating and posturing about the civil war victory in the Bolshevik Party had to stop. Stalin was one of the worst offenders. Lenin appealed for modesty, a recognition of how little the Bolsheviks understood not just about industrial reconstruction but about industrialisation itself. Marxism contained no magical solutions for addressing the Bolsheviks' crisis, he warned. He attacked the petty privileges and indeed the outright corruption afflicting the growing party bureaucracy. Lenin's defence of bourgeois culture and his disdain for claims of a proletarian culture were part of his wider argument. Ali comes close to linking Lenin's repeated strokes, which would eventually kill him, to his increasing realisation that the continuing isolation of the revolution would destroy it. And in a passage that serves as an important marker for this thesis, we learn that the Bolsheviks' worker cadres had disappeared. Those who had not perished "were interspersed in the party and state bureaucracy... workers' control in the factories had to be abandoned" (Ali, 2017: 311-12).

Marcel van der Linden has described the events of 1968 as part of "one great transnational cycle of contention", which began in the late 1960s and continued to the mid-1970s. He agrees with Giovanni Arrighi and others who have likened 1968 to 1848—revolutions which failed but nevertheless left legacies which changed the world: increased self-confidence of former colonial peoples in the southern hemisphere, the wave of democratisation which put an end to many dictatorships, the increased assertiveness of workers' movements worldwide and the diminished power of "dominant status-groups" over "subordinate status-groups", youth, women, ethnic minorities (van der Linden 2003: 117). The revolutions or near-revolutions I describe in Poland, South Africa, Iran, and Brazil between 1979 and 1989 fit this pattern very well but one very troubling legacy has to be included. The democratisation wave was a factor in the implosion of Soviet Communism and its satellite states in 1989. But was the very idea of communism also a victim of this implosion? And are we not still grappling with *this* legacy today? We will have to return to these questions.

As the International Socialists began to grow amongst the would-be revolutionary students at the LSE in the late 1960s, organised by the university Socialist Society, familiarly known as LSE SocSoc, Tony Cliff became an ever more frequent visitor. He held a particular fascination for me because of his self-identity as a Palestinian Jew who had eschewed Zionism. I was a British middle class Jew who took Zionism for granted. Cliff, real name Ygael Gluckstein, had been born into a well-established, prosperous European Jewish Zionist settler family in British-controlled Palestine in the early part of the last century. His remarkable journey from this start-point to leading what became, in the latter part of the last century, Britain's largest Trotskyist organisation, cannot concern us here.[6] Nevertheless my encounter with him led to one of two turning points at the LSE which would set me on a life-time path in both the theory and practice of revolutionary socialism.

The first turning point came when LSE SocSoc organised a debate in response to the June 1967 war between Israel and Egypt and Syria. Jewish students sympathetic to LSE SocSoc were shocked. The debate took for granted that Israel was the villain, so it centred on whether Nasser, Egypt's world-famous anti-imperialist leader, would prosecute the war effectively by mobilising the Arab masses, workers and peasants across the Middle East or would be compromised by his dependence on the Soviet Union. Tony Cliff argued the latter point, predicting correctly that Nasser would lose the war. His main antagonist, Ronnie Kasrils, simultaneously a mature LSE student and secret underground operative for the ANC, the African National

Congress, the banned national liberation movement fighting South African apartheid, was far readier to defend Nasser. But it wasn't this argument that startled me the most (startling though it certainly was for a wannabe socialist who had worked enthusiastically on Israel's "socialist" kibbutz system the summer before), as much as the fact that Cliff and Kasrils were both Jews. Over the next few months as I became friendly with both of them, I discovered both to be completely at ease with their Jewish heritage. I was about to join their tiny, but nevertheless not un-influential, internationalist unofficial club of anti-Zionist, pro-Palestinian Arab Jews.[7]

The second turning point was France, May 1968, when the student revolt, and particularly the fierce fighting with the police in Paris, triggered the ten-million strong workers' occupation of French factories. "Students of the World, Ignite!", "Autogestion!" (self-management), were amongst the many slogans which caught the mood of that incredible moment. It was also the moment that I joined the International Socialists. Tony Cliff was fond of repeating to his student followers one of Marx's most famous aphorisms that the emancipation of the working class was the task of the working class itself. In my head what had seemed an abstraction, to use the jargon, had suddenly become "concrete". Cliff's enthusiasm for this statement was very much rooted in his anti-Stalinism. Workers' self-activity was counter-posed to reliance on great leaders. For sure workers needed leaders but workers would choose and test leaders through their own struggles, democratic accountability being absolutely essential. Two words, "workers' control", summed it up for Cliff. Workers' control of their own organisations, trade unions and workplace committee delegates tasked with negotiations with management, workers' control of their own political parties and, ultimately, workers' control of the means of production, with or without management,[8] and workers' control of the state. Cliff viewed the disintegration of workers' control, described by Tariq Ali, during the civil war following the October 1917 Revolution in Russia, as a fundamental weakening of the revolution, paving the way to its bureaucratisation and reversible only by its internationalisation, especially in Germany.[9]

In fact, the aphorism and its application to the "French May" raised more questions than it answered. The French working class did not emancipate itself in 1968. One reason was the conservative role played by France's most left-wing mass-based political party, its Communist Party which had long abandoned any perspective of socialist revolution. But that argument, in turn, raised the question of the role of a Marxist political party in the self-emancipation of the working class. Alongside that question, the workers' occupations of the French factories had raised another. Were we witnessing the first act of a socialist revolution, preparing the way for the formal seizure of the means of production by the working class? Certainly, as I discuss in much detail in Chapter 1 below, with one especially important qualification, this may be a legitimate application of a vital argument in Marx's and Engels's 1848 *Communist Manifesto*. And, indeed, the slogan of "Autogestion!", self-management, appeared to support this perspective. But that qualification raises the role of the state. Unarmed workers' occupations of factories face the prospect of a stand-off not just with the riot police but also with the army.[10]

As I was to learn over the following few days, weeks, months—for good reason LSE was earning the reputation as the University of Revolution, hundreds of its students engaged daily in hours of intense discussion in the bars, canteens, corridors, streets, often overflowing into the classroom whether the lecturers liked it or not—workers occupying their factories in the Hungarian Revolution of 1956 faced Soviet Russian tanks. Those tanks returned to demolish the "Prague Spring" in the Soviet Communist satellite state of Czechoslovakia in 1968. This was the antidote to the "French May" and it left 1968 very much as unfinished business.

But the International Socialists had taken off. High levels of activity were complemented by high levels of theoretical discussions. What amounted to a theoretical challenge to liberate

Marxism from its Stalinist straitjacket was as exhilarating intellectually as the constant round of student sit-ins, demos and increasing visits to striking workers' picket lines were exhilarating politically. The questions which were raised in the last paragraph were debated almost daily, remain partly unresolved, and form the basic intellectual framework of this thesis. Amongst the LSE students, the International Socialists' Chris Harman was the most talented, intellectually and politically. Tragically he died aged 66 in Cairo, following a cardiac arrest. Michael Rosen, Oxford University student in 1968, poet, broadcaster and former Children's Laureate, knew him well, and his *Guardian* obituary gives good insight into Chris's under-recognised significance:

> In 2005 Chris Harman was writing about how the 30-year project to publish the collected works of Marx and Engels was done. It is 50 volumes long and he was reviewing Vol. 50, having read the previous 49 one by one as they had appeared. Of course, he had read them all. Harman was never satisfied with second-hand summaries.
>
> I remember hearing Chris speak at LSE, one moment alongside Danny Cohn-Bendit, the next with a shop steward from the occupation of the Renault factory in France, another at a demonstration against the Vietnam war. At one meeting, I recall how it seemed incredible to some that he could support Vietnam's fight against the US but be critical of Ho Chi Minh's Communist party. The events in Paris and the rest of France, he would claim, proved the point: existing parties claiming to be Marxist were unwilling and unable to make a revolution.
>
> Everything Chris did over the next 40 years was geared towards creating a political party that was able and willing. With IS and its successor, the Socialist Workers Party, he spent his life speaking, writing, editing, organising and campaigning. He was editor of the *International Socialism*

Journal from 2004 and had previously edited *Socialist Worker* for more than two decades. In conversation his eyes would move between the middle distance and the floor, his ears picking up on every word, his replies indicating that he was relating what you were saying to the library in his head.

He didn't finish the PhD but produced a constant stream of articles, editorials and books: the book that would become *Class Struggles in Eastern Europe* (originally published in 1974 as *Bureaucracy and Revolution in Eastern Europe*), which developed the theory that the Soviet bloc was "state capitalist"; a history of the German revolution in *The Lost Revolution: Germany 1918 to 1923* (1983); and the Marxist classic *A People's History of the World* (1999). At various times, his articles, which mostly homed in on the economics of the moment, coagulated into books: *Explaining the Crisis* appeared in 1984, and this year he produced *Zombie Capitalism.*

His style of speaking was rapid but analytic, good on irony and contradiction; his lifestyle frugal in the extreme. He was never tempted by academe or celebrity. It was always a regret and an irritation to me why newspaper and TV debates about wars or the state of global capitalism did not call on him (Rosen, 2009).[11]

In 1968 Chris Harman had grappled with what seemed to be 1968's spontaneous call for a student-worker alliance, following France's May '68. Yet it was notoriously short-lived and, in any case, arguably, it failed. Yet the idea had caught the imagination. Chris addressed it in a pamphlet essay, "Party and Class" (Harman: 1996), which also deserves to be ranked as a classic 1968 text. He argued that the best way to unite workers and students was in a new revolutionary party where the interaction between students and workers would benefit both groups. He built a powerful case for the creation of worker-intellectuals, juxtaposing and dovetailing several celebrated passages about the crowd in history, from the writings of Italian Marxist philosopher Antonio Gramsci.[12]

Chris also contributed to a document which definitely does rank as a classic 1968 text, The "Open Letter to the Polish Communist Party" by Jacek Kuroń and Karol Modzelewski. Kuroń and Modzelewski were young Communist dissidents in one of Soviet Communism's most strategically important military outposts in Eastern Europe, its Warsaw Pact ally Poland. Their *Open Letter*, written in 1964, was a closely argued critical Marxist analysis of Polish society. It identified bitter social class divisions, with the Polish "Communist" state bureaucracy playing the equivalent role of a capitalist ruling class, extracting surplus value from Polish workers on shockingly low pay and terrible working conditions with no control either of the work process or the product of their labour. In 1965 Kuroń and Modzelewski were thrown into jail for this "provocation", the Polish government thereby dramatising the prestige and authority of the *Open Letter*. It began its travels across the Polish border, in various forms, to an increasingly receptive audience on both sides of the so-called iron curtain.

In Britain, the International Socialists enthusiastically welcomed the *Open Letter*. Its analysis was strikingly similar to the state capitalist analysis of Stalin's Russia, pioneered by the IS founder Tony Cliff (Cliff, 1988). Cliff had argued that Stalin's industrialisation drive in Russia in the 1930s not only consolidated his very personalised totalitarian dictatorship but also that the state bureaucracy became "an extreme and pure personification of capital" (Cliff, 1988: 168). The need to catch up with the West, both economically and especially militarily, exerted competitive pressure to accumulate, similar to the competitive pressure on capitalist firms. Accumulation of capital by the state, based on the forcible extraction of surplus value from workers, at the expense of their consumption needs, was also dependent on the crude "expropriation of the peasantry" (Cliff,

1988: 50-55). In *Capital*, Marx had called this process "primitive accumulation...a history...written...in letters of blood and fire" when describing it in Britain (Cliff, 1988: 54). Cliff noted that "Stalin accomplished in a few hundred days what Britain took a few hundred years to do" (Cliff, 1988: 54). The language of "Socialism in One Country" masked the genocidal exploitative processes unleashed. Lenin had explicitly warned against any attempt at socialism in one country (Cliff 1988: 144-45).[13]

The IS published an English language version of the *Open Letter* in 1966.[14] Confirmation of the group's most iconic political perspective could hardly have sprung from a more authoritative source. It helped enhance IS's reputation and influence in the UK student movement. Chris Harman wrote an introduction to the *Open Letter* and helped its promotion among students. It also intensified the already infectious campus arguments, with several questions reoccurring: why had "Communism" failed to live up to its ideals? How can "Communism" be an answer to the failures of capitalism and the barbarities of its offspring, imperialism? The *Open Letter* provided a platform in the search for answers.

In the 1970s I worked as an unpaid then paid full-timer for the International Socialists. I helped build a workplace IS branch amongst the engineering and maintenance workers at Heathrow Airport. I also worked as a journalist on *Socialist Worker* and was briefly one of the paper's editors during the upheavals which afflicted all the post-1968 revolutionary groups in the late 1970s, as it became apparent that the much awaited revolution had, shall we say, been postponed... In the 1980s I tried my luck as a freelance journalist writing regularly about the 1984-5 miners' strike for the *New Statesman*. But I needed a proper job and drifted into teaching sociology at a further education college. In fact, I was becoming more and more preoccupied with the Israeli oppression of the Palestinians. For the next 20 years I was to become in effect the SWP's "Comrade Anti-Zionism", its Jewish "expert" on the Israeli-Palestinian conflict.[15]

But in the last few years I became increasingly frustrated with this political role. As the beginning of this Introduction suggested, 1989, and the collapse of Soviet Communism, transformed the political landscape. And whilst I contest the extreme pessimistic conclusions drawn, there is no doubt that the non-Stalinist Marxist Left took part of the hit and has been on the ideological defensive ever since. This was both proved and exacerbated by the 2008 financial crisis which, whilst it may have lent itself to claims of the continuing relevance of Marx's theoretical analyses of the intrinsic crisis-prone character of contemporary capitalism, it in no way significantly revived Marxist influence on contemporary workers' movements. On the contrary, the much famed "global elite" succeeded in imposing harsh austerity measures on the working class globally, making the poor pay for *their* crisis. This has allowed a spectacular rise of the far right, manipulating anti-globalisation sentiment, redirecting the legitimate popular hostility towards the "global elite" by mobilising nation-state nationalism as the vehicle for opposition. They have often succeeded in dragging along sections of workers, left rudderless by their traditional organisations, trade unions, and parliamentary labour and socialist parties alike.

A series of defeats for left wing movements especially in Latin America and southern Europe has exacerbated this situation. The most serious defeat, though, was that of the "Arab Spring" which erupted in 2011. The revolt in Egypt was its spearhead and whilst Egyptian workers played a significant part, neither they nor the independent Marxist left were able to provide leadership to the movement (Alexander and Bassiouny, 2014). One consequence of both the movement and its failure in Egypt was to test an important theory of the SWP's Tony Cliff in relation to the liberation of Palestine. Cliff had argued that the Palestinians could not defeat Israel alone, that they were ultimately dependent on the Arab workers and peasants simultaneously rising against their own despotic rulers. He popularised a slogan that the road to the liberation of Jerusalem ran through

Cairo. Momentarily the "Arab Spring" seemed to fulfil this prediction. Certainly, the cry "Free Palestine!" was a familiar slogan on the Arab streets during the uprising. But this aspiration, alongside all the others, was crushed.

These events alongside two massive internal crises in the SWP, which seriously weakened the organisation in the 2010s, brought me to the conclusion that a fundamental re-think was required on my part. Why was the Marxist left in such a precarious state, especially when the proverbial crisis of capitalism, including its fossil fuel dependency posing an existential environmental threat to the very survival of humanity on the planet, was so serious? I began writing a series of articles for *International Socialism* revisiting a number of our basic arguments. This included inadvertently becoming embroiled in a sharp argument about Chris Harman's *The Lost Revolution: Germany 1918-1923* when I challenged Chris's conclusion that socialist revolution had been possible in Germany in October 1923.[16] Irrespective of the merits of that argument, it served as a warning about the institutionalisation of cadres in small revolutionary socialist organisations over such a long period of time. We can reinforce each other with a comfortable and relatively sophisticated world-view without it necessarily being subject to the kind of rigorous independent tests that must surely be essential at a time of such crisis.

One reason for pursuing the PhD thesis on which this book is based was to subject my "1968" assumptions to just such an independent test. The research project was partly designed with this objective in mind: three revolutionary upheavals against totalitarian regimes in the three countries, Poland, South Africa, Iran, on three different continents with three very different political and cultural histories at roughly the same time. Brazil was added for this book at the suggestion of the PhD examiners, Steve Smith and Marcel van der Linden. Each one of these events made a major contribution to 20th century history. They also, I would argue, both separately and together, showed how modern history has at least the potential to expand the promise of the Enlightenment understood as the pursuit of human freedom. Each one of these events simultaneously opened an opportunity to test a prediction about industrial capitalism made in *The Communist Manifesto* by Karl Marx and Frederick Engels in 1848: that the class divisions of modern capitalist society, and its compulsion to exploit workers to extract surplus value, would force workers to organise themselves both to challenge capital's rule at the point of production and assert themselves as alternative rulers as the first step towards a communist classless society. In each of these countries, independent workers' movements did indeed play a decisive part in toppling the tyrannies. In addition, these workers' movements developed far-reaching aspirations for workers' control of production precipitating some remarkable if short-lived experiments. In each case Soviet Communism whether through its satellite state, Poland, its satellite Communist Parties in South Africa and Iran, or simply its negative example, for example, in Brazil, directly or indirectly helped thwart these experiments.

Unravelling these complexities of course is the challenge. I sum it up in my research question: how and why did independent workers' movements that played a decisive role in removing tyrannies in these countries but then lose the political initiative.[17] But a further question is buried in the phrase "lose the political initiative". What does that mean? The implicit implication is that workers could have carried forward the political struggle in their own interests. But that would have required self-belief in such an audacious challenge to the new post-revolutionary status quo which, in different forms, emerged in all four countries, and in different forms capitulated to neoliberalism. Lenin argued that there can be no revolutionary movements without revolutionary theory. In each of the four countries, the revolutionary movements were dominated by approaches more or less hostile to the ideas of communism summarised by Marx and Engels in the 1848 *Communist Manifesto*. Chapter 1 of the thesis explores these ideas, explaining how they, and, in particular, the organisational form they took, evolved, between 1848 and the Russian Revolution of 1917. It is argued that the organisational form is crucial, raising the question of what type of political party was required. The following chapters, addressing the revolutionary crises respectively in Poland, South Africa, Iran, and Brazil, argue that the failure to understand and learn the lessons from this earlier period was a major contributory factor to the workers' movements losing the political initiative.

An additional question raised by this argument is how workers develop the revolutionary socialist ideas they need for their struggles. What is it that makes them susceptible to join an appropriate revolutionary socialist or communist party? Chapter 1 emphasises the role of worker intellectuals stressed by Antonio Gramsci, the Italian philosopher and communist. David Mandel, discussing the revolutionary factory committees in the Russian Revolution in Chapter 1, also identifies individual worker intellectuals or worker cadres and how they emerged. He gives the example of A. Buzinov, a member of the Social Revolutionary Party in Petrograd, "a self-made agitator" (Mandel, 2018: 6). Self-made agitators tended to be drawn from the growing layer of skilled workers, especially in the metal working industries. Forced to think for themselves by the nature of their work, this spilled over into a growing self-awareness about their own role in workplace politics and in the wider society consumed by multiples crises. Mandel cites Buzinov: "Among the worker masses, one now [1906-7] heard the word 'conscious'." These were not necessarily members of political parties. They were far more numerous, ten times as many, says Buzinov. "Each was, in a way, a 'legally reasoning individual' capable of understanding everything around him ... Life transformed them into the vanguard of the worker masses. Their native keen wit and worker sensitivity did not fail them when they exposed the hidden ends behind this or that manoeuvre of management." Buzinov describes how these self-made agitators both reflected and encouraged "class separation". "Life," he says, "had hammered a wedge between workers and owners ... This self-made agitator spoke of that which each worker had in his head but, being less developed, was unable to verbalise. After each one of his words, the workers would exclaim: 'That's it! That's just what I wanted to say!'" (Mandel, 2018: 17-8).

Mandel also cites a liberal journalist, S-skii, who became fascinated by the Petersburg workers led by the metal-working industry. Turners, founders, blacksmiths, mechanics, machinists, S-skii engaged them in conversations. "They are almost indistinguishable from our intellectuals. In my opinion, they are more interesting because their judgments are fresher, and their convictions, once established, are very firm" (Mandel, 2017: 14). Again, citing an unnamed observer, writing for a Russian periodical: "The spiritual process is an active one ... the voice of an individual has begun to speak in the worker ... [releasing a] ... dynamism: the upper strata of the proletariat raise up the backward strata to their own level. Questions of honour and conscience are the first small bridges on which the proletarian shakes the hand of the semi-proletarian" (Mandel 2018: 19).

It was the equivalents of these men (and unfortunately far fewer women) that I wanted to interview in Poland, South Africa, Iran and Brazil, as well as those activists and intellectuals who worked with them politically and knew them well, for my research into the revolutionary events in these countries. Of course, there were obvious methodological limitations. Nearly 40 years have passed transforming former young revolutionary firebrands into, in almost every case, far more conservative senior citizens. This undoubtedly compounded the problem of selective and fading memories. Nevertheless, there are a number of mitigating factors. A wealth of secondary sources confirm, amplify and qualify these primary sources, in some cases tracking and recording the same individuals during the period of their revolutionary interventions. In some cases the individuals had either written their autobiographies or recorded their experiences much closer to the period under examination with scholars and professional journalists.

But a further factor is in play which I hadn't anticipated but proved to be common to all the interviewees in all four countries, irrespective of the disappointing and, indeed, extremely demoralising political outcomes. This is the enormous pride in their personal participation in the events, truly historical ground-breaking events, they describe. The experiences remain burned in their memories. This led to intriguing contradictions. It was suggested that I ignore for an interview a particularly important former bus drivers' leader of workers in a Solidarity region in Poland, despite his heroic role in the Solidarity underground after martial law had been declared in December 1981. It was advice which I, in turn, ignored. Today, he is a managing director of a private fleet of commercial vehicles. To put it discreetly, some of his current industrial relations practices are called into question by his critics. Whether this is true or not, his enthusiasm for the "revolutionary" period of his life, which he continues to describe as revolutionary, remains undimmed, as will be noted both in the unedited interview and the extracts I used in the chapter. I could report almost identical experiences from all the former worker leaders, irrespective of their politics and social position today.[18]

Finally, I discover that I may be inadvertently making a contribution to what van der Linden describes as "an exciting transition to a truly Global Labour History" (van der Linden, 2008: 1). Certainly, my research can in no way be described as "Eurocentric", one of the factors inhibiting such a transition in the past. It also identifies "global interconnections" essential to this approach (van der Linden 2008: 372). At the same time, I think my approach is simultaneously both less and more ambitious than that demanded by a truly Global Labour History. It is less ambitious in the sense that it does not devote enough attention to what van der Linden describes as the importance of what have been traditionally called, and too easily dismissed as, "the self-employed (part of the 'petty bourgeoisie') and poor outcasts (the 'lumpen-proletariat')". Van der Linden argues that these classifications simply do not apply in the Global South (van der Linden, 2008: 10). I am not able to address his argument properly. However, these groups are absolutely essential in all four chapters. In Poland, the Solidarity workers' movement succeeded in uniting these groups behind the workers in the large workplaces organised in the newly independent trade union, including at an absolutely pivotal potentially revolutionary moment, rural peasant farmers. In South Africa and Iran, the opposite was the case. At the risk of over-simplification, I designate these groups the urban poor. As we shall see, in the case of South Africa, there was tension between the newly organised black trade unions in the workplaces and the urban poor in the black townships. Similarly, in Iran there was tension between the workers' "shoras", workers' councils, in the advanced modernised workplaces and the urban poor, unemployed, semi-employed or working in tiny traditional workshops in the bazaars. Similarly, a limitation of the workers' movement and the party that emerged from it in Brazil was its failure to bridge the gap between the organised workers and the "shirtless", the inhabitants of the *favelas*, or settlements of the poor. This tension had decisive implications for the politics of the period which I most certainly do address. And this brings me to where I think my project stretches beyond the limits of a Global History or at least has to insist on a tight focus on two dimensions of global politics in the latter part of the last century. The first one is the implications of revolutionary processes once unleashed in these four societies, comparing and contrasting the strategic central role of the organised workers' movements. The second one is the impact on the revolutionary processes of the conservatism of Soviet Communism as expressed through its satellite state in Poland, its satellite communist parties and organisations in South Africa and Iran, and the negative example it offered in Brazil.

In an earlier study, van der Linden writes about the limitations of making formal transnational comparisons: "Time and again researchers are discovering that, although formal methods are useful, it is in-depth ideographic knowledge that is decisive in the end" (van der Linden, 2003: 189). I understand this to mean that the unique aspects of a social phenomenon take precedence over aspects that might be comparable.[19] But in a footnote, van der Linden proposes a solution to this problem: "counterfactuals might also be important since each comparative hypothesis logically contains a counterfactual: if one believes Y is caused by X it follows that one presumes Y would not have occurred without X. One way in which a researcher can test the plausibility of his or her hypothesis is to convert the hypothesis into a counterfactual argument" (van der Linden, 2003: 196, n76).

I interpret this argument to allow counterfactuals to make at least a limited contribution to a research investigation. To return to hypotheses already signalled in my research, I argue that Soviet Communism, manifest in different forms, is a conservative factor in the revolutionary processes unleashed in Poland, South Africa, Iran, and Brazil. This is not a counterfactual, since I claim to provide empirical evidence to prove it. It follows that without the malign influence of Soviet Communism, different outcomes might have been possible. Framed in this way, the problematic aspect of counterfactuals, if presented as dogmatic certainties, is addressed. An alternative outcome is presented only as a possibility.

To make this "concrete", I argue that one of the reasons why in each of the countries the organised workers' movements failed was because they were unable to build their own independent workers' political parties. Two counterfactuals are present. First, this failure was contingent on the presence of already-existing communist parties. Second, independent workers' parties may have helped guide the workers' movements to reshape the outcomes following the removal of the dictatorships. But these are offered only as tentative possibilities, not certainties, hence, they have a legitimate place in the overall argument.

CHAPTER 1

A workers' political party for a workers' revolution? From the 1848 Communist Manifesto to the world's first socialist revolution, Russia October 1917

Introduction

The *Manifesto of the Communist Party*, written by Karl Marx and Frederick Engels, must rank as one of modernity's greatest historical documents. Published on the eve of revolutionary upheavals that swept across Europe in 1848, over one hundred and fifty years later it is has lost none of its vitality. Its indictment of the capitalist system retains an extraordinary contemporary relevance. True, its call to arms for the working class to overthrow capitalism is likely today to generate caution, scepticism, even cynicism, in the shadow of the apparent failure of communism in Russia in the last century.[20] The reforms also in the 20th century seemed to ameliorate at least some of the more grotesque excesses of capitalism that Marx and Engels had identified. Yet an intense curiosity lingers about the roots of Marx and Engels's most audacious prediction. Was *The Communist Manifesto* a manifesto aimed directly at the workers' movements in the 1848 revolutions or for a political party that would intervene in these movements? Both the questions and the answers evolve over time. The chapter attempts to track the process.

The Communist Manifesto provides strategic and tactical guidelines for accomplishing the ultimate goal of a classless society. Marx and Engels's insights here, developed in many of their earlier and later voluminous writings, chart a route to a unique post-Enlightenment vision of human freedom, justice and economic, social and political equality. And yet the decisive mechanism of the role of political organisation remains underdeveloped in their writings. The 19th century's greatest communists never satisfactorily resolved how to create an organisation that both attracted and created fellow communists. Nor did they satisfactorily resolve, either in theory or practice, how such an organisation would enhance the revolutionary potential of the working class. This chapter will attempt a fuller understanding of this problem.

It will trace how Marx and Engels responded to a number of decisive events as industrialising capitalism transformed 19th century Europe and a working class political and trade union movement began to emerge as a permanent outcome of this process: the Chartist movement in the UK of the 1830s and 1840s—the world's first mass revolutionary workers' movement, the 1848 revolutionary upheavals in Europe, the Utopian Socialists, the launch of the First International in the 1860s, the Paris Commune of 1871, the emergence of the German socialist party in the 1870s, the world's first mass-based workers' political party. All of these events helped shape and consolidate what appeared to be a particularly important, even conclusive, achievement of Marx and Engels towards the end of the 19th century, the founding of the Second International. Here was an internationally based working class political party, insisting that it spoke in the name of Marx and Engels following their deaths in this period. It had even helped invent and promote a new word and then proudly declare itself to be its living expression: Marxism. Here, then, was the political instrument that would help achieve the international socialist or communist working class revolution in the 20th century, so confidently predicted by *The Communist Manifesto* the century before.

Alas, the opposite turned out to be the truth. In 1914, the Second International would face its greatest test. Britain and Germany were about to plunge the world into an unprecedented bloody carnage, literally, the world's first world war. The cause was well understood by Marxists. Britain and Germany were the two principal imperialist countries. They were about to go to war over colonial possessions. Millions would perish. The Second International had a clearly defined responsibility to try and halt the slaughter before it began. That, after all, was the purpose, the raison d'être, of the International, to defend the interests of the international working class against the warring national interests of the capitalist class in each country, in each nation state. Workers should refuse to become soldiers, and, if they were already soldiers, they should refuse to fight. All eyes were on the German Social Democratic Party (SPD) and its leading Marxist theoretician, Karl Kautsky, both a decisive influence in the Second International. But Kautsky and the parliamentary party had for some time been expressing illusions in the German national state and the prospects for reform. There was a grim logic in the SPD's support for the war. But that made their decision no less shocking, a capitulation of such magnitude that it would inevitably shatter the Second International.

Two of the most famous names in 20th century Marxist history would now attempt to pick up the pieces, Rosa Luxemburg and Vladimir Lenin. The latter part of the chapter will trace how Lenin in particular, and, to a much lesser extent, Luxemburg, now responded to the calamity. Luxemburg was already the German party's most outspoken critic, hostile to its illusions in the nation state and the parliamentary process as an agency of change, and the increasing institutionalisation of the trade unions as a curb on workers' self-activity. Luxemburg would remain in the German socialist party, but by 1916 had formed with Karl Liebknecht the anti-war Spartacus faction within it. They would both be jailed for their anti-war resistance. Lenin continued to build his anti-war Bolshevik Party amongst workers and soldiers in the conspiratorial circumstances dictated by the repressive conditions in Tsarist Russia.

Both Luxemburg and Lenin predicted correctly that the war would trigger revolutionary upheavals across Europe. But they differed about the type of political party that was now required. Kautsky's approach, the German socialist party and the Second International, had been the taken-for-granted model for both of them. Lenin famously returned to the great 19th century German philosopher Hegel, who had so influenced Marx, in his effort to identify the flaws that had wrecked the Second International.

Later his *State and Revolution* would complement *The Communist Manifesto* as one of the great founding documents for international socialism in the 20th century.

Both Russia and Germany did indeed experience revolutionary upheavals as the carnage of the First World War dragged to its bloody conclusion. Lenin and his Bolshevik Party would lead a successful socialist revolution in Russia, based on workers' and soldiers' and peasants' councils, the soviets. Luxemburg, originally unconvinced about the need for an independent Communist Party, helped form one too late for intervention in the workers' and soldiers' councils in Germany in 1918. The lessons to be learned from Lenin's Bolsheviks' victory in the 1917 Russian Revolution, before it was engulfed by civil war, will conclude the chapter. In particular, there is an attempt to decipher a well-worn shibboleth on the revolutionary left—nationalisation under workers' control.

This is nothing less than a summary of a famous passage from the *Communist Manifesto*: "the first step in the revolution by the working class is to raise the proletariat to the position of ruling class ... to centralise all instruments of production in the hands of the state ie the proletariat ... and to increase the total of productive forces as rapidly as possible" (Marx and Engels, 1998: 60). This is sometimes also described as "workers' power" and for a few months it was a reality in revolutionary Russia—a precious historical moment demanding the closest attention both for its own sake, but also for the light it throws on later revolutionary working class upheavals—not least the four case studies under investigation here. Common threads too often ignored in so much of the discourse that passes for serious scholarly commentary on the apparent failure of communism. Democratically elected rank and file workers' leaders at the point of production with mandates to pursue deepening aspirations for workers' control—self-management, "*autogestion*", the slogan particularly associated with the French "events" of May 1968, accompany all these revolutionary upheavals. Workers' leaders as well as many of their militant supporters, already revolutionary cadres, took part in constant discussion about the theory and practice of socialism and communism, prospects and challenges. As we shall see, with good reason, Antonio Gramsci insisted that these were worker intellectuals—an intellectual of a new type, that the older intellectuals from the middle class professions, even if they were on the left, had to understand, engage with, learn from, as well as encourage, helping to raise the worker activists' newly discovered intellectual self-confidence.

But their workplace committees at the high points of revolution had to be linked to the wider revolutionary movement engulfing the rest of society. Workers' self-emancipation, the foundation for a communist society as Marx and Engels understood it, cannot be restricted literally to the point of production. Economic power had to be accompanied by political power and this meant control of the state, a workers' state displacing the capitalists' state. Even workers seizing control of the means of production and creating their own state is an insufficient condition for its success. A workers' political party, already understanding this "line of march", is an essential ingredient. As we shall see in this chapter, Lenin's Bolsheviks fulfilled these conditions. Alas, in three of the case studies in the following chapters, the revolutionary upheavals in Poland, South Africa, and Iran, with independent workers' movements centre stage, the Communists, who claimed the mantle of Lenin's Bolsheviks, undermined them, and in the fourth, Brazil, the USSR gave a negative image to the revolutionary alternative. A disconnect, arguably the single most important, and least understood, development of the 20th century, had occurred between Soviet Communism, its satellite states and communist parties, and the original vision of the 1848 *Communist Manifesto.*

I. The 1848 *Communist Manifesto*, the working class and the role of a communist party

Marx and Engels regarded workers' power as the essential pre-condition for establishing the foundations for a communist society, as is clear from the passage from *The Communist Manifesto*, cited above. But *The Communist Manifesto* itself was a pre-condition for workers' power. The Communists had to "publish their views, their aims" in "a manifesto of the party itself" (Marx and Engels, 1998: 34). The Communists were indispensable to the revolutionary development of the working class, "the most advanced and resolute section of the working class ... theoretically, they have ... the advantage of clearly understanding the line of march, the conditions, and the ultimate general results of the proletarian movement" (Marx and Engels, 1998: 50-51).

There had been since the French Revolution of 1789 differing interpretations of communism. But it was the interpretation of Marx and Engels, with the launch of their *Communist Manifesto* by the Communist League, on the eve of the 1848 Europe-wide revolutionary wave, which would come to dominate the communist perspective in the growing workers' movements around the world. A formulation from Marx and Engels's *Communist Manifesto* appears to interpret working class organisation and political party organisation as interchangeable "This organisation of proletarians into a class, and consequently *into a political party*" (Marx and Engels 1998: 46).

This is conditioned by another passage:

> All previous historical movements were movements of minorities, or in the interest of minorities. The proletarian movement is the self-conscious, independent movement of the immense majority, in the interests of the immense majority. The proletariat, the lowest stratum of our present society, cannot stir, cannot raise itself up, without the whole superincumbent strata of official society being sprung into the air (Marx and Engels 1998: 49).

The last quotation could be interpreted to imply that the proletariat spontaneously erupts and overthrows its oppressors.

Except that we have the phrase "self-conscious". Is this self-consciousness or class consciousness developed through struggle alone or is there a decisive role for a party, "the Communists ... [who understand] the line of march"? As we shall see, Marx and Engels never satisfactorily resolved this question.

It's true they ask: "In what relation do the Communists stand to the proletarians as a whole?" But the answer is ambiguous: "The Communists do not form a separate party opposed to other parties. They have no interests separate and apart from those of the proletariat as a whole. They do not set up any sectarian principles of their own, by which to shape and mould the proletarian movement" (Marx and Engels, 1998: 50).

In his excellent discussion of Marx, Engels and their concept of the party, Monty Johnstone argues that they left no systematic theory of the party. They tended to evolve their ideas about the proletarian party as they went along, relating them to their analyses of very different historical situations (Johnstone, 1967: 121). This is a helpful approach provided we recognise two underlying trends that remain, even if contradictory, consistent in Marx and Engels's thinking about "the party". First, that the principal theoreticians, the communists who most fully understood the line of march, were Marx and Engels themselves. Marx and Engels "presented themselves and the Communists as the theoretical vanguard of the class" (Johnstone, 1967: 123). They maintained consistency in this position even when they were detached from any form of workers' organisation and, confusingly, continued to describe themselves as "a party".[21] This brings us to the second principle. The "theoretical vanguard" does not organise "the working class to constitute itself as a political party". It seeks to influence, to become an organic part of, whatever political form mass-based working class organisation takes. The mass-based working class organisation then itself becomes "the party".

Marx had the Chartists in mind when he wrote against the French philosopher Proudhon's hostility to strikes in *The Poverty of Philosophy*.[22] Marx described how workers in struggle first formed trade unions and then a "large political party under the name of Chartists" (Marx and Engels, 1975-2005, vol. 6: 210). This informed that phrase in *The Communist Manifesto*, "This organisation of proletarians into a class, and consequently *into a political party*" (Marx and Engels, 1998: 46, Johnstone, 124). Or as Stathis Kouvelakis has put it recently, "[the] 'communist party', for Marx and Engels is not ... a separate organisation but rather a tendency within the labour movement considered as a whole (the 'class party')" (Kouvelakis, 2016: 82). But this still begs the question about how Marx and Engels conceived of "the Communists". Marx and Engels never settled it. Certainly, their ambivalent relations with the Communist League, discussed in section IV of this chapter, offered little clarity. This crucial question is only finally and convincingly addressed in the 20th century by both Lenin and Gramsci. Lenin describes *purposive workers*. "Genuine heroes", says Lenin, who show a "passionate drive toward knowledge and toward socialism" (Lih, 2008: 344-45). These were the worker cadres of the Bolshevik Party. We might even describe them as worker intellectuals.

This is an argument developed by Gramsci drawn partly from his experience in the Italian city of Turin as editor of *L'Ordine Nuovo* "the paper of the factory councils", as Gramsci described it (Fiori, 1990: 120). Gramsci's knowledge of the flourishing of workers' soviets or councils in the early stages of the 1917 Russian Revolution allowed him to intervene directly in the Italian factory council movement of 1918-20. He and the paper became very popular with the workers, and he spoke regularly at their meetings. This dynamic of interaction between intellectual and worker helped propel the movement forward, both on a learning curve. The expectation was nothing less than the workers replacing the capitalists and organising production (Fiori, 1990: 119). Gramsci explains:

> The weekly *L'Ordine Nuovo* worked to develop certain forms of new intellectualism and determine its new concepts...The mode of being of the new intellectual can no

> longer consist in eloquence, the external and momentary arousing of feelings and passions, but in active participation in practical life, as constructor, organiser, "permanent persuader" (Gramsci, 1971: 9-10).

These permanently active persuaders are "*elites* of intellectuals of a new type who arise directly from the masses through remaining in contact with them" (Gramsci, 1971: 340). Nothing less than changing the "ideological panorama" of an age is at stake. At the same time Gramsci accepts that a "hierarchy of ... intellectual competence" is inevitable. "The culmination of this can be a great individual philosopher. But he must be capable of re-living concretely the massive ideological community of the masses ... and must succeed in giving formal elaboration to the collective doctrine in the most relevant fashion, and the one most suited to the modes of thought of a collective thinker" (Gramsci, 1971: 340-1).

This passage requires close inspection. The phrase "hierarchy of intellectual competence" and the introduction of "a great individual philosopher" at first sight seems to reflect the old order re-appearing in the workers' movement, directly at odds with Gramsci's perspective. In part this may be about some deliberate obfuscation, Gramsci shielding himself from the prison censor, these are, after all, writings from his prison notebooks. But a stronger explanation is necessary. First, it is a statement of the obvious. There is inevitably a hierarchy of intellectual competence, reflecting capitalism's division of mental and physical labour, with particularly inspired and inspiring intellectuals, not least Gramsci himself (though he probably had Lenin in mind), for whom philosopher and political leader are interchangeable, displaying outstanding leadership roles. But secondly, attention needs to be paid to the last sentence. The objective is to develop the modes of thought of "a collective thinker". This suggests dynamic interaction with the intention of minimising the effects of hierarchy, working together to equalise thought and action, where the workers' experience fuses with the greater knowledge of the more developed intellectual to the benefit of both. We have an interesting example with the role played by *L'Ordine Nuovo.* Gramsci explains why workers loved the paper, "They found something of themselves, their own better selves." The paper "was permeated with their own spirit of self-searching." It endeavoured to answer all questions in a manner that avoided "cold intellectual construction but flowed out of our own discussions with the best workers..." (Gramsci, 2016: 24). The "collective thinker" is *The Modern Prince,* the workers' political party (Gramsci, 1971: 129). Gramsci also issues a warning about the isolated workers' leader who lacks this organised political and intellectual support:

> The active man-in-the-mass has a practical activity, but has no clear theoretical consciousness of his actions ... His theoretical consciousness can indeed be historically in opposition to his practical activity. One might almost say that he has two theoretical consciousnesses (or one contradictory consciousness), one which is implicit in his activity, which unites him with all his fellow-workers in the practical transformation of the real world, and one, superficially explicit or verbal, which he has inherited from the past and uncritically absorbed. But this verbal conception is not without consequences ... often powerful enough to produce a situation in which the contradictory state of consciousness does not permit any action ... and produces a state of moral and political passivity (Gramsci, 1971: 333).

Gramsci goes on to describe the struggle between two "hegemonies" in the worker's mind: the pull of a vision of the future, and its potential strategies and tactics, constantly being fashioned and re-fashioned with his comrades, tested in struggle, as part of a collective thinking and highly practical process: and the pull of the past inducing passivity:

> Critical understanding of self takes place therefore through a struggle of political "hegemonies" and of opposing directions ... in order to arrive at the working out at a higher level of one's own conception of reality. Consciousness of being part of a particular hegemonic force ... is the first stage towards a further progressive self-consciousness in which theory and practice will finally be one (Gramsci 1971: 333).

As Peter Thomas has put it, the permanent persuaders are in an "organic integration with the masses, in a reciprocal relationship ... where they are at least as often 'the educated' as 'the educators' ... working out ... principles and problems which the masses have posed in their own practical activity" (Thomas, 2010: 436). The result is "a theory that, coinciding and identifying itself with the decisive elements of the same practice, may accelerate the historical process taking place rendering practice more ... coherent ... setting it to work" (Gramsci, 1995: 384; Thomas, 2010: 380).

This is a re-working of *revolutionary practice*, key to Marx's Third Thesis on Feuerbach:

> The materialist doctrine concerning the changing of circumstances and upbringing forgets that circumstances are changed by men and that it is essential to educate the educator himself. This doctrine must, therefore, divide society into two parts, one of which is superior to society. The coincidence of the changing of circumstances and of human activity or self-changing can be conceived and rationally understood only as revolutionary practice (Marx, 1975: 422).

Thomas argues that the Third Thesis exerts an enormous pull on Gramsci's thinking. The argument is underlined with the stunning image of the Aeolian harp, invoked by the young Marx: "a sounding board that absorbs the cacophony of existing contradictions and attempts to 'tune' them or reorganise them into more harmonious forms" (Thomas, 2010: 435).

Here, as in revolutionary Russia, we have worker cadres or worker intellectuals. But were they also the cadres of the Chartist movement who influenced Marx's and Engels's thinking about communism? And were they also the cadres who led the revolt that formed that early experimental form of communism, the Paris Commune in 1871? Individual workers' leaders will be briefly tracked here, observing whether they anticipate "communist" cadres in what with hindsight we might describe as the Marxist and Leninist pre-Stalinist communist party tradition.

II. Marx and Engels and the world's first workers' mass movement: The Chartists[23]

The Chartists demanded universal manhood suffrage as well as vastly improved pay and conditions. Their methods of struggle, strikes, led to the general strike of 1842. The movement's most famous national leaders were not drawn from the vast mass of the new factory workers, but most of its rank and file local leaders were. The most talented amongst them became nationally known not least through the pages of the extraordinary Chartist newspaper, the *Northern Star*. Furthermore, some of them equated universal suffrage with workers' power replacing the competitive economic system and its private owners. Generally, though, the politics of Chartism were contradictory, its leadership divided and unstable.

Here is one of these local leaders, Richard Pilling, power loom workers' leader in Lancashire, well known throughout northwest England, addressing a 6,000 strong workers' meeting in Stockport. His speech was scrambled by the police reporter taking notes but the thrust is still clear: "Had the working people been in the legislature by their Charter this Nation would now have been the most prosperous Nation in the world. The working people as the origin of the arts, improvements, ingenuity and wealth, of the empire are the only fit persons to govern this or any other nation" (Chase, 2007: 230-1).[24]

There is no ambiguity here. Pilling is indeed calling for transformed social relations with workers, as the wealth creators, in power. Pilling's speech at his trial in 1843, after the failed general strike (59 defendants facing charges which included conspiracy and sedition), is well known to historians. Malcolm Chase argues that here at least he was more effective than national Chartists' leader Feargus O'Connor. It concluded with the words: "the masters conspired to kill me, and I combined to keep myself alive" (Chase, 2007: 233).

Neville Kirk insists that the speech was nothing less than "an indictment of the factory system run on capitalist lines" (Kirk 1985: 19; see also Charlton 1997: 49). Pilling detailed, on the basis of personal experience the evils of the system: overproduction; intolerably long hours of labour; competition and the beating down of wages; unemployment and poverty in the midst of plenty; the employment of child and juvenile labour and the break-up of the family; lack of independence and control; the reification of human beings under commodity production; tyrannical and hypocritical actions of the cotton manufacturers—their insensitivity to the sufferings of the operatives, blind adherence to the tenets of orthodox political economy, opposition to combination amongst workers, their frequent victimisation of labour activists and their abhorrence of Chartism.

This is Kirk's interpretation of Pilling's speech. Remarkably, a version of the transcript of the trial has survived.[25] It seems reasonable to conclude that Pilling was a potential cadre, a worker intellectual. Kirk adds that these arguments were common amongst many of the other defendants. And that there is a broad consensus amongst Chartist historians, including Dorothy Thompson, that the grievances articulated by Pilling lay at the heart of Chartism's appeal to the factory population of the North of England.

The early influence on the Chartists of James "Bronterre" O'Brien deserves exploration. The Irish radical was main "mentor" to George Julian Harney, one of the very few Chartist leaders, at least for a period, close to Marx and Engels (Foot, 2005:

94). Harney published the first English translation of *The Communist Manifesto* in November 1850 (Fernbach, 1973: 22). We catch an important glimpse of O'Brien in E P Thompson's classic study *The Making of the English Working Class*, "a theorist of stature to define the working-class predicament" (Thompson, 1968: 903). "He sought with considerable genius, to twist together the tradition of democratic ultra-radicalism with that of Owenism,[26] into a revolutionary Socialism," demanding "the expropriation of the propertied classes, and a network of Owenite communities." O'Brien identified with Gracchus Babeuf and the Conspiracy of Equals, the extreme left wing of the radical republicans of the French Revolution (Thompson, 1968: 903). "His writings are a central thread through the abundant agitations of the early 1830s." (Thompson, 1968: 905). When Feargus O'Connor launched what would become the movement's most famous newspaper, the *Northern Star* in 1837, O'Brien was its editor (Foot, 2005: 97).

Thompson goes so far as to suggest that Chartism's revolutionary intellectuals like O'Brien explicitly anticipate Marx: "When Marx was still in his teens, the battle for the minds of trades unionists, between a capitalist and a socialist political economy had been (at least temporarily) won ... 'What is capital?' asked a writer in the *Pioneer*. 'It is reserved labour!' ... A 'Parliament' ... could be formed, delegated directly from the workshops and the mills" (Thompson 1968: 912).

But O'Brien turned out to be politically unstable.[27] By 1842, the year of the general strike, O'Brien was no longer a revolutionary, preaching conciliation instead (Foot, 2005: 123-4). There can be no doubt about the revolutionary potential of the world's first mass workers' movement—with some ideological sense of challenging fundamentally the emerging capitalist order. But there most certainly is a case for doubting its value as a model for a working class political party.[28]

III. The Utopian Socialists

Engels's pamphlet *Socialism: Utopian and Scientific*,[29] introduced and promoted by Marx, though published much later, highlights one of the most influential political traditions that immediately preceded "communism" as Marx and Engels would develop it. In different forms it would continue to offer a competitive challenge, ultimately justifying conciliation between the social classes and thus contributing to the reformist socialist tradition which would so powerfully take root in the 20th century. Nevertheless, Marx and Engels were keen to acknowledge the achievements of the Utopian socialists, before explaining their criticisms. They were particularly complimentary about England's most famous Utopian socialist, Robert Owen.

Owen had broken with his class, turning his back "on getting rich quickly ... From 1800 to 1829 he directed the great cotton spinning mill of New Lanark in Scotland. He transformed a population, which originally consisted of ... very demoralised elements into a model colony, in which drunkenness, police, magistrates, lawsuits, poor law relief ... charity were unknown" (Engels 1993: 70). Owen is even praised as one of the first genuine communists.[30] But Engels, at the same time, develops the argument that first appeared in the *Communist Manifesto*'s criticism of the Utopian socialists. They saw the working class as a "suffering" class (Marx and Engels, 1998: 73), unable to act on its own behalf. In its infancy, they argue, that might have been true, but the "progressive historical development" of the working class meant that it can and does fight for its own interests. Communists had to place their visionary ideas, their talents at the disposal of the movement and not see the working class as dependent on them, leading inevitably to a new form of elitism. Marx and Engels drew the following distinction, "Therefore, although the originators of these systems were, in many respects, revolutionary, their disciples have, in every case, formed mere reactionary sects ... The Owenites in England ... oppose the Chartists" (Marx and Engels, 1998: 74-75).

IV. 1848, "Springtime of Peoples", *The Communist Manifesto* and the Communist League

"A spectre is haunting Europe—the spectre of Communism. All the powers of old Europe have entered into a holy alliance to exorcise the spectre" (Marx and Engels, 1998: 34). With these famous lines at the start of *The Communist Manifesto*, Marx and Engels fired the opening polemical shots of the 1848 "Springtime of the Peoples" (Hobsbawm, 1977: 21). The Pope and the Russian Tsar, notorious Austrian and French statesmen were identified in the alliance. But interestingly so were "French Radicals". Perhaps unwittingly, Marx and Engels here had also identified the potential strength of the alliance and the weakness of the communist "threat". "French Radicals" symbolised the radical bourgeoisie and their political and intellectual representatives. But weren't they supposed to be on the revolutionary side of the barricades?

The Communist Manifesto often surprises first time readers with its many early pages appearing to celebrate the achievements of capitalism: "during its rule of scarce one hundred years, [it] has created more massive and more colossal productive forces than have all preceding generations together" (Marx and Engels, 1998: 40). The bourgeoisie is even presented as a revolutionary class which "cannot exist without constantly revolutionising the instruments of production, and thereby the relations of production, and with them the whole ... of society" (Marx and Engels, 1998: 38). In one of the most brilliant passages, which has stood the test of time like perhaps no other part of the *Manifesto*, we learn that "all fixed, fast frozen relations, with their train of ... prejudices and opinions, are swept away ... All that is solid melts into air, all that is holy is profaned, and man is at last compelled to face with sober senses, (the) real conditions of life" (Marx and Engels, 1998: 38-9).

In his biography of Marx, Jonathan Sperber makes the interesting observation that the original German version of this passage included "elements of the society of orders evaporate" (Sperber, 2013: 206). It is the economic power deriving from the capitalists' steam engines that will "evaporate" or "terminate the anachronistic society of orders that [King] Friedrick Wilhelm IV [of Prussia] and his supporters idealised," (Sperber, 2013: 207), the world before the 1789 French Revolution (Sperber, 2013: 206). Sperber highlights these revolutionary expectations of Marx and Engels on the eve of the European-wide 1848 revolutions. A decisive revolutionary democratic breakthrough by the bourgeoisie is anticipated in alliance with the proletariat which will then, in turn, challenge bourgeois dominance. This is because:

> modern industry also created the proletariat, not only increasing in number, but becoming concentrated in greater masses, its strength grows, and it feels that strength more ... workers begin to form combinations (trade unions) against the bourgeois; they club together to keep up the rate of wages ...
>
> Now and then the workers are victorious, but only for a time. *The real fruit of their battle lies, not in the immediate result, but in the ever-expanding union of workers* ... This organisation of proletarians into a class, and consequently *into a political party* is constantly being upset by the competition between the workers themselves. *But it ever rises up again, stronger, firmer, mightier. It compels legislative recognition ... Thus the Ten Hours Bill was carried* (Marx and Engels, 1998: 45-6).

Legislative recognition was a double-edged marker. It would sap revolutionary energies but it was also a symbol of the potential power of the working class, workers "rising up again, stronger, firmer, mightier".[31] And it was the latter that terrified not only the anachronistic feudal rulers like Friedrick Wilhelm IV and their hangers-on across Europe but much more importantly the would-be "revolutionary" republican bourgeoisie. As Count Cavour of Piedmont, the future architect of united Italy, observed in 1846, if the "social order were to be genuinely menaced ... many of the most determined republicans would be ... the first to join the ranks of the conservative party" (Hobsbawm, 1977: 28). The barricade fighting that gripped Paris for three days in February 1848 ended with the overthrow of the monarchy and the proclamation of the republic. "Electrifying" the whole of Europe (Sperber, 2023: 214), it appeared to signal the much anticipated European-wide revolutionary upheaval.

Marx and Engels headed for Cologne which would simultaneously be a centre for the Communist League (CL) to organise workers and for Marx to edit the "bourgeois" liberal democratic newspaper, *Neue Rheinische Zeitung* (*NRZ*). Cologne had a particularly active communist-led workers' movement as well as what appeared to be a vibrant middle class agitating for full democratic rights. Marx and the *NRZ* would be the bridge between the two movements. *NRZ* would call for the creation of a revolutionary German republic, a German version of France 1792-94, the "bourgeois revolution", in Marx's terminology. The nationwide network of workers' associations would support such a revolutionary initiative, but it would also prepare for the next stage ... the communist workers' revolution (Sperber, 2013: 217-8).

However, there was a problem. The CL in Cologne was led by "True Socialist" Andreas Gottschalk (Sperber, 2013: 220). In the *Communist Manifesto*, Marx and Engels had devoted a whole section exposing, as they saw it, competing tendencies or strands of misleading socialist and communist thought and organisation. No less than three pages were devoted to the German based strand of "True Socialism", associated with their former comrade, Moses Hess. The most damning accusation was that by opposing bourgeois demands like "freedom of the press ... liberty and equality" it served the interests of reactionary German governments "as a welcome scarecrow", "a weapon" for the reactionaries to "fight the German bourgeoisie" (Marx and Engels, 1998: 68, 69). Although Gottschalk's opposition to liberals and democrats appeared to come from the left, his refusal to cooperate with them in constituent assembly elections, even refusing to stand communist candidates in this "bourgeois farce" of elections (Sperber, 2013: 220-21), meant that the main beneficiaries were the conservatives. Again, on the one hand Gottschalk called for a workers' republic, on the other hand he insisted that no action was necessary to bring about such a republic. This was the echo of his mentor, Moses Hess who had argued that the vast majority of the population could be won by argument to these ideas (Sperber, 2013: 221). This also echoed the early "Utopian socialist" Engels's writing about the Chartists mentioned above (Kouvelakis, 2003: 228).

This led Marx to concentrate all his efforts on *NRZ*. The paper campaigned for full democracy, damning the Prussian Constituent Assembly in Berlin and the German National Assembly in Frankfurt for failing to bring Germany's authoritarian monarchies under control. *NRZ* demanded a "German Republic, one and indivisible", "a telling phrase from the slogan of the Jacobins during the Reign of Terror in the French Revolution" (Sperber, 2013: 225). However, Marx found himself a victim of the old English proverb warning of the impossibility of changing horses in midstream. When *NRZ* campaigned in defence of the "June Days" in Paris 1848, taking the workers' side in the fierce barricade fighting with the republican government and predicting communist revolution, Cologne's democrats rounded on him. Uncharacteristically Marx performed a political somersault and repudiated his own writings (Sperber, 2013: 227). Everything was to be subordinated to a multi-class alliance aimed at destroying authoritarian Prussian rule. It was a strategy that would come to haunt Marx, again in the shadow of 1789.

Well beyond the scope of what it is possible to analyse here, the complex series of events that then followed didn't alter the fundamental character of what became the failed 1848 revolutions (Sperber, 2013: 227-236). The problem Marx faced was rooted in the accuracy of the Italian Count's prediction cited earlier. In 1848 the working class movement that erupted, in different forms and with differing degrees of intensity, across Europe wasn't strong enough to make a revolution in its own interest, but was sufficiently strong to unnerve the bourgeoisie who came to regard this would-be ally with deepening suspicion and hostility, preferring in the end to rally to the conservative authorities in the hope of some meagre gains.

Two very different and immensely authoritative documents authored by, or contributed to, by Marx, find him grappling with the consequences of 1848. In the first one, the March 1850 "Address to the Central Committee of the Communist League", Marx and Engels cast doubt on their 1848 strategy. The Address opens with criticism of the way the workers' movement had become subordinate to the (failed) democratic revolution. "This situation cannot be allowed to continue. The independence of the workers must be restored" (Marx, 1973a: 320).[32] But Marx goes much further than this. Using a concept later developed by Trotsky, he closes the Address by calling for "Permanent Revolution" (Marx, 1973a: 330): "Workers must be armed and organised ... they must try to place themselves not under the orders of the state authority but of revolutionary local councils set up by workers" (Marx, 1973a: 326).

Marx appears to be anticipating a form of *dual power* similar to the period between the February and October revolutions in Russia where democratic workers' assemblies, the soviets, co-existed with the Provisional Government that had replaced the Tsar. Independent workers' candidates would also stand for the constituent assembly. Wherever possible they should be members of the Communist League (Marx 1973a: 327). Even when there was no prospect of winning the election, they should stand "to gauge their own strength and to bring their revolutionary position and party standpoint to public attention" (Marx 1973a: 327). A range of demands would be placed on the constituent assembly. For example:

> the workers can force the concentration of as many forces of production as possible—means of transport, factories, railways etc—in the hands of the state ... if purchase is proposed, workers must demand railways

> and factories be confiscated without compensation ... if the democrats propose ... a moderate progressive tax, workers must demand a tax ... so steep ... that big capital is ruined by it (Marx, 1973a: 329-30).

The Address concludes by recognising that German workers "cannot come to power ... without passing through a protracted revolutionary development" and "by informing themselves of their own class interests" (Marx, 1973a: 330). The distinction between the workers learning for themselves and their party, the Communist League, accelerating the learning process, is blurred. The role of the party is not here made explicit, though it could be argued there is an implicit assumption about its role. But, in any case, and crucially, the argument seems to expect a lengthy period of co-existence with the constituent assembly.

Finally, do workers take power in the revolutionary councils or in the constituent assembly? And do they take power through their party, the Communist League? Alan Gilbert interprets Marx as anticipating the Paris Commune by saying, "in effect, the armed workers and ... councils would become the real power. Though the formal state structure would remain in the hands of the democrats, this state would lose its cutting edge and dwindle into a political shadow" (Gilbert, 1981: 243). Again, that is a legitimate interpretation, but Marx and Engels nowhere explicitly exclude the possibility that workers take power by forming an electoral majority in the constituent assembly, in other words by taking over the existing state administration. As we shall see it is only with the experience of the Paris Commune that they call openly for workers to establish their own state administration, a "dictatorship of the proletariat" (Callinicos 1983: 155-162).[33]

In the second document, the pamphlet *The Eighteenth Brumaire of Louis Bonaparte,* "a literary masterpiece ... a drastic example of Marx's practice of engaging in self-criticism through the criticism of others" (Sperber, 2013: 286-7), Marx analysed the defeats of the 1848 revolutions with a focus on the

Napoleonic pretender who seized power in France in 1852. The stunning one-liner showing how the traditions of the past can be "like a nightmare on the brain of the living" (Marx and Engels, 1975-2005, vol. 11: 103) applied to Marx himself, as he had joined most of the other 1848 revolutionary intellectuals, partly cloaking the 1848 events in the mantles of 1789. The 1789 revolutionaries had before them adopted "Roman costumes and Roman phrases", similarly "Cromwell with the English people had borrowed speech, passions, and illusions from the Old Testament for their bourgeois revolution" (Marx and Engels, 1975-2005, vol. 11: 104).

Marx notes the problem with this:

> The social revolution of the 19th century cannot draw its poetry from the past, but only from the future. It cannot begin with itself before it has stripped off all superstition in regard to the past. Earlier revolutions required recollections of past world history in order to drug themselves concerning their own content, the revolution of the nineteenth century must let the dead bury the dead. There the phrase went beyond the content; here the content goes beyond the phrase (Marx and Engels, 1975-2005, vol. 11: 106).

The poetry of the future, *The Communist Manifesto* had noted, depended upon the "Communists ... theoretically ... clearly understanding the line of march". This passage fits in an interesting way with the passage from Gramsci cited earlier about the contradictory consciousness of workers' leaders:

> The active man-in-the-mass has a practical activity, but has no clear theoretical consciousness of his actions... His theoretical consciousness can indeed be historically in opposition to his practical activity. One might almost say that he has two theoretical consciousnesses (or one contradictory consciousness), one which is implicit in

> his activity, which unites him with all his fellow-workers in the practical transformation of the real world, and one, superficially explicit or verbal, which he has inherited from the past and uncritically absorbed. But this verbal conception is not without consequences ... often powerful enough to produce a situation in which the contradictory state of consciousness does not permit any action ... and produces a state of moral and political passivity (Gramsci, 1971: 333).

"Theoretical consciousnesses ... implicit in his activity and which in reality unites him with all his collaborators in the practical transformation of reality" is only strengthened decisively against the conservative consciousness "inherited from the past" by a vision, "poetry", of the future, "the line of march", constantly subjected to debate and discussion "with all his collaborators in the practical transformation of reality" and how it informs the immediacy of strategy and tactics. That is the role of the revolutionary or communist party.[34]

V. Marx and the First International, the "Great Lever" [35]

How does the birth and development of the First International, the *International Working Men's Association (IWMA)*, in 1864 fit in with this argument? Marx, in his "Inaugural Address" (1864) to the International, speaks of "numbers ... united in combination and led by knowledge" (Marx ,1974: 81). Here Marx was "broadly paraphrasing his party concept of the fusion of Socialist theory with the labour movement", (Johnstone, 1967: 131), and hence adopting the broad concept of party. There is a strong hint that Marx sees the International as "the party". We'll return to this argument later. Defeat and impoverishment had stalked the fledgling workers' movement both in England and throughout Europe since 1848. Alternative political tendencies competed with Marx and Engels's vision of communism and the means to achieve it. The International had to accommodate them.[36] One of the most interesting was the persistence of the Owenite-inspired co-operative movement—also influential with some of the English trade union leaders, "the backbone" of the IWMA (Sperber, 2013: 357). Marx in his *Inaugural Address* begins by praising it:

> But there was ... a still greater victory of the political economy of labour over the political economy of property[37] ... the co-operative factories raised by the unassisted efforts of a few bold "hands". By deed, instead of by argument, they have shown that production on a large scale, and in accord with ... modern science, may be carried on without the existence of a class of masters ... [38] like slave labour, serf labour, hired labour is but a transitory and inferior form, destined to disappear before associated labour plying its toil with a willing hand, and a joyous heart ...

However, Marx adds, "co-operative labour, if kept within the narrow circle of the casual efforts of private workmen, will never be able to arrest the growth ... of monopoly ... to free the masses, nor even to perceptively lighten the burden of their miseries". Co-operative labour could only succeed if fostered "by national means" and that meant "conquering political power has therefore become the great duty of the working classes" (Marx, 1974: 80).

At the same time Marx stressed internationalism: "That bond of brotherhood which ought to exist between workmen of different countries, and incite them to stand firmly by each other in all their struggles for emancipation ... This was the pre-condition for emancipation. Disregard it and the efforts will be doomed. This, after all, was the purpose of an International" (Marx 1974: 81).

Marx concludes, re-enforcing this appeal for internationalism by praising the lead given by organised workers in England to the rest of Europe by taking sides in the US civil war and resisting the "infamous crusade for the perpetuation ... of slavery" (Marx 1974: 81). Working class solidarity was similarly required with the fighters for the liberation of Poland from the empire of Russia. Marx's dispute with the Owenites also led to a bitter clash over their refusal to support strikes, their claim that trade unions were harmful and that wage rises induced from trade union pressure would in effect be wiped out by price rises. Marx presented a paper to the General Council of the International, which later became the pamphlet *Wages, Price and Profit*, refuting these arguments. He applauded trade unions "as centres of resistance against the encroachments of capital". But the trade unions didn't go far enough. "They fail partially from an injudicious use of their power ... limiting themselves to a guerrilla war against the effects of the existing system, instead of ... using their organised forces as a lever for the final emancipation of the working class" (Marx, 1996: 120).

Class struggle was the only route to a genuinely communist society. The chapter "The Working Day" in the first volume of *Capital*, also published for the International, would describe it as "an antinomy of right against right ... between equal rights, force decides. Hence, in the history of capitalist production, the establishment of a norm for the working day presents itself as a struggle over the limits of that day, a struggle between collective capital ie a class of capitalists, and collective labour, ie the working class" (Marx, 1990: 344).

Marx's analogy of the "lever" in his formulation of his criticism of the trade unions—failing to use their power as "a lever for the final emancipation of the working class"—had an unintended consequence. It exposed both the strengths and weaknesses of his position in the IWMA and his alliance with the English trade unions. Based in London, together they effectively administered the IWMA.

On the one hand the English trade union leaders had enormous respect for Marx, his "erudition, powers of creative thought and political acumen" (Collins and Abramsky, 1965: 42). They had, after all, accepted the *Inaugural Address* and signed up to its *Provisional Rules* which began with the statement, "That the emancipation of the working classes must be conquered by the working classes themselves" (Marx, 1974: 82, Collins and Abramsky, 1965: 53). The *Inaugural Address* had made clear, as reported earlier, this meant the organisation of "production on a large scale ... without the existence of a class of masters employing a class of hands"—although how that was to be organised was "left deliberately open" (Collins and Abramsky, 1965: 53). These were words the union leaders could live with. The role of parliament, for example, was simply not discussed. In any case the:

> most effective actions of the IWMA, with the greatest public resonance and working class support, centred on labour disputes. The International raised funds from trade unionists across Europe to support the strike of Berlin printers and typesetters in 1865, Paris bronze workers in 1867 and Geneva construction workers in 1868 ... This intervention to prevent workers of one nationality from breaking strikes in another country was repeated on a large number of occasions (Sperber, 2013: 358).

At one level, the International more than justified both its name and existence. Trade unionism was spreading across Europe as a direct result of its influence (Collins and Abramsky, 1965: 92). On the other hand, at another level, it failed completely to live up to Marx's expectations for it. Marx fully understood the political limitations of his English trade union comrades on the GC, General Council, of the IWMA. Whilst "the class struggle and the organisation of the working class by the trade unions have acquired a certain degree of maturity and universality" in Britain, Marx wrote in a confidential note, "the English ... lack ... the *spirit of generalisation* and *revolutionary ardour*". However, his intervention to ensure the GC provided leadership, in combination with anticipated revolutionary upheavals in Europe, he argued, would make the trade unions a "*great lever of proletarian revolution*" (Marx and Engels, 1975-2005, vol. 21: 118; Collins and Abramsky, 1965: 85).

The industrial analogy of the "lever" came with another one, the "great engine." Again, in the expectation of renewed revolutionary outbreaks in Europe, Marx had told Engels that the GC and the IWMA was a "mighty engine in our hands" (Marx and Engels, 1975-2005, vol. 42: 424; Collins and Abramsky 1965: 78, 98). Yet when the anticipated revolution burst in Europe in 1871 in the entirely unanticipated form of the Paris Commune, the International most certainly did not fulfil Marx's expectations for it. It was already clear that his English trade union comrades were far more pre-occupied with the Reform League and even with Gladstone's Liberal Party. This culminated in the 1867 Reform Act which, for all its limitations, enfranchised a working class majority (Collins and Abramsky, 1965: 146). These developments highlighted the limited support for the IWMA. By now hundreds of thousands of workers had joined trade unions, but only a minority of these affiliated to the IWMA. This factor seriously restricted its fund-raising capacities. "What our party lacks is money," Marx wrote to Engels (Marx and Engels, 1975-2005, vol. 42: 455; Collins and Abramsky, 1965: 88). The remark revealed both the IWMA's weakness as well as emphasising Marx's blurring of his own role, the IWMA and his idea of the party.

The English trade union leaders of the International were not revolutionaries. If they were willing to support revolutions abroad it was because they wanted to see the internationalisation of the few democratic and trade union rights that they had secured at home (Collins and Abramsky, 1965: 153-4, 291). The politics of the most left wing workers' leader on the GC of the IWMA, Robert Applegarth, Secretary of the ASCJ, Amalgamated Society of Carpenters and Joiners, formed earlier out of a bitter building workers' strike, are briefly worth exploring to illustrate Marx's dilemma. Applegarth was one of the very few trade union leaders on the GC to support, albeit hesitatingly, Marx's perspective on the Paris Commune. Was Applegarth, then, a potential "Marxist" cadre? Marx and Engels certainly regarded him as one of their closest comrades. He had publicly supported their views on land nationalisation. They were delighted when Applegarth was invited by both houses of parliament, as a leading representative of trade unionism, to offer advice (Collins and Abramsky, 1965: 173). Yet Applegarth lacked consistency as an international socialist. A sometimes narrow view of trade unionism could spill over into dangerously reactionary politics. He lent public support to the launching of the Emigration League which sought "to remove by emigration the superfluous hands from the labour market ... and strengthen the British empire through the extension of prosperous colonies" (Collins and Abramsky, 1965: 173).

This lack of consistency, instability of opinion, went to the very core of his politics. He might have agreed with Marx's lines in the *Inaugural Address* denying the need for "a class of masters employing a class of hands". Yet in the tenth annual report to his union the ASCJ in 1870, he praised both employers and workers for meeting as equals, settling their differences through arbitration and together introducing reforms like technical schools for the building trades (Collins and Abramsky, 1965: 176). But lack of consistency is a limited explanation. What we are witnessing here is a development, in embryo, that would become only too familiar in the 20th century: trade union leaders, as well as the parliamentary representatives of organised labour, who believed they were socialists, even Marxists. Yet they staked their futures, and that of the trade unions, on reforming capitalism rather than overthrowing it. It was a development that would make Marx and Engels increasingly uneasy but they never fully understood it, and certainly never attempted to theorise it. As we shall see, Rosa Luxemburg was the first Marxist of the stature of Marx and Engels fully to comprehend it.

VI. Marx and Engels, the International, and the Paris Commune

In his "Address to the General Council of the IWMA on the Civil

War in France" (1871), Marx provided the International with documentary evidence from the Paris Commune which in pamphlet form complements the *Communist Manifesto*. We now had the first example of working class revolutionary practice overthrowing capitalism, at least in one city, and laying the foundations, however rough and incomplete, for a communist society. But we also saw the limitations of the IWMA, the International, as a facilitator of that process.[39] Marx could only comment with hindsight on what he believed to be the first major mistake of the communards: "the [National Guard] Central Committee made themselves ... guilty of a decisive mistake in not at once marching on Versailles, then completely helpless" (Marx and Engels, 1975-2005, vol. 22: 326).

The complicated politics of the outcome of the Franco Prussian war, the capitulation of France to Bismarck, which had precipitated the siege of Paris, and the Commune as a response, are beyond our scope here. Nevertheless, a case can be made that the weak and defeated French government, propped up by Prussia, and based at Versailles, was susceptible to an immediate military advance by the Communards. This was the position recommended by Duval (Gluckstein, 2011: 118), a young iron founder, established popular local working class leader and Blanquist (Lissagaray, 1976: 60).[40] But the Blanquists' conspiratorial and elitist political history put them at odds with the spirit of the Commune which wanted mass participatory democracy. The tension between the military and political objectives of the Commune was never satisfactorily resolved. Duval was clearly a Commune cadre but not a communist cadre in the tradition that would develop in the 20th century from the ideas of Marx and Engels. The National Guard may have made a mistake but nevertheless it came to symbolise the new politics that the Commune represented. "The first decree of the Commune was the suppression of the standing army, and the substitution for it of the armed people." This was now the National Guard, "the bulk of which consisted of working men", electing its own officers (Marx and Engels, 1975-2005, vol. 22: 331):

> The Commune was formed of the municipal councillors, chosen by universal suffrage ... and revocable at short terms.[41] The majority of its members were naturally working men,[42] or acknowledged representatives of the working class. The Commune was to be a working, not a parliamentary, body, executive and legislative at the same time. Instead of continuing to be the agent of the Central Government, the police was at once stripped of its political attributes, and turned into the responsible, and at all times revocable agent of the Commune. So were the officials of all other branches of the Administration. From the members of the Commune downwards, the public service had to be done at *workmen's wages* (Marx and Engels, 1975-2005, vol. 22: 331).

Marx had earlier underlined the significance of this development: "The working class cannot simply lay hold of the ready-made state machinery, and wield it for its own purposes" (Marx and Engels, 1975-2005, vol. 22: 328.). The state had to be overthrown. The Commune "breaks the modern State power" (Marx and Engels, 1975-2005, vol. 22: 333). This led Marx and Engels to make a rare change to the *Communist Manifesto*, the preface of the 1872 edition, after the Commune had been crushed. That single sentence was also the inspiration for Lenin's *The State and Revolution* (Hobsbawm 1998: 10). It was a "dictatorship of the proletariat" or "proletarian dictature" as Marx would describe the Commune during a speech at a special dinner in London on the seventh anniversary of the International in October 1871, just a few months after the bloody destruction of the Commune (Marx 1974: 272).[43]

The Commune "aimed at the expropriation of the expropriators". It wanted to transform "the means of production, land and capital ... into mere instruments of free and associated labour. But that is Communism!" Here Marx is distinguishing between the Commune's intentions and what it could achieve in its brief two months of existence:

> If co-operative production is not to remain a sham and a snare; if it is to supersede the Capitalist system; if united co-operative societies are to regulate national production upon a common plan, thus taking it under their own control, and putting an end to the constant anarchy and periodical convulsions which are the fatality of Capitalist production—what else ... would it be but Communism ...? (Marx and Engels, 1975-2005, vol. 22: 335).

This is a call for socialisation of production under workers' control and the Commune did offer some examples where it occurred. Lissagaray writes of the postal system under Albert Theisz, a manual worker and prominent member of the International. He "found the service quite disorganised, the divisional offices closed, the stamps hidden away or carried off ... Theisz acted with promptitude and energy ... ". He opened discussions with the employees "and the direction of the services was entrusted to the head clerks ... in 48 hours the collection and distribution of letters was re-organised" (Lissagaray, 1976: 176; Gluckstein, 2011: 9). Lissagaray writes of other departments including the Telegraph and National Printing Press "ordinarily reserved to the great bourgeoisie ... managed with skill and economy ... by workmen, subordinate employees; and this is not the least of their crimes in the eyes of the Versaillaise bourgeoisie" (Lissagaray, 1976: 177-78).

Yet "its special measures could but betoken the tendency of a government of the people by the people" (Marx and Engels, 1975-2005, vol. 22: 339). The Commune used a range of measures against the "expropriators". Private employers were subject to the equivalent of what Marx had called on earlier occasions "legislative interference", but imposed by a workers' government not a capitalist government. Night work was abolished for journeymen bakers. Employers were banned from finding excuses for reducing wages. Associations of workers replaced those employers who had abandoned their workshops or factories. Nevertheless, the Bank of France remained untouched, as Engels stressed:

> The hardest thing to understand is certainly the holy awe with which they remained standing outside of the Bank of France ... The bank in the hands of the Commune ... would have been worth more than ten thousand hostages. It would have meant pressure of the whole of the French bourgeoisie on the Versailles government in favour of peace with the Commune (Marx and Engels, 1975-2005, vol. 27, 187).

What we can conclude though is that despite the mass democratic Communal pressures on both Blanquists and Proudhonists, the dominant political tendencies, which curbed or even reversed their "doctrines", as Engels put it, the Commune leadership were unclear about their political objectives (Marx and Engels, 1975-2005, vol. 27, 187).[44] Eugene Varlin, who had led a book binders' strike in 1864 and became one of the International's best-known representatives in the Commune and part of its leadership, personified the problem. A "Left Proudhonist", influenced by, and in communication with, Marx (Nimtz, 2000: 214), he was ready to criticise Proudhonism as "abstract scientific sociology" (Gluckstein, 2011: 74). Yet as assistant delegate for Finances in the Commune he, too, opposed seizing the Bank (Gluckstein, 2011: 143).

Varlin is a good example of a potential "communist" cadre, a cadre in embryo, unstable in opinion.[45] Lissagaray went so far as to write that the Commune leaders were "without a military plan, without a programme, without general views" (Lissagaray, 1971: 154). His concluding poetic flourish exposed even more the political vacuum, "O Revolution! Thou dost not wait the well-timed day and hour. Thou comest suddenly, blind and fatal as the avalanche. The true soldier accepts the combat wherever hazard may place him" (Lissagaray, 1971: 154). Engels would write, "the Commune was the grave of the Proudhon school of

Socialism ... The Blanquists fared no better" (Engels, 1968: 15).

For Engels, Elizabeth Dmitrieff, "the spiritual daughter of the International", personified the Commune's potential (Ross 2015: 27). A Russian, one of the tiny number of "Marxists", with evolving ideas about the emancipation of the peasantry, she represented both Marx and the International in the Commune.[46] Her lasting achievement in the Commune was the founding of the Women's Union, "the Commune's largest and most effective organisation ... the Union envisioned a full re-organisation of women's labour and the end of gender-based inequality" (Ross 2015: 27-8).[47] Dmitrieff also personified Marx's insistence that the Commune was "emphatically international", admitting "all foreigners to the honour of dying for an immortal cause" (Marx and Engels, 1975-2005, vol. 22: 338).[48]

VII. Marx and Engels and the world's first workers' mass political party: Germany's Socialist Party

The defeat of the Paris Commune was, in effect, also the trigger for the disintegration of the First International. Marx's *Civil War in France* had made him famous, indeed infamous. It was seized upon by all of the Commune's enemies as proof of an international insurrectionary conspiracy inspired by Marx and "his" International. This was amplified by the media of the day and had the, no doubt intended, effect of undermining the weak coalition ties that held together the IWMA. Bismarck even proposed a European alliance against the International (Fernbach, 1974: 43). It was a phantom. Marx may have helped make the International a symbol for the Commune but it had most definitely not been able to provide it with political leadership, which was indeed a vital missing ingredient. Marx and Engels recognised the weakness. It helped inform Resolution IX, drafted by Marx and Engels in 1871, for the September conference of the IWMA, the First International, once more calling for the working class to organise itself as a political party.

This resolution was also precipitated partly by the bitter battles with the anarchist Mikhail Bakunin over the future of the

International. The fight with Bakunin and his supporters would consume a huge amount of Marx's and Engels's time and energy and, arguably, contributed to the International's demise.[49] Amongst the exchanges of bitter polemics, one in particular, stands out. Engels's "On Authority", a challenge to Bakunin and the anarchist assertion that all authority, even the authority of workers' democratically elected representatives, must inevitably become authoritarian. Engels's argument is particularly relevant because he locates it in the workplace. Engels asks the question, "suppose a social revolution has dethroned the capitalists ... and the instruments of labour have become the collective property of the workers who use them. Will authority have disappeared or ... only have changed its form?" (Marx and Engels, 1975-2005, vol. 23: 423). Engels describes how in a cotton spinning mill several technical and mechanical operations are required to transform the cotton into thread, and that these operations, for the most part, take place in different rooms. Steam is the energy source. And "the workers ... are obliged to begin and finish their work at the hours fixed by the authority of steam, which cares nothing for individual autonomy." So how do the workers control the productive process? "The workers must first come to an understanding on the hours of work; and these hours, once they are fixed, must be observed by all." In addition, "particular questions can arise in each room," concerning the technical process, "which must be settled by a decision of a delegate placed at the head of each branch of labour, or, if possible, by a majority vote, the will of a single individual will always have to subordinate itself, which means that questions are settled in an authoritarian way" (Marx and Engels, 1975-2005, vol. 23: 423).

Authority is essential for the successful operation of the mill, but it has been democratised. Workers have taken part in and have agreed the framework for the minute by minute, productive operations. Engels leaves open the question whether it is the elected delegate, or majority voting, that establishes the framework for agreeing the procedures. Indeed, the majority may well decide to trust their delegate with the day to day decisions, using the Paris Commune principle: if the delegate betrays their trust, they can always be replaced. Certainly, in Engels's other example of the ship, he warns, especially in times of danger on the high seas, "lives of all depend ... on obedience", the immediate response to instructions from the person charged with the ship's management (Marx and Engels, 1975-2005, vol. 23: 424). Engels adds "if man by ... his ... inventive genius, has subdued the forces of nature, the latter avenge themselves upon him, by subjecting him ... to a veritable despotism independent of all social organisation. Wanting to abolish authority in large scale industry is tantamount to wanting to abolish industry itself, to destroy the power loom in order to return to the spinning wheel" (Marx and Engels, 1975-2005, vol. 23: 423-4).

At the same time, he makes the interesting observation: "Authority and autonomy are relative things whose spheres vary with the various phases of the development of society. If the autonomists confined themselves to saying that the social organisation of the future would restrict authority solely to the limits with which the conditions of production render it inevitable, we could understand each other" (Marx and Engels, 1975-2005, vol. 23: 424). This helps define the route to one of communism's most inspirational objectives, cited in the *Communist Manifesto:* an "association, in which the free development of each is the condition for the free development of all" (Marx and Engels, 1998: 62), the complementary freedoms dependent on the development of the immense potential of socially controlled modern productive forces. First, though, we have to make the revolution, "certainly the most authoritarian thing there is" (Marx and Engels, 1975-2005, vol. 23: 425).

Here is a direct challenge to the anarchists. How will your revolution avoid any exercise of authority? A revolutionary upsurge may begin spontaneously. But it quickly comes up against well organised conservative forces. Our side needs to organise in response. There will be a range of different views on the best strategies and tactics. Organisation is required for these strategies and tactics to be thoroughly and fairly discussed: even more so when a strategy is agreed upon and then implemented, especially if this requires the use of force, and rapid on-the-spot decision-making. The anarchist confuses authority with authoritarianism. Engels is playing with this confusion almost satirically, confident, unlike the anarchists, that authority and organisation can be exercised democratically. If objective circumstances momentarily impose constraints on democratic practice, say, an anticipated military attack, then an ingredient binding together democratically elected leaders and and those they lead comes into play, misunderstood or perhaps never understood by the anarchists: trust.

Meanwhile, the roots of the world's first mass-based working class political party were already being laid in Germany, quite independently of the International and the Paris Commune. They were planted not by Marx and Engels but by an extremely eccentric, indeed dangerous follower of theirs, Ferdinand Lassalle. Lassalle was the founder of the General German Workers' Association in 1863. Marx had been suitably impressed (Sperber, 2013: 353), although wary of Lassalle's obsessive leadership cult (Johnstone, 1967: 136). They had worked together on the *Neue Rheinische Zeitung* in 1848 (Sperber, 2013: 338). Lassalle combined support for Marx with support for, and even secret meetings with, the Prussian premier Bismarck (Sperber, 2013: 353-4).

Nevertheless, Lassalle's initiative was historically unprecedented. Rosa Luxemburg's quite extraordinary tribute in 1913 gives us a sense of his continuing impact even into the early years of the 20th century: "The emergence of an independent class party of the proletariat was a historical necessity ... [That it] ... appeared at the gates with such radiance and splendour fifty years ago, more than two decades before all other countries, and acted as a role model for them, is thanks to Lassalle's life work and his maxim: 'I dared!'" (Luxemburg: 2009).

Lassalle's early death in a bizarre duel in no way diminished his influence, or weakened the dispute of principle between Marx and the leadership of the new workers' party. German national unity, yes, said Marx, but it "could only be achieved by a German revolution ... sweeping away the Prussian dynasty" (Sperber, 2013: 362), not by allying with it. Marx looked instead to two of his most ardent supporters, Wilhelm Liebknecht and a young August Bebel[50] who, by taking control of the federation of German workers' educational societies in Saxony, provided the base for a second German workers' party (Sperber, 2013: 367). But here too was almost a mirror-image problem. Liebknecht was ready to support the anti-Prussian monarchs in Hanover and Hessen (Sperber, 2013: 368). Both groups were fixated on the *national* state.

German unity under Bismarck in 1871 superficially resolved, or rather shelved, the problems. The two workers' parties came together for a unity congress in the German city of Gotha in 1875. But Lassalle's posthumous influence weighed heavily. Hence Marx's famous *Critique* of the Gotha unity programme,[51] and, at first, a refusal to support the new party. Here was the major dilemma for Marx and Engels in the shadow of the First International. They would not stay with a given organisational form if they thought the real movement had outgrown it and it had become a "fetter" on its further development. They could not save the First International but it "did help provide the political and organisational principles for the new parties that were to emerge" (Johnstone, 1967: 135). And they, in turn, provided the basis for the Second International formed in 1889. Yet these were national parties with a political orientation on existing national states. At the same time Marx recognised in a letter about the *Critique,* "Every step of a real movement is more important than a dozen programmes ... " (Marx, 1974: 341). But that didn't resolve the dilemma and Marx's *Critique* was harsh. He saw Lassalle's influence stamped all over the programme, Liebknecht and Bebel had effectively capitulated to the idea of a national state.

According to the Gotha Programme, "the working class must initially work for its emancipation *within the framework of the present-day national state*" (Marx, 1974: 349, emphasis in original). Marx thundered in response: "In contrast to the *Communist Manifesto*" (which "Lassalle ... knew by heart"), "Lassalle approached the workers' movement from the narrowest national point of view—and this after the work of the International!" (Marx, 1974: 349, 350). German nationalism tainted the new party. "Bismarck's *Norddeutsche*[52] was perfectly right when it declared to the satisfaction of its master, that the German workers' party had renounced internationalism in its programme" (Marx 1974: 350-1).

Indeed, Lassalle had effectively ignored the workers' movement altogether by substituting the national state as socialism's agent, opposing the trade unions in favour of state sponsored workers' co-operatives (Sperber, 2013: 526). The Gotha Programme also reflected Lassalle's reactionary and exclusive focus on the capitalist component of the ruling class alone, deliberately ignoring the landlord component. It states that "the capitalist class has a monopoly of the instruments of labour". Wrong, and as Marx pointed out this was because "Lassalle only attacked the capitalist class and not the landowners" (Marx, 1974: 343). Lassalle "wanted to extenuate his alliance with the absolutist and feudal opponents of the bourgeoisie" (Marx, 1974: 349).

Raya Dunayevskaya has noted:

> The *Critique* ... is not just a criticism of a programme, but a comprehensive analysis of Lassalle's doctrines. It contains a theory of the state and, more importantly, of the non-state-to-be (as he [Marx] called the Paris Commune), which was to be the model for the future breakup of the capitalist state ... Not only was capitalism a transient stage, but so was the "revolutionary dictatorship of the proletariat" which was to replace it (Dunayevskaya, 1981: 156).[53]

Sensing the danger, prophetically as it turned out, that the new party would lose sight altogether of communist objectives,

Marx felt compelled to spell them out, sometimes in passages which outline a communist society in ways not previously attempted (Callinicos, 1983: 170, Dunayevskaya, 1981: 157). After the state had withered away:

> in a more advanced phase of communist society, when the enslaving subjugation of individuals to the division of labour, and thereby the antithesis between intellectual and physical labour, have disappeared; when labour is no longer just a means of keeping alive but has itself become a vital need; when the all-round development of individuals has also increased their productive powers and all the springs of co-operative wealth flow more abundantly—only then can society ... inscribe on its banner: From each according to his abilities, to each according to his needs! (Marx, 1974: 347).

However, the new united party proved to be a great success. In the 1877 national elections it doubled the vote of the previous socialist parties "and emerged as a significant political voice against Bismarck" (Sperber, 2013: 528). Marx and Engels, in any case, had withdrawn their threat to disown the new party. The press viewed it as genuinely socialist, even revolutionary. More importantly, so did workers. Engels noted, "It is *this circumstance alone* which has made it possible for Marx and myself not to dissociate ourselves publicly from a programme such as this" ("Letter to Bebel", 12 October 1875, in Marx and Engels, 1975-2005, vol. 45: 98). They even began referring to it as "our party" (Marx and Engels, 1975-2005, vol. 27: 227; Johnstone, 1967: 137). But Marx still always blamed Liebknecht for compromising with the Lassalleans (Sperber, 2013: 528).

Nevertheless, the influence of Marx and Engels on the new party made its mark. Bismarck certainly thought so and "unleashed his fury" against it as the party appeared to become "really receptive to Marxism" (Schorske, 1983: 3; Blackledge, 2014: 91). This coincided with the publication of Engel's

Anti-Dühring (1878).[54] And, rather like the *Critique of the Gotha Programme*, *Anti-Dühring* deliberately contained a more detailed, though inevitably speculative, vision of a future communist society both as an innovation in itself, but also as propaganda weapon. Consolidation of what would become known as *Marxism* in the new party accelerated, especially after Marx's death in 1883.[55]

Although Engels welcomed the revised party programme at the Erfurt Congress of 1891 as an improvement on Gotha, he identified the same fundamental weakness—ambiguity about the role of the state in the transition to socialism. He raised objections that Rosa Luxemburg would build upon in her later criticisms. He warned against "the forgetting of the great principal considerations for the momentary interest of the day. ... regardless of later consequences, this sacrifice of the future of the movement for its present, may be 'honestly' meant, but it is and remains opportunism" (Marx and Engels, 1975-2005, vol. 27: 227). He reminded comrades that socialism could only be realised by a revolutionary regime similar to the Paris Commune: "Our party and the working class can only come to power under the form of a democratic republic. This is even the specific form for the dictatorship of the proletariat" (Marx and Engels, 1975-2005, vol. 27: 227).[56] Carl Schorske points out that the Erfurt Programme contained two related messages distinguishing revolutionaries from reformists. To the revolutionary left it said be "patient". To the reformists it said, "reforms are the first task, pursue them" (Schorske, 1983: 6). But the die was cast and the question that Rosa Luxemburg would force to the surface was raised, even though, at the time, she didn't answer it. Can reformists and revolutionaries co-exist in the same party?

The economic boom of the 1890s simultaneously gave rise to increased living standards, momentarily eased tensions between reformists and revolutionaries, and, above all, saw a massive expansion of trade unionism. The leaders of the unions began to play an increasingly important role in the party. They represented in some ways the late 19th century German equivalent of the English trade union leaders who had so shattered Marx's revolutionary illusions in them in the First International. They certainly strengthened the social base of reformism within the German party.

Rosa Luxemburg, in one of her most famous pamphlets, *The Mass Strike, the Party and the Trade Unions*, published in 1906, would describe the trade union leaders as part of the "opportunist wing of social democracy" which wanted to reduce "the political struggle of the working class to the parliamentary contest" and turn "the revolutionary proletarian party into a petty bourgeois reform one". She attacked:

> the specialisation of professional activity as trade union leaders, as well as the naturally restricted horizon which is bound up with disconnected economic struggles in a peaceful period, [and] leads only too easily, amongst trade-union officials, to bureaucratism and a certain narrowness of outlook ... There is ... the overvaluation of organisation, which from a means has gradually been changed into an end in itself ... From this comes that openly admitted need for peace which shrinks from great risks ... to the stability of the trade unions ... from the concealment of the objective limits drawn by the bourgeois social order, to the trade-union struggle, there arises hostility to every theoretical criticism which refers to these limits in connection with the ultimate aims of the labour movement (Waters, 1970: 209, 214-15).

Instead, we are asked to accept "an illimitable vista of economic progress to the trade union struggle within the capitalist system". Adding to this major threat to working class democracy in the movement, another loomed, nothing less than a counter "revolution in the relations of leaders and rank and file. In place of the direction by colleagues through local committees, ... there appears the business-like direction of the trade union officials.

The initiative and power of making decisions thereby devolve upon trade union specialists ... and the more passive virtue of discipline upon the mass of members .... The dark side of officialdom" (Waters, 1970: 215-16).

In fact, Luxemburg under-estimated just how damaging would be this undermining of rank and file workers' democracy with the concentration of bureaucratic control in the hands of both parliamentary and trade union leaders. She believed the conservatism would be broken by a revolutionary mass strike movement: "Whether they stand aside or endeavour to resist the movement, the result of their attitude will be that the trade union leaders, like the party leaders ... , will simply be swept aside by the rush of events, and the economic and political struggles of the masses will be fought out without them" (Waters, 1970: 207).

But the 1918 German Revolution proved the opposite. The eruption of mass strikes and mass-based revolutionary Workers' and Soldiers' Councils were immediately and successfully undermined by the reformist political and trade union leaders (Hoffrogge, 2014). Undoubtedly, Luxemburg's faith in the spontaneous creative capacities of the masses was one of her great strengths and a refreshing contrast to the nightmare bureaucratic politics of official German trade union and nation state socialism that had tied it to the Kaiser's war machine. Yet there was a fatalism built into this perspective. Arguably, it reflected both the legacy of party organisation, and even an analytical weakness about the class struggle itself, left by Marx and Engels, a degree of fatalism about the dynamics of the working class movement (Callinicos 1983: 153).

Marx's *Capital* had encouraged the fatalism. In its closing chapters in Volume 1 we read, "But capitalist production begets, with the inexorability of a natural process, its own negation" (Marx, 1990: 929). This encouraged the inter-changeability perspective of working class and political party, common to Marx, Engels and Luxemburg. It was one of the reasons why it took such a long time for Luxemburg to break with the German socialist party. This has led Paul Le Blanc to formulate the division between Luxemburg and Lenin over the legacy of Marx and Engels's conception of the party in the following way. Lenin saw "the party not as *embracing* the working class, but as *interacting* with it for the purpose of influencing it in a revolutionary direction. For Luxemburg ... the point is to blend into the working class as it exists, the better to contribute to its organic development as a revolutionary force" (Le Blanc, 1999: 95-6).[57]

VIII. Lenin's *State and Revolution*: theory

The political consequences of this kind of fatalism were exposed in August 1914, when the German Social Democratic Party, along with almost all the other parties of the Second International, reacted to the outbreak of the First World War by supporting its national government. 1914 shook Lenin, the leader of the world's first socialist revolution in Russia in October 1917, to the core. Famously, it forced him to return and re-examine the basic roots of Marxism including a return to Feuerbach and especially Hegel. Lenin would come to emphasise more forcefully that subjective practical activity lay at the centre of the "objective" world, and that social scientific laws should not be "fetishised" as things distinct from conscious human activity but instead be recognised as "necessarily, incomplete, and approximate" and open to attempts to frame political intervention (Kouvelakis, 2007: 174, 186). Kouvelakis quotes a Lenin marginal note on his re-reading of Hegel: "Man's consciousness not only reflects the objective world, but creates it" (Kouvelakis 2007: 193). The result is Lenin's intervention to change the course both of the war (or at least Russia's involvement in it) and the revolution that erupted as a result of the war: "a mass initiative under proletarian leadership aimed at the conquest of political power, that is, breaking the existing state apparatus and replacing it with a contradictory state" (Kouvelakis, 2007: 195).

Lenin's pamphlet *The State and Revolution*, written during 1917, provided the theoretical framework, although his conception of proletarian leadership, and the way the Bolshevik Party would relate to the wider workers' leadership, would evolve in response to how the revolutionary process unfolded, especially at the point of production. One further qualification must be added. *The State and Revolution* was never intended to provide theoretical perspective for an exclusively *Russian* revolution. It was a challenge to all the socialist parties linked to the Second International, especially the German one. "But this revolution as a whole can only be understood as a link in a chain of socialist proletarian revolutions being caused by the imperialist war" (Lenin, 1965e, Preface).[58]

The structure of the pamphlet is based upon Lenin re-visiting two of Marx's writings—on the Paris Commune as developed in his *Address to the General Council of the IWMA on the Civil War in France, 1871* and his *Critique of the Gotha Programme*—both of which emphasise the necessity of a complete revolutionary break with the existing nation state, indeed all the warring imperialist national states. Lenin's direct quote of a single sentence from Marx's writings on the Paris Commune dominates the discussion of the subject in *State and Revolution* "that the working class cannot simply lay hold of the ready-made state machinery, and wield it for its own purpose" (Lenin 1971a: Chapter III). As Lenin notes, this had led Marx and Engels to make a rare change to the *Communist Manifesto*, the preface of the 1872 edition after the Commune had been crushed. Lenin attempts to summarise Marx's arguments[59] and project them on to the anticipated international socialist revolutions:

> We, the workers, shall organise large scale production on the basis of what capitalism has already created, relying on our own experience as workers, establishing strict, iron discipline backed up by the state power of the armed workers. We shall reduce the role of state officials to that of simply carrying out our instructions as responsible, revocable, modestly paid "foremen and accountants" (of course, with the aid of technicians of all sorts, types and degrees) ... Such a beginning ... will of

> itself lead to the gradual "withering away" of all bureaucracy, to the gradual creation of an order ... bearing no similarity to wage slavery ... under which the functions of control and accounting, becoming more and more simple, will be performed by each in turn, will then become a habit and will finally die out as the special functions of a special section of the population (Lenin, 1965e: Chapter III).

This, of course, is an immensely ambitious projection—on a heavily concertinaed timeline. It should be understood as providing flexible principles or guidelines, inevitably to be conditioned by the real historical circumstances of the actual revolutions, not least the isolation that would be the fate of the Russian Revolution. Nevertheless, there is clarification of a much-misunderstood and controversial formulation—dictatorship of the proletariat:

> Simultaneously with an immense expansion of democracy, which for the first time becomes democracy for the poor, democracy for the people, and not democracy for the money-bags, the dictatorship of the proletariat imposes a series of restrictions on the freedom of the oppressors, the exploiters, the capitalists. We must suppress them in order to free humanity from wage slavery (Lenin, 1965e: Chapter V).

This is the one of the rare occasions where we have a hint, a projection, about the role of capitalists in the transition phase. Capitalists, and hence capitalism, are to be suppressed by "a series of restrictions": not eliminated either as individuals or even as capitalists. Later in the chapter, Lenin returns to this point where he equates "the expropriation of the capitalists, with the establishment of workers' control over the capitalists" (Lenin, 1965e: Chapter V, Part 4).

In other words, dictatorship of the proletariat is not about a general society-wide dictatorship over the entire population that would become so associated with the Stalin period. It is about dictatorship over the remnant of the capitalist class whose functions cannot be eliminated overnight but must be forced to serve the interests of the vast majority. We also have in this section the first mention of how the dictatorship of the proletariat will express itself: the Soviets of Workers' and Soldiers' Deputies:

> Naturally, the exploiters are unable to suppress the people without a highly complex machine for performing this task, but the people can suppress the exploiters even with a very simple "machine", almost without a "machine", without a special apparatus, by the simple organisation of the armed people (such as the Soviets of Workers' and Soldiers' Deputies, we would remark, running ahead) (Lenin, 1965e: Chapter V).

Lenin would learn very quickly that this ultra-optimistic forecast of "a very simple [state] 'machine', almost without a 'machine'", was misplaced. Nevertheless, his interpretation of Marx's outlines of "the transition" would still provide elementary ground rules for the phase immediately after the October Revolution in 1917. In September 1917, just before the October Revolution, Lenin wrote a pamphlet, *The Impending Catastrophe and How to Combat It*. Arguably it translates *The State and Revolution* into a transitional programme for the immediate post-revolutionary period, similar to the programme in the *Communist Manifesto.*[60] The title signals Lenin's recognition of the appalling circumstances that threatened the revolution from the start. The impending catastrophe was a spreading famine exacerbated by capitalists "deliberately ... sabotaging production" (Lenin, 1965d).

The transitional programme was about the new state, the "workers' state", imposing urgent measures to seize control of the economy but not necessarily displacing the previous private owners, rather compelling them to co-operate. Interestingly, it also shows Lenin pre-occupied with the question of the peasantry from the start. Here were the revolution's allies, indispensable to the revolution's victory, as well as to resolving the food shortage catastrophe. However, peasant support for a workers' dictatorship could not be taken for granted. The peasant question overshadowed the demand to nationalise the banks. The language surprises: "The advantages accruing to the whole people from nationalisation of the banks—*not* to the workers especially (for the workers have little to do with banks) but to the mass of peasants and small industrialists—would be enormous ... The availability of credit on easy terms for the *small* owners, for the peasants, would increase immensely" (Lenin, 1965d).

There is no ambiguity here. The market will continue to operate. However, at the same time the state "would for the first time be in a position first to *review* all the chief monetary operations, which would be unconcealed, then to *control* them, then to *regulate* economic life, and finally to *obtain* millions and billions for major state transactions, without paying the capitalist gentlemen sky-high 'commissions' for their 'services'." Nevertheless, Lenin expected co-operation from the displaced—overthrown—social class, albeit under coercion.

"Nationalisation of the banks has only to be decreed and it would be carried out by the directors and employees themselves ... It would be enough, for example, to organise the poorer employees *separately* and to reward them for detecting fraud and delay on the part of the rich for nationalisation of the banks to be effected as smoothly and rapidly as can be" (Lenin, 1965d).

We have an insight here into how Lenin conceived nationalisation or socialisation under workers' control. In a later section headed "Compulsory Association", Lenin describes how manufacturers and industrialists in every branch of production would be amalgamated, this included the "big shareholders (for they are the real leaders of modern industry, its real masters)". Yet the approach to them was to be double edged. On the one hand:

> They shall be regarded as deserters from military service, and punished as such, if they do not work for the immediate implementation of the law ... workers and their trade unions ... (will) institute the fullest, strictest and most detailed accountancy, but chiefly to *combine operations* in the purchase of raw materials, the sale of products, and the *economy* of national funds and forces. When the separate establishments are amalgamated into a single syndicate, this economy can attain tremendous proportions, as economic science teaches us and as is shown by the example of all syndicates, cartels and trusts (Lenin, 1965d).

On the other hand:

> it must be repeated that this unionisation will not in itself alter property relations one iota and will not deprive any owner of a single kopek. This circumstance must be strongly stressed, for the bourgeois press constantly "frightens" small and medium proprietors by asserting that socialists in general, and the Bolsheviks in particular, want to "expropriate" them—a deliberately false assertion (Lenin, 1965d).

Again, Lenin is conscious of the peasant looking over his shoulder. The very next sentence reads: "Socialists do not intend to, cannot and will not expropriate the small peasant *even if there is a fully socialist revolution*." Nor is the underlying revolutionary principle the immediate abolition of the capitalist class. "In point of fact, the whole question of control boils down to who controls whom, ie, which class is in control and which is being controlled" (Lenin, 1965d). Herein lies the meaning of the dictatorship of the proletariat in the transition period following the socialist revolution.

IX. Lenin's *State and Revolution*: practice—"All Power to the Soviets!"[61]

Orlando Figes's ferociously anti-Bolshevik *A People's Tragedy, The Russian Revolution 1891-1924* has been a dominant text in the post-1989 scholarship on the subject, translated into 28 languages. Eric Hobsbawm, arguably the most able and certainly the most famous Marxist historian of the late 20th century, gave the book the most extraordinary and virtually unqualified stamp of approval: "*A People's Tragedy* will do more to help us understand the Russian Revolution than any other book I know of written since the end of the Soviet Union" (Hobsbawm, 1996).[62] What interests us here is that the serious scholar in Figes is compelled to concede the main argument in 1917 of Lenin and the Bolsheviks: the main argument, indeed, of *The State and Revolution*:

> The rising fortunes of the Bolsheviks during the summer and autumn [of 1917] was essentially due to the fact that they were the only major political party who stood uncompromisingly for Soviet power (Figes, 1997: 460).

Although Figes claims that the October insurrection was a coup, he insists that it took place:

> amidst a social revolution which was centred on the popular realisation of Soviet power as the negation of the state and the direct self-rule of the people ... The popular demand for Soviet power had never expressed itself in a preference for the dictatorship of any particular party. The torrent of resolutions, petitions and declarations from the factories, the army units and the villages in support of a Soviet government after the Kornilov crisis[63] invariably called on all socialist parties to take part in its establishment, and often displayed a marked impatience with the factional disputes

> between them ... The dominant sentiment was one of anger and frustration that nothing concrete had been gained, neither peace, nor bread nor land, six months after the February Revolution ...
>
> What the workers saw in Soviet power, above all, was the chance to control their own factory environment. They wanted to regulate their own shop floor relations, to set their own wages and working conditions, and combat the "sabotage", the conspiratorial running-down of production by profit-conscious employers, which many workers blamed for the industrial crisis ... In this heightened atmosphere of class war, impatience was growing with the Mensheviks' leadership[64] of the labour movement: their policies of mediating labour disputes and conciliating the employers had failed to stop the rising tide of unemployment. Many workers, especially those under the influence of the Bolsheviks, saw the solution in the sequestration (or nationalisation) of their factory by a Workers' State, called "Soviet Power", which would then set up a management board of workers, technicians and Soviet officials to keep the factory running.[65] It was part of the growing political consciousness of workers, the realisation that their demands could only be met by changing the nature of the state itself (Figes, 1997: 460, 461).

Figes reports on the deepening strike wave involving far wider groupings, "unskilled labourers and semi intelligentsia ... hospital, city and clerical workers". And the strikes were far more political, "no less than a battle for control of the workplace and the city economy as a whole ... they spilled on to the streets and sometimes even ended in bloody conflicts between workers—armed, trained and organised by the Red Guards [the Bolsheviks' militia]—and government militias." If employers resorted to lock-outs, their factories would be stormed and occupied by workers. "Some strikes spread to involve residents of whole urban districts in attacks on bakeries and shops ... whom the crowd suspected of hoarding food" (Figes, 1997: 462).[66]

Remarkably, at this point in his narrative, Figes adopts, what is in effect, an explicit pro-Bolshevik analysis. Figes even concedes through gritted teeth that Lenin, though, according to Figes, always harbouring an ultimate desire for a one-party (one-man ie Lenin) dictatorship, also favoured soviet power through a soviet coalition of all the socialist parties (Figes, 1997: 466):[67]

> The mass of workers and peasants were moving inexorably towards their own localist conceptions of Soviet rule. Only a Soviet government could hope to command any real authority in the country at large. This had been the case since the February Revolution. But time and again the [non-Bolshevik] Soviet leaders had chosen to ignore it—their dogmatic faith in the need for a "bourgeois stage of the revolution" had tied them to the hopeless task of trying to keep the coalition [with the capitalist parties in the Provisional Government] going—and every time the streets had risen to the cry of Soviet power they had chosen to cover their ears (Figes, 1997: 464).[68]

Steve Smith's *Red Petrograd* remains one of the most important studies of "workers' power" in the months immediately before and during the October 1917 Russian Revolution, at least in its main industrial centre, Petrograd.[69] At its core were the democratically elected factory committees, which challenge, with increasing intensity and ambition, management's right to manage at the point of production from the February Revolution onwards.[70] Workers in Russia had added a further potentially explosive demand to the elementary liberal democratic demands supported by the moderate socialist parties: Democratise the factory order! (Smith, 1983: 54):[71]

> Factory committees dealt with every aspect of life, as an examination of the minutes of any factory committee will reveal. In the first two weeks of its existence the committee at the 1886 Electric Light Company dealt with matters as diverse as food supplies, the factory militia,[72] arbitration of disputes, lunch breaks, overtime and the factory club. In a typical week the committee in the gun shop at Putilov dealt with the hiring of workers, wear-and-tear of machinery, wage fixing, financial help to individual workers and the experiments of a worker-inventor trying to invent a new kind of shell (Smith, 1983: 85).

Smith investigated diverse areas of factory committee policy and practice, including food supply, labour discipline and campaigns against drunkenness. They illustrate a paralysed management increasingly dependent on the factory committees. Smith's conclusion on food supply illustrates not just this point but the sheer scale of what Lenin described as the "impending catastrophe". The factory committee initiatives were "puny compared to the colossal scale of the food crisis ... worse[ning] through the winter of 1917-18 until mass starvation drove hundreds of thousands out of the capital. Nevertheless, one day's dinner meant a great deal to a hungry worker ... that the factory committees did all in their power to provide such meals, immeasurably enhanced their prestige" (Smith, 1983: 88).

Hunger, absenteeism, petty theft, drunkenness, disruptive behaviour, an understandable desire to ease the pace of production: issues that the factory committees did not evade. But their efforts to resolve them were infused by the spirit of mass democratic control. After all, their authority depended upon the rank and file worker, hence "disciplinary measures were agreed by a general meeting of the workforce" (Smith, 1983: 91). Also, despite the claims of enemies of the Bolsheviks that they had so poisoned the psychology of workers that they were corrupted by sheer idleness, "the Bolshevik dominated factory committees seem to have been just as concerned as committees dominated by moderate socialists to maintain labour productivity—even before October." Nevertheless, there was one important difference, put bluntly by Yu Larin in the Bolshevik press: "Whoever talks about labour discipline and does not demand workers' control of capitalist enterprises is a hypocrite and a windbag" (Smith 1983: 92).[73]

Smith notes, apart from the Bolsheviks, it was axiomatic in 1917 that workers "did not possess a level of culture adequate to establishing their hegemony throughout society" (Smith, 1983: 94). The factory committees saw it as their responsibility to rise to the challenge implied, establishing cultural enlightenment commissions. The Putilov works committee encouraged evening classes with an appeal to "gain scientific knowledge ... We need not only to catch up with the classes with whom we are fighting, but to overtake them" (Smith, 1983: 95).[74] At the Baltic works the education commission sponsored theatre, arranged for women workers to be given some teaching by women students, gave financial help to the apprentices' club and to a school for soldiers and sailors. At the Sestroretsk works the commission gave the house and garden of the former director to local children as a kindergarten. Similar examples alongside musical, theatrical and wider artistic endeavours and experiments sprang up everywhere, though the line dividing education from entertainment was sometimes the source of bitter controversies. But binding all sides in these arguments was a democratic awakening of poor people who suddenly felt both the power and now taken-for-granted moral right to take part in such debates. No longer just the victims of history, they were helping to shape it (Smith, 1985: 95-98).

Smith devotes a chapter analysing the relations between factory committees and trade unions, introducing the Bolsheviks' most senior worker activist cadre, metal workers' union leader, Alexander Shlyapnikov.[75] Shlyapnikov played a pivotal role during this period negotiating the metal workers' contract, a model for all industries and particularly notable for achieving unity between the skilled men (and they were nearly all men) and the *chernorabochie*, the appallingly low paid, semi and unskilled men and women workers. The *chernorabochie* had been understandably tempted to form their own union. This would have had dire, deeply divisive consequences not just for the burgeoning trade union movement but also for the factory committees which tended to be dominated by skilled workers. Smith devotes justifiably much attention to just how Shlyapnikov and his comrades managed to bind the *chernorabochie* to a single contract for all, reducing but by no means eliminating wage differentials. This included confrontation with particular layers of skilled workers, the "small trades" like welders where "particularism" and "craft consciousness" was quite ingrained (Smith, 1983: 129). But the "one united contact" approach won the day which Smith attributes to "class unity" overwhelming "craft particularism" (Smith, 1983: 129).

What about relations with the *sluzhashchie,* white collar workers, also experiencing rapid trade union growth and militancy? Clerical to technical personnel, sometimes including foremen as well as highly qualified professionals like accountants were involved. But tension between the *sluzhashchie* and manual workers was never satisfactorily resolved. The Putilov works committee warned against "the erroneous view that people not engaged in physical labour are ... basically drones and parasites. Comrades who argue this lose sight of the crucial fact that in industry, in technical production, mental labour is as indispensable as physical labour" (Smith, 1983: 137). Though there were some outstanding examples of unity between the two sectors—Smith cites the Skorokhod shoe factory and the Petichev cable works—the problem remained. It would later compound the crises for the fledgling Bolshevik administration, leading to short term improvised—and as Lenin saw it, retrograde solutions, "bourgeois" salaries for "bourgeois" specialists (see below).

Smith notes the limited significance that Lenin accords to workers' control in his *The Impending Catastrophe and How to*

Combat It (Smith, 1983: 154). Yet it is the economic breakdown and the catastrophe of fuel and food shortages that, as it stimulated Lenin to write the pamphlet, separately deepened the urge of the factory committees to take control of production. In fact, although the factory committees developed independently of the Bolsheviks, and reflected a wide range of political opinion from anarchist to Menshevik, Bolshevik influence grew as they grew. The factory committee movement had increasingly recognised the need to link their demand for workers' control to soviet state control. This was reflected in a key clause in the Bolshevik resolution passed by the First All-Russia Council of Factory Committees (ARCFC), immediately following the October Revolution:

> The workers' control being implemented in the localities through the factory committees must be organised into a state-wide system ... A majority (2/3) for the organs of control must be workers, delegated by the factory committees, trade unions and the Soviet of workers' deputies. As well as workers' representatives, there must be scientifically-educated technical personnel (engineers, technicians etc)[76] (Smith, 1983: 157).

In fact, it was pressure from Lenin who helped make explicit and unambiguous the ARCFC October Revolution position on workers' control by publishing the *Draft Regulations on Workers' Control* (Lenin, 1917f):

> This ... decree on workers' control ... breathes a spirit of libertarianism which reflects Lenin's profound faith at this time in the creativity of the masses. It recognised the right of workers ... to control all aspects of production ... to bind employers by their decisions ... This awkward fact makes nonsense of the claim in Western historiography that, once power was in his grasp, Lenin, the stop-at-nothing centraliser, proceeded to crush the

'syndicalist' factory committees. In fact, the reverse is true (Smith, 1983: 209-10).[77]

"Control was envisaged as taking place at both state level and factory level and local initiatives were to be organised into a hierarchy of local and regional Councils of National Economy ... topped by the Supreme Council of National Economy" (Smith, 1983: 212). Lenin saw the factory committee as the "organisational cell" for the new revolutionary soviet state system. Economic organisational planning must emerge from the masses' "own experience ... We must begin immediately from above and from below" (Smith, 1983: 156).

David Mandel's study of the Petrograd workers, updated with more recent archival research, reinforces Smith's perspective. The TsIK, the All-Russian Central Executive Committee of Soviets of Workers' and Soldiers' Deputies adopted a law on workers' control unanimously (24 in favour, 11 abstained). Guidelines based on the law, published in December 1917, show just how far reaching it was intended to be:

> Workers' control of industry, as an integral part of control over the entire economic life of the country, should not be understood in the narrow sense of simple inspection but, on the contrary, in the broad sense of *intervention* into the disposition by the entrepreneur of capital, inventory, raw materials and finished goods in the enterprise; [it should be understood as] *active monitoring* of the correctness and expediency of the fulfilment production orders, the use of energy and of the work force and [in the sense of] *participation in the organisation of production itself on a rational basis* (Mandel, 2018: 399; emphasis in the original).

There were accusations of anarchism and anarcho-syndicalism, not least by the trade unions. Mandel dismisses them as disingenuous since every conference of factory committees before and after October had insisted that workers' control had to be exerted within the framework of state regulation exercised on a national level. In other words, centralisation of economic authority was taken for granted (except by the real anarchists). The problem was implementation of such a major undertaking in such devastating conditions—conversion of military industry to peacetime production with increasingly scarce fuel and raw materials. The factory committees, far from resisting state regulation, saw themselves as its representatives until such time as implementation was feasible (Mandel, 2018: 401).

It was just such a principle that was adopted by the Sixth Petrograd Conference of Factory Committees in January 1918. The need for regional economic councils, including regional soviet and trade union representation, was accepted to help frame factory committee policy. And while the factory committees would continue to execute the will of the workers' general assembly, the Conference agreed, "at the same time, it ... answers to government authority ... for the rational conduct ... of the enterprise, in accordance with the needs of the entire working people and also for the integrity of the property of the given enterprise" (Mandel, 2018: 401-2).

N A Skrypnik, a Bolshevik and member of the Central Council of Factory Committees, observed, "Workers' control is not yet socialism but only one of the transitional measures that bring us closer to socialism" (Mandel, 1968: 405). Tseitlin, from the Kersten Knitwear mill, (incidentally partly representing unskilled workers, including women workers, often considered far less politically active than the skilled workers, [Mandel, 2018: 26-38]), delegate to the First Conference of Petrograd Factory Committees in June 1918, came up with a novel solution to the relations between the factory committees and the state: "We need a strong centre of factory committees that will be the Ministry of Labour of the proletariat of all of Russia" (Mandel, 2018: 171).

The Opticheskii factory committee reported in September 1918 that it had taken over the main functions of management, an independent initiative but one ultimately dependent on support from the new revolutionary state administration. During the war, the factory's optical operations were diminished to make way for the production of grenade detonators. But when the time came to demobilise in January 1918, the supply of electricity was cut. The factory committee reacted by building its own generating plant. Meanwhile, it worked on the development of new models of cinematographic equipment. Eventually, the factory obtained contracts to build projectors for the Commissariat of Education. The report explained:

> The factory committee and its control organ, taking management of production into their hands, they knew that they were overstepping by several degrees all the guidelines issued by the higher organs of power to workers' organisations ... Feeling their strength ... they were able ... to create discipline, to organise production on a new basis, and to save the treasury of the People's government many millions in funds that, had the workers' organisation not been up to the task, would have floated away into the pockets of the foreign imperialists, as happened in many other cases ... Based on all the foregoing, the factory committee and the control commission ... declare that the time has come ... to take fully into the workers' hands the enterprise that they have put in order, and for that they have people who are prepared to assume the tasks of managing (Mandel, 2018: 415).

The phrase "take fully into workers' hands" is understood as the completion of workers' control, generalised from the workplace to the state. As M N Zhivotov, a Bolshevik electrician at the 1886 Electric Lighting Co explained at the January 1918 conference of factory committees, "A series of requests are being received from factory committees on the need to take the factories into the workers' hands, and so unexpectedly there arises the practical question of nationalisation of enterprises." He went on to explain that the requests were made in response to the owners' refusal to recognise workers' control or to their refusal to run their factories for other reasons (Mandel, 2018: 416).

Alas, this revolutionary creative fusion of liberated local rank and file initiative and centralised state necessity was to be effectively stillborn. The post-revolutionary crises proved too deep and intractable and immediately so, partly anticipated by *The Impending Catastrophe and How to Combat It*, but much, much worse. Smith describes it as nothing less than "economic catastrophe" and "the dissolution of the working class" (Smith,1983: 242-45).[78] It was exacerbated by the threat posed to Petrograd in particular, both by the German military high command, and the eruption, or as some would argue, the intensification, of civil war.[79]

Implementing the demand for "peace" was given added urgency by the literal threat of a German military occupation of Petrograd at the beginning of 1918. Thousands of workers, already facing job losses as a result of the agreed running down of the war industries, now faced a cut in the bread ration so serious that "mass starvation" threatened. The metal section of the newly formed Council of National Economy reported: "The workers hurried ... to get out of Petrograd as quickly as possible, to escape starvation and the threat of invasion."[80] In the first six months of 1918 over a million people left Petrograd (Smith, 1983: 243). Within a matter of months, the proletariat of Red Petrograd, renowned throughout Russia for its outstanding role in the revolution, had been decimated. By April 1918 the factory workforce of the capital had plummeted to about 40 percent of its January 1917 level, and it shrank still further thereafter (Smith, 1983: 243).

Civil war added to the exodus. Many of the most committed Bolshevik workers, some of whom could have stayed in the remnants of the factories, nevertheless chose to leave:

> in order to serve the new soviet government. They enlisted in the Red Army, assumed posts of responsibility within the government and party apparatuses, or joined food detachments ... [81] Young workers, fired by revolutionary elan and without family commitments, were especially eager to quit the factories in order to defend soviet power ... by April the proportion of youths in the factory workforce was only half of that the previous year ... It would seem ... that at least the keener Bolsheviks among the "cadre" of workers left the factories in the early months of 1918 (Smith 1983: 244).[82]

The Brest-Litovsk peace treaty that the Bolsheviks felt compelled to sign with Germany in March 1918, and which produced one of the deepest splits in the Bolshevik Party's history, consolidated the trap that now ensnared the beleaguered regime. "It was massively punitive: the Baltic provinces, a large part of Belorussia, and the whole of the Ukraine were excised from the former empire, with the result that Russia lost one third of its agriculture and railways, virtually all its oil and cotton production, three quarters of its coal and iron" (Smith, 2017: 157). So punitive, that another contemporary scholar of the Russian Revolution has concluded that "by the summer of 1918, Soviet Russia had shrunk to the size of the medieval Moscovy state and had lost almost all grain producing regions" (Murphy, 2007: 64).

That the Red Army would reverse these defeats and rescue the revolution was an astonishing achievement. But a very heavy price was paid. At the 1921 Third Congress of the Communist International (Comintern), Trotsky, the Red Army's founder, reported its demobilising, following the civil war victory: "I can now reveal this secret ... During the period when we were fighting on four fronts, our army numbered 5,300,000 men, of which no less than three-quarters of a million were skilled workers. That was an extremely heavy and unbearable loss for the economy" (Trotsky 2016: 117).

Trotsky could have added that it was also an unbearable

loss for the revolution. The factory committees and soviets' workers' cadre had been the willing conscripts which formed this Bolshevik workers' backbone of the Red Army. But it had left a political vacuum in the shrivelled industrial base of the economy, now dependent on newly recruited workers with little or no trade union and political experience. This is why Isaac Deutscher, Trotsky's principal biographer, titled his chapter on the civil war victory, "Defeat in Victory". And it is why the biography later contains one of the most damning indictments of the immediate post-civil war period: Shlyapnikov's taunt to Lenin at the Tenth Congress of the Bolshevik Party, 1921, "Permit me to congratulate you on being the vanguard of a non-existing class." (Deutscher, 1970b: 15, n1).[83]

On several occasions in this period, Lenin effectively conceded Shlyapnikov's underlying argument:

> Our enemy ... in the present period is not the same one that faced us yesterday ... He is everyday economics in a small-peasant country with a ruined large-scale industry. He is the petty-bourgeois element which surrounds us like the air, and penetrates deep into the ranks of the proletariat. And the proletariat is declassed, ie, dislodged from its class groove. The factories and mills are idle—the proletariat is weak, scattered, enfeebled ... (Lenin, 1965j).

This is the context for understanding Lenin's abrupt change in policy as early as March–April 1918: "Lenin quickly became aware of the impossibility of saving the country from the rapid slide toward economic ruination through authentically socialist forms of administration ... as it became increasingly clear to him that the European revolution, which he had expected as an almost immediate repercussion of the Russian Revolution, was not maturing as expected" (Harding, 1981: 188). Or to put it more bluntly, the context was increasingly becoming a "burnt out proletariat" (Cliff, 1978: 112-15).

Lenin and the other Bolshevik leaders were forced into compromises with capitalism far beyond anything he had imagined in his effort to adapt Marx's transition phase, and Marx's understanding of the dictatorship of the proletariat, in the *Critique of the Gotha Programme*. This was less about workers controlling those remnants of the capitalist class deemed necessary for socialist reconstruction of the economy and more about a state partnership with capital, however unwillingly conceded, and however much its temporary character was to be emphasised.

Here is an unexpected Lenin writing in late April 1918. Its turnabout political character speaks for itself, including Lenin's quite intriguing warning that workers are not ready for nationalisation because they are not yet ready for workers' control:

> I told every workers' delegation with which I had to deal when they came to me and complained that their factory was at a standstill: you would like your factory to be confiscated. Very well, we have blank forms for a decree ready, they can be signed in a minute ... But tell us: have you learnt how to take over production and have you calculated what you will produce? Do you know the connection between what you are producing and the Russian and international market? Whereupon it turns out that they have not learnt this yet; there has not been anything about it yet in Bolshevik pamphlets, and nothing is said about it in Menshevik pamphlets either.
>
> The situation is best among those workers who are carrying out this state capitalism:[84] among the tanners and in the textile and sugar industries, because they have a sober, proletarian knowledge of their industry ... They say: I can't cope with this task just yet; I shall put in capitalists, giving them one-third of the posts, and I shall learn from them (Lenin, 1965h).

"The enlistment of bourgeois experts by means of extremely

high salaries" also became essential, though it was "a retreat from the principles of the Paris Commune" (Lenin, 1965g):

> Without the guidance of experts in the various fields of knowledge, technology and experience, the transition to socialism will be impossible, because socialism calls for a conscious mass advance to greater productivity of labour compared with capitalism ... Had our proletariat, after capturing power, quickly solved the problem of accounting, control and organisation on a national scale (which was impossible owing to the war and Russia's backwardness) then we ... would also have completely subordinated these bourgeois experts to ourselves ... It is ... *a step backward* on the part of our socialist Soviet state power (Lenin, 1965g).

Expertise also meant introducing the novel American capitalist technique known as Taylorism for raising labour productivity:

> The Russian is a bad worker compared with people in advanced countries. It could not be otherwise under the tsarist regime and in view of the persistence of the hangover from serfdom. The task that the Soviet government must set the people in all its scope is—learn to work. The Taylor system, the last word of capitalism in this respect, like all capitalist progress, is a combination of the refined brutality of bourgeois exploitation and a number of the greatest scientific achievements in the field of analysing mechanical motions during work, the elimination of superfluous and awkward motions, the elaboration of correct methods of work, the introduction of the best system of accounting and control, etc. The Soviet Republic must at all costs adopt all that is valuable in the achievements of science and technology in this field (Lenin, 1965g).

One-man management was also introduced. Here, though, Lenin seeks to, or rather hopes to, retain some revolutionary principles:

> Given ideal class-consciousness and discipline on the part of those participating in the common work, this subordination would be something like the mild leadership of a conductor of an orchestra. It may assume the sharp forms of a dictatorship if ideal discipline and class-consciousness are lacking. But be that as it may, *unquestioning subordination* to a single will is absolutely necessary for the success of processes organised on the pattern of large-scale machine industry. On the railways it is twice and three times as necessary (Lenin, 1965g).

Lenin, though, seeks a democratic mandate for these changes which he hopes will retain mass worker democratic principles, reminiscent of Engels's *On Authority*:

> The "mania for meetings" is an object of the ridicule ... of the bourgeoisie, the Mensheviks ... But without the discussions at public meetings the mass of the oppressed could never have changed from the discipline forced upon them by the exploiters to conscious, voluntary discipline. The airing of questions at public meetings is the genuine democracy of the working people, their way of unbending their backs, their awakening to a new life, their first steps along the road which they themselves have cleared of vipers (the exploiters, the imperialists, the landowners and capitalists) and which they want to learn to build themselves, in their own way, for themselves, on the principles of their own *Soviet* ... to the conscious appreciation of the necessity for the dictatorship of the proletariat, to unquestioning obedience to the orders of individual representatives of the Soviet government during the work (Lenin, 1965g).

Lenin still hoped "to draw *the whole of the poor* into the practical work of administration ... *every* toiler, having finished his eight hours' 'task' in productive labour, shall perform state duties *without pay*; the transition to this is particularly difficult, but this transition alone can guarantee the final consolidation of socialism" (Lenin, 1965g). Alas, it proved wishful thinking in the context just described: the decimated former workforce, its leadership enlisted in the Red Army, now a rump, surly, hungry, diminished workforce, often newly recruited, desperate for work, disillusioned with the revolution.

Conclusion

In his 2017 centenary book on the Russian Revolution, Steve Smith describes how "the idea of the working class as the agent of socialist revolution gave way gradually to the party and the Red Army as the guarantors of the workers' state" (Smith, 2017: 380). This observation implies a major distortion of the original principles underpinning the route to communism, that the emancipation of the working class is the task of the working class. Political parties and revolutionary armies are supposed to be part of that process, not substitutes for it. The isolation of the Russian Revolution built in this distortion to communist development almost from the beginning. It set the seal on what would become Official Communism for the rest of the 20th century. But a "Communism" that claims to speak and act on behalf of the working class, without their active participation, cannot be the same communism that Marx, Engels and Lenin originally intended.

Thus, in the course of the Civil War, a bureaucratic regime crystallised in what became, after Lenin's death in 1924, the Soviet Union. Its legitimacy derived from the Revolution that its real functioning increasingly negated. The conditions were created for full-scale counter-revolution at the end of the 1920s, when, under the pressure of geopolitical competition from the imperialist West, Josef Stalin led the forced industrialisation of the country, based on the expropriation of the peasantry and the super-exploitation of the new working class forming around rapidly thrown up factories. The political tensions generated by this brutal process found expression in the Great Terror that eliminated most of the old Bolshevik Party in the late 1930s. The socio-economic order that crystallised from this enormous upheaval was what Cliff called bureaucratic state capitalism, in which workers were as exploited as they were in the West, but the logic of capital accumulation was imposed by military rivalry with the advanced capitalist countries (Cliff, 1988). Stalinist Russia emerged from the Second World War with enormous prestige thanks to its central role in defeating Nazi Germany. It also reproduced itself in Central and Eastern Europe, using its military power to install state capitalist regimes there—for example, in Poland, the setting of the next chapter. The expansion of Stalinism as a state system boosted the influence and membership of the international Communist movement, but in reality it was a brutal caricature of real communism.

At the same time, we shouldn't lose sight of the unique historical breakthrough that had been momentarily achieved in October 1917, or of the decisive role of Lenin's Bolshevik Party and its worker cadres. Red Petrograd was at the centre of an experiment in workers' power, rooted in a workers' state based on soviets or workers' councils. The humble factory committee at the point of production, democratically elected, organisational cell of the soviet, played a strategically central role. The resurfacing of the factory committee in later revolutionary upheavals in the 20th century is the subject of this investigation.

CHAPTER 2

The Lost Revolution in Poland 1980-81

Introduction

In the 16 months from August 1980 to December 1981, one of the least understood revolutionary upheavals of the 20th century came close to toppling the so-called Communist government of Poland, part of the Warsaw Pact constellation of satellite countries tied to the former Soviet Union. This moment, centred on the insurgent trade-union movement Solidarity (*Solidarność*), followed a succession of workers' revolts in Poland, in 1956, 1970-1, and 1976. Was it an anti-Communist revolution, a Polish nationalist revolt against Soviet Russian domination? Or, controversially, the beginnings of a genuine communist revolution as Marx and Engels would have understood it, fulfilling predictions made in their famous *Communist Manifesto* of 1848? Certainly, it would become a major contributor to the implosion of "Soviet Communism" in 1989. That this was indeed a revolution remains the view of many former leaders of the Solidarity movement. This is forcefully expressed in interviews I carried out with some of them, illustrated in this chapter, in September and November 2017.

TIMELINE POLAND

1939: Poland is invaded and partitioned by Nazi Germany and Stalinist Russia following the Hitler-Stalin Pact agreed in August.

1941: As part of Operation Barbarossa, the Nazi invasion of the Soviet Union launched on 22 June, Germany seizes the rest of Poland.

1944-5: As the Nazi war machine collapses in the climax of the Second World War, Poland is occupied by the Red Army and incorporated into what becomes a system of Stalinist satellite states. The Communist Party, known as the Polish United Workers Party (PZPR), became the sole governing party.

1951-2: As part of a general clampdown in response to the escalation of the Cold War and Yugoslavia's break with Moscow, the PZPR is purged.

1956: Against the background of Soviet leader Nikita Khrushchev's secret speech denouncing Stalin and the Hungarian Revolution, a workers' revolt in Poznań forces in October the selection of a new PZPR leadership headed by Władysław Gomułka, a victim of the earlier purges, who promises de-Stalinisation.

1968: Student demonstrations at the University of Warsaw in March lead to more repressive policies and an antisemitic wave.

1970: Rising food prices provoke workers' riots in December in the cities of the Baltic coast—Gdańsk, Gdynia, Elbląg, and Szczecin. Gomułka is removed and replaced by Eduard Gierek.

1976: Food price rises lead in June to more workers' riots centred on the Ursus factory at Radom. The regime reacts with concessions and repression, provoking the formation of the Workers' Defence Committee (KOR).

1979: The newly elected Pope John Paul II, a Polish prelate, visits Poland in June, leading to huge gatherings to greet him and attend the masses he gives.

1980: Mass strikes starting in mid-August at the Lenin shipyard in Gdańsk force the regime to accept the formation of the independent union *Solidarność*, Solidarity, led by Lech Wałęsa. Gierek is removed and replaced by Stanisław Kania.

1981: Solidarity's failure to respond to the beatings of leaders and activists at Bydgoszcz in March mark the beginning of the movement's decline. General Wojciech Jaruzelski, the defence minister, becomes first prime minister and then party leader. On 13 December he imposes martial law, bans Solidarity, and orders the arrest of its leaders.

1986: Amid growing economic difficulties and the increasing reliance of market mechanisms, Jaruzelski announces a general amnesty.

1988: A strike-wave led by young workers is halted thanks to the intervention of Wałęsa, who is seeking negotiations with the regime.

1989: Between February and April Round Table talks take place between the regime and the ex-Solidarity leaders, and result in the legalisation of Solidarity and multi-party elections in which Solidarity triumphs and the PZPR is humiliated. In August, Jaruzelski, now President, appoints the liberal Catholic intellectual Tadeusz Mazowiecki prime minister. His finance minister, Leszek Balcerowicz, imposes "shock therapy", accelerating Poland's transition from state to market capitalism.

INTERVIEWEES POLAND

Wladysław Frasyniuk

Former bus drivers' trade union leader from Wroclaw who became leader of the city regional Solidarity. After martial law, he led the underground resistance in the city until his arrest in 1982. Today he is Managing Director of *Fracht*, a lorry fleet company. The interview took place in his Wroclaw office in November 2017.

Andrzej Gwiazda and Joanna Duda-Gwiazda

Andrzej Gwiazda and Joanna Duda-Gwiazda were amongst the original founders of the Free Trade Union movement which preceded Solidarity in Gdańsk. The interview took place in November 2017.

Zbigniew Kowalewski

Zbigniew Kowalewski was a Solidarity leader in the Łódź region. He regarded himself as a revolutionary socialist in the original tradition of the principles of the *Open Letter* of Jacek Kuroń and Karol Modzelewski.

Karol Modzelewski

Karol Modzelewski was jailed along with Jacek Kuroń for jointly authoring the *Open Letter to the Polish Communist Party* in 1964. Both men were Communist Party members. The *Open Letter* challenged the credentials of the Polish Communist regime and its claim to be communist by applying a Marxist analysis. A generation later both men played a major part in founding, and then leading, Solidarity, though by that time they had rejected the *Open Letter* and its underlying Marxist principles. Modzelewski served as a senator in 1989-91. The interview took place at the University of Warsaw, where he was Professor of History, in September 2017.

Józef Pinior

Józef Pinior, former Solidarity leader from the Polish city of Wroclaw and the movement's National Treasurer. Famously, he concealed Solidarity's funds when martial law was declared in December 1981. He was a member of the European Parliament in 2004-9, and helped to expose Polish government complicity in allowing NATO's so-called "black sites", used for the "rendition" programme of torture of terrorist suspects, on Polish territory. He served as a Polish Senator in 2011-15.

Jan Rulewski

Solidarity leader in the Bydgoszcz region. He and other activists were assaulted by the police during negotiations between Solidarity and government officials in March 1981 for 3 million peasant farmers to join Solidarity. This became the major flashpoint, or turning point, in the clash between Solidarity and the government in the period 1980-81. A planned general strike in response was unilaterally suspended by Solidarity leader, Lech Wałęsa. Jan Rulewski, a professional bicycle design engineer, was a member of the Sejm (Lower House of the Polish Parliament) 1991-2001, and has served as a Senator for *Platforma Obywatelska, Civic Platform* since 2007. The interview took place in his Senator's office in Bydgoszcz in November 2017.

Andrzej Słowik

Former bus driver and workers' leader for Solidarity's Łódź region. In late 1981, in response to major food shortages, he was one of the organisers of a highly successful "Hunger March" in the city. This was immediately followed by a plan to implement the active strike strategy where workers threatened to take control of food production and distribution. He was Deputy Minister of Labour and Social Policy in 1992-3.

Section I of the chapter analyses the importance, and relevance to the Solidarity movement, of the *Open Letter* to the Polish Communist Party written in 1964 by two dissident Polish Communist students, Jacek Kuroń and Karol Modzelewski. Applying Marxist assumptions, it challenged Poland's communist credentials, identifying a class-divided society with a state bureaucratic ruling class oppressing and exploiting its workers. They were thrown in jail for their efforts. This remarkable document, rarely given the attention it deserves by historians, might even lay claim to be the basis for a *Communist Manifesto for the late Twentieth Century*. Certainly, a claim can be made that it predicted the emergence of the Solidarity workers' movement a generation later. The second claim is complicated by the fact that both Kuroń and Modzelewski, although they became very important leaders of Solidarity, had, by then, rejected, in its entirety, the highly innovative (some would say "Trotskyist") Marxist premises of the *Open Letter*.[85] Kuroń, in particular, opted instead for what he described as a self-limiting revolution, believing that the Polish "Communist" state could be reformed and should not be overthrown. This argument, and its flaws, goes to the heart of this chapter. It finds its expression in the role of KOR, *Komitet Obrony Robotnikow*, the Workers' Defence Committee, analysed in section II. KOR was decisive in both helping to initiate and then shape Solidarity's development.

Section II goes on to discuss the rise and fall of Solidarity during its brief but spectacular history before the imposition of martial law in December 1981. This includes the movement's high point, its "October" moment, at the Polish city of Bydgoszcz, in March 1981, when the revolutionary seizure of power came tantalisingly close. Solidarity would not recover. Martial law completely destroyed its revolutionary potential. Karol Modzelewski did not join KOR. Although no longer a revolutionary, unlike Kuroń he maintained a much stronger identification with the workers' movement long after it was fashionable for intellectuals to do so.

An outstanding passage from his autobiography, *Riding*

History to Death, captures the essential significance of this history, and with it the demand for workers' self-management, both of the workplace and the wider society:

> The attitude of the masses toward the leaders during the "first" Solidarity was also emotional, but there was no blind trust. Activists at all levels—from factories to the Countrywide Commission—and rank-and-file members wanted self-governance above all. They would entrust themselves to nobody, not even to Wałęsa. In order to effectively manage this movement, it was necessary to constantly talk to crowds who wanted to decide for themselves, the Union, and Poland. In January 1990 at the Hydral meeting hall in Wrocław, I saw with my very eyes that this spirit of self-determination had vanished without a trace. This was a different Solidarity. The problem was not that 80 percent of its former members had not returned when the Union was reactivated. The main thing was that the overwhelming spirit of self-determination had been broken by the armed forces, and it had never returned. The rare phenomenon of the common independent activity of millions of people had been destroyed beyond repair. The myth had survived, and it had revealed itself in the 1988 strikes. When "our" government emerged, "our" prime minister and his people naturally became the legitimate standard-bearers of the myth. But a myth neither expresses the aspirations of the masses for self-determination nor does it possess the instruments or will to control the chosen few. Where a myth reigns, its priests' hands are not tied. Their decisions are met with no resistance (Modzelewski, 2021: 425-6).

Was there an alternative strategy? Section III analyses the importance of the rising threat of "active strikes" between March and December 1981, pioneered by workers in Poland's second largest city, Łódź, and in particular by Łódź's bus driver worker leader Andrzej Słowik and the revolutionary socialist intellectual Zbigniew Kowalewski. "Active strikes" were seen as a response to catastrophic food shortages in the city where tens of thousands of women had taken part in a hunger march. It raised the question of workers taking control of food production and distribution in the city and had the potential to spread across the country. But Solidarity nationally was unable to unite around the demand for "active strikes" at its one and only National Congress in the autumn, despite Congress committing itself to "Workers' Self-Management in a Self-Governing Republic". Zbigniew Kowalewski concludes section III with a powerful analysis of Solidarity's theoretical, strategic and tactical weaknesses. Those weaknesses were exposed by the breakdown of relations between Solidarity's workers and intellectuals, examined in section IV, following the imposition of martial law. This provided an opening for Polish nationalism to fill the vacuum when the Soviet inter-state system imploded in 1989.

The conclusion, section V, returns to the *Open Letter* and observes that despite its rejection by its authors, Kuroń and Modzelewski, it had provided the framework for an alternative strategy for Solidarity. To be sure, the *Open Letter* required some major amendments following the failure of the revolutionary wave in 1968. In particular, it required an adaptation of its economic analysis to Poland's deepening crisis in the 1970s. Poland's state bureaucratic ruling class was increasingly relying upon Western capitalism and especially its banks for its very survival. This suggests that the economic crisis that precipitated the eruption of Solidarity in 1980 was, in part, a response to a Western economically induced recession, intensifying the pressures that would implode the entire Soviet "Communist" satellite state system. In other words, Solidarity needed much greater ideological clarity at the outset: an explicitly anti-capitalist, as well as anti-Soviet "Communist" perspective which, paradoxically, the rejected premises of the *Open Letter* could have provided.

I. *An Open Letter to the Party* by Jacek Kuroń and Karol Modzelewski

Jacek Kuroń and Karol Modzelewski were young Communist dissidents in one of Soviet Communism's most strategically important military outposts in Eastern Europe, its Warsaw Pact ally, Poland. Their *Open Letter*, written in 1964, was a closely argued critical Marxist analysis of Polish society. It identified bitter social class divisions with the Polish "Communist" state bureaucracy playing the equivalent role of a capitalist ruling class. It extracted surplus value from Polish workers on shockingly low pay and terrible working conditions with no control either of the work process or the product of their labour. In 1965 Kuroń and Modzelewski were thrown into jail for this "provocation", the Polish government thereby unwittingly dramatising the prestige and authority of the *Open Letter*. It began its travels, in pamphlet form, across the Polish border, to an increasingly receptive audience on both sides of the so-called Iron Curtain, which divided Soviet Communist dominated Eastern Europe from Western Europe and North America. Though they don't use the term, the analysis of Kuroń and Modzelewski is similar to the state capitalist analysis of the Stalinist societies that has surfaced at different times following Trotsky's break with the Soviet regime.[86]

In the opening paragraphs of the *Open Letter*, Kuroń and Modzelewski expose the gulf between the ruling Communist Party in Poland and the country's working class. State nationalisation of the means of production serves to consolidate that gulf, undermining the ideological pretence that state nationalisation is by definition the equivalent of a workers' state:

> In our system, the Party elite is ... also the power elite; all decisions relating to state power are made by it ... [it] has at its disposal all the nationalised means of production; it decides on the extent of accumulation and consumption, on the direction of investment, on the share of various social groups in consumption and in

the national income; in others words, it decides on the distribution and utilisation of the entire social product. The decisions of the elite are independent, free of any control on the part of the working class and of the remaining social classes and strata. The workers have no way of influencing them, nor have Party members in general ... This Party-state power elite ... we shall call the *central political bureaucracy* (Kuroń and Modzelewski, 1966: 7).

Later this argument is strengthened, making explicit the ruling bureaucracy as a ruling class:

> To whom does the worker ... sell his labour? To those who have at their disposal the means of production ... the *central political bureaucracy*. On account of this ... it is a ruling class. It has at its exclusive command the basic means of production. It buys the labour of the working class. It takes away from the working class by force and economic coercion the surplus product and uses it for purposes which are alien and hostile to the worker in order to strengthen and expand its rule over production and society.
>
> It is said that the bureaucracy cannot be a class, since the individual earnings of its members do not come anywhere near the individual earnings of capitalists ... This is quite wrong ... the property of the bureaucracy is not of an individual nature, but constitutes the collective property of an elite which identifies itself with the state ... Its class character depends ... only on its relationship—as a group—to the means of production and to other social classes (above all the working class) (Kuroń and Modzelewski, 1966: 15).

Discussing the origins of the system in the context of the

outcome of the Second World War, and the ceding of Poland (and other Eastern European countries) to Stalin's sphere of influence as part of the post-war settlement, the *Open Letter* identifies Poland's post-war industrialisation drive as the mechanism which created this new state-based bureaucratic ruling class: "The nature of the task of industrialising a backward country called to life as a ruling class a bureaucracy which was able to achieve this task, since it alone, through its class interest, represented the interest of industrialisation under the conditions—production for the sake of production" (Kuroń and Modzelewski, 1966: 27).[87]

The *Open Letter* had an additionally good reason for predicting the emergence of a mass-based revolutionary workers' movement, resulting directly from its class analysis of "Communist" Polish society (Kuroń and Modzelewski, 1966: 50-1). There was a famous historical precedent. Although not on the same scale as Hungary 1956,[88] Polish workers in that year not only went on strike but developed democratically elected workers' councils which, momentarily at least, appeared also to challenge the authority of the Polish state-system. However, the state would, partially at least, successfully neuter them by integrating them into its own industrial power arrangements. Kuroń and Modzelewski called on this experience not simply to demand genuine workers' democracy in Poland but to locate the demand very specifically in the lessons of 1956. The following passage from the *Open Letter* is particularly remarkable because it also unwittingly pinpoints with extraordinary accuracy the key debate in Solidarity in late 1981 about workers' control in the workplace, workers' democracy and state power:

> Workers' democracy cannot limit itself to the level of an enterprise. For when economic and political decisions, the actual rule over the surplus product, and the labour that creates it, do not belong to the working class, then participation of the workers in managing the enterprise must also become fictitious. Workers' self-rule in an

> enterprise, therefore, requires full workers' democracy in the state. The working class organised under such conditions will set the goals of social production, guided by its own interest, the interest of the people living today at subsistence level. The goal of production will then be, of course, consumption for the broad masses. This signifies the overthrow of existing production and social relationships and, with them, the bureaucracy's class rule (Kuroń and Modzelewski 1966: 22-3).[89]

Finally, again based on the 1956 experience, and again in extraordinary anticipation of potential weaknesses in the Solidarity movement, the *Open Letter* called for workers to organise their own independent political party:

> The so-called October Left—a political current made up in large measure of the natural leaders of the working class, youth and intellectual opinion—could have been a substitute for the political vanguard of the mass working class movement. The October Left differed from the liberal current, especially in its views on the Workers' Councils, in which it saw the basis for new production relationships and the nucleus of a new political power. But it was not a uniform movement. The Left did not separate itself from the technocratic current in the Workers' Council movement (the demand that factories be run by the Councils did go beyond the programme of the technocracy) nor from the liberal bureaucracy, in the political showdown on a national scale. It did not set itself apart from the general anti-Stalinist front as a specifically proletarian movement. In this situation, it was evidently unable to formulate its own political programme, to propagate it in an organised manner among the masses, to create a party. Without all this, it could not become a politically independent force, and therefore, had to transform

> itself into a leftist appendage of the ruling liberal bureaucracy (Kuroń and Modzelewski, 1966: 45).[90]

The legacy of the *Open Letter* and the legacy of the events of 1968, or the class of '68, have become deeply intertwined (Ash, 1983: 22). Unravelling this process is essential both to understanding the birth of Solidarity, Kuroń and Modzelewski's roles in the movement and their rejection of the Marxist premises of the *Open Letter*. 1968 was a year, certainly, but also a mood, an expectation, a world, it seemed, bursting with a promise of revolutionary possibility. A world-wide student movement, world-wide street demonstrations against the US war in Vietnam, the Black Power movement in the US, a widespread sense of cultural dislocation amongst young people, the "Prague Spring", symbolising protest against Soviet Communism. And above all, a focus provided by the unprecedented students' and workers' demonstrations in France which climaxed in May 1968 when 10 million workers occupied their factories and de Gaulle, the French President, temporarily, fled the country.

Modzelewski provides the link in his autobiography:

> The "Open Letter" was better known abroad than in Poland. I saw the French, Italian, German, Swedish, and Japanese translations; however, there were many others, such as ones in Czech and English. The "Letter" was issued largely, if not exclusively, by short-lived publishers of the radical left between 1966 and 1968. This was a time of youthful rebellion in Europe and America. The participants were rebelling against the conformism of bourgeois societies but equally against their bureaucratized communist parties with their Mecca in Moscow (Modzelewski, 2021: 136).

Modzelewski identifies "Adam Michnik's circles"[91] for its international promotion in 1968:

It was published in Polish in August 1966 by Jerzy Giedroyc's Instytut Literacki in Paris. Subsequently it reached the intelligentsia in Poland who read the Paris-based journal *Kultura*, in particular a small number of public intellectuals critical of the system ... This manifesto by two rebellious Marxists from Warsaw was met with great interest and sympathy. When young Daniel Cohn-Bendit[92] stood up in court he proudly answered the judge's question, "What is your name?" with, "Kuroń Modzelewski" ... The "Open Letter" addressed to the members of the Warsaw University Party and ZMS [Union of Socialist Youth] cells was a must-read for young people who in 1968 and 1969 were erecting barricades in university towns across Western Europe. I was jealous—why was it so popular there, but not in Poland? (Modzelewski, 2021: 136-7).

The obvious and entirely understandable pride that Modzelewski exhibits for the *Open Letter* illustrates a wider truth about its impact on 1968. It is arguably the single most important historical document of both the movement and its year of climax. Yet Modzelewski's comment here ends on a negative note. This is because the *Open Letter* also proved a failure that year. It had no impact in Poland, as noted by Modzelewski, where antisemitism was explicitly used by the regime to drive a wedge between students and workers.[93] The *Open Letter* had also played down—almost to the point of explicitly denying—the possibility of Soviet tanks destroying incipient revolutionary uprisings against Soviet power.[94] If the student uprisings and the ten-million strong workers' occupations of factories in France in May proved to be the highpoint of 1968, then the outcome of what is sometimes called the "Prague Spring" proved its low point, when Soviet tanks moved in to crush the mass-based student-led insurgent movement for democratic reform in Czechoslovakia. Kuroń and Modzelewski, together with Adam Michnik, issued a famous and classic 1968 leaflet, "Time and again great powers preserve the existing social order using tanks":

> Vietnam's cause is our cause. A right to a revolution, abolish social slavery ... freedom from exploitation ... from Great Powers' dictatorship over small nations. We—the Polish left—cannot be silent ... Because we remember ... the foreign interventions, stifling the Hungarian Revolution ... Che Guevara laid down his life for the thousands who die every day in Latin America and Vietnam ... Fighting for a sovereign and socialist Vietnam means fighting for sovereign and socialist Poland. A nation cannot be free if its government oppresses other nations ... We send our solidarity to the American left, whose fight for peace and freedom for Vietnam means fight for human rights and democracy in their country. We send our solidarity to the Soviet left. We send our solidarity to West German students, French left and Czech intellectuals. Alien to us, the great powers, trading in Vietnamese nation's blood. Alien to us, the provocative politics of the Chinese bureaucracy. To all who trample the sovereignty of working people in any country, we follow the Spanish antifascists: NO PASARAN (Friszke, 2010: 493).

But Modzelewski soon concluded that a literal interpretation of the *Open Letter* could not be defended:

> After the experience of crushing the Prague spring through the involvement of the Soviet Union and five countries of the Warsaw Pact, including Poland, as well as the earlier experience with the Hungarian revolution, I stopped imagining that when a revolution starts in one country, its flames could be spread to other countries immediately, especially in the case of the Soviet Union (A-KM: 270).[95]

Herein lies one of the roots of Solidarity's appeal for a *self-limiting* revolution, the vital qualifying restriction imposed by Solidarity leaders on their movement. Discussing the background to the recognition of Solidarity by the Polish authorities over ten years later, Modzelewski concluded: "I thought that the most important thing for us, as we already had some recognition, some sort of authority, was to prevent Soviet military intervention in the event of any revolutionary movement. Such an invasion was still possible ... no revolutionary movement would have withstood it. And that would have been tragic for our country" (A-KM: 270).

Yet in his autobiography he remains ready to link the *Open Letter* to the rise of Solidarity. Some of the *Kultura* magazine intellectuals, referred to earlier:

> collaborated in the 1970s with the Committee for the Defense of Workers, KOR, and even more later actively participated in Solidarity. In 1980–1981 this social movement was infused with the idea of forging a brotherhood between intelligentsia and workers. If Kuroń and my 1964–1965 writings had any impact on the attitudes of *Kultura* readers toward the largest workers' movement in Polish history, then our efforts and imprisonment were not in vain. But the true lasting impact remains an open question (Modzelewski, 2021: 136).

But this begs the question that goes to the heart of this chapter. The *Open Letter* is based on Marxist premises. "Workers and intelligentsia collaboration and fraternity" in 1980-81 explicitly rejected this perspective, imposing the ideological constraints of the *self-limiting* revolution. Two of the key authors of this alternative approach were Kuroń and Modzelewski. Kuroń was quite explicit at a Solidarity meeting: "Marxism 'was a nineteen-century philosophy ... and is long outlived,' he told a general assembly of delegates of Solidarność of Łódź region, in the last months of 1980."[96]

Modzelewski came to regard the *Open Letter* as "Utopian," because he began to reject Marxism as utopian:

> any vision which is sort of a radical contestation of the existing order is by definition Utopian. Just as every other intellectual tradition in Europe, Marxism as well, Marxist philosophy has Christian roots ... Utopia can be compared to eschatology ... The kingdom on earth in the Christian sense is—was—necessary in order to formulate a radical criticism of the existing ... order at the time. By the same token, the utopia ... set out in the *Open Letter* was an axiological condition necessary in order to formulate a radical criticism of the existing social and economic regime at the time (A-KM: 271).

This seems to be an attempt to re-fashion the *Open Letter*, indeed Marxism itself, as a moral appeal, moreover a moral appeal in a Christian context. But this weakens it. The *Open Letter's* greatest strength and most obvious characteristic is its closely argued Marxist economic analysis of Stalinism as a class-divided capitalistic system and its accurate (indeed prophetic) prediction of a workers' revolt.[97] Nevertheless, the assertion of an alleged Christian and Utopian context provides a powerful insight into the political trajectory then followed by Kuroń and Modzelewski, and Kuroń in particular. It finds its expression in KOR, *Komitet Obrony Robotnikow*, the Workers' Defence Committee, the movement which preceded and helped precipitate Solidarity. The roots of Solidarity's *self-limiting* revolution, and ultimate defeat, are to be found in KOR.

II. KOR, *Komitet Obrony Robotnikow*, the Workers' Defence Committee, and the Rise and Fall of Solidarity

In December 1970, price rises precipitated mass strikes and demonstrations in the Baltic coastal shipyard cities of Gdańsk and Szczecin. The security forces responded with unrestrained brutality, killing hundreds of workers. Leszek Kołakowski, at that time considered Poland's most prominent exiled dissident Marxist philosopher, wrote a seminal article "Theses on Hope and Despair" for *Kultura* in 1971.[98] In it, he chastised potentially critical Polish intellectuals for "allowing themselves to be convinced of the total rigidity of the shameful system under which they live". This led to the "passivity which they manifested at the time of the dramatic struggle undertaken by Polish workers in December 1970". Kołakowski had been an influential figure with Poland's 1968 generation. He had been expelled from the Polish Communist Party for speaking in solidarity with the 1956 revolt in Poland at Warsaw University on the occasion of its tenth anniversary. A number of students were suspended for attending and taking part in the discussion, including Adam Michnik (Lipski 1985: 15).[99] Michnik, along with Kuroń, was one of the key founders of KOR in 1976. Kołakowski, in exile, was also one of its founding signatories (Lipski: 114).[100] Michnik attributes two of KOR's founding values to Kołakowski, the need to live in "dignity ... striving not so much for a better tomorrow as for a better today" (Michnik, 1987: 148). And, rather revealingly, "inconsistency" (Michnik, 1987: 89), a value transferred to Solidarity that would contribute to its chronic instability at its most critical test at Bydgoszcz in March 1981.[101]

This emphasis on KOR's founding *values* reflects the new movement's assertion of the primacy of morality over politics. Its activities "would appeal above all ... to general moral standards rather than political attitudes" (Lipski, 1985: 44). The personal but deliberately very public and open activity of KOR activists would exhibit behaviour of the highest moral standards and would seek to confront the "opportunist" passivity of the intellectuals that Kołakowski had identified (Lipski, 1985: 44). This approach would be combined with attempts to stay within the law, always to tell the truth and renounce violence (Lipski 1985, 45, 68, 70). Jan Józef Lipski cites a remarkable essay by Kuroń, KOR's most prominent spokesperson, "A Christian Without God", written under a pseudonym, where Kuroń embraces Christian ethics, rejects ethical relativism and views ethical values "as if they were transcendent" (Lipski, 1985: 75).

But there was a glaring contradiction built into this movement from the outset. Kuroń had rejected Marx, an apparently out-dated 19th century philosopher, only to turn to 2000-year-old biblical fables about a preacher called Jesus who, as well as leading an exemplary personal life, made a virtue of helping the poor because the poor could not help themselves. However, let's for a moment concede the profound political as well as moral significance of the dramatic public appearance of intellectuals, rallying to the workers' cause, fearless of any personal risk to themselves. And that this did indeed immediately mark them as targets for the security forces which made life hell for them.[102]

It was the strikes at the Ursus tractor complex in Warsaw and in the city of Radom in June 1976 that provided take-off for KOR. It supported the striking workers at their trials, raised funds and publicised the cases of victimised workers. As a sporadic strike movement developed between 1976 and 1980, in response to the deepening economic crisis, KOR would widen the scope of its intervention, breaking the state's censorship monopoly and providing news of workers' struggles. KOR would also break the state's monopoly over education. Its contribution to the impressive initiative known as the Flying University, providing lecturers like Michnik and Kuroń, used supporters' homes as unofficial classrooms. Topics such as the History of the People's Poland would explicitly challenge the official "line" (Lipski, 1985: 208). Government efforts to disrupt the Flying University were complicated by the intervention of the Catholic Church which attacked restraints on "the human spirit freely creating cultural values" (Lipski, 1985: 212). In Cracow, home base of the Polish Pope, John Paul II, the church offered to accommodate the lectures.

This coming together of the "Christians without God" with the traditional church found its very personal and public expression in John Paul II's much acclaimed visit to Poland in June 1979. Michnik would quote Tadeusz Mazowiecki in his essay of celebration for the visit, *A Lesson in Dignity* (Michnik, 1987:

160-168). Mazowiecki was editor of a liberal Catholic magazine who would become one of Solidarity leader Lech Wałęsa's closest advisors (Ash, 1983: 20), and Poland's first non-Communist, and indeed neoliberal, prime minister in the 1990s. According to Michnik, Mazowiecki captured the intellectual and spiritual moment of the Pope's visit by grasping the way the Pope fused the teachings of Jesus Christ "with the most important values of European culture" and so becoming "for everyone the source of moral norms and the light of hope" (Michnik, 1987: 166).[103] Some militant workers were drawn towards KOR's activities leading to the production of underground leaflets and newspapers, the most important of which was *Robotnik* (Worker). The demand for a free trade union movement had already begun to grow. KOR's influence on this development was thus well rooted—including its theory of a self-limiting revolution.

The glaring contradiction is this. Perhaps the suffering poor of biblical times could not help themselves. But when KOR activists rallied to workers it was by striking they were beginning to help themselves. KOR's support was most welcome but, as the workers' movement developed, they demonstrated a capacity for self-help that would ultimately bypass KOR. Certainly the workers' movement needed their own intellectuals but the ideology, masquerading as a non-ideology, an eclectic mix of barely concealed Christian values, of the KOR intellectuals would prove itself to be backward and a drag on the movement. There is an uncanny reminder here of Marx's and Engels's *Communist Manifesto* criticism of the 19th century Utopian socialists.[104]

Sociologist David Ost makes a convincing case that the non-ideology was indeed an ideology which he labels "Anti Politics", and that it very successfully, and arguably, disastrously, laid down guidelines for Solidarity in 1980-81. "When KOR and Solidarity claimed they were not 'political' movements, what they meant was that they did not want to challenge the Party's control of the state" (Ost, 1990:1.):[105]

The class of '68 ... thought they discerned a new way

forward ... "bureaucratic socialism" would not be transformed from above ... its internal contradictions made it susceptible to pressure from below ... this autonomous "civil society" would reassure Soviet leaders, whose control of Poland's foreign and defence policy would not be challenged. This strategy was elaborated in a series of essays by KOR members like Jacek Kuroń and Adam Michnik ... Kuron's slogan "Don't burn down the Party committees, found your own!" could hang as a motto over all the workers' protests in 1980 (Ash, 1983: 22-3).

Ost captures the contradiction that would doom this strategy very well: "Unlike revolutionaries ... their goal was not to seize state power, but to secure conditions in which they could interact with the government. They had to act illegally, but their goal was to have independent institutions exist legally ... Yet the oppositionists, aware that the state could not be ignored, nonetheless kept emphasising that it should be ignored" (Ost, 1990: 71, 72).

This made Kuroń and Michnik extraordinarily cautious from the beginning. When faced with the prospect of the mass-based independent workers' movement at Gdańsk in 1980 that might threaten the state and the ruling Communist Party's monopoly control of it, they opposed it. KOR's conservatism was immediately exposed. Not for the first time in history, the workers were far in advance of the intellectuals ...[106] Michnik would concede this in a remarkable statement:

> Jacek, like me, was very uneasy about the situation in Gdańsk ... The "wildest" idea was ... that independent and self-governing trade unions could be formed. Jacek knew this was impossible in a communist system ... I was supposed to go to Gdańsk ... Since I was known and rather liked there ... perhaps I might have convinced them. Fortunately, I was arrested ... and so Solidarity was created ... That's how Solidarity arose, without us

> and against us, although we always considered it to be our [KOR's] child. An illegitimate one, you might say (Ost, 1990: 77).

In 1980 KOR dissolved. With the launch of Solidarity, it believed its work to be complete (Lipski, 1985: 452-6). But, of course, its key activists became part of the Solidarity leadership helping to shape Solidarity's political outlook. The breakthrough had come at the Baltic port city of Gdańsk. Anna Walentynowicz, who would become internationally famous as the militant crane-driving grandmother in the shipyard, had helped produce *Coastal Worker*, a KOR newspaper. She was sacked. A strike movement erupted which not only closed the giant, unfortunately named, Lenin Shipyard, but began spreading to workers across the city. It seemed as though the moment to turn the idea of a "free trade union" movement into a reality had arrived. A strike committee was formed which included Lech Wałęsa, previously sacked from the yard and who had climbed over the wall to address striking workers, along with Anna Walentynowicz.

The government was forced to negotiate. Political demands were added to the economic demands, the release of political prisoners, the erection of a monument at the shipyard gates to the workers murdered by the regime in 1970, which were conceded. Demands for full scale democratisation from the workplace and local communities to all the economic and political institutions of the state simmered just beneath the surface. Not all were agreed, nevertheless the final outcome was a humiliated government forced to recognise, for the first time in a "Communist" country, a mass-based independent free trade union. In any case, the government understood, in no uncertain terms, that the dynamic of democratisation, sometimes referred to as self-determination and workers' self-management, was now unstoppable. Implicit in the KOR strategy was the belief that the government could be forced to compromise, opening political space for democratisation. The outcome of the Gdańsk negotiations seemed to endorse this perspective. But the newly born confident, independent, militant workers' movement was in no mood for compromise.

Andrzej Gwiazda, a name virtually unknown in the West, was one of Solidarity's chief negotiators with the government. Along with his wife Joanna Duda-Gwiazda, Anna Walentynowicz and Lech Wałęsa, he had formed the free trade union movement in Gdańsk, independently of KOR. Tracking his political journey from Gdańsk 1980 to Bydgoszcz 1981, both the high point and moment of defeat for Solidarity, gives us a unique political insight into both the strengths but also the fatal political weaknesses of the new movement.[107] At Gdańsk, Gwiazda symbolised the mood of no compromise.

His extraordinary personal history, deported with his family to Siberia at the age of five at the beginning of World War Two as a result of the Hitler-Stalin pact, had made him an implacable foe of the regime. Polish nationalism was one inevitable result of his hatred of Soviet Communism. But his commitment to an independent workers' movement also meant he was open to socialist ideas—providing they were untainted by Stalinism. In his own words: "If someone asked me in the 1950s, I would position myself as a right wing nationalist. And then we landed on the left—without changing our set of beliefs. At the moment, we're back on the right side.[108] So one can say our beliefs are constant, it's the political scene that's spinning around. But because of that spinning and our standing still, we're sometimes on the left, and sometimes on the right" (A-AG: 249).

The liberal journalist and historian Timothy Garton Ash observed Andrzej Gwiazda's dominant role both in the negotiations and the early mass campaigning days of Solidarity. There had been an internal argument. Should the Interfactory Strike Committee, which would dissolve into Solidarity, insist on the release of all political prisoners, including the detained KOR activists? The argument was effectively decided by Gwiazda: "Of course we must get them free" (Ash, 1983: 65).[109] A last minute panic over the government's agreement formally to register

Solidarity gave way to a bitter row between Lech Wałęsa and Andrzej Gwiazda over the call for a warning general strike. Gwiazda added his own warning, "Wałęsa will have to go along with it if he wants to keep his position" (Ash: 82).

Gwiazda also had an uncompromising view of workers' democracy that gave unprecedented power to rank and file workers, resembling the "instant recall" principle of the Paris Commune. Solidarity's strength rested on this approach, as Modzelewski also testifies.[110] Gwiazda argued that workers should not vote for "Franek or Gienek" but for a programme:

> that protective clothing should always be provided ... or that proper cupboards should be fitted in the changing-rooms. And after six months people can say to Franek: What's happened to the cupboards? You made a promise ... you haven't done anything, you creep. We're going to get rid of you ... Gwiazda was not a natural practitioner of the art of the possible: if he had been, he would never have begun the struggle for what seemed to everyone impossible in the 1970s. He was a fighter for fundamental principles, with more than a streak of intransigence. Yet no one who travelled around the country in this week could doubt that Gwiazda was more closely in tune with the mood of the workers than the counsellors of caution (Ash, 1983: 77, 82-3).

Fast forward to March 1981 and we find Andrzej Gwiazda and Solidarity facing their biggest test—the crisis at Bydgoszcz, simultaneously the high point of the movement and the moment of its defeat (see section after next). And we find Gwiazda, now the chief counsellor of caution, paralysed by indecision and inconsistency. Gwiazda, speaking on behalf of Wałęsa, unilaterally abandoned the general strike, which had been called to force recognition of Rural Solidarity and bring to justice all those responsible for the police assaults on Jan Rulewski and other Solidarity leaders. We will return to the Bydgoszcz moment shortly but first let us record and indeed celebrate the flowering of the revolution that was Solidarity's first few months.

The revolution had grown out of shipyard workers' strikes at the Polish port cities of Gdańsk and Szczecin on the Baltic coast, which laid the foundations for *Solidarność*, Solidarity. At its height Solidarity, simultaneously a social and political mass movement as well as a trade union, could legitimately claim 10 million worker activist supporters, backed by passive support of the vast majority of Polish society. The renowned Polish journalist Ryszard Kapuściński was amongst the first writers to sense the importance of what was happening:

> The workers on the Coast have smashed the old stereotypes of the "dumb prole" ... The young face of a new generation of workers has emerged: thoughtful, intelligent, conscious of its place in society, and most importantly, committed to drawing all the consequences of the ideological foundations of this system, according to which it is their class that plays the leading role in society. Kapuściński describes Gdańsk and Szczecin as "cities in which a new morality took control. No one drank, no one caused trouble ... Crime fell to zero, aggression disappeared. People became friendly, helpful and open to one another. Total strangers suddenly felt they needed one another". People were motivated not by 'wage demands', but 'the dignity of man'." Kapuściński saw the 1980 events as "an attempt to create new relations between people, in every location and at every level ... the guiding theme ... the principle of mutual respect".[111]

"The Lost Treasure of the Revolution"

Former Solidarity leader and the movement's national treasurer, Józef Pinior, also insists that 1980-81 was "a real revolution" (A-JP: 287).[112] Like Modzelewski, Pinior sees the settlement in 1989 as a major defeat for the movement. Deep disillusion was the result, paving the way to the present "nationalistic, populistic government, xenophobic and a hybrid of authoritarianism".[113] "People, society, had in their mind that a real alternative works. It work[ed], in 1980, 1981." To understand the Polish revolution, Pinior recommends Hannah Arendt's reflections on "the lost treasure of the revolutions", from 1789 to 1956.[114] Similarly "we lost treasure". In people's minds, something very precious was lost. "The degeneration of Polish politics today ... is a result of this disillusion, that it was not possible to really provide this revolution ... a real alternative not only to Stalinist regime but to global capitalism, markets" (A-JP: 287).

Władysław Frasyniuk is a former bus drivers' trade union leader from Wroclaw who also became leader of the city regional Solidarity.[115] After the imposition of martial law in December 1981, he led the underground resistance in the city until his arrest in 1982 (Bloom, 2015: 400). He experienced the revolution as lifting the burden of ignorance:[116]

> Anyway there was an enormous thirst for knowledge, everyone at the time was seeking to learn more ... something like a university operated and run like a trade union, it was actually founded at the workplace ... the thirst for knowledge was just bursting on all sides amongst young people. And this of course came out during the period after the political transformation in a more free, liberated Poland...The key was understanding that in order for democracy to function there are certain tools that you need to be able to use ... So very quickly in September 1980, we organised a sort of trade union university. And there were so many people that we couldn't fit them all even into a large concert hall. We took the decision to decentralise this education, to hold those courses in different places in order to give everyone the chance to participate and take the knowledge (A-WF:234).

It was a tremendous revolution in an intellectual sense ... During those 16 months ... we had a stronger civil society, and compared to today when we have democracy, parliament and market economy ... Polish society has never been so free as it was then, and free of complexes, as well, after the events of August 1980 ...

In Solidarity we didn't ask people where they came from, it was a place where people could come and gather and participate, because they all wanted to achieve something better ... After 1989 this never happened again. When it comes to the martial law period, I don't have the biggest problem with the fact that I was a prisoner for four years and I was treated as one of the most dangerous people, and I was heavily beaten on several occasions, that's not the biggest problem for me. The martial law killed a sort of decency and positivity that had emerged among Polish society. And the martial law period taught me that poverty and suffering demoralised people, it wasn't a ground for any sort of noble attitude. Not in the sense that Catholic Church hierarchs would say it, but with August 1980 there was a kind of moral renewal of Polish society. Yes, I feel I am a representative of that moral revolution, moral renewal of August 1980 ...

There's one other thing that people would say about those 16 months, everyone calls it—the Carnival of Solidarity. Not because vodka was flowing down the streets. Because people were open, joyful, they wanted to learn about the world around them and beyond borders, and they believed that they were better, and they wanted to be better. After 1989 that never returned, never happened again (A-WF: 240-242).

Bydgoszcz—high point of the revolution

Both the high point and turning point of the Solidarity Revolution was at the city of Bydgoszcz, March 1981. This is where the leaders of private peasant farmers, representing three and a half million members, occupied the headquarters of the United Peasant Party (ZSL), widely understood as a government agency, demanding recognition of Rural Solidarity (Ash, 1983: 112,151). They were joined by regional Solidarity leader Jan Rulewski. Negotiations were agreed but then abruptly adjourned. Later in the day, government officials asked the Solidarity group to leave the premises. When they refused 200 uniformed policemen arrived to enforce the request. What followed was recorded on tape, including a suggestion from Rulewski that the police were like those in the West "who truncheon people at the bequest of the bourgeoisie" (Ash, 1983: 152). Finally, they were dragged out of the building, some, indeed, pushed down a corridor of truncheon-wielding police, with a shout heard from police ranks: "Get Rulewski!" (Ash, 1983: 152). Rulewski and several others were badly beaten and hospitalised. The pressure from below for an all-out general strike and workplace occupations was overwhelming. It became a moment of truth for Solidarity when the question of political power seemed tantalisingly within their grasp, as Jan Rulewski ruefully here recalls:[117]

> We had ... a peaceful revolution, in mass and general scale, unknown in Poland, and probably in Europe ... so utterly surprising, shocking ... it had to surprise everybody and it did. It absolutely exceeded all our expectations here in Poland and internationally, and it can be compared, if to it only, the revolution in Iran.[118] During the revolution in Iran nobody listened to the king anymore.[119] Similarly in Poland, nobody listened to the government ... The most important ... moral result was the fight for human dignity ... of the worker ... who performs all the heavy work using machines, get his hands dirty up to his elbows. He is the one that the director

> needs. The Communists used to say, that "he is a planning unit. We will throw people here, some materials there, we will mix them and then we will thrive." This is how the central planner managed things. The workers' ambitions, their imagination, their dreams, were just ignored ... Because the first secretary of the party was the one who decided whether a worker could have any dreams, what is his right to have dreams, imagination, expectations, even moderate ones (A-JR: 290-1).

Rulewski then drew a parallel with Poland's new private capitalism today. Nothing had really changed. The state central planner had been replaced by the private owner, but in the workplace "the human being is not what he dreamed of". He is "a personalised business cost". Jan Rulewski was very keen to integrate his professional occupation with this opinion: "I was an engineer mechanic, a constructor in Romet Bicycle Works, a semi-scientific institution, a research and development centre. I voluntarily acted as the head of trade unions" (A-JR: 289).

He was, and remains fascinated "for the general good of society, of developing a new concept of a bicycle, because the one we still use originates from the 19th century." He explained in some detail how it was completely unsuitable for modern 21st century conditions.[120] His commitment to developing a modern environmentally friendly bicycle is such a passion that he continues his research part time, at the age of 73 at the time of the interview, as well as continuing his duties as a Senator in the Polish Sejm, or Parliament.[121]

I suggested a link between his revolutionary commitment to workers' human dignity and to a new bicycle design. That he worked alongside the workers who made the bicycles he designed, and in combination they were a very powerful technologically innovative force that might have been a symbol for the Solidarity Revolution: a force which could design an economic model and find a way of not just producing, but also distributing to people's needs. This is neither the "Communist model" of the Soviet type, nor the Western European capitalist model. He replied "*Tak, zgadza się*. Yes, exactly" (A-JR: 297).

Rulewski fully expected Bydgoszcz to take the revolution forward. The proposed general strike was posing the question of political power for Solidarity. Lech Wałęsa understood this only too well and was resisting.

Andrzej Słowik, Łódź Solidarity workers' leader,[122] and also a member of the negotiating team, recalls the historically significant moment only too vividly:

> I took Gwiazda and Jurczyk [another negotiator] on a side and made an agreement with them that we're not accepting the text, proposed by Wałęsa ... Gwiazda walked away from us. And then I could see that down the hall TV cameras' lights were turned on ... For a moment I was considering doing some kind of prank—jumping on a table and bringing cameramen's attention to myself. But eventually I joined the group surrounding Gwiazda, heard what he read and asked him why he did it. "Because I can read"—that was his reply. Why he was earlier against? Till this day I cannot understand this ... it was a crucial moment ... we could not achieve such a degree of mobilisation and determination any more (Warzecha, 2014: 86-7).[123]

And Gwiazda knew it. Almost immediately he sent Wałęsa an Open Letter, widely published throughout Solidarity, attacking the decision! "Not going into an evaluation of whether or not it was a just decision, we were not authorised to make such a decision." (Persky and Flam, 1982: 171, 172). Gwiazda described the decision as nothing less than a threat to Solidarity's *moral revolution* in Poland.[124] Superficially this seems to reflect the earlier KOR perspective. But there is an important difference. The workers' movement was not relying on others. It was generating both its own morality and crucially its own politics. This was seen in the preparations for the general strike over Bydgoszcz when workers had begun to organise self-defence ready to combat a police and military intervention. Gwiazda continued, "Each shadow that falls upon the union painfully hurts the hearts of Poles. Internal democracy is our union's prerequisite" (Persky and Flam, 1982).

And that internal democracy, described earlier, had led the union to a very advanced level of self-organisation. Ash summed it up: "Workers' power was at its height ... popular mobilisation complete" (Ash, 1983: 297). Ash had earlier quoted Leon Trotsky's use of the idea of *Dual Power*, where elements of capitalist and workers' power coexist in unstable combination, to set the scene for just such a crisis (Ash, 1983: 99). US sociologist Jack Bloom also quotes Trotsky's *History of the Russian Revolution* on "revolutionary turning points" to emphasise the momentous implications of Bydgoszcz (Bloom, 2015: 219-20). Solidarity's earlier four-hour warning general strike, on Friday 27 March, curtain-raiser for the threatened unlimited all-out version, had been a spectacular success. It was the largest strike in the history of the Soviet bloc (but not the longest—that was in Budapest in 1956 where the general strike lasted two months following the Soviet invasion: Ash, 1983: 157).

"For the Party leadership the most shattering feature ... was the almost universal participation of Party members, against the explicit orders of the Politburo ... the base of the Party was in open revolt" (Ash, 1983: 157). The Church had put immense pressure on Wałęsa. The Pope sent him a special letter pleading for the general strike to be called off (Ash, 1983: 159). The government thanked the Pope for his intervention (Barker, 1986: 55). Many of Solidarity's best activists publicly criticised the Church's role and afterwards its influence began to wane (Touraine, 1983: 69-70). Modzelewski summed up the dilemma now facing Solidarity's impending showdown with the Soviet state satellite system. On the one hand, maximum readiness on the Solidarity side, backed by the vast majority in Polish society including the bulk of the police and military. On the other, unambiguous signals that Soviet military intervention was underway.

Just before the planned strike, Modzelewski recalls that members of the regional Solidarity committee stayed and slept at one of the larger factories in Wrocław called PaFaWag. It had around 11,000 workers. He also visited many of the different factories and workplaces and shops in the city, to get a sense of the atmosphere:

> And at these different facilities, there were gates. And the gates were open during the time of the warning strike. Generally, they would be guarded by sort of, say, state official guards. Industrial guards, we could translate them into English. These guards were relieved of their responsibilities, and the gates were guarded by workers from different organisations which were represented by armbands they were wearing ... you can find, for example, there would be three workers, one would have an armband representing Solidarity, another with an armband of the government-aligned trade unionists, and yet another had an armband representing [Communist] Party membership. What this was [was] a symbol that the government had no support, had no leg to stand on, that all of these different centres, all of these different groups were participating in the strike, against the government ... It should be emphasized that the threat of Soviet intervention was not an empty one. Apart from two Czechoslovakian divisions and two East German divisions, also 14 divisions of the Soviet Army amassed on the Eastern border, and they were kitted out and prepared for war. They had field kitchens, field hospitals, these were armoured divisions. This was a real and immediate threat at the time, one year before the imposition of martial law (A-KM: 274-5).[125]

Nevertheless, Jan Rulewski opposed calling off the strike: "Calling off ... the trade union paid too high a price compared to what it achieved, hence I support the opinion ... at the time, that this compromise ... was a rotten compromise" (A-JR: 290). Rulewski also argues that the anticipated international consequences of a Soviet invasion acted as a deterrent (A-JR: 290). Moscow was indeed in a far weaker position than at the time of Prague 1968. Its military intervention in 1979 in Afghanistan was having a profound demoralising effect. Like Poland's, its economy was destabilising from the unstoppable pressures emanating from the global economy (see below the concluding section V of this chapter).

In any case, the Soviet military intervention in the Hungarian Revolution of 1956 provides some unexpected guidelines. Moscow had been in no hurry to dismantle by force the Hungarian workers' councils that had developed after workers had occupied their factories. Better to pressurise the Hungarian government to seek out conciliatory elements amongst the workers councils' leadership. Of course, Moscow may well have been playing for time before the arrests of the workers' leaders began. But the time lag is important. The stand-off provided an opportunity for the workers' councils to assert their strength. They controlled production, not the government. See the outstanding 3,000-word statement issued by the Central Workers Council of Central Budapest, confronting Soviet military forces, on 6 December 1956 (Harman 1988: 177). The outcome of a stand-off between a much-weakened Soviet military and Solidarity in Poland's industrial centres, rallying almost the whole of Polish society behind it, was by no means a foregone conclusion.

For Joseph Pinior, Bydgoszcz:

> was a climactic ... revolutionary moment ... There was a nuclear bomb shelter in the basement. I used this shelter because I was formally leader of a trade union ... [here] ... I organised a strike committee for this March mobilisation for all offices, all workshops around the old market. I even prepared food for three months. So I had everything prepared for these strikes ... It was a classical dual power situation. There was still a state with

> military apparatus and police ... But the real power, day by day, went to workers' factory councils. In the fall with Karol Modzelewski, we organised a plebiscite in the biggest factories in Wrocław about who has the power to choose the director, manager, the Party or workers' councils? And in every factory we won this plebiscite ... We had the power but gave way to "demobilisation" and "demoralisation" (A-JP: 284).

Again, Jan Rulewski agreed. He emphasised key demands within Solidarity's grasp—a guarantee of "the security of the trade union, the registration of peasants' unions, access to the media, some kind of control over security forces and the security apparatus" (A-JR: 291). With this last demand, Rulewski breaks with the self-limiting revolution perspective, a position he makes explicit in July 1981 (Ash, 1983: 193).

Andrzej Słowik backed Rulewski: "He was one of the 'radicals'—always sharp, loud, determined and fully convinced that he's right ... As a leading 'extremist' Rulewski was not the authorities' favourite. I had a good working relationship with him ... One could count on Rulewski" (Warzecha 2014: 85).

Władysław Frasyniuk took a very different view, supporting Lech Wałęsa: "We were prepared for confrontation in the workplaces. We looked for ways to prevent the tanks from getting in, we put oxygen bottles. We pulled up many different objects on the roof if we found them suitable for defence, among them these acetylene-oxygen bottles, because we are from the generation who served in military as conscripts." But Frasyniuk says that the young workers were naïve, with "no complexes" but also lacking "knowledge and a sense of threat". He argues that the movement was:

> too weak ... for a tough fight ... Wałęsa's Bydgoszcz decision was an ultimate foundation for a different way of thinking about Solidarity ... in terms of compromise, securing yourself with time, space, and opportunities

> for building a civil society. A ground-breaking decision, and for that alone Wałęsa deserved a Nobel prize. Don't forget that we are brought up in Polish history. One unsuccessful uprising after another. These uprisings are deeply within us, and there is always a hero who ends up on the barricade. We were the first generation that said, "Enough, we are going to draw the right conclusions of the lessons from Polish history" (A-WF: 237).[126]

But perhaps the most telling remark came from none other than Jacek Kuroń, who asked at Solidarity's National Commission in July whether the revolution should continue to limit itself. He was responding to mounting pressure, following the debacle at Bydgoszcz and a deepening sense that the government had lost control. If the ship is floundering, delegates demanded, then why "not take over the running of the ship"? Kuroń appeared to agree, observing: "that is what, on the model of previous European revolutions, they would have already done. The revolutionary power would have taken over state power" (Ash, 1983: 183). Exactly the strategy he and Modzelewski had laid out in their *Open Letter...*

After Bydgoszcz, the next major focus for Solidarity was what turned out to be its one and only National Congress in the autumn of 1981. Though its main resolution confirmed the continuing revolutionary potential of the movement, there was a sense that rhetoric was beginning to substitute for strategy and tactics, exposing the movement's political weakness. Certainly, the main resolution was very impressive. It is summarised in the following statement: "The fundamental unit of the national economy is to be the social enterprise, managed by the workers' council and operationally led by the director appointed by the council on the basis of a contest and revocable by the former ... The reform must socialise planning ... True workers' self-management must be the fundament of the Self-Managed Republic" (Kowalewski, 2011: 203). Yet it found little inspiration amongst Congress delegates on the day that it was discussed. According to Andrzej Friszke, Solidarity's most authoritative Polish historian, "The discussion lacked cohesion and clarity ... Besides neither the union leaders nor—obviously, the experts took part in the discussion. It was without doubt, one of the most boring days of the Congress; best reflected by the delegates themselves, who were not paying great attention, many left" (Friszke, 2014: 962-3).

George Sanford, the only British historian to have observed and written about the Congress, noted that the programme had been hailed as Solidarity's *Magna Carta* (Sanford, 1990: 21). But Sanford also expressed reservations about its potential impact, recommending as a "readable interpretation" Colin Barker's *Festival of the Oppressed, Solidarity, Reform and Revolution in Poland 1980-82*, "the most cogent, if inevitably partisan, political analysis, establishing common ground with the radical Fundamentalist tendency within Solidarity itself" (Sanford, 1983: 2).[127] Barker acknowledges that the programme was indeed "an inspiring even noble document", but "remained at the level of dreams ... as long as the ... issue of power (was) not openly addressed" (Barker, 1986: 114, 117). Even the "Fundamentalists" avoided the demand for Solidarity to take power or become a political party (Barker, 1986: 118, Ash, 1983: 217).[128] This decisive argument forms the focus of the concluding parts of the chapter.

That's not to say the Congress lacked real drama. As at Bydgoszcz, Solidarity President Lech Wałęsa came under fire. Despite a Congress vote, a Wałęsa-backed deal allowed the regime to deny workers in defence and other "key" industries the right to select top managers, possibly involving as many as half of Poland's workplaces: a breach of an absolute cornerstone of the entire workers' self-management strategy (Barker, 1986: 114). Wałęsa's re-election as National Chairman faced more radical opponents, including Andrzej Gwiazda and Jan Rulewski. Yet he hung on with 55 percent of the vote. His opponents had not "presented clear alternatives" (Barker, 1986: 119).

Nevertheless, perhaps we should be wary of dismissing too

easily rhetorical intention—even if there is no defined strategy for moving beyond the rhetoric.[129] Policies to be agreed by Congress delegates were first discussed and debated in Congress Commissions. These were committees, given the time to thrash out the details of any proposed policy, and then make recommendations to Congress. One of the Commissions, Friszke argues, debated a position very similar to the *Open Letter*: "After a two-day session the common programme agreement was not reached and the Congress was to be presented with two variants: fundamentalist and pragmatic." According to Friszke, the post-Marxist philosopher Leszek Nowak was one of the leading "Fundamentalists":[130]

> Their proposal was characterised by stressing class aspects and the workers' movement traditions: "The ideas and mottos that had led the workers' movement for centuries in their fight for social and economic liberation have been re-appropriated by the ruling system." It was stressed that the party apparatus became the ruling class as it holds the main attributes of power: property, coercion measures and propaganda. "Instead of the promised classless society the most class-polarised society in history was created; a society where one side of the social spectrum holds all the political, economic and ideological power over deprived powerless masses at the opposite extreme." These words strongly resemble the 1965 *Open Letter* (Friszke, 2014: 919-921).

But Kuroń now claimed that Solidarity had:

> crushed the party's monopoly of power. Kuroń kept stressing the latter on several occasions. The Fundamentalists did not agree. "Defending the current regime, the ruling party cannot be a trustworthy partner for the society, and therefore for our Union". This statement was, as it appears, unacceptable to the "Pragmatists",

> who took into consideration the need of seeking compromise, even if preceded by confrontations, with the government. Less disputable for the "Pragmatists", nonetheless tactically problematic, was the demand of social and political pluralism: multi-party system and freedom of choice between different political programmes. The "Fundamentalists" shared a belief in the need of "the real socialisation of the means of production through the transfer of the means of production in the hands of shop floor workers", yet at the same time they supported the withdrawal of "party committees" from the workplace, which, from the perspective of the PZPR [Polish United Workers Party, the ruling Communist Party], would have been a revolutionary postulate, therefore unacceptable for the "Pragmatists". The "Pragmatists" group was bigger in numbers, but also more diverse. This included both commissions' leaders, Modzelewski, Siła-Nowicki, Gwiazda, Lis, Seweryn Jaworski, Jan Strzelecki, as well as Kuroń. They were quite divided, both in their ideological beliefs as well as the level of determination and proposed tactics (Friszke, 2013: 919-921).

Kowalewski has challenged Friszke's overall interpretation and claim about the influence of Leszek Nowak. He also downplays the division between Fundamentalists and Pragmatists. However, he agrees with Friszke that ideas similar to those of the *Open Letter* seemed to be stimulating some Congress delegates. He offers a different explanation:

> A more or less rough or crude idea of a new ruling class and a new class system was a popular idea among Solidarność militants and expressed the level of their spontaneous class consciousness. It is wrong to attribute it to this or another thinker; working-class militants were perfectly able to arrive to such an idea without theo-

> rists, intellectuals, and so on. There is a strong tendency among intellectuals writing about Solidarność (and about other mass movements) to attribute the production of ideas and the ideological leadership to intellectuals, but it is wrong: working-class militants are producing ideas, too, and during great working-class upheavals they are very active in this field.[131]

Kowalewski's point here expresses one of the core arguments of this book. That revolutionary workers' movements like Solidarity throw up their own leaders. Intellectuals who support the movement need to relate to them, not substitute for them.

III. Was there an alternative strategy?

An "active strike" is not really a strike at all. It is a far more revolutionary development where workers begin to reorganise production and distribution in their own interests. Zbigniew Kowalewski was a Solidarity leader in Łódź, Poland's second largest city, sometimes described as Poland's "Manchester" because of its long association with textile manufacturing. It concentrated some of the largest numbers of women workers in the country. As reported earlier, Kowalewski identified with Kuroń and Modzelewski's *Open Letter*, despite the hostility from Kuroń for doing so. Hunger stalked Łódź in the summer of 1981, the city under siege from serous food shortages. Solidarity leaders including Kowalewski and workers' leader Andrzej Słowik were compelled to develop a more radical strategy that went beyond the strike movement. A "hunger march" was called which attracted 50,000 women workers, many coming with their children. Placards and banners were made in the factories. Slogans included attacks on a "Communism" where "socialism is the doctrine of hunger, poverty and filth". Some were warnings. "Hunger deprives people of reason. It can deprive you of power" (Kowalewski, 1988: 25).[132] This was no idle threat. Słowik warned the local authorities that Solidarity intended, as from now, to check on the food production and distribution process, implicitly hinting that they were ready to take it over themselves. As Kowalewski put it: this was to be "social control over distribution". The government also understood this as a political threat. Deputy Prime Minister Rakowski responded: "He who controls the production of food ... holds power. Your demand ... constitutes a programme for the seizure of power" (Kowalewski, 1988: 27).[133]

Nevertheless, the Łódź Mayor found a legal pretext to respond to Solidarity's demands. He issued authorisations for Solidarity to check on the city's food production and distribution network. Wholesale centres in the countryside, the slaughterhouses, the depots, the retail establishments, all were inspected. "It was soon discovered that large amounts of meat left the central slaughterhouse for unknown destinations" (Kowalewski, 1988: 28). Data were presented to the Mayor that he said he was unaware of. He was thus forced to issue requests to central government directing stocks to consumption needs. In October Solidarity's Łódź regional leadership raised the stakes when it introduced the idea of "active strikes" (work-ins) where workers would independently re-organise production to meet urgent consumption needs, especially in response to food shortages. In response, local Solidarity was given control of the production and distribution of food ration cards, previously a state monopoly (Kowalewski, 1988: 30). This represented a fundamental deepening of Solidarity's encroachment on state power. Kowalewski insists that one immediate result was that food queues got shorter, and food supplies improved (Kowalewski, 1988: 31).

Andrzej Słowik has described these developments as follows:[134]

> the Hunger March was supposed to be seen as a warning and a last step before an active strike... [especially] in the meat industry. It was our original concept, prepared in details by Grzegorz Palka.[135] We proposed also to cover with trade union supervision purchasing of

> cattle, food factories, food distribution, transport and sales. For sure, it was a Bolshevik way, but no other one was available in that situation. We already experienced instances where goods in shops' storages didn't show up on shops' shelves ...What we proposed was seen by the authorities as a threat. They accused us of trying to take over control. An active strike was not started, but me and Grzegorz Palka were considered ... extremist activists. On top of that we presented our concept of kicking out the PZPR from workplaces, and leaving there only trade unions taking care of workers' interests. A workplace is not a place for a political activity. And if one political party was supposed to be there, why not other ones? Such claims were ... a kind of heresy, because a leading role of the PZPR was written down in the constitution (Warzecha 2014: 111).

Nobody in Poland had ever tried an active strike before: "We envisaged taking under our supervision the whole production cycle of selected goods, including securing delivery of raw materials and semi-finished fuels for transport purposes" (A-AS:299). Słowik goes on to describe why an active strike was potentially much more popular than a traditional strike. Government propaganda was having some success convincing workers that strikes were the cause of shortages in the shops. All right, he says, workers will stay at work, but we'll control production and distribution: "We treated the whole action and publicity about our preparations for an active strike rather as a form of propagandist pressure than a real threat to the authorities. The reason was that starting such an action would mean a necessity of gradual extension of the active strike, practically on the whole economy"[136] (A-AS: 299-300). In other words, it had the potential to undermine the economic and therefore the political power of the state.

This point was grasped immediately when the active strike strategy surfaced at the National Congress.[137] Bogdan Lis said that in regard to the demands for self-government all available means of exerting pressure would need to be used, but the tactic would have to be carefully thought through.[138] An active strike, as proposed by Łódź—taking over control of factories and production by workers—would, in reality, mean the seizure of power and the state of emergency would definitely have been declared. A pressure tactic needed to be developed as much as attempts of coming to an agreement with the government needed to be made (Friszke, 2014: 704). The stakes were indeed high. Andrzej Gwiazda would urge "rationality" and warned that an active strike would mean rebellion and it would require recreation of the entire machinery of state (Friszke, 2014: 1092-3). Frasyniuk spoke against the active strike that would need huge structural resources, which Solidarity didn't have. There was a choice: "either general strike, if the resolution is passed, or ... the government will take a step back and we will present our key political demands, or simply, if the government persists, the national uprising, and there is nothing else left to do in this situation" (Friszke, 2014: 1269).

Modzelewski thought the project of an active strike unrealistic. An active strike in a national economy means taking over economic power. The union lacked the apparatus to do that. "Let's imagine that now; our union has—on the scale of national economy—to divide resources and supplies. On the scale of national economy. Who will do this? Factory councils? The Presidium of the National Commission?" He was also against the idea of tribunals. When it comes to this, "we will decide, whether we choose the revolution way, appoint security guards, get armed with whatever we can and use physical force to smash all these institutions, or not. Because if not, let's not play with power. Simple. The basic weapon our union possesses, let's not delude ourselves, is a strike, not an active strike" (Friszke, 2014: 1270).

Andrzej Słowik wanted to test the strategy in the food industry in the Łódź region. Such a strike would result in "the government seeking opportunities to start talks with us" (Friszke, 2014: 1332). However, his motion for the National

Commission's support for active strike in selected industry sectors was not accepted (Friszke, 2014: 1354). Nevertheless, after Congress, the following plan was put forward by the National Commission, KK, at Gdańsk on 22-24 October, threatening traditional strikes over the food shortages with the warning of active strikes to come:

> on 28 October 1981 at 12.00 in all workplaces in Poland work will be stopped, public transport will be stopped. Strike action will last for 60 minutes. At the same time we demand the government immediately:
>
> makes all efforts—in accordance with provisions of "Solidarity"—to increase livestock purchasing;
>
> makes the level of meat ration supply equal all over the country;
>
> stops any repression of union activists;
>
> recognises and gives appropriate powers to the Social Council for the National Economy [Społeczna Rada Gospodarki Narodowej—SRGN] and the unions' social control commissions.
>
> If these demands are not met by the end of the month, the union will be forced to prepare for an *active strike* across the selected sectors of the economy. The date and scope of strike will be decided by the National Commission (KK) (Friszke, 2014: 1094-5).

In effect, despite the misgivings of the National Congress, Solidarity was giving every impression of preparing for a campaign of active strikes. Andrzej Słowik was amongst the most prominent working class militants moving towards such a revolutionary position. In early December, just before the imposition of martial law, and after mass meetings in the 12 largest Łódź factories, he told Kowalewski:

> After the Bydgoszcz provocation in March we entered a revolutionary situation, but we did not know how to make use of it. We reached a compromise and gave up the idea of a general strike. The situation is now once again revolutionary ... This is what the factory workers told me today ... This meant [Słowik] demanding the go-ahead from the National Commission for an active strike in his own region. It seemed that Łódź region would then draw other regions into an active strike (Kowalewski, 1982: 28).

The stakes were now very high. Kowalewski cites General Wojciech Jaruzelski, the defence minister, warning against active strikes in the Sejm and quotes the party paper *Trybuna Ludu* attacking his pamphlet *The Active Strike Tactic* for preparing a scenario for a seizure of power by Solidarity. (Kowalewski, 1982: 27).[139] The following month, December 1981, General Jaruzelski would impose martial law. Poland's Revolution would not recover.

There was nothing inevitable about Solidarity's defeat. Kuroń and Modzelewski's *Open Letter* in their explanation and remedy for the Polish workers' defeat in 1956 provided the lessons and the guidelines for what was required by Solidarity in 1980. They wrote: "The so-called October Left in 1956—a political current made up in large measure of the natural leaders of the working class, youth and intellectual opinion...was evidently unable to formulate its own political programme, to propagate it in an organised manner among the masses, to create a party" (Kuroń and Modzelewski, 1966: 45). Here Zbigniew Kowalewski gives a detailed explanation of the difficulty of implementing this perspective.[140] He begins by explaining the importance of the impact that Andrzej Słowik, Łódź region's workers' leader, had on him:

Andrzej Słowik had a strong class instinct and class reactions to the situations, and I learned a lot from him, because I had a Marxist formation but, being an intellectual, I lacked the working class instinct.

Concerning intellectuals and Solidarity: the fact is that sectors of "intelligentsia" active alongside or behind Solidarność or trying to lead politically this workers' movement were not socialists and, often, were even anti-socialists. But, in itself, it is neither strange nor specific for Poland in 1980-81. The problem is that there was no socialist intelligentsia (if there was one before it disappeared during the two decades preceding 1980) and not only that there was no organised socialist political current, but also that there were no dispersed individual socialists you could try to group and organise. Or if there were individual socialists, they were extremely rare, extremely dispersed and isolated among them. It was a huge contradiction of this political situation: an enormous upsurge of the working class, and even a workers' revolution, but at the same time a total lack of any, even incipient socialist political organisation.[141] There was no organisation that could materialise a revolutionary programme and strategy. And it was impossible to form such an organisation during the 16 months of Solidarity.

I was a self-made or self-formed Marxist (Third Worldist and Althusserian) becoming Trotskyist,[142] but a Trotskyist without any contact with Trotskyists. I met first Western Trotskyists only in October '81, during the First National Congress of Delegates of Solidarity. And I joined immediately their organisation, the Fourth International, FI, strongly engaged in the support for Solidarity and relatively well informed about our movement.

The level of Marxist theoretical knowledge of the Soviet bloc as social formation was pitiful. There was not even a Marxist knowledge of the forms and particularities of the exploitation of the working class in the societies of the Soviet bloc. There was not a serious Marxist knowledge of the functioning of their economies and societies. There was not a serious theory of workers' democracy. Marxism was in crisis, but Marxists, with some rare exceptions, were not aware of it. In those first 16 months, it was not possible to form a party or even an independent organisation for Solidarity's left wing. There was not a left wing. There was growing an elementary differentiation, not even between the left and the right, but only between radicals and moderates, between those looking for negotiation and compromise and those looking for mass struggle; those looking for a coexistence of an independent mass movement and the bureaucratic power, or (Kuroń) a "self-limited revolution" and those tending (tending only, not even consciously) toward an overthrow of this power, without any idea about what to establish after the overthrow of this power. Ideas of a political organisation were still rejected by the most radical militants of Solidarity, fundamentally as an effect of the generalised discrediting of the idea of a party by the regime. For them such an organisation was seen as divisive of the movement, manipulative, looking for minority power over the masses, etc. For this reason the first independent party we had in Poland in this period, the right-wing Confederation of Independent Poland (KPN), and the KOR, seen by many people as a secret party, were considered by the radical workers, including specifically people like Słowik, as "alien" to Solidarity: "alien" not due to their political orientation, but due to their (actual in the case of the KPN, and supposed in the case of KOR) party form.

I had been elected to the Łódź regional leadership of Solidarity and to its executive, together with the majority of members of this executive, on the base of a platform (with elements of an immediate programme) we presented for the internal regional elections. We, the militants regrouped around this platform, the most advanced collective paper produced in this time (the spring of 1981) inside Solidarity, by a group of its plant and regional activists, called ourselves Independents, because we declared that we would defend the independence of Solidarity from any political party (the ruling one, but it implied also the KOR, the KPN, and so on). It is obvious that radical militants needed to be regrouped in different manners, and this platform was one of such steps, but they needed also to overcome progressively, learning fundamentally from their own experience, their anti-party prejudices and understand that a radical left-wing political organisation is not only necessary for them, but also compatible with and useful for their militancy inside Solidarity, as well as compatible with the independence of Solidarity from political parties. On the first level of the public discourse, there was a tacit agreement inside Solidarity to not speak the same language the ruling bureaucracy and its party spoke: not to use terms appropriated by the official ideology. For these reasons, in the programmatic resolution adopted by the First National Congress of Delegates of Solidarity, in October '81, we invented the term, "Self-Managed Republic". There was also a tacit agreement to not use, publicly and internally, an anti-Communist language. Of course, these consensuses were not universally respected, but in general it was the case, with the special (but, obviously, not a unique) exception of Kuroń and his comrades from the KOR, who spoke about "Communist regime". The majority of leaders and militants avoided it.

On the second level, inside Solidarity, a lot of militants said: we struggle for a "true socialism", a "democratic socialism", or a "workers' socialism", and—in any case this is my personal experience—there were never hostile or negative reactions to it. In the fall and the beginning of the winter of 1980, I represented the Solidarity regional leadership at founding meetings of Solidarity in 40 factories and enterprises, and always I said there that we were fighting for a "true, workers' and democratic socialism", and later, when the movement for workers' self-management began, I said that we were fighting for a "workers', democratic and self-management socialism". When I presented myself as a candidate to the regional leadership of Solidarity, during the internal electoral campaign, in the spring of 1981, I said that I am "Marxist, supporter of workers' democracy, workers' power, workers' and democratic socialism, and, finally, a partisan of building a classless society, in Poland and elsewhere". There is an important document: "The Electoral Program of the Group, 'The Independents'", presented on May 7, 1981, by 14 candidates, including me, to the regional leadership of Solidarity. It was not a program of a political organisation, but of a current formed inside the union. The first chapter was an "ideological declaration", where we explained why we are for socialism, why there is no socialism in Poland, and what socialism means for us. It stated: "It is our conviction that the regime we have until now cannot be considered as a socialist one. (...) The ideology of this regime affirmed that socialism means the passage of fundamental means of production to the society and the passage of political power to the working class. In reality, during the last 36 years, all political and economic power belonged to a centralised bureaucracy alienated from the society. The working class was submitted to a regime of factory despotism, an exploitation destroying it physically and morally, and a police repression, while the whole society was deprived of the right to self-determine its destiny. (...) What will spring from the social revolution initiated in August by the working class will be a truly humanist socialism (...) oriented toward the satisfaction of material and intellectual needs of the society, This revolution opens the road toward the self-organisation and self-management of the society, ends with the omnipotence of the bureaucratic apparatus and breaks its monopoly on the disposition of the means of production, and makes possible the establishment of political democracy. (...) We conceive the historical task ahead of Solidarity as a general union of working people and as a powerful social movement unequivocally: it consists in assuring the victory of the moral and social revolution, and thereby in realizing a true socialism."

Thus, "The Independents" spoke openly about socialism. They were successful in this electoral campaign: finally four of them became members of the nine-person regional executive committee; all other members of the executive were elected individually, without a common platform. Even ideologically non sophisticated workers believing that the country was ruled by a Communist regime had a manner to solve the problem: often they said that they wanted socialism, but without Communist dictatorship. But at the mass level the most important thing was not the terminology, but the overwhelming sentiment inside the working class that the factories belonged legitimately to this class. They didn't demand bureaucrats: give us your factories; they demanded them: give us back our factories. It is a critical difference.

Kowalewski was a revolutionary socialist leader, a lone voice in Solidarity with some influence in the strategically important Łódź region of the movement. He struggled to find appropriate ways of developing genuine Marxist principles, strategies and tactics for a "Left" position in Solidarity. But fighting a "Communist" government made this task daunting, if not impossible. The very language needed to communicate ideas was sabotaged, or at least contaminated, by official Communist discourse. Promoting an argument for a new Marxist party, in the short time available, proved not possible, the idea of "party" burdened by totalitarian implications. Being accepted as a "democratic socialist" activist committed to workers' self-management in a "self-governing republic" probably pushed the limits of possibility.

IV. Workers and Intellectuals

"From Fawning to Discarding": it's a memorable phrase of David Ost's, summing up the changing relationship between the intellectuals and workers in the 1980s, before martial law and then after it (Ost 2005: 39). With Solidarity's launch in 1980, the "intellectuals first proclaimed an inseparable connection of labour and democracy, thus establishing the claim they would spend most of the rest of the decade trying to dismantle":

> For in 1980 Polish workers suddenly found themselves overwhelmed by the affection of intellectuals ... In August 1980, intellectuals in the political opposition [ie KOR] greeted the general strike in Gdańsk with nothing short of awe ... Gdańsk seemed to lay to rest the pervasive image of worker as *robol* (the uncultured brute who cares only about his next drink), revealing instead a citizen who cared for dignity and autonomy—precisely the values that intellectuals saw as their own. Even more, the strike showed that workers knew how to win, too. The Warsaw intellectuals advising the Gdańsk strikers famously urged them not to press the demand for free trade unions, and Solidarity came about only because the strikers ignored this

> advice ... Workers, it appeared, had the courage and tenacity to bring about the changes that intellectuals only talked about. Gdańsk set in motion a deferential exaltation ... One can see it in the difference between Andrzej Wajda's two films, *Man of Marble* (1977) and *Man of Iron* (1981). The heroine of the first film is a young filmmaker who cuts through bureaucratic obstacles to learn the truth about the Stalinist past. In the second film, the same woman comes to realize that her struggles are nothing compared to those of the average worker. The intellectual gives up her craft to become a wife to the Gdańsk shipworker valiantly fighting for social justice (Ost, 2005: 39).

But the liberalism of the intellectuals would all too easily degenerate into neoliberalism. Suddenly there is a change, a somersault, articulated most dramatically by Adam Michnik in 1985:

> In 1980 we may have thought of them [worker activists] as sensible and rational actors. In fact, says Michnik, they are really irrational hotheads, hostile to reason and common sense, contemptuous of the notion of compromise, and incapable of recognizing the "limits and realities" of the real world ... Local Solidarity leaders ... blinded by the ambition to become petty despots themselves ... Michnik is particularly harsh on their meagre intellectual qualifications—they resorted to easy slogans in order to speak to the masses and win their support ... the building blocks of a new totalitarianism. Michnik stands as a strong defender of Solidarity, but only if led by intellectuals. A Solidarity outside of their control, he suggests, is a dangerous one (Ost, 2005: 41).[143]

At the same time Michnik and Kuroń were involved in a disastrous flirtation with the Catholic Church (Ost 1993). Ost's damning indictment is powerfully endorsed by Karol Modzelewski. The Kuroń-Modzelewski partnership had broken up by the 1970s. Modzelewski was not involved in the founding of KOR. When he joined Solidarity in 1980, he remained friends with Kuroń but there was a difference in their politics. Albeit ambiguously, he remained closer to the spirit of the *Open Letter* than Kuroń, although he was as explicit in his public rejection of it—as is clear from my interview with him. Nevertheless, his distance from the KOR intellectuals gave him a critical eye on their capitulation to neoliberalism. He was appalled by their attitude towards their 1980-81 revolutionary workers' base. This is the context for his mildly ironic yet courteous tribute to Kuroń's supporters, and Kuroń himself after Kuroń's long overdue recognition, by the mid-1990s, that something had gone seriously wrong:

> Some of them were Jacek Kuroń's students and still influenced by his charisma. It must have hurt them that Jacek reassessed his participation in the post-Solidarity governments. He blamed himself (excessively in my opinion) and no one else. In 1994 he wrote that the Solidarity movement—or rather its symbolic potential—had been "destroyed by the government and the administration between 1989 and 1993 . . . The fall of real socialism did not bring workers freedom or empowerment. To the contrary, they not only lost their privileges, but also their prestige" (Modzelewski, 2021: 447).

In his autobiography Modzelewski reflected on the impact on working class consciousness of Poland's rapid and brutal transition from state to neoliberal capitalism after the Round Table Agreement of April 1989 ended Communist Party rule and brought in a Western-oriented government under the Catholic intellectual Tadeusz Mazowiecki:

> the frustration and aggression of the millions of people

> hurt by the transition turned against the elites who had initiated the Great Change. At a crucial stage of the transition, the reformers used the myth of Solidarity as a political shield. This was effective, but nothing comes free of charge. The myth wore out, and the trauma of the people who felt cheated remained ... During martial law most of them gave up when confronted with violence, and not all of them voted in the 1989 elections. But after those elections, almost all of them felt the taste of victory—"Finally we won!" And then they started to lose. Their earnings decreased, they faced layoffs, and they lost ground in the community as their factories were eliminated. Their prospects for tomorrow and prestige in society were compromised. They had to ask, "What happened? We won, and now my friends and I have lost out. Who stole our victory? They did—they climbed to power on our backs, entered into murky deals with strangers, and now are stealing our national wealth" (Modzelewski, 2021: 432-3).

Modzelewski expresses no surprise that workers started "desperately seeking those who are responsible for their situation" (Modzelewski, 2021: 446), even though this opened up the dangerous political route taken by the Gwiazda group.[144] Modzelewski spells out the perspective motivating him: "I put loyalty to people from giant state-owned factories whom I did not know personally over loyalty to my colleagues and friends from the democratic opposition. They had now started to govern and regarded these factories and their workers as the wreckage of socialism. Do not lecture me about who was right in this controversy" (Modzelewski, 2021: 429). Simultaneously, he anatomises the shift in attitudes by pro-Solidarity intellectuals such as the economist Waldemar Kuczyński, minister of ownership 1990-1, when he worked closely with deputy prime minister and finance minister Leszek Balcerowicz, the architect of neoliberal shock therapy in Poland:

> When Kuczyński became involved in Balcerowicz's transition, the passive resistance of the workers' councils, trade unions, and the administrations of large factories became annoying obstacles on the way to the great goal. This logic caused the reformers to perceive factory workers as their opponents, practically as enemies. In government circles, the workers' councils, trade unions, and factory administrations were called the "Bermuda triangle" because they could run the ship of the great reform aground, or even sink it without a trace. The workers' councils, a leftover from the 1981 success, worked in the workers' interests and tried to protect their factories. The reformers' objectives were exactly the opposite. No wonder that the workers' self-governance became a target for Balcerowicz and his people (Modzelewski, 2021: 428).

Modzelewski describes a meeting with Kuczyński in December 1989, where the latter defended the *popiwek*, under which firms were taxed if they allowed their employees' wages to rise faster than inflation:

> The example of Kuczyński is especially telling. He had been closely involved (as well as emotionally tied) with the workers' revolution of the first Solidarity. In 1989 he convinced Mazowiecki to put Balcerowicz at the helm of economic change, and then, as a trusted advisor to the prime minister, he secured the smooth collaboration between the two. This was a very important and politically crucial role. I have known Kuczyński for a long time. I have the right to call our relations friendly, and I am positive his change of economic views was not opportunistic. I have a high regard for his stubborn struggle in writing in defence of Polish democracy ... Kuczyński attempted to convince me of his (and the government's) arguments ... He was so convinced of his

logic that he did not see in his words what was turning me off. He was enthusiastically arguing, as if talking to himself, what a great idea the *popiwek* was. According to him, the *popiwek* was a trap to prevent the state-owned enterprises from compensating inflation with pay increases. Should the factory administration give in to the union pressure, then "their workers would bite their own asses."

> I remember this juicy phrase verbatim because it shocked me. Kuczyński always talked with a flair, but in these words I felt a complete reversal of his sympathies. During the great Solidarity, we swore by the workers in large industrial factories. We were linked with them by seemingly unbreakable anchor chains of unconditional loyalty. By the way, in my case these links were much older ... (Modzelewski, 2021: 427-8).

This reflected an ideological transformation that had taken place under martial law:

> The great Solidarity of 1980–1981 was a collectivist, egalitarian, and in fact socialist movement. Two years after the introduction of martial law none of these epithets reflected the ideological makeup of the underground Solidarity. This applied to intellectuals as well, especially the economists who had served as union advisors. Solidarity continued to be their reference point, or rather they looked toward what was left of it, but they spoke a different language and thought differently than in 1981 when they coedited the program "The Self-Governing Republic" during the union's Congress. Now their compasses pointed to different poles. The eyes of the Polish intelligentsia looked toward the West—but it was no longer the time of John Maynard Keynes and Willy Brandt but that of Milton Friedman,

Margaret Thatcher, and Ronald Reagan (Modzelewski, 2021: 352-3).

For a highly appropriate conclusion, here is Andrzej Słowik, former Solidarity Łódź workers' leader:

> The period of the martial law and after was a time of bureaucratisation of the union's structures, of much slower pace of developments and regaining control by the government side. The authorities started then to select from the so-called social side partners convenient for themselves. The final result of that process was the team which sat at the Round Table. The martial law was used to eliminate so-called extremists and radicals from a circle of potential negotiating partners. What started just after the imposition of martial law reached its apex by the Round Table when accusations of selling out workers' interests were raised on daily basis toward that side, which usurped for itself the right to represent the whole community in the negotiations. That claim was false because as I've mentioned all currents called by the government radical and extreme were removed. Here a mechanism repeated itself, which is known since the beginnings of human history. One can see it in slaves' uprisings in the Roman times, in the Reformation with Luther and peasants' rebellions, in the Spring of Nations, and then in the whole pseudo-revolution in Russia. In all cases the mechanism is the same: contain masses at the moment when they threaten those holding power—whether it's economic power and wealth, or political power. In order to do it and pacify masses, bogus leaders are created and concessions are made to bring some comfort, but the essence of exercising power remains unchanged. This is what happened in Poland. We were left without our workplaces, which were sold out in order to heal

> the ailing economy; without jobs, because our factories were sold out. Banks are in foreign hands, loans are going elsewhere, taxes are not coming to Poland because somebody made some kind of a deal and found a temporary way for making our system and country look better on the outside (A-AS: 306-7).

There is a tremendous irony here in Słowik's comments. Earlier in the interview he denies he is a worker intellectual. Now he proves himself to be one, albeit, and perhaps understandably, a pessimistic one.

V. Conclusion:

(i) "Poland: weakest link ... of Russian bureaucratic imperialism"

Let's return to the Bydgoszcz crisis of March 1981, when the Solidarity movement began the retreat that led to martial law and eventually to the neoliberal upheaval of the 1990s. Zbigniew Kowalewski approached it in a very different way from those who argued that Solidarity was right to avoid provoking a Russian invasion:

> you did not need suppositions about the inevitability, possibility or improbability of the Soviet military intervention, because both ... could be reasonably supposed ... what you needed was a good Marxist knowledge of the social nature and phase and tendency of development of the Soviet Union; you needed to know if this state was relatively stable on a long term or close to a collapse, and why. In the Marxist literature of this period you had practically nothing about it. What Marxists rather inertly ... supposed ... was a relative stability of the USSR. I said [it] in Poland in 1981, and it was one of the most important bases of my reflection on strategic issues, intertwined with the idea that Poland was the weakest link in the international chain

> of domination of Russian bureaucratic imperialism. So the problem, for me, was how this chain can break in Poland, what can be expected as a result of this break for the whole chain, and how the fall of the bureaucratic rule can be combined with the rise of the workers' power establishing a regime of the workers' and socialist democracy (A-ZK: 260-61).

Kowalewski's perspective fits well with the argument developed by Alex Callinicos that by the 1970s "globalisation of capital" was beginning to "leave the Stalinist states stranded ... What Chris Harman calls 'the shift from national capitalism to multinational capitalism' created powerful external forces threatening the USSR with stagnation, even collapse, until its closed economy was somehow broken up." (Callinicos, 1991: 45, 46).[145]

Harman had been the principal British student activist promoting Kuroń and Modzelewski's *Open Letter* in the late 1960s. He went on to build upon the analysis in the *Open Letter*, a decade after Kuroń and Modzelewski had abandoned it, to analyse the specific crisis in Poland which emphasised Poland as "the weakest link...of Russian bureaucratic imperialism", as Kowalewski had put it.[146] He showed the astonishing penetration by Western capitalism, both its corporations and its banks, into the Eastern European economies, and Poland in particular. It showed that Polish "Communism" increasingly morphing into a hybrid between the Western and Eastern systems, but with a dependency that was increasingly tied to the dangerously unstable rhythms of the global economy. The centre piece of the Polish government's next "five-year plan" in the 1970s was to be the expansion of Polish copper production through a massive £250 million (£1.87bn today) investment. This was to be provided by a consortium of Western banks but they had demanded as a condition for the loan the power "to demand changes in the copper export strategy as necessary", the *Financial Times* reported (15 December 1975; Harman, 1976). So we had the extraordinary spectacle of the classic model of Stalinist

'Command' economic planning, dictated not from Moscow but from the boardrooms of the Western banks!

The Wall Street Journal reported, "Foreign bankers are as happy to lend to Communist governments as to a family business. Happier. They've found in governments like Poland who will pay at rates western industrial powers would scorn" (7 December 1981; Harman, 1988: 255). Expanding trade with the West but also borrowing heavily from Western banks might have benefitted Poland from Western economic growth but the converse was also true. Western European recessions would now become exaggerated in the Eastern European economies, especially Poland. Just servicing the Western bank debt, which cost Poland nearly a quarter of its export earnings, triggered the red warning lights. At the start of the 1980s Poland's production fell by nearly a third, prices increasing by 24 percent in 1981, 100 percent in 1982, as real wages fell by about a fifth (Harman, 2009: 206).

The burgeoning mass movement of Polish workers that became Solidarity was a direct outcome of these circumstances. Confirming the implications of this analysis, Jane Hardy cites a Polish source describing the *nomenklatura*, Polish state bureaucrats who managed the economic enterprises, benefitting from the partnership with Western capital by the late 1970s, just before the eruption of Solidarity: "The communist doctrine was dead... the *nomenklatura* [were] getting rich" (Cieochinska 1992: 215, Hardy 2009: 25). KOR exposed the *nomenklatura* after a government censor fled the country to seek asylum in Sweden. The resulting publication of secret documents revealed a Polish government desperate to keep silent its cultivation of Western capitalism.[147]

We have here an intriguing, frustrating and admittedly highly speculative glimpse of the implications, and the high stakes at issue, if Kuroń and Modzelewski had developed this 1970s Marxist analysis. We might have had a recognition that Polish workers were in revolt against a fast-changing global capitalism, as well as the Polish state as simply an extension of the Soviet state satellite system. This just might have forced a reconsideration of political objectives, strategies and tactics. An open debate about global capitalism could have become part of the "Polish" debate. And it might have made the embrace of neoliberalism by the Solidarity leaders at the end of the 1980s, with the background applause from Reagan and Thatcher, far less likely. What we can conclude with confidence is that both Poland and the Soviet Union had entered that era of chronic political and economic instability, induced by globalisation, which would climax in the implosion of the entire Soviet state satellite system in 1989. This also contextualises the prospects for Soviet military intervention in Poland in response to Bydgoszcz in 1981, suggesting a far less certain outcome compared to Hungary in 1956, exactly the implication of Kowalewski's argument.

(ii) Explaining Solidarity's defeat through the failure of the worker-intellectual relationship

Progressive intellectuals were amongst the leaders of the new workers' movements struggling with the emergence of industrial capitalism in the 19th century. In Chapter 1, we saw Marx and Engels attempt to assert theoretical dominance amongst the several competing intellectual and political strands. I argued in Chapter 1 that Lenin and Gramsci refined the approach of Marx and Engels in the early 20th century, following the polarisation in the workers' movements between the reform of capitalism and its revolutionary overthrow. A different relationship was required between the revolutionary intellectuals and the most militant worker activists who had no illusions in the reformist alternatives. Chapter 1 introduced Gramsci's idea of the "democratic philosopher", which insisted on breaking down the distinction between worker activists and intellectuals. Gramsci's newspaper *L'Ordine Nuovo* in 1919, "the paper of the factory councils", was one of the most important bridgeheads between worker activists and intellectuals. *L'Ordine Nuovo* developed "certain forms of new intellectualism ... actively involved in practical life, as a builder, an organiser, 'permanently persuasive'" (Gramsci, 1971: 9-10).

Worker activists would become not just leaders at work but intellectual and political leaders in the wider society, Lenin's "Tribunes of the People".[148] A united political organisation was essential. Appropriate political strategies and tactics would be developed together to maximise the effectiveness of intervention in the wider movement. In other words, the wider movement itself was no longer perceived as adequate to be the exclusive canvass, as it had seemed to be in the 19th century. Two levels of intervention were now required. Developing strategic and tactical foresight as an organised minority political and intellectual strand or political party was a condition for competing for political leadership of the wider movement. This perspective was reflected in the *Open Letter* of Kuroń and Modzelewski. But when they rejected it, they seemed to return to the older 19th century approach of relating only to the movement as a whole (KOR was dissolved but its intellectuals became some of Solidarity's most prominent leaders). But something unprecedented happened to its intellectuals during Solidarity's downward spiral following Bydgoszcz and the imposition of martial law. Some of Solidarity's former leftist intellectuals turned on the worker activists, their former comrades, with extraordinary hostility and ferocity. It not only set the seal on the outright victory for neoliberalism when "Communism" finally imploded in 1989, it marked the route for Poland's rightward nationalist drift right up until the present day.

Dramatically underlining this process was the inability of the intellectual left to theorise the failure of Soviet Communism in the 20th century. This was essential and needed to be followed by a socialist perspective which demonstrated on the one hand, the unambiguous exposure and complete break with Soviet Communism, but on the other, a sophisticated adaptation of Marx's and Engels's perspectives, strategies and tactics for the establishment of communism in the late 20th century. Revitalising the ingenuity of Marx's and Engels's original shattering critique of capitalism, haunting the much famed but far from secure "global elite" and its neoliberal "globalisation" strategy, even before its puncturing in the 2008 financial crash which seemed to flash straight out of the pages of Marx's *Capital*, was perfectly possible. Kuroń and Modzelewski had seized upon just such an initiative with their *Open Letter*. It might indeed have laid the basis for a *Communist Manifesto for the late Twentieth Century*.

This remains an essential project. We need a *Communist Manifesto for the Twenty-first Century*. The lessons of Solidarity's failed but potentially socialist revolution against "Communism" would be central to it, alongside putting on the historical record some of the experiences of its leading activists. Jan Rulewski's continuing preoccupation, despite his Senator's duties, with technological innovation and his enthusiasm for it to be placed under workers' self-management, provides fascinating insight into a crucial aspect of what the contemporary content of a modern *Communist Manifesto* might look like. Equally, Józef Pinior's aggressive and very public internationalist exposure of NATO's sinister "black sites" in Poland, alongside his declared hostility to the usurping of Solidarity's legacy by a narrow national Polish populism, illustrates the need for an internationalist and socialist counter claim on that legacy—as Pinior put it: "a real alternative not only to the Stalinist regime but to global capitalism". Unfortunately, demonstrable proof that Marxism has been liberated from its Stalinist straitjacket is a pre-condition for achieving this, and it is a marker of the continuing failure of the remnant of the internationalist Marxist left that this remains elusive a generation later.

Paradoxically, Modzelewski, despite his protestations to the contrary that he rejected Marxism because he concluded that it was "Utopian", and based on "myth", seemed unable to shake off its influence—not least Marx's core postulate *that the emancipation of the working classes must be conquered by the working classes themselves*, as we see in the passage cited earlier where he says he "put loyalty to people from giant state-owned factories whom I did not know personally over loyalty to my colleagues and friends from the democratic opposition"

(Modzelewski, 2021: 429). Even more surprising is his veiled compliment to Lenin's Bolsheviks, also from his autobiography:

> in Marxism the myth of the working class was connected with the myth of the revolution. The Bolshevik revolution was the model, an example of how the proletariat changes into a power capable of overthrowing capitalism—not by itself, but by the missionary work of the conscientious intelligentsia. The intelligentsia brought a revolutionary consciousness to the workers. This lesson was not lost on us and became the compass for our activism when we started our fight against the Communist dictatorship. In our case, indoctrination did not serve the system well (Modzelewski, 2021, p92; translation altered).

Read carefully, he doesn't believe it to be a myth at all. On the contrary, despite the ironic undertone, this appears to be an application of Lenin's principles of revolutionary organisation at least as Modzelewski has understood it. But there is a flaw. Modzelewski fundamentally misunderstands Lenin's approach and "the missionary work of the conscientious intelligentsia ... [who] brought a revolutionary conscience to the workers". There is of course some hyperbole here, but it reflects the same mistaken principle that caused Modzelewski to write about the Solidarity worker mass movement: "In order to effectively manage this movement, it was necessary to constantly talk to crowds who wanted to decide for themselves" (Modzelewski, 2021: 425). Didn't the crowds themselves produce some leaders? Lenin's *purposive workers*: worker leaders, "genuine heroes... with a passionate drive toward knowledge and toward socialism" (Lih 2008: 344-45). Modzelewski seems to have forgotten that this was also his view. Kuroń and Modzelewski's *Open Letter* had described them as the "natural leaders of the working class", to be recruited alongside "youth and intellectual opinion", and able to formulate [their] own political programme, to propagate it in an organised manner among the masses, to create a party" (Kuroń and Modzelewski, 1966: 45).

Wladysław Frasyniuk's description of workers' overwhelming enthusiasm for education in the Wrocław region, for the establishment of workers' universities, also gave expression to the suddenly liberated desire of workers to create the intellectual tools they required to control their own lives in 1980-81. And, as we saw earlier, according to Kowalewski, "natural leaders of the working class" were present at Solidarity's National Congress as they had been present in their thousands, if not hundreds of thousands, since the birth of Solidarity. Kowalewski also provided convincing explanations for the immense difficulties over recruiting these worker militants, to use the formulation of the *Open Letter*, "in an organised manner ... to create a party". But those difficulties do not alter the absolute centrality of attempting to implement such a perspective or of appreciating that the failure to do so lost Poland its revolution in 1980-81.

CHAPTER 3

The black workers' challenge to South African apartheid in the 1980s: how the struggle was lost

Introduction: The Historic Twentieth Century Struggle Against Apartheid

The fall of apartheid and the election of Nelson Mandela as South Africa's first black president on the basis of one person one vote majority rule in 1994 was justifiably celebrated as one of the most spectacular victories for democracy over racial oppression in the 20th century. But behind this victory lay the spectacular rise of a powerful black workers' movement, starting with mass strikes in Durban in February 1973 and leading to the formation of the Congress of South African Trade Unions, COSATU, in 1985. The forward march of black labour forced white capital eventually to support a political deal with Mandela's African National Congress, ANC. This makes the culmination of the struggle against apartheid an important case-study for this book. South Africa in the 1980s was marked by a political struggle within the anti-apartheid camp between "workerists" based in the new black unions and "populists" supporting the ANC that illustrates the hard choices that all the new labour movements of the late 20th century faced in translating economic power at the point of production into a distinctive working class politics (Callinicos, 1988, chapters 4 and 5).

The ANC was the oldest nationalist movement on the African continent. Its long history of struggle against colonialism and internal racial oppression sustained its legitimacy during the worst of the apartheid years in the second half of the last century. This was a period when the ANC was banned, its leaders killed, jailed or forced into exile. Two very important landmarks stand out from the earlier period which would have a decisive impact as the internal struggle to overthrow apartheid in the 1980s intensified. The first one is the endorsement of the ANC's Freedom Charter by some 3,000 delegates at an open-air meeting in 1955, representing African, Indian, Coloured[149] and anti-racist white organisations, as well as the multiracial SACTU, the South African Congress of Trade Unions (Johns and Davis, 1991: 27). The second one is the Rivonia Trial, 1963-64, of Nelson Mandela and nine others, on charges of sabotage (SAHO:1). They were members of the High Command of Umkhonto weSizwe, Spear of the Nation (MK), which the ANC, along with members of the South African Communist Party, SACP, had formed as part of the armed wing of the resistance movement against apartheid.

SOUTH AFRICA TIMELINE

1910: The Union of South Africa is established as a self-governing part of the British Empire, with political power in the hands of the white settler population, Afrikaans- and English-speaking, and the African majority disenfranchised and subject to an increasingly refined system of segregation.

1948: The Afrikaner supremacist National Party (NP) wins the white elections and begins to implement a radicalised version of segregation known as *apartheid* (separation). It will hold power till 1994.

1950: The Suppression of Communism Act is passed, banning the Communist Party. Eventually it is reformed underground as the South African Communist Party (SACP).

1952-8: The African National Congress (ANC) and its allies launch a Defiance Campaign against apartheid that is met with increasing repression.

1955: The ANC launches the Freedom Charter, advocating a non-racial democracy in place of apartheid.

1960-1: Pass law protests initiated by the Pan-Africanist Congress (PAC), a breakaway from the ANC, lead to massacres at Sharpeville and Langa and huge stay-aways. The NP regime reacts by imposing a state of emergency and banning the ANC and the PAC. In 1961 South Africa becomes a republic, breaking with the Commonwealth.

1961-4: The scale of repression leads the resistance to turn to armed struggle, mainly by sabotaging infrastructure. The ANC and SACP led by Nelson Mandela and Joe Slovo initiate Umkhonto weSizwe, Spear of the Nation (MK). In July 1963 the Security Police capture most of the MK high command in

Rivonia, near Johannesburg. They, along with Mandela, are sentenced to life imprisonment in June 1964, after a lengthy trial.

1973: Mass strikes in Durban in February open a new period of resistance, much more powerful than that of the 1950s and 1960s.

1974: The Portuguese Revolution that begins on 25 April is provoked by the wars in Portugal's African colonies. The independence of Angola and Mozambique fatally undermines the security of the white settler colonies in Zimbabwe and Namibia and puts increasing pressure on apartheid South Africa.

1976: On 16 June school students in Soweto, Johannesburg's main African township, rebel against having to use Afrikaans as the language of instruction. This is the beginning of a year-long wave of revolt that is only broken by further repression, including the murder of the Black Consciousness leader Steve Biko.

1978: P W Botha takes over as Prime Minister (and later State President). He pursues a strategy that combines the militarisation of the state apparatus and selective reforms. The most important of these is the legalisation of African trade unions following the 1979 Wiehahn report.

1979: The Federation of South African Trade Unions (FOSATU) is formed.

1983: The United Democratic Front (UDF), a coalition of ANC-sympathising civic organisations, is formed to coordinate resistance to Botha's new constitution, which seeks to perpetuate apartheid by offering economic and political concessions to the black middle class.

1984-7: A new wave of township risings develops, interacting with the rapid growth of the black workers' movement. The ANC launches from exile the slogan "Make South Africa Ungovernable!" The Congress of South African Trade Unions (COSATU) is launched in December 1985. Botha's belligerent "Rubicon speech" the preceding August—defying international pressures to start dismantling apartheid—provokes a massive flight of capital from South Africa. In June 1986 he imposes a nation-wide state of emergency that succeeds in temporarily abating the township resistance. The workers' movement retreats after the Chamber of Mines defeats the National Union of Mineworkers in August 1987.

1985-90: Nevertheless, Botha initiates negotiations with the imprisoned Mandela after he refuses to be released without them. The secret talks, also with the exiled ANC leadership, are encouraged by Western governments. F W de Klerk, who replaces Botha as State President in August 1989, decides to take the leap. In February 1990 he announces Mandela's release and the unbanning of the ANC and SACP. Nevertheless, the security apparatus continues to wage a campaign of assassination and to encourage supporters of the Zulu tribalist Inkatha Freedom Party (IFP) to attack ANC and COSATU activists.

1989: The defeat of a South African Defence Force invasion of Angola by the combined forces of Cuba and Angola, which pursue it to the border with Namibia, increases the pressure on the NP regime.

1993: SACP leader Chris Hani is assassinated in April. This provokes an extraordinary explosion of popular anger that Mandela uses to force key concessions from de Klerk.

1994: Between 26 and 29 April South Africa holds its first democratic elections. Mandela and the ANC win a sweeping victory and take office, initially in a "government of national unity" with the NP and IFP.

1996: In June Finance Minister Trevor Manuel unveils his neoliberal economic programme, known as GEAR (Growth, Employment, and Redistribution).

INTERVIEWEES SOUTH AFRICA

Ronnie Kasrils

Ronnie Kasrils was a commander in Umkhonto weSizwe, Spear of the Nation (MK), armed wing of the ANC, African National Congress, member of the Central Committee of the South African Communist Party and an ANC government minister from 1994 until his resignation in 2008. He is author of his memoir *Armed and Dangerous*, of the memoir of his deceased partner Eleanor, *The Unlikely Secret Agent*, and of *A Simple Man, Kasrils and the Zuma Enigma*.

Makoma Lekalakala

Makoma Lekalakala, woman shop steward, CCAWUSA, Commercial, Catering and Allied Workers Union of South Africa, the second largest union in the country, largest union organising thousands of women workers, member of an anti-ANC socialist faction of the union in 1989. As a COSATU affiliate in 1990 it became SACCAWU, South African Commercial, Catering and Allied Workers Union. Today Makoma is Director of the environmentalist NGO Earthlife http://earthlife.org.za/contact/ She was recently the joint winner of a prestigious environmentalist award https://www.goldmanprize.org/recipient/makoma-lekalakala-liz-mcdaid/

Bethuel Maserumule

Bethuel, former "workerist", former shop steward with Barlow aluminium production until 1986 when he became a full time organiser with the Metal and Allied Workers Union, MAWU, and then the National Union of Metalworkers of South Africa, NUMSA. COSATU had just replaced FOSATU as the main trade union federation. NUMSA was often seen as its most militant and socialist union.

Moses Mayekiso
"Workerist" leader, later member of the South African Communist Party, metalworker shop steward, chair of the Alexandra Action Committee 1985-6, lead defendant in the 1986-9 treason trial, elected successively as General Secretary of MAWU and NUMSA 1986-7. He joined the ANC and the South African Communist Party in 1990, and served as ANC Member of Parliament 1994-6.

Darlene Miller
National Education Office-bearer 1990-93, for SACCAWU, South African Commercial, Catering and Allied Workers Union.

James Motlatsi
Motlatsi, working miner, and lawyer Cyril Ramaphosa, together played decisive roles in building the National Union of Mineworkers, NUM, in the early 1980s. At the start of the 1987 miners' strike, Motlatsi was NUM President, Ramaphosa General Secretary. Motlatsi, a migrant miner, came from Lesotho, the tiny independent impoverished state, landlocked in South Africa and economically dependent on its émigré miners.

Rob Petersen
Rob Petersen was a member of the Marxist Workers Tendency, a Trotskyist current within the African National Congress, who were expelled from the ANC in 1985. He returned to South Africa in 1990, and resumed his practice as an advocate (barrister). He has a website here https://rob-petersen.info/

The ANC Freedom Charter of 1955 was a powerful, rallying manifesto, unambiguous in its commitment to end racial oppression. But almost immediately it aroused bitter controversy. A central clause asserting the right for the ordinary people to control the country's wealth seemed far from unambiguous. It stated:

> The People Shall Share in the Country's Wealth! The national wealth of our country, the heritage of all South Africans, shall be restored to the people. The mineral wealth beneath the soil, the banks and monopoly industry, shall be transferred to the ownership of the people as a whole. All other industry shall be controlled to assist the well-being of the people. All people shall have equal rights to trade where they choose, to manufacture and enter all trades, crafts and professions.

Within months the ANC felt obliged to publish a second document, *Does the Freedom Charter Mean Socialism?* hoping to clarify the controversial clause. It made clear that the transfer of "wealth ... to the people as a whole" meant "nationalisation of the basic wealth". At the same time, though, it stated explicitly that "socialism and ... nationalisation ... are not synonymous terms".[150] This, then, left open the question of the ANC's attitude to economic inequality, which, as we shall see in the conclusion, the ANC visited again at its Morogoro conference in 1969.

However, this internal debate made the ANC no less of a threat as far as the apartheid government was concerned. And Sharpeville, where on 21 March 1960 police opened fire on an unarmed African crowd objecting to the notorious racist pass laws, killing 69, eliminated any illusions about a peaceful transition (Johns and Davis, 1991: 6).[151] The Rivonia trial was seen as a way of decapitating the ANC. Mandela's speech in the court would secure his lasting status as one of the movement's most outstanding leaders. This was not simply a blistering attack on the evils of apartheid, it was an open defence of the use of political violence to destroy it (Johns and Davis, 1991: 93). Mandela, and the others, were expecting the death sentence but instead received the infamous life sentence of hard labour on Robben Island. How the ANC understood the strategic objective of Umkhonto weSizwe has an important bearing on the later struggles. At the trial Mandela stated that there were four possible forms of violence—sabotage, guerrilla warfare, terrorism and open revolution. Umkhonto started with sabotage hoping "it would apply pressure for change while at the same time keeping bitterness to a minimum ... holding out the possibility of accommodation rather than irrevocable confrontation" (Johns and Davis, 1991: 90).

Rivonia and the wave of repression of which it was part briefly shattered the organised resistance movement. But the 1970s saw an upsurge of spontaneous mass black action on an unprecedented scale which would now shape the resistance movement right through to the collapse of apartheid in the early 1990s. It took two forms, the Durban strike wave of 1973 and the Soweto township uprising of 1976. Both laid the groundwork for the distinctive political perspectives referred to above that came to be known as "workerism" and "populism". "Populists" tended to argue that "racial oppression is the central contradiction within society". Class contradictions, whilst acknowledged, were seen as less important, "downplayed in the interests of the broadest possible anti-apartheid unity". "Workerists" by contrast, tended to see "racism and apartheid as a mask concealing capitalist exploitation". "Populists" prioritised "the national democratic revolution", "workerists" "the class struggle ... the working class alone on an anti-racist and socialist programme, can effect real change ... class alliances were not ruled out in principle ... [but were viewed] with suspicion" (Baskin, 1991: 96).

Despite the tension between the workerist and populist currents, in combination they posed a direct, arguably fatal challenge to the apartheid regime, drawing in both the exiled SACP and ANC. The potential of "workerism" additionally posing a left-wing political challenge to the authority of both the

ANC and SACP is the central theme of this chapter. The Durban strike wave witnessed tens of thousands of workers walking out of their factories and securing increased wages and improved working conditions for the first time since the 1940s. It was only a matter of time before the government was forced legally to recognise independent black trade unions. Its Wiehahn Commission and the resulting labour relations legislation of 1981 hoped to restrict severely the scope of the new trade unions (Johns and Davis, 1991: 187,189). But there was no escaping the implications of this startling new development. Apartheid had been breached in the workplace, at the point of production. White bosses and their deeply racist managerial subordinates were forced to negotiate with black workers' democratically elected leaders.

The Soweto township uprising was sparked by a government attempt to impose Afrikaans as the mandatory language of instruction in African secondary schools. In response, secondary school student activists, many of whom had been active in the South African Student Movement, SASM, part of the black consciousness (BC) movement asserting black pride, black culture and ultimately black power, called protest demonstrations. Tear gassed and shot at, the demonstrations spread rapidly to other urban centres. The "stay-away" tactic was introduced.[152] Township workers were encouraged to refuse to go to work on dates announced for demonstrations. Over 500 were killed but Soweto quickly became the symbol of a new defiance. This was underlined when black consciousness leader Steve Biko was brutally murdered by security police in 1977 and immediately attained status as one of the anti-apartheid movement's great fighters.

Whilst the ANC was weak on the ground in Soweto, it was the immediate recipient of many youthful volunteers who went into exile to join Umkhonto weSizwe (Johns and Davis, 1991: 188-9). Soweto was also the stimulus for one of the most important mass-based grassroots organisations that emerged in the 1980s, the United Democratic Front, UDF. In August

1983, 12,000 South Africans from all ethnic backgrounds met in Cape Town and agreed a campaign of civil disobedience and disruption to minor constitutional reforms, designed to soften the public face of apartheid without changing its fundamental structure. Particularly offensive was the government plan to provide the franchise to those classified as Coloureds and Asians but not Africans. The UDF also supported the "charterist movement" that developed in the early 1980s, promoting the ANC's Freedom Charter (John and Davis, 1991: 195, 196).

The UDF campaign was a tremendous success. The apartheid-imposed political structures in the African townships came under relentless assault. Roving demonstrations challenged police patrols. Africans collaborating with the new local Community Council system came under intense pressure to withdraw. School student boycotts over a range of grievances quickly spread as a mass movement. The UDF provided coordination to a movement that was able successfully to call the 800,000 strong Transvaal "stay-at-home" for two days in November 1984. The ANC had issued a call to make the townships ungovernable (SAHO: 2). "Ungovernability" was about to move from the townships to the workplace.

Meanwhile Umkhonto sabotage attacks escalated. The apartheid government was able to force neighbouring Mozambique to close its transit facilities for Umkhonto guerrillas but its sense of losing control was deepening. Simultaneously it prepared to declare a State of Emergency whilst developing channels of communication with Nelson Mandela. In January 1985, South Africa's President P W Botha offered to free Mandela (who by now had been removed from Robben Island to a mainland prison) in return for his renouncing the use of violence. Mandela's response deliberately deepened the government's dilemma. Not only did he refuse the government's conditions, he chose a public rally of the UDF for his daughter Zindzi to deliver it. Unconditional unbanning of the ANC, freeing all political prisoners and moves toward full democracy were amongst his conditions for negotiation. Botha refused. But the idea of a negotiated solution had been firmly placed on the political agenda (Johns and Davis, 1991: 198, 199).

At the same time the government was about to face an even more dangerous threat to its authority—a rapidly growing and self-confident independent and politicised black trade union movement, already in the making with black trade union federations like the Federation of South African Trade Unions, FOSATU, the Council of Unions of South Africa, CUSA and the black consciousness Azanian Confederation of Trade Unions, AZACTU. All three would be linked, directly or indirectly, to the much larger Congress of South African Trade Unions, COSATU. As Cyril Ramaphosa[153], general secretary of South Africa's recently formed National Union of Mineworkers and Convenor at the launch of COSATU, 1985, proclaimed: "Never before have workers been so powerful, so united and so poised to make a mark on society... We all agree that the struggle of workers on the shop floor cannot be separated from the wider political struggle for liberation in this country" (Baskin, 1991: 54).[154]

The launch of the new trade union federation had the potential to transform the struggle against apartheid in South Africa. It was the largest black trade union federation ever formed in the country, representing affiliated unions with a combined membership of nearly half a million workers. It brought together the two wings of the internal resistance to apartheid, the "workerists" in the workplaces and the "populists" in the townships. But it also provided a covert link to the banned and exiled African National Congress, the ANC, and the South African Communist Party, SACP. Several ANC and SACP supporting trade unionists were elected to the COSATU executive. From now on, COSATU leaders would be in regular covert contact with the ANC. In other words, it seemed COSATU could threaten the apartheid government with maximum unity of resistance forces in a period where the struggle against it was increasingly taking on an insurrectionary character.

"A massive strike wave accompanied COSATU's birth" (Baskin, 1991: 77). On New Year's Day 1986, 30,000 workers downed tools at four Impala Platinum mines in Bophuthatswana. Strikes were triggered across South Africa's coal, gold and precious metal mines which would climax in the great national miners' strike of August 1987. The strikes spread to the manufacturing industry, as well as other sectors, particularly involving MAWU, the Metal and Allied Workers Union. The escalating struggle triggered new forms of action like the "siyalala" or sleep-in strike (Baskin, 1991: 83). Managerial authority was fast eroding. This was the moment that the "ungovernability" of the townships came to the workplace, analysed in microscopic detail in one of the most important studies of the period to which we will return (Von Holdt 2003: 124). It was "a climate of uprising and even insurrection" (Baskin, 1991: 89).

A successful test of strength for the new federation was its call to recognise 1 May, May Day, as a workers' holiday. Without using the words, COSATU had effectively called for a one-day general strike, although it was called "a national stay-away ... probably the largest ever in the country's history" (Baskin, 1991: 125).[155] Over one and a half million workers took part. Planned rallies were met by government bans, enforced at venues by heavily armed police and soldiers. Some, like at Soweto, nevertheless went ahead where thousands of illegal SACP pamphlets were distributed (Baskin, 1991: 124-6). Pressure now grew from the employers, and even sections of the apartheid press, to make May Day a public holiday. But the government refused to recognise a date which was so obviously "Communist" (Baskin, 1991: 127). Instead, it suggested a compromise, the first Friday of every May would be a public holiday known as "Workers Day". Now COSATU refused. But at least in 1987 both sides "won". The first Friday in May 1987 was May Day, 1 May.

Alas, the growing power of the workers' movement, symbolised by the May Day victory, was about to be rapidly curtailed. The deepening of the industrial revolt in the following year climaxed with the great miners' strike of August 1987 (see section II below). It went down to crushing defeat. A month later the government published changes to its Labour Relations Act, severely restricting the right to strike (Baskin, 1991: 261-275). Although COSATU would mount an extremely impressive campaign resisting the changes, culminating in a three-day stay-away from work in June 1988, involving between two and a half and three million workers, (although with a very poor response from mineworkers; Baskin, 1991: 287, 288), the government would impose the new legislation anyway (Baskin, 1991: 291).

The period immediately following the defeat of the miners' strike, 1987-88, has been described as "a state onslaught" (Fine and Webster, 1989: 272, Legassick, 2007: 537). COSATU had suffered a strategic defeat which would significantly shift the balance within the movement. "Implicit in this broad-front conception of unity" that had defined COSATU was "the view that class contradictions are secondary to the national democratic struggle" (Fine and Webster, 1989: 272).[156] This now became increasingly explicit and unchallengeable. Why this happened and its implications is the subject of the rest of this chapter. It is the moment that the workers' movement decisively lost the political initiative and hence any prospects of political independence.

"Workerism" had failed to develop politically and had rejected the necessity of an independent workers' political party. It will be argued that the implications were fatal for its project, and this will be analysed in four distinct ways. First, it was unable to resist the pressures of the SACP, the South African Communist Party, as the latter emerged from the underground in the late 1980s. Secondly, it missed an essential strategic opportunity to strengthen its position by failing to deliver any meaningful solidarity to the 1987 miners' strike, the high point of the strike wave of the period. Thirdly, the treason trial of Moses Mayekiso, "workerism's" most accomplished leader, decapitated the movement, his own political trajectory at this time and afterwards reflecting "workerism's" impasse. Finally, how the limitations of "workerism", tending to confine its political perspective to the workplace alone, were spectacularly exposed at one of its most important power-bases, Highveld Steel on the edge of Johannesburg.

Meanwhile the apartheid government was about to be seriously weakened on the military front. This raised the question of the armed struggle and its relation to the deepening mass internal struggle. The battle at Cuito Cuanavale in May 1988, previously a little-known town in Angola, was so dramatic and significant that Nelson Mandela would describe it "as a turning point for the liberation of our continent and my people".[157] Cuban military intervention tipped the battle in the tiny town in the bitter war in favour of the Angolan military and against the SADF, South African Defence Force, and SADF-backed Angolan "rebel" UNITA forces. South Africa's attempt to destroy Angola's independence would end, as would its opposition to Namibia's independence. Its military self-confidence was severely shaken and would hasten apartheid's demise. Cuito Cuanavale has even been compared "to the great turning point in the second world war, when the Nazi forces were halted at Stalingrad" (Kasrils 2008: 6). Namibia's liberation forces led by SWAPO, the South West African People's Organisation, were also involved at Cuito Cuanavale. Namibia would become independent in 1990. Cuito Cuanavale clearly justified the 15-year Cuban presence in Angola. Nor can Cuba's military role be dismissed as a Soviet proxy. Moscow wasn't even consulted "over Havana's massive intervention" (Kasrils, 2008: 8). Cuba lost over 2,000 soldiers during that period; Umkhonto, its key South African ally during those years, 130 (Kasrils 2008: 10).

International diplomacy was also intensifying. 1989 is the year that saw the beginning of the end for apartheid. The OAU, Organisation of African Unity, representing independent African nations across the African continent, met in Harare, capital of the newly independent state of Zimbabwe. The OAU endorsed a document known as the Harare Declaration, prepared in advance by ANC leaders, which spelled out the conditions for a negotiated settlement, leading to elections for a one person one vote constituent assembly. The Harare Declaration received world-wide attention and was the subject of a special session at the United National General Assembly in

December—a convenient forum for Western governments to signal their support, albeit couched with diplomatic ambiguities (Johns and Davis, 1991: 207-9). It was also the year that the Soviet empire started to disintegrate, easing the way for the fall of apartheid to take place on terms set by the West.

COSATU's 1989 Congress captured the mood as well as the politics which were now hardening in its leadership:

> The spirit of the congress was unusually defiant. Delegates' most popular songs lauded the ANC's military wing, Umkhonto ... Flags of the banned Communist Party and ANC were in evidence. So too were hundreds of posters calling for Nelson Mandela's release. SACP members covertly distributed the party's newspaper, *Umsebenzi* ... [the atmosphere conveyed] a sense that the government was unable to contain the tide of resistance (Baskin, 1991: 345).[158]

Nelson Mandela would be freed in 1990 along with all other political prisoners. The ANC and SACP would be unbanned.

How the independent workers' movement lost the political initiative 1985-1989

I. The "workerist" movement and its collapse into the SACP

Cyril Ramaphosa's COSATU launch speech, cited above, reflected the two components of the rapidly developing mass movement against apartheid in the mid-1980s: "the struggle of workers on the shop floor" and "the wider political struggle for liberation in this country". The ANC was accepted as the leader of that wider political struggle for national liberation. But what were the politics of the shop floor workers? How did their politics become associated with the idea of "workerism"? Did "workerism" pose a challenge to ANC leadership?

In 1982, Neil Aggett, a white trade union organiser with FCWU, the Food and Canning Workers Union, was tortured to death in a police station. FOSATU, the recently formed

Federation of South African Trade Unions, which preceded COSATU, called strikes on the day of his funeral. More than 100,000 workers responded (Baskin, 1991: 35-6). The solidarity strike helped inspire the "legendary" speech by FOSATU general secretary Joe Foster at the Federation's April 1982 conference. It also made the solidarity strike, at least in principle, a strategic part of the FOSATU and "workerist" armoury. The Foster speech is generally regarded as a manifesto for the "workerist" movement. And as another former "workerist" leader, Alec Erwin, has recently explained, it was the product "of months of meetings and laborious drafts (usually hand written) by one or other scribe" involving intellectuals, shop stewards and union organisers (Erwin, 2017: 237).[159]

The speech was indeed "a strident assertion of independent politics" (Forrest, 2011: 329). Whilst Foster respected "the international presence of the ANC ... essential to a popular challenge to the present regime", this placed "certain strategic limitations on the ANC". Perhaps the most damning claim by Foster was that to the Western powers, the ANC "had to appear anti-racist but not anti-capitalist" (Foster, 1987, 227). This was essentially a reminder that the ANC's Freedom Charter was not a programme for socialism. Foster also noted because of its friendly relations with the Soviet bloc, the ANC could not appear to support socialist alternatives. Foster had already signalled support for Solidarity in Poland (Foster, 1987: 221). "It is therefore essential that workers ... build their own powerful and effective organisation even whilst they are part of the wider popular struggle ... to ensure that the popular movement is not hijacked by elements who will in the end have no option but to turn against their worker supporters" (Foster, 1987: 228). The base of the organisation was to be "located where workers have most power and authority and that is where production takes place". Foster stressed the democratic base of the worker shop floor representatives and unambiguously cited class struggle as the driver of the new movement, even though the phrase is not used.

"Capital's hostility to factory organisation forces members and shop stewards to struggle continuously or else to have their organisation crushed ... [The objective was] greater worker participation in *and control over* production (Foster, 1987: 231).[160] Finally, Foster made clear the objective of using "the strength of factory based organisation to allow workers to play an effective role in the community." There is a strong indication that Foster saw workers playing a leading role, "otherwise workers will be entirely swamped by the powerful tradition of popular politics" (Foster, 1987: 231, 232).[161]

In his recent review of FOSATU's position, Erwin elides this tension. "The FOSATU leadership eschewed syndicalist and 'socialism now' positions as they realised that a mass struggle was essential to defeat apartheid, and that restricting organisation to factories would not achieve that goal" (Erwin, 2017). Here Erwin fudges the central question: who will lead "the mass struggle against apartheid", the workers' movement or the ANC? Erwin also implicitly opens up the so-called two-stage theory of the ANC and SACP, that national liberation from apartheid must precede the struggle for socialism.

Erwin's elision here is underlined with his claim that exiled SACP leader Jo Slovo's "famous paper" in 1988, "The South African Working Class and the National Democratic Revolution", which addresses the two-stage theory, was a reason why many former "workerist" leaders joined the SACP when it was unbanned in 1990 (Erwin, 2017: 250).[162] Paradoxically Slovo answers the question that Erwin raised but didn't answer: who will lead "the mass struggle against apartheid?" Whether Slovo answers it satisfactorily is another matter. Nevertheless, Slovo's paper amounted to an ideological onslaught on the "workerist" position that the "workerists" were ill equipped to deal with. It would have been helpful if Erwin had admitted this rather than present Slovo's paper as a somehow seamless development of the "workerist" position.[163] Slovo argues that the presentation of the SACP two-stage theory has often crudely misrepresented the party's position. He re-fashions it as follows: "There is ... both a distinction and a continuity between the national democratic and socialist revolutions; they can neither be completely telescoped nor completely compartmentalised" (Slovo: 1988). The absolute key to the continuity between the two revolutions, writes Slovo, lies in the working class emerging "as the dominant social force in a truly democratic post-apartheid state".

This is the point which exposes the SACP's failure. Both in practice and in theory SACP politics led to the working class becoming a subordinate social and political force in the post-apartheid state.[164] But before attempting to develop this crucial proposition, it is important to contextualise it in Slovo's legitimate argument about the national democratic revolution and the struggle to maintain national integrity in the post-apartheid state, as a *unitary* nation state. By 1987 Botha's apartheid government was already searching for a "negotiated" solution. As Slovo writes, "the growing demand for democracy and majority rule in a united South Africa continues to be met by the diabolically simple answer that 'South Africa is a multi-racial country'. There is no majority. There are only minorities, all of whom must retain their economic, geographic and cultural 'heritage'". Slovo quotes a BBC monitored South African government broadcast statement "explaining" that "there are ten African nations plus whites, coloureds and Indians, and all insist on their right to self-determination" (Slovo, 1988).

As Slovo rightly pointed out, promotion of this "multi-nationalism", a development of the original "Bantustan" strategy, was a "device for continued national domination". Worse, it encouraged in particular "the Buthelezi-backed Kwa Natal proposals". This would lead to the apartheid government backing Mangosuthu Buthelezi's Zulu nationalist Inkatha Freedom Party with the explicit aim of splitting the internal anti-apartheid resistance movement and its agreed objective of black majority rule in a post-apartheid democratic South Africa (Slovo, 1988).[165] So the elementary objective—the struggle for black majority rule in a post-apartheid state—could not be taken for granted and

Slovo was absolutely justified in raising this. Furthermore, as we shall see shortly, the "workerists" were very vulnerable to criticism on this point.

But would the working class be leading this struggle for black majority rule in a post-apartheid state? Metal workers' union historian Kally Forrest has succinctly captured the political and historical moment that preceded Slovo's paper: "The banning of the UDF and the imposition of the 1986 State of Emergency moved COSATU to the centre of the political stage" (Forrest, 2011: 416). This seems to have left Slovo floundering about the meaning of working class leadership at this critical juncture in the struggle against apartheid. The section of his paper entitled "Trade Unions and the Working Class" treats COSATU as an abstraction. He makes a general argument without any mention of COSATU or its constituent unions' struggles, apart from two very brief footnote references. This contrasts sharply with Slovo's very concrete and arguably "populist" defence of the UDF in the townships, apparently undermined by democratic "workerist" principles.[166] Slovo argues that the "UDF is the umbrella of the broad legal liberation front", though he does add a footnote: "The relationship between trade union federations and organisations such as the UDF does need to be worked out more precisely." But what he is certainly not saying is that COSATU should be at centre stage in that "umbrella", the argument of the best of the "workerists" like Mayekiso. Indeed, his treason trial was precipitated precisely because he put that perspective into practice.

Furthermore, Slovo ignores the most important strike of the period, the miners' strike, the politicised strike wave that preceded it and the political implications of the miners' defeat. The following is typical of Slovo's general argument about trade unions and politics:

> The very fact that the workers' economic struggle cannot be separated from the struggle against national domination has helped to blur the borderline between

> trade union and political leadership of the working class as a whole. It is, however, vital to maintain the distinction between trade union politics and overall revolutionary leadership. A trade union cannot carry out this dual role; if it attempted to do so it would have to change its basic character and risk committing suicide as a mass legal force. In addition, the very nature and purpose of trade unionism disqualifies it from carrying out the tasks of a revolutionary vanguard (Slovo: 1988).

First, we're discussing a trade union federation not a single trade union, with a legitimate claim to represent the working class as a whole. Secondly, trade union federations certainly can play political roles—as we saw in Poland with the example of Solidarity. Thirdly, whether trade union federations can play revolutionary roles does indeed depend on the interventions of "revolutionary vanguards". But here Slovo's argument descends into pure obfuscation. This is not about "revolutionary vanguards" becoming or replacing the trade union federation but about revolutionaries raising demands within the federation which advance the workers' movement and, in the case of apartheid South Africa, simultaneously the wider liberation struggle. Furthermore, the principle underlying such an intervention was developed by communism's most outstanding leader: Lenin.[167]

"Revolutionary vanguards" are, of course, revolutionary socialist parties with strong workplace and community roots. Remarkably, Slovo's discussion about "revolutionary vanguards" is restricted to just five brief paragraphs, the shortest section in his paper. Here was an opportunity—missed—to show how a "revolutionary vanguard" would assist the working class emerging "as the dominant social force" in the struggle for "a truly democratic post-apartheid state". Translated into the practical politics of late 1980s South Africa with its apartheid-state structure on the brink of disintegration, this would have meant a COSATU deeply influenced by revolutionary socialist politics: a COSATU ready to rally maximum solidarity to the striking miners, a COSATU ready to exert extreme pressure on an ANC if perceived ready to make unacceptable compromises, rather than "becoming a conveyor belt for the ANC" (Erwin, 2017: 251).

In fact, Slovo's proposed "revolutionary vanguard" is a completely inadequate version of what was required. Slovo seems trapped in the Lenin of *What Is To Be Done* in 1902 rather than the Lenin of *The State and Revolution* of 1917.[168] This is not to argue that South Africa was comparable to Russia in 1917. But when Slovo tells us that "a vanguard party, representing the historic aspirations of the working class, cannot (like a trade union) have a mass character, it must attract the most advanced representatives of the working class; *mainly professional revolutionaries* [my emphasis] with an understanding of Marxist theory and practice", he misrepresents the development of Lenin's party in Russia.[169] As Chapter 1 illustrated, "the most advanced representatives of the working class with an understanding of Marxist theory and practice" in Lenin's party in 1917 were not only the professional revolutionaries. They were the democratically elected shop floor worker leaders in the workplaces, on the factory committees at the point of production, who had joined the Bolshevik Party. To be sure, they were in political and intellectual dialogue with the professional revolutionaries who arranged education classes and prepared political pamphlets, newspapers and other appropriate forms of propaganda. But this was now a mass party with a worker cadre as part of its leadership.

Paradoxically as soon as the SACP was unbanned in 1990 it too became a mass party. The "workerists" were in political disarray. They had failed to respond to the miners' strike in 1987 (see section II below). And they had failed to form a political party of their own.[170] And, as an alternative, Slovo's rhetorical claims for a working class political leadership were given credibility by Chris Hani, the charismatic ex-chief of staff of MK and, increasingly, the link with former "workerists" who were now close to the SACP. Hani's role is examined in the conclusion of this chapter. Nevertheless, the opportunity to create a politically trained worker cadre at the point of production from the existing factory committees was squandered. Preoccupation with the ANC alliance and the prospect of a negotiated settlement took priority. Many of the "workerist" leaders who joined the SACP would leave, making a mockery of Slovo's frankly outrageous claim that "there is no organised force in our country's history which has matched our Party's contribution to the spread of genuine workers' organisation at the point of production. We can truly claim to be the parent of black trade unionism" (Slovo: 1988).

The political evolution of Bethuel Maserumule in the 1980s illustrates the significance of the showdown between Slovo, the SACP and the "workerists". Maserumule was a former shop steward with Barlow Aluminium until 1986 when he became a full-time organiser with MAWU and then NUMSA, the metal workers' union.[171] My interview with Maserumule opened with the exposure of an immediate weakness of the "workerist" movement. Although both Poland's Solidarity movement and the Workers Party in Brazil at different periods served as inspirational models, "we never clarified the relation between unions as a political movement and a political party". This weakness is discussed in the concluding section of this chapter. This lack of clarity spilled over into the wider discussion of the workers' movement as a political movement and the ANC:

> A lot of us were persuaded about the potential power of the industrial proletariat but we weren't sure about the requisite political force needed in order to achieve transformation. And so we realised there were other forces which constituted the broader working class in order to make this class a meaningful agent of change. In the initial stages I was in MAWU and NUMSA [the metal worker unions], heavily critical of the ANC, very resentful actually. Our understanding of the history of the ANC was that it did not inspire any hope in transforming the country in any meaningful way. They had a

heavily reformist character and inclination into incorporation into the political and economic structures. This meant to us that we'll have an outcome, a political dispensation which would favour any other social class except the working class. And so we were heavily sceptical about any prospects of change coming through the ANC as the leading force.

But the reality was that the ANC had established itself strongly in South Africa, that it influenced all militant mobilised formations within society ... youth ... students, community structures, rural movements, the leading cadres ... owed their loyalty to the ANC. So, you had this dilemma where the more consciously socialist elements are few and outside the ANC. And those within the ANC are good at organising struggles, building structures, fighting campaigns and battles against the regime.[172] If you really want to advance a meaningful concept of socialist change you had to connect to those forces who, unfortunately, were loyal to the ANC. That began to influence and moderate some of the resentment towards the ANC.

And it gave us the opportunity to actually start interrogating them. What is the ANC? So, for some of us it became interesting to develop this sense that the ANC is a broad movement led by middle class forces, heavily influential, but vulnerable to the movement and development of its constituencies. This broad movement consisted of people in urban areas, people in the industrial sector, people in the rural movements. And they were heavily radicalised, and at the height of the radical mobilisation, they would push the ANC to the left. But as soon as the radical flow would decline, the middle-class leadership would assert itself once again. So, this made us appreciate an orientation towards the ANC—not in terms of its politics and policies but more in terms of the forces from below that were loyal to it and would follow it (A-BM: 326-7).

Maserumule was to be surprised not so much by how the workers' movement might influence the ANC-led movements outside the workplaces, but the extent to which the ANC was beginning to influence the workers' movement. He describes the "shock" of some "workerist" NUMSA leaders when they learned about a particularly militant and loyal "workerist" NUMSA organiser from the township, Katlehong, just outside the airport, in the industrial heartlands of South Africa, East of Johannesburg. One evening the NUMSA organiser was nearly caught by police at a roadblock with heavy weapons and members of Umkhonto weSizwe, MK. Again, Maserumule describes a comrade, an activist in a young Christian workers movement, influenced by "workerism", discovered also to be part of SACP initiatives. "Just around the 1990s ... revelations about who was in NUMSA and associated with either the ANC or the SACP were multiplying by the day" (A-BM: 329).

The SACP was pivotal in organising the MK intervention. Maserumule describes how his relationship with the SACP developed:

> They used to get their newsletter to us ... I was initially critical of them because of their closeness to the ANC. I could not understand how a party of socialism would ... subordinate itself to the nationalism of the ANC. But the more I read their documents I found them inviting us and sensitising us to the national question in South Africa ... And that's where they neutralised the influence of workerism—because they demonstrated that workerism neglected the national question ... and national oppression. I joined SACP but very late on ... my sense was that the way you deal with the national question was by settling the class question. There were no prospects for resolving racial inequalities without

> assuming control, the working class assuming political and economical control of society ...[173] But the battle against the ANC was lost. The battle against the ANC would have required a resolutely and strongly organised industrial proletariat rooted in point of production that would show and say to the ANC, we are an all-round political force able to take our destiny into our own hands. Without that I think the ANC would always have outmanoeuvred us (A-BM: 329).

Here again was the political question challenging the "workerists" in relation to the ANC: the Slovo promise of the working class emerging as "the dominant social force in a truly democratic post-apartheid state". How could the "workerists" have risen to that challenge? The Great Miners' Strike of August 1987 had posed that challenge in the most practical and dramatic way.

II. The Great Miners' Strike of August 1987 and the failure of the wider workers' movement

Strike statistics for the period 1984-1994 illustrate the escalation of the workers' strike movement, in the wider context of the rising internal struggle against apartheid, climaxing sharply with the three-week strike of 325,000 miners in August 1987 (Ceruti, 2021: 99-107).[174] The National Union of Mineworkers (NUM) was the largest trade union in the country, based in the most important sector, and this was to be its largest and longest national strike involving the loss of production of coal, gold and other precious metals, threatening the national economy, "mining...its backbone" (Baskin, 1991: 232). The NUM had been built quickly in the early 1980s primarily by the lawyer Cyril Ramaphosa, its first general secretary, and Lesotho migrant worker-miner James Motlatsi, the union's first president. Several spectacular workers' victories immediately preceded the miners' strike, including the mainly women workers' strike at the Anglo American owned OK Bazaar chain called by their union, the Commercial, Catering and Allied Workers Union of South Africa, CCAWUSA, the second largest union in the country; and the rail workers who succeeded in forcing the South African Transport Services to reinstate a sacked leader and stayed on strike defying earlier advice from their leaders for a return to work. Other strikes at the time, including the post office workers, helped create a climate of generalisation of struggle and "mass politicisation" (Baskin, 1991: 224). On the other hand, NUMSA, the metal workers' union, and main "workerist" union, called off their planned national strike because it was deemed illegal.[175]

COSATU convened OK Bazaar striker solidarity meetings of shop stewards from non CCAWUSA unions throughout Anglo American companies. There were solidarity demonstrations and short stoppages. The Food & Allied Workers Union refused to make deliveries to OK. Sixty percent of black customers stopped buying at OK, even though the union had not called a consumer boycott. In January, a bomb exploded at OK head office—believed to be the work of MK. Eventually OK capitulated (Forrest, 2005: 66). The rail workers' strike was notoriously violent with the police killing or injuring hundreds of workers and some strikers killing strike-breakers. COSATU HQ became an important strike centre with police storming the building, holding strikers at gunpoint for hours and systematically wrecking the building, room by room, destroying union records and equipment (Baskin, 1991: 177). Solidarity action in the wider community helped tip the balance: boycotts, black train commuters refusing to pay for tickets and riding free, attacks on train coaches and other South African Transport Services' property. At some factories workers refused to unload railway trucks (Baskin, 1991: 175, 179).

The miners' strike was also preceded a year earlier by the Kinross gold mine disaster which killed nearly 180 miners in September 1986. Between 1973 and 1984 more than 8,500 miners had been killed in South Africa's notoriously unsafe mines. The motto of the newly founded NUM was "Organise or Die". The NUM called a one-day national strike on 1 October 1986 in protest. COSATU called brief solidarity strikes of between one and two hours for workers to attend memorial services (Baskin, 1991: 150). More than a quarter of a million workers took part, making it the largest solidarity stoppage of its kind.

The NUM leadership called the 1987 national strike over pay and conditions. For the government and mining employers this strike was about who controlled the mines and the urgent need to refashion industrial relations in favour of the employers (Baskin, 1991: 226, Botiveau, 2017: 60). Government and employer violence dominated the strike from the start. Three months earlier COSATU HQ had been bombed, seriously disrupting both union federation and NUM administration—the building was also the NUM HQ. The State of Emergency anyway prohibited meetings outside the mining compounds, soliciting sympathetic strikes or mobilising opinion in the townships. The gold mines looked more like military installations. Armoured vehicles crammed with steel-helmeted soldiers and police patrolled the main road (Allen, 2005: 306, 316-17). Strike organisation was meticulous, though miners' leaders' suggestions that miners leave their hostels and return home for the duration of the strike were largely ignored (Allen, 2005: 309, 320). Vic Allen, commissioned by the NUM to write its history and a life-long supporter of Soviet Communism, nevertheless was sufficiently impressed by the magazine of the Trotskyist Marxist Workers Tendency, MWT, *Inqaba Ya Basebenzi*, to quote its account of the secret and highly effective room by room strike unit organisation in the massive hostels, sometimes sleeping up to 10,000 miners (Allen, 2005: 322).

After a week, negotiations between union and mining employers resumed. During the meeting Ramaphosa received news that 15 unarmed strikers had been injured by the police, without any provocation. Ramaphosa, well known for his calm demeanour, exploded and led the NUM delegation out of the meeting. He had placed rubber bullets and cartridges on the negotiating table and then with his arm swept them on to the floor (Butler 2007:197). But at issue wasn't simply police violence. Ramaphosa felt betrayed by Anglo American, the main mining company in the consortium, with whom he had previously enjoyed very good relations.[176] Ramaphosa's personally dictated NUM press release afterwards waås uncompromising. He accused the Anglo American Corporation of treachery, cowardice and deceit. The cowardice accusation was the most damning: "Cowardly in that they have now firmly come to depend on the state and its forces to assist them in breaking the legal strike..." (NUM Press Release, quoted in Allen, 2005: 356-7).

This was the moment of truth for both sides. For the mining companies relying on government authorised state violence, the collusion was there for all to see. For the NUM and COSATU, the strike could no longer be interpreted as a straightforward industrial dispute bound by industrial relations legislation and practice. The State of Emergency would also have to be defied. This meant serious COSATU solidarity action designed to secure a miners' victory. As we have seen, there were precedents with the OK Bazaar and rail strikes, but the action was not forthcoming and in the third week the miners succumbed to the employers when mass dismissal notices were issued. The most recent independent study of the NUM describes the defeat as "catastrophic" (Botiveau, 2017: 61), with mass dismissals of up to 60,000 mineworkers, including all the most active shaft stewards and other known NUM activists, locally and nationally.

The wider "massive strike wave" subsided (Baskin, 1991: 242). The following year COSATU nearly fell apart (Baskin, 1991: 239). *Inqaba Ya Basebenzi*, the Trotskyist MWT magazine cited by Allen earlier, carried a detailed analysis of the strike, including interviews with mineworkers, pinpointing the failure of COSATU solidarity. It quoted COSATU leader Elijah Barayi at the COSATU Congress earlier in the year warning that "COSATU was ready to bury P W Botha", South Africa's President, suggesting a readiness by COSATU for an all-out fight. *Inqaba Ya Basebenzi* criticised an earlier decision of the NUM leaders to disband the shaft stewards' councils, a crucial organised tier of rank and file miners' leaders which could have strengthened the strike and helped organise local appeals for solidarity.[177]

At the end of the miners' strike, Jay Naidoo, COSATU general secretary said: "Black workers in this country have few weapons, but one of those weapons is the withdrawal of labour... A general strike is not a last resort ... The mine owners have made it a test of strength and that is what it is going to be and we are determined to win it" (Allen, 2005: 384). But "it was...too late" (Baskin, 1991: 232). COSATU leaders knew what was needed but they seemed to lack the political will to carry it out.[178]

In May 2018 I put this and related issues to James Motlatsi, NUM president at the time of the 1987 strike. At first, he was unwilling to admit the seriousness of the scale of the miners' defeat, even denying it was a defeat. He also defended COSATU's relative passivity in terms of their "inexperience", although, as we saw, in the earlier strikes COSATU did provide solidarity. But, in any case, during the interview, Motlatsi seemed to shift his position as though recalling his former militancy and anger. He told me: "If COSATU [had taken] that strike as a platform not only for bread and butter issues [but also] for general political changes in the country, if in the second week in the strike, COSATU had taken a decision to say 'an injury to one is an injury to all', I can tell you, not only could they have saved the dismissal of 50,000, we could have seen a lot of changes within the country, within the industry" (A-JM: 358).

Motlatsi then made an unexpected comparison with the successful miners' strike in Britain in 1972. He pointed out that the British miners' victory in 1972 was secured through solidarity by other workers helping miners block the movement of coal to the power stations. He was presumably referring to the climactic moment in February 1972 when thousands of engineering and transport workers joined miners' pickets in the Birmingham city area to force the closure of Saltley depot and stop coal going to the power stations.[179] He continued: "Yes, so if quite a number of unions, maybe without going on strike could have stopped the services which they were running to service the mining industry, we wouldn't be where we are now" (A-JM: 359).

Two political strands in the wider workers' movement, though at loggerheads, had an interest in helping COSATU build solidarity with the miners, the "workerists" and the SACP.[180] But the main "workerist" union, NUMSA, showed little or no interest in the miners' strike in August 1987 (Forrest, 2011). This had serious implications for the strong "workerist" base in the steel industry generally and, in particular, at the Highveld steelworks in the region of Witbank, 150km east of Johannesburg. This was one of South Africa's biggest industrial companies, producer of precious metals, also owned by Anglo American, the main mining company. The Witbank region also produced 80 percent of the country's coal. Eight power stations burned this local coal which produced half of South Africa's electricity (von Holdt, 2003: 14). During the 1987 miners' strike, Witbank collieries were "the most tightly organised..." (Allen, 2005: 322). I return to this argument in section IV below, where I analyse Von Holdt's detailed and outstanding investigation of the workers' trade union and shop steward organisation at Highveld steelworks (von Holdt: 2003).

Bethuel Maserumule recognised this fundamental, arguably fatal, weakness in the "workerist" position:

> a really important question. The steel industry and the mining industry are really closely connected. In NUMSA we organise the steel factories which means we produce the equipment that is used in mining. So the direct way we are connected to mining existed and should and could have been used as a basis of waging solidarity with the miners. Because we could simply have stopped producing or sending the equipment needed for mining production. But that didn't happen. 1987 was the year NUMSA was formed. A more moderate union had just joined it. [In] 1987, the union was caught in internal organisational consolidation processes to integrate

> this more moderate element but also to merge different organisational and political cultures that came with the merging union. To organise its power and its united members the union wasn't available at that time, the year of its formation, to take up such major militant struggle. I don't remember thinking about it. We may have sent symbolic support messages but we never really discussed it in terms of a stronger role we could play ... it was a serious mistake ... (A-BM: 331-2).

Ronnie Kasrils in his interview with me provides a forceful defence of the SACP's view of the rising industrial struggle in 1986-87, citing a comprehensive statement issued by the SACP Central Committee in January 1988, titled "Leading Role of the Working Class in the Present Situation" (SACP, 1988).[181] The statement referred to the extraordinary growth and achievements recorded by COSATU in the two years since its creation and its rise in membership to 1 million members; its composition of 13 federated industrial unions, with 31 shop stewards councils, and according to the CC statement "an industrial army marshalled by 50,000 shop stewards in the factories and 20,000 shaft stewards in the mines". The influence of both the ANC and the SACP would have been profound on that organised core of the working class. The statement highlighted the rising tide of workers' militancy as reflected in the growth of the strike movement, "the highest figures in South Africa's history", evident through 1985-86, and the 6 and 7 May, and 16 June general strikes in 1987, which were by far the biggest and most highly organised ever recorded. Identifying the most significant strikes during 1987 the statement listed the ten-week national strike at OK Bazaar—the country's leading department store chain; the 12-week railway workers' strike; two major strikes in the postal sector; strikes in the country's sugar mills and tea estates; a massive one-day strike on 14 July by metalworkers called off when it was declared illegal. "Then", the statement continued, "there was the largest strike in South

Africa's history—the August 9 miners' strike involving 340,000 workers led by the NUM which lasted three weeks." The report did not include on which of these strikes the workers had won their demands and where they had failed—as in the case with the NUM strike which was defeated.

The cause of that failure was not analysed—in that statement at any rate (A-RK: 315). But the ANC magazine *Sechaba* in its October 1987 issue did analyse the strike in some depth in an article presumably written by a SACP member, who referred favourably to Lenin calling for the capitalist state to be shaken by violent revolution. The writer described the conclusion of the strike as a tactical retreat rather than a defeat, even claiming the union "scored tremendous victories". Astonishingly it applauded COSATU for "fast gaining strength" and emerging "from every action with greater resilience". Not a word about COSATU's failure to provide solidarity to the miners.[182] The failure to admit and analyse the miners' defeat contrasts with the detailed analysis in *Inqaba Ya Basebenzi*, the Trotskyist MWT magazine mentioned earlier. The SACP needed to be more than cheerleaders for COSATU. If there was a fundamental problem of organising solidarity for the miners (Baskin, 1991: 232), then the SACP needed to address it.

Kasrils now recognises the potential of the MWT and, whilst using very cautious language, thinks that their expulsion from the ANC was mistaken.[183] A retrospective view that sees the MWT growing alongside, or even inside, a re-emerging SACP, disoriented by the collapse of Soviet Communism in 1989, might have provided the political focus that "workerism" so obviously lacked. The necessity of a left-wing challenge to the SACP is developed in the conclusion. Finally, we know that Kasrils as a member of Operation Vula was part of an apparently secret ANC/SACP group, recognising the limitations of the armed struggle as well as the enormous potential of the internal and industrial struggle. Did the earlier militaristic perspective still affect the SACP internally even as it re-emerged?[184] There is also the question of SACP over-dependency on the ANC. Again,

Kasrils, though couching the argument with extreme caution, hints at the possibility:

> Whilst there is a growing critique that much that is wrong with the ANC and liberation movement today, stems from ... [the SACP] tailing behind the ANC in service of a skewed nationalist agenda in a two-stage march to socialism. My view (without dismissing the criticism outright) would argue that the main deficiency in the Party's involvement in the 1987 miners' strike related more to the concrete exile limitations (A-RK: 319).

Ramaphosa's own complex relations with the ANC and SACP at the time are succinctly summed up in the chapter title of his biographer that addresses them: "Becoming ANC" (Butler, 2007: Chapter 13).

III. The Treason Trial and political transformation of Moses Mayekiso, "workerism's" most accomplished leader

At the height of the township uprisings in 1984, FOSATU mandated Moses Mayekiso to represent its interests on the Transvaal regional stay-away committee where he sat with activists from the Soweto Youth Congress committee, the Release Mandela Committee and the UDF-affiliated unions. The stay-away call resulted in nearly a million workers from the Witwatersrand and Vaal Triangle absenting themselves from work for two days in November (Baskin, 1991: 45). Mayekiso, former miner and metal worker and now organiser with MAWU, the Metal and Allied Workers Union, which preceded NUMSA, was the best known, and most political, of the "workerist" activists. He was seen as a major threat to state security and would be put on trial for treason along with his younger brother, Mzwanele, and three others from the Alexandra township. The apartheid state had reason to worry. The potential fusion of township and workplace struggles, "populism" and "workerism" was indeed insurrectionary:

> My politics were developing now to say ... not only mobilise metal workers, but all workers across industries to have power ... I looked at [our] shop stewards' committees ... I thought these are grand structures that can really give power to workers, not only ... for wages, better conditions...but also to change the system of capitalism ...The perspective was that for any revolution to succeed the workers must be able to seize power in the factories. And working together with the communities seizing power in the residential areas—merged that to mount a real revolution (A-MM: 342).

It was the most high profile trial of the period and it provoked major protest struggles, illegal solidarity strikes and demonstrations, led by NUMSA in South Africa and a worldwide international campaign (Bell, 2009, Forrest, 2011: 421). The trial and its background—the uprising in the Alexandra township in February 1986—have been analysed by Moses's brother, Mzwanele, (Mayekiso, 1996).[185] For a few days, after fierce fighting, "The Six Day War" (Mayekiso 1996: 61-64), the puppet black civic authorities and the white police were marginalised. The Alexandra Action Committee became the real authority, with Moses Mayekiso its leading figure. It was a formidable expression of the ANC's 1985 call to make South Africa "ungovernable" (Mayekiso,1996: 53).

The ANC magazine *Sechaba* even compared Alexandra to the Paris Commune, in an article written by a SACP member (Mayekiso, 1996: 83). It was a superficially attractive comparison but revealingly misleading. Alexandra was a black township suburb of apartheid-era Johannesburg, South Africa's metropolis with modern industrial production located outside the township in the wider city region. In Paris, France's capital city, in 1871, the year of the Commune, the communards momentarily controlled the whole city including its rudimentary, early industrial productive system. It was precisely this distinction that made Moses Mayekiso so threatening to the government. He understood only too well the limitations of the township uprising he was leading:

> With those shop stewards' councils, we began looking beyond the realm of those workers' areas. We asked where are the workers staying? They are staying in squalid conditions in the townships. Let's bring our structures. Organise the communities, the poor, in the townships to really topple apartheid and capitalism later ... I got labelled as the workerist because of my emphasis on the worker power at the point of production. You can do whatever outside the factory, but if you cannot stop production then you cannot mount a revolution (A-MM: 343).

At the same time the ANC, its main supporter in the townships, the UDF, and the SACP wanted the political initiative to stay with the townships and not the workplaces.[186] The trial was also subject to a lengthy analysis by legal writer Richard Abel. This provides a different and unexpected insight both to the trial and the fluid politics of the time. Abel makes it clear that the trial was about Moses Mayekiso and the entire labour movement: "Unable to outlaw the unions, the state sought to discourage links with community organisations, remove a militant leader of the second largest union, and encourage a return to economism" (Abel, 1995: 374).

Abel, however, claims Mayekiso deliberately moderated his position as a legal defence tactic. He reinterpreted his actions to present responsible citizenship rather than revolutionary challenge. Abel gives numerous examples but one in particular stands out: "The most embarrassing language appeared in the [British] *Socialist Worker* [4 May 1986] ...which he now tried to explain" (Abel, 1995: 354). Abel then addresses the several often quite ingenious ways Mayekiso used to distance himself from the article. In reference to a related exchange, Abel comments, "Mayekiso gratefully accepted less threatening interpretations of his words suggested by the judge. He had embraced the two-stage theory of revolution, first nationalist then socialist (Abel, 1995: 348):

> Judge: "So, you want a mixed, socialist and capitalist state or to put it another way, a capitalist state in which the worker has more say?"
>
> MM: "Yes ... and the model that we saw ... in Sweden ... seems to be giving something to the worker and there would be no super exploitation."

This explicitly contradicts Mayekiso's position in the pamphlet *Comrade Moss* written and published by respected South African journalist Terry Bell, where he counter-poses a "Workers' Charter" to the ANC's Freedom Charter rejecting the stages theory (Bell, 2009: 34-5).[187] The encounter infuriated Abel:

> Mayekiso bowdlerized his own political philosophy ... he was not a communist or even a socialist but just a Swedish social democrat, and even that was a utopian aspiration ... Such repudiation of achievements, ideologies and loyalties may be one of the most insidious attributes of treason trials. Whereas punishment affirms moral purity and confers martyrdom, strategic denials are a degradation ceremony (Abel, 1995: 377).

When I interviewed Moses Mayekiso, I put to him some of Abel's observations. He burst out laughing at every one. He accepted that it was a legal defence tactic and described the choices that confronted him: a revolutionary defence, a politician's defence or a coward's defence. A politician's defence accepted the evidence when accurate but did indeed re-interpret it to "soften" its impact. The question for Mayekiso was simple, which defence would take him back to the struggle and which defence would take him to Robben Island. In 1988 he and the other defendants would be acquitted. I gave Moses Mayekiso a copy of the offending *Socialist Worker* article and asked him to re-read it. He told me later that he stood by every word. It is indeed a unique account of "workerism" providing leadership in the Alexandra township uprising. Mayekiso describes the breakdown both of the court system and police authority in Alexandra: "People are sick and tired of the court system, they don't want to take their cases to the state. They want to discuss their own cases, and be able to mediate" (Mayekiso, 1986).[188] The article also gives a fascinating account of the shifting relations between COSATU and the UDF: "The UDF is supported widely by many people. Say in the unions we decided we were going to have a stay away ...then we communicate with the UDF ... like the May Day now approaching" (Mayekiso: 1986). As we saw earlier the 1986 May Day strike-stay-away was the largest in the country's history.[189]

Moses Mayekiso nevertheless leaves a conflicted legacy for the period. On his release, he resumed his duties as NUMSA general secretary. When the SACP was unbanned, he would declare himself a member. He would rapidly become one of its most important worker leaders. He accepted the negotiating strategy pursued by the Triple Alliance, ANC-SACP-COSATU. And he became very much part of its apparatus, leading a mass movement with a leadership expectation of a government-in-waiting. His legal defence tactic had indeed become his politics, even if he rationalised it as an inevitable short-term compromise in the interest of unity with the wider movement necessary to destroy apartheid. In his own words...

> FOSATU became COSATU. MAWU became NUMSA—the beginnings of the broad working class movement. We (had earlier) got in touch with the Communist Party guys, for example, Sipho Kubeka[190] in Alexandra ... I went along with their politics, but not the commandist, the top down approach. I didn't agree with that, but, for the sake of unity, then let's work together. [But] I was

> adamant—you cannot have two stages of revolution. That's what happened. You use the power of the workers to get the elite into government, then once they are in government they will stifle. We were looking at the ANC, the ANC wants to get into government, once they are in government they will forget about the workers—even gun down the workers. Marikana is a good example.[191] I opposed this but with the politics of COSATU I said let's allow this as a trial stuff. I would say a majority of the shop stewards got sucked into CP politics. This all happened with the formation of COSATU. It was a compromise on my side. That this may not work. But the unions were a mass moving in that direction of accepting the CP, accepting the ANC as liberators. We thought let's get in and change the way things work. With people like Chris Hani, I was very close to him, to change the way the CP is working.[192] Hani was a real revolutionary. He believed workers should take power at the point of production. I joined the CP... after meeting people like Chris Hani after the CP was unbanned ... His approach was that if we leave the CP led by people who are leading it now, not by the working class, the workers, therefore it's not going to address the issues of the workers. Well, that was a good argument. But I was still sticking to the fact that the two stages is not going to work. I don't think I was appreciated much (A-MM: 343-4).

I told him I thought he was appreciated. He was now on the steering committee of the SACP. He was playing a leading role. For example, he had gone with Joe Slovo and another ANC leader to Mercedes-Benz in East London and persuaded striking workers to go back to work.

Mayekiso left the CP in 1993, the year Chris Hani was assassinated:

> I could see that it (the CP) was going to lose the plot—

> before the final settlement. I lost interest and my membership lapsed. I doubted the interest of the CP leadership to represent the workers in the way Chris Hani was dedicated. The leadership that was left didn't impress me to be able to do what Chris Hani could do to mount the revolution ... Yes, he was in the ANC structures but I don't think he believed in the two-stage theory of the CP (A-MM: 346).

IV. "Workerism" implodes: the case of Highveld Steel

As reported earlier, Highveld steelworks was owned by the main mining company Anglo American and located in Witbank, a key coal and electricity producing region. The NUM-organised Witbank mines were amongst the most militant in the country. The steelworks was a model of NUMSA "workerist" shop floor organisation, democratically elected shop stewards' committee constantly challenging pay, conditions and the petty apartheid, the grotesque bullying, often violent, from white foremen and white skilled workers. Black workers lived either in the township, KwaGuqa, or if they were rural migrant workers, and often from distinctive ethnic or tribal backgrounds, in hostels. The struggle to overcome this split between urban and migrant workers, institutionalised by the apartheid system, signalled one of the first victories for united shop floor trade union organisation.

The company's desperate need for black semi-skilled workers had also opened an unintended route for the new unionism. The first major strike successfully reinstated a shop steward, sacked after he had assaulted a white foreman in response to persistent racial harassment. Both sides understood that industrial relations were inseparable from the apartheid structure (Von Holdt, 2003: 72-3). Unrest in KwaGuqa led to the township's "ungovernability", its demands for stay-away strike action coupled with a dangerously divisive demand for township employment only, sometimes led by the unaccountable township youth and unemployed, drew the shop stewards into the action, demanding democratically-based unity. After its formation, COSATU locally took the lead, based on the steelworks shop stewards, described by von Holdt as "social movement unionism" (von Holdt: 101-9, 119).[193] The focus of the struggle also shifted to the workplace.

In 1987 "ungovernability" came to the steelworks with strikes every week. According to a migrant worker, "we never negotiated, we would just go into the bush" (von Holdt, 2007: 122). The remark captured the mood. "Release Mandela" became a strike demand. Strikers increasingly saw themselves as liberation fighters. Collective bargaining, as well as managerial authority, broke down completely: "ungovernability prevailed" (von Holdt, 2003: 122). A spectacular victory was achieved out of the chaos caused when NUMSA leaders called off the national strike in July 1987. Highveld shop stewards accepted the decision but workers at the Witbank Ferrometals smelter, owned by a separate company, did not. Some strikers there were sacked. Threats of strike action at Highveld forced their reinstatement. Von Holdt describes not just the solidarity but "an extraordinary display of worker power" (von Holdt, 2003: 128). But this moment was to prove short lived. Immediately after the August miners' strike was defeated, Anglo American imposed a lock-out at Highveld, as with the miners, threatening mass dismissals. The shop floor union organisation was "smashed completely" (von Holdt, 2003: 137). Anglo American, fresh from its victory over the miners, had felt sufficiently confident to break the union at one of its most important steelworks. "The parallels" between "ungovernability" in the mines and Highveld "are obvious" (von Holdt: 133, 145, n26).

Yet von Holdt records not a single instance of solidarity from Highveld steelworkers to the miners in August despite the "extraordinary display of worker power" the month before: and despite his earlier reports about the militant miners of Witbank as the "general unrest" in both community and workplace mounted (von Holdt, 2003: 92). A year before the miners' strike, several NUM officers, including the regional treasurer, were "arrested after a clash with police at Bank colliery when workers commandeered the store owner's vehicle, and workers at Landau colliery 'set upon' a police car carrying two black police officers and burnt it after they fled" (von Holdt, 2003: 92). The NUM regional treasurer was also a member of the Witbank Youth Congress. We also learn that the first attempt to build political structures linking township to workplace with a Co-ordinating Committee included a key shop steward from Highveld and a former NUM shop steward from Rietspruit Opencast Collieries, who had been dismissed during a strike at the beginning of 1985 (von Holdt, 2003: 96-7).

But it is an extraordinary earlier incident that most commands our attention. Weeks before the miners' strike, the Highveld strike committee, "armed" with their *sjamboks* (rawhide whips), organised an expedition to the Mapochs mine to bring it out on strike in solidarity with one of the steelworkers' strikes (von Holdt, 2003: 151). The *sjambok* and what Von Holdt calls "revolutionary bullying" (von Holdt, 2003: 173) holds the key both to the failure of Highveld steelworkers' solidarity with the miners and the implosion of "workerism" at Highveld. Charles Makola, active in community structures, chairperson of COSATU locally, and vice chair of the shop stewards committee, describes the political mood in 1987: "The aim was political ... to overthrow the government ... there was no differentiation between the state and the companies. Apartheid was more practical in the working environment ... Negotiations were not strictly speaking negotiations ... our approach was one of confrontation ... We strike whether it's legal or illegal" (von Holdt, 2003: 121).

There were so many strikes that a separate strike committee was formed "from the most militant workers amongst the rank and file" (von Holdt, 2003: 148). The strike committee rapidly grew to be a movement within the union. "At its height anywhere between 800 and 1,800 members and supporters, identified by their distinctive maroon T-shirts and *sjamboks*, ... consisted of migrant workers from the hostels, and militant young workers from hostels and township" (von Holdt, 2003: 152). It was an unmitigated disaster. It re-opened the split between migrant and township workers, it exacerbated tensions between literate and illiterate workers. In short, "workerism" imploded. Bunny Mahlangu, militant chair of the shop stewards, who had displaced a more moderate chair, was shocked by the development: "We saw a very big giant ... uncontrollable ... attacking us viciously. Can you imagine 800 people coming from one side with sticks and everything ... And if one person talks and the 800 clap hands, the rest get frozen. They scare the shit out of you" (von Holdt, 2003: 151, 153).

It was also a gift to management; the shop floor union was already effectively broken before they imposed the lockout. Von Holdt's explanation criticises core assumptions of social movement unionism:

> community and workplace struggles [were] woven together by a discourse of national liberation struggle. In effect, the community was inside the union. In place of the democracy and open debate [associated with social movement unionism] this study highlights a coercive approach to solidarity ... and the failure of democracy to empower the unskilled migrants in the union ... At its height, this struggle broke into open violence between factions ... the failure of union democracy to empower the less literate migrant workers led them to resort to coercion to empower themselves (von Holdt, 2003: 148, 175).

The breakdown of the shop floor union reflected the breakdown or absence of politics. In a revealing footnote von Holdt writes:

> The issue of socialist beliefs is scarcely mentioned in this study, despite its significance to the culture of social movement unionism, because shop stewards referred so seldom to it in relation to the struggles in the 1980s. This may have been because Witbank was somewhat

> remote from the main urban centres where socialism was most discussed—which itself casts doubt on the depths of such beliefs, or at least the meaning of these beliefs (von Holdt, 2003: 295, n28).[194]

"Workerism" proved incapable of politically theorising its own crisis or even understanding its own limitations. This was exposed when the point of maximum militancy within the workplace was achieved, cloaked in a narrow one-dimensional version of the ideology of national liberation. The SACP exacerbated the "workerism" crisis by prioritising the national liberation struggle over class struggle, prioritising community struggles over workplace struggles (Slovo: 1988). The distortion of the miners' strike outcome displayed in the SACP article in *Sechaba* was a symptom of this flaw. This absence of political, and especially socialist, discussion meant that the rhythm of class struggle in winter 1987, dramatically rising with the miners' strike, and hence understanding the need to generalise the struggle, was ignored. Its potential blow against apartheid was not recognised.

The explosive revolutionary mood that had penetrated the factories had no outlet. Not even the strike committee with their *sjamboks* proposed an immediate overthrow of the factory management. Yet an outward direction for that mood was essential—not least to avoid the inward implosion that would substitute for it. "Ungovernability" had come to the steelworks. A victory for the miners offered the prospect of destabilising still further the apartheid regime's entire productive system—making it increasingly "ungovernable". Recall miners' strike leader, Motlatsi's understated remark: "I can tell you, not only could they have saved the dismissal of 50,000, we could have seen a lot of changes within the country." It seems that the need to fight simultaneously for national liberation and workers' power was not understood (Legassick, 2007: 408). Recall Foster's speech. It was implicit in "workerism" but remained politically undeveloped.

It is impossible retrospectively to spell out the strategic and tactical significance of Witbank metal workers' solidarity with the miners. Could the movement of coal to those power stations been halted? Could the apartheid government have faced a shut-down of half its electricity supply? We will never know. A former miner writing for the MWT's miners' strike special feature in its *Inqaba Ya Basebenzi* magazine described a strike at his Kloof mine a year before. Local township youth had spoken to the striking miners. Shaft stewards knew the activists following visits to the township. Even township taxi owners had offered free transport to the striking miners.[195] Witbank's KwaGuqa township rallying in support of the miners would have strengthened both their resolve as well as encouraging Highveld steelworkers' solidarity actions. Was this possible? Again, we'll never know. But the point is that not only was any of this not attempted, it seems that no one even thought about it.

Conclusion: "South Africa ... one of the highest inequality rates in the world", World Bank, South Africa, 2018 [196]

How has it come about that after more than 20 years, following "South Africa's peaceful transition ... one of the most remarkable political feats of the past century", according to the same World Bank report, it is one of the most unequal societies in the world? This outcome, according to Ronnie Kasrils, not only betrays the expectations of the vast majority of South Africans following the fall of apartheid, but also the ANC's own Freedom Charter. Although, as noted earlier, the Freedom Charter explicitly rejected socialist solutions, nevertheless it anticipated a significant reduction of apartheid's extreme economic inequality. Kasrils has pointed to refinements to the Freedom Charter elaborated at the ANC's Morogoro Conference in 1969:

> It is inconceivable for liberation to have meaning without a return of the land to the people as a whole ... To allow existing economic forces to retain their interests intact is to feed the root of racial supremacy and does

> not represent even the shadow of liberation. Our drive towards national emancipation is therefore ... bound up with economic emancipation ... The argument was forcefully repeated by ANC president Oliver Tambo in 1981 (Kasrils, 2017: 226).

Whilst avoiding the word "betrayal" but in no sense denying his own responsibility, as part of the ANC and SACP leadership, Kasrils summarises the calamitous implications which included the unprecedented corruption of Jacob Zuma's presidency (2009-18), the focus of his most recent book: "Formal political independence without economic emancipation ... provided a stepping stone for all manner of predatory rogues to use power for self-enrichment" (Kasrils, 2017: 227).

He spells it out point by point:

> *The repayment of the $25bn apartheid-era foreign debt. This denied Mandela money to pay for the basic needs of apartheid's victims.
>
> *Giving the South African Reserve Bank formal independence. This resulted in the insulation of ... the bank's officials from democratic accountability. It led to high interest rates and the deregulation of exchange controls.
>
> *Borrowing 850 million dollars from the International Monetary Fund in December 1993 with ... conditions ... scrapping import charges that had protected local industries, state spending cuts, lower public sector salaries and a decrease in wages across the board ...
>
> *Reappointing apartheid's minister, Derek Keys[197], and the Reserve Bank governor, Chris Stals, who retained neoliberal policies.
>
> *Joining the World Trade Organisation on adverse

> terms, as a "transitional", not a developing economy. This led to the destruction of many clothing, textiles, appliances and other labour-intensive firms.
>
> *Lowering primary corporate taxes from 48% to 29% and maintaining white privileges ...
>
> *Privatising parts of the state ... Telkom telecommunications company.
>
> *Relaxing exchange controls. This led to sustained outflows to rich people's overseas accounts and a persistent current account deficit even during periods of trade surplus, and raising interest rates to unprecedented levels.
>
> *Approving the "demutualisation" of the two mega-insurers, Old Mutual and Sanlam ... privatisation ...
>
> *Permitting most of South Africa's ten biggest companies to move their headquarters ... abroad. The results were a permanent balance of payments deficit and corporate disloyalty ... (Kasrils, 2017: 225).

Kasrils then recalls the fateful day in 1992 when ANC leaders were called together to listen to Trevor Manuel, the ANC's future Finance Minister, make a presentation of the possible "scenarios" facing a future ANC government. "The technique of scenario planning was introduced in South Africa by Anglo American Corporation guru, Clem Sunter ... to massage protagonists onto a common ground ... Nelson Mandela ... looked sombre. His face was an expressionless mask" (Kasrils, 2017: 228). The fundamental message could hardly have been more candid: "quickly redistributing wealth from rich whites to poor blacks would not work" (Kasrils, 2017: 229). This included land distribution which is still over 70 percent white-owned. Instead,

Manuel described the perspective which would lead to the policies described above.[198] There were only two dissenting voices, Kasrils and Pallo Jordan.[199] Chris Hani was not present: "Joe Slovo ... gave the presentation a very polite hearing ... angry with Pallo for the roughness of his response. Slovo ... had taken to accepting that there was only one man driving the bus and that was Mandela. He in all likelihood would have found the opportunity to whisper privately in the bus driver's ear ... Mandela was not amused at our reaction. He tore strips off us and at the conclusion stalked out" (Kasrils, 2017: 230).[200]

But what had happened to Joe Slovo and his commitment to the working class emerging as "the dominant social force in a truly democratic post-apartheid state"? Had the SACP's perspective on post-apartheid South Africa shrivelled so much that it was to depend upon Slovo, presumably the political representative of the working class, managing the occasional whisper in Mandela's ear? In fact, Slovo himself was one of the architects of the fateful compromise both with the representatives of international capital and the apartheid state. In 1992 he wrote: "We are clearly not dealing with a defeated enemy and an early revolutionary seizure of power by the liberation movement could not be realistically posed." Instead, he proposed the so-called "sunset clauses" as a compromise: transitional power-sharing with a compulsory government of national unity; no purge of civil service or security forces (Legassick, 2007: 433).[201]

ANC and SACP leaders justified such compromises in terms of MK forces being "too weak" to secure an alternative (Legassick, 2007: 434). The possibility of the working class resisting such compromises is simply forgotten or ignored. A comprehensive discussion of the disorientation of SACP leaders following the collapse of Soviet Communism is not possible here, though it is an essential component for fully understanding the process of capitulation to neoliberalism that was unfolding. Slovo's pamphlet *Has Socialism Failed?* (1990) exposes a deep demoralisation with the authoritarianism of the former Soviet Union but offers no serious explanation. As Pallo Jordan wrote at the time,

Stalinism needed to be called by its name and thoroughly analysed (Legassick, 2007: xxi) not least for its bureaucratic interpretation of the working class as a dominant social force—a point to which we will return. Meanwhile in 1992 the working class may not have been that dominant social force, but, as represented by COSATU, it was still a force to be reckoned with by the compromisers on both sides (Ceruti, 2021).

But was there an alternative to it becoming "a conveyor belt for the ANC" (Erwin, 2017: 250-51) in the Triple Alliance of ANC-SACP-COSATU? As we have seen, former "workerist" activists and trade union leaders, like Moses Mayekiso and Bethuel Maserumule who joined the SACP when it was unbanned in 1990, certainly thought so. They cite the name of Chris Hani, former MK Chief of Staff and at the time new General Secretary of the SACP. Hani seems to have exuded confidence that the SACP would now open up, responsive to the democratic awakening sweeping the country, and the demands of its new worker members.[202] Here is an extract from Chris Hani's last interview, one week before he was assassinated by a supporter of the neo-nazi party Afrikaaner Weerstandsbeweging (AWB) in April 1993. As part of the exiled ANC leadership, Hani describes his underground role in Lesotho from 1975. He was secretly meeting individual trade union activists from unions which would form FOSATU:

> In FOSATU we had elements which were pro SACTU, pro ANC, pro CP. You had syndicalists, you had elements which were hostile to the old tradition of the trade union struggle ... So there was a struggle, say about the tendencies within FOSATU. But our approach was that... we must form one federation in SA ... weld together, all these tendencies ... Our approach has always been ... the trade union struggle is part of the broad national liberation struggle. That the victory of the national liberation struggle would actually create better conditions for the workers in this country, and that the workers had

to participate in the struggle. They would not have to remain on the sidelines as spectators ... (FOSATU led to COSATU) ... We didn't say because some elements rejected us ... no, no, no, to hell with them. We felt that it was our duty to engage ourselves in the struggle... To contest the influence with the New Left, with neo-liberal elements, because FOSATU (and then COSATU) was a mixture of all things. And I think ultimately we succeeded in building a federation which ... became close to the national liberation struggle ... from Lesotho we began also to build the CP. We set up cells. We influenced comrades from the trade union movement, and we influenced the youth, and that is why again you see a lot of the comrades who were in the Black Consciousness Movement also opted for the Party, and today they are outstanding leaders of the Party.[203] Through ... the ideology of the Party, through the politics of an alliance, they saw the relevance of the ANC, as a broad national liberation movement ... as a left-inclined nationalist movement (Callinicos: 1993)

His biographers help enrich these comments:

privately those closest to him had an understanding that his need to intensify the role of the SACP, and to entrench socialism in the communities wherever he went, was beginning to dominate his engagement. The revolutionary consciousness was not enough. Slogans were shallow. Only true mobilisation to roll back poverty could lead to the complete political transformation that the country needed. Nearly two decades later, Hani's voice on this is as loud as ever. It echoes, but the echo may be too late (Smith and Tromp, 2009: 234).

According to Moeletsi Mbeki, brother of former ANC president Thabo Mbeki, the (unbanned) SACP offered Hani:

the first opportunity to construct his own vision as the top person...Within days of his election, he was burrowing away with his characteristic energy and enthusiasm and, above all, his openness of mind and spirit. He was trying to make his mark on the SACP and South Africa as a socialist not as a military man. M. Mbeki said Hani—whom he described as "a strategist for a socialist South Africa"—was "emphatic" that he no longer saw the SACP as the vanguard party of the working class, with the right to define what was or was not true socialism.[204] At the same time, he did not agree with those—like Thabo Mbeki—who were critical of the Communist Party, particularly after the fall of the Berlin Wall. That communism had failed in Europe did not have meaning within the South African context. But he was equally forthright about COSATU. At the time, its leadership was vacillating between positions—trying to do deals with capitalists on macroeconomic issues and trying to secure a better life for the working class. "Instead", said M Mbeki, "he stressed the need for unions to fight for democracy at plant level. He said he got the impression that this aspect of working class aspiration was being abandoned by the union movement in return for a search for a deal with capital—something he did not think was feasible" (Smith and Tromp, 2009: 269).[205]

The attraction of Hani to former "workerists" seems obvious. Hani, in shifting away from former SACP orthodoxy, seemed ready to inject a healthy sprit of openness and internal democracy into party structures focused on working class interests.[206] But he never sought to develop theoretical clarity about the past or develop an innovatory Marxism to provide guidelines for what was then the immediate post-apartheid present. However, his status as a former MK Chief of Staff, perhaps surprisingly, may also have been a factor attracting former "workerists".

There will be an attempt to address these questions shortly

and that will conclude this chapter, but first some further brief comments about the scale, the potential as well as the limitations of the "workerist" challenge and its allies in other trade unions, apart from NUMSA. A history of the emergence of independent textile unions in the Durban area and beyond following the 1973 Durban strike wave has been written by one of its principal (white) organisers, Johnny Copelyn. A number of these unions finally came together in 1990 to form SACTWU, the South African Clothing and Textile Workers Union. Perhaps its most significant achievement "was that for the first time it brought large numbers of Indian and Coloured workers into COSATU's ranks" (Baskin, 1991: 394), many of them women.

Copelyn was its assistant general secretary. Known as an "arch workerist" (Copelyn, 2016: loc. 4506), Copelyn is a further illustration of the limitations of workplace shop floor democratic unionism bereft of political anchorage. On the one hand he describes the impressive union structures he helped establish and which might have propelled serious advance for a left that knew what it was doing. He and his comrades:

> focused on building a shop steward movement. The highest policy making structure ... was a national shop steward congress comprised of a set number of elected shop stewards from each branch of the union proportional to the membership of the branch. It was a structure made for large representative gatherings of activists capable of taking resolutions calling for mass action (Copelyn, 2016: loc. 1312).

At the same time, he praises two NUMSA officials writing for the *South Africa Labour Bulletin* in 1992 who no longer "spout socialist rhetoric" and recognise "that some social pact with capital was inevitable" (Copelyn, 2016: locs. 4869-4877).

As reported earlier, the Commercial, Catering and Allied Workers Union of South Africa, CCAWUSA, the second largest union in the country and the union with the largest number of women workers, won an important strike against Anglo American's OK Bazaar chain in 1987. But as it grew it faced a bitter and prolonged political split, "it was hell, a divided union" (Forrest, 2005: 91-99). Apolitical regional, factional and personal rivalries undoubtedly complicated and clouded the roots of the split. Nevertheless a polemical leaflet by the socialists attacking what might legitimately be called the pro ANC faction exposes the more serious political divide:

> The opportunists ... have adopted the programme ... which calls merely for reforming present-day racial capitalism to a more "Democratic Capitalism"... [but] this will not mean the emancipation of the working people, it will only open the road for the oppressed petty bourgeoisie, the small businessmen, the petty proprietor ... the working class must have its own programme, its own policy, its own class leadership, distinct from and opposed to all nationalist leadership.

The leaflet made clear it was not opposed to an alliance with the nationalists, but resolutely opposed the "subordination of the working class to nationalism".[207] Interestingly, the socialist faction attracted support from potentially critical political movements. Makoma Lekalakala, CCAWUSA shop steward at the time, has described her political background: "I grew up in the black consciousness ideological movement. I was a student before I joined the workforce, I was part of the Azanian youth organisation. So when I got into the union my drift was more towards the socialist faction" (A-ML: 323).

COSATU intervened and managed to bind the factions (Forrest 2005: 97) and as a COSATU affiliate in 1990 it became SACCAWU, South African Commercial, Catering and Allied Workers Union. But according to Darlene Miller, National Education Office-bearer 1990-93, for SACCAWU, the political divisions continued: "You had these large company union councils, I think they were called, for example in the retail industry you've got

Woolworths, Checkers. So it would be known that Checkers would be sympathetic to the socialist faction, Woolworths to the ANC faction" (A-DM: 350). Thus, the question forcefully and finally confronting us is whether an independent left might have developed and what it would have looked like.

Kally Forrest, NUMSA's historian, records that in her interviews with metal workers, two political theorists were often mentioned, the Italian Marxist Antonio Gramsci and the South African political philosopher Rick Turner.[208] She provides a powerful summary of Gramsci's position showing why the "workerist" factory committees in South Africa might have thought they would benefit from applying Gramsci's arguments about the factory councils in the Italian city of Turin in the revolutionary upheavals after the First World War. She shows how Gramsci understood the role of communists, before the Stalinist era, helping to facilitate an "embryonic form of worker democracy with the potential to become organs of worker power". But the implication was also that an independent Marxist party was necessary—a conclusion rejected by NUMSA "workerists": "The NUMSA unions appreciated the importance of rank and file engagement and the need to build national power but made no attempt to launch a socialist party which would develop worker political cadres and coordinate the national mobilisation of workers for political power" (Forrest, 2011: 484).

This was to be a recipe for failure. As Maserumule put it:

> Yes, one fundamental weakness in building the industrial working class as a political force for change. The situation had fragmentation, fragmented thinking. The "workerists" were so inward looking in terms of union role which was still incomplete in the way I am trying to explain that while the union pronounced against nationalism and for socialism, it had little by way of guiding or empowering its members on the shop floor on what that vision meant (A-BM: 332).

The weakness was ideological and it undermined political strategy.[209] "Militarism" and "guerrilla-ism" filled "workerism's" ideological and political vacuum after the defeat of the miners' strike in 1987. Joe Foster in his famous "workerist" speech at the FOSATU Congress created an opening when he compared favourably the workers' struggle and the guerrilla struggle. At COSATU's 1989 Congress, "delegates' most popular songs lauded the ANC's military wing Umkhonto weSizwe" (Baskin, 1991: 345). As we saw in the preceding section, von Holdt concluded after his Highveld steel investigation: "Community and workplace struggles [were] woven together by a discourse of national liberation struggle. In effect, the community was inside the union." Maserumule had read Lenin, Luxemburg, Trotsky, yet said, "strangely I found Maoism ... and guerrilla-ist concepts and approaches to struggle (more helpful)" (A-BM: 333). Maserumule also approved of the division between the shop stewards and the strike committee at Highveld steelworks.

It is easy to see Chris Hani's appeal. He combined his former MK Chief of Staff status with a genuine interest in understanding and addressing workers' questions—though, through no fault of his own, he was politically ill-equipped to provide the guidance that was needed. MK understandably symbolised the struggle for national liberation against apartheid. It became a workers' motif. But the final step was missing. Workers could only transform the motif into a real struggle for national liberation if they combined it with the struggle for their own liberation as workers. This was never understood and Marxist parties and groups across the board must share some of the responsibility.

Baskin has provided an outstanding illustration of how this expressed itself. The East London plant of Mercedes-Benz was a notorious NUMSA "workerist" stronghold even in the early 1990s. On one occasion both Joe Slovo and Moses Mayekiso had to persuade striking workers to return to work and give up plant bargaining for national bargaining (A-MM: 344-5, 346). NUMSA members wore MK machine gun emblazoned T-shirts. They independently resolved to build a special bullet-proof luxury model as a gift for Mandela. Union power in the plant was such that management rapidly agreed. Mandela's car came off the production line with nine faults. "In this company cars don't come off the line with less than 68 faults," commented the company chairman. "Normally it takes 14 days to build that car. Mandela's was built in four days! Only nine faults!" A tribute indeed from one of international capital's most prestigious corporations: it confirmed a prediction of Karl Marx more than one hundred and fifty years ago that uninhibited workers' power is far more productive than workers controlled by capitalists' power:

> The cost of the vehicle was covered by each employee working a few hours of unpaid overtime ... "We look to comrade Mandela to initiate a ... political settlement which will incorporate the needs and aspirations of workers," said NUMSA's general secretary Moses Mayekiso. Cynics noted that Mandela would be driving a luxury car and saw in it the premature emergence of a privileged "wabenzi" class. Others saw in it a sign of workers' expectations ... After all, workers had insisted that Mandela's car be painted not black, but red (Baskin, 1991: 421).[210]

Once again motif and gesture, indeed a great gesture, but no politics: cynics might warn against the rise of a "*wabenzi*" class, but there was no political movement signalling this danger. Was that possible? A new political party, rooted amongst the best of the worker activists at Mercedes-Benz and across the country which would organise immediately against this threat—and to keep within the spirit of the times—to save Mandela from himself?

But how might this political party have been formed? As suggested earlier during the discussion about Gramsci, the "workerist" factory and shop stewards' committees would have provided an excellent base to root a small non-Stalinist Marxist party and contest prevailing ideas, strategies and tactics or lack of them. But, most important of all, it would have insisted that Slovo's claim about the working class emerging as "the dominant social force in a truly democratic post-apartheid state", found political and practical expression.

Von Holdt formulated exactly the political and practical strategy that was required. In 1989, anticipating successful elections for the ANC in a future constituent assembly, he proposed that the first sessions of the assembly coincide with factory occupations "by militant workers demanding their immediate nationalisation".[211] By arguing for such a strategy the new party might have strengthened the former "workerist" voice in the SACP and galvanised support.

Certainly, an independent, uncompromising and frankly intimidating, expression of workers' power was urgently required by the time those elections arrived in 1994. Not only was nationalisation off the agenda, but, as we have seen, the ANC was ready to endorse an economic neoliberal programme which, in effect, tolerated the persistence of economic apartheid. That stark warning issued by the ANC's own Freedom Charter, reaffirmed at the Morogoro Conference in 1969 that "to allow existing economic forces to retain their interests intact is to feed the root of racial supremacy and does not represent even the shadow of liberation", was simply forgotten or ignored. Both the SACP and COSATU capitulated. Chris Hani's own warning that COSATU might be abandoning the struggle for workers' democracy at plant level "in return for a search for a deal with capital" was similarly ignored. A wave of factory occupations challenging the new ANC government's abandonment of its earlier commitments could only have been led by a new left workers' party.

CHAPTER 4

How workers helped make and then lose the Iranian Revolution 1979

Introduction

The 1979 Iranian Revolution has been described both as an Islamic Revolution and a people's revolution. Whatever the merits of these two descriptions, and the chapter attempts to scrutinise both of them very carefully, it is the under-stated role of organised workers in the revolution that is the chapter's main focus. Indeed, the argument is that organised workers held the key for the secular left both to address the Islamic content of the revolution and to transform it in a socialist direction. Strikes by workers, and especially oil workers, were decisive in toppling the Shah of Iran. But it was the unexpected development of workers' shoras (councils), briefly springing up in modern workplaces around the country immediately afterwards, that offered a potential political challenge to the revolutionary leadership of Ayatollah Khomeini, and his determination to install an "Islamic Republic". Workers' shoras were democratically elected workplace councils where manual and non-manual workers united in an attempt to control the productive process. Managements had either fled or were replaced or put under intense pressure to accede to workers' demands over wages, conditions and, crucially, control over the goods or services produced.

Comparisons and contrasts with the early soviets of the 1917 Russian Revolution will inform an important part of this investigation, although the conclusion argues that it is the failed German Revolution of 1918 that possibly offers more important lessons. The new regime certainly understood the threat. In less than a year, the shoras were brought under control through a mixture of repression and ideological confrontation with the minority, but highly influential, secular leftists who were playing a significant role in the shora leaderships. The ideological confrontation pitted Khomeini's version of political Islam against the heavily Stalinised version of Marxism dominant among the secular left. At the same time a separate struggle was unfolding over Khomeini's determination to install an Islamic Republican constitution on post-revolutionary Iranian society. But was it to be a theocratic or a democratic constitution? Explaining the relatively swift victory of the political Islamists in both of these struggles, and their connection, is one of the most demanding tasks of this chapter.

The chapter is divided into five sections. I. The historical background and political context of the 1979 Iranian Revolution. II. Analysing the claim that the 1979 Revolution was an Islamic Revolution. III. Analysing the role of the left in the Revolution. IV. Analysing the rise and fall of the shoras in 1979. V. A conclusion which probes the failure of the left to link the struggle for workers' democracy in the workplace with the struggle for popular democracy in the wider society.

TIMELINE IRAN

1941: Britain and the Soviet Union invade Iran, depose its ruler, Reza Shah, a Cossack officer who had proclaimed himself Shah, and install in his place his son Mohammed-Reza Shah Pahlavi.

1951-3: Prime Minister Mohammad Mossadeq, leader of the National Front, nationalises the oil industry and forces the Shah into exile. The CIA and the British Secret Intelligence Service organise a coup that restores the Shah and reverses the nationalisation.

1963: The Shah launches the "White Revolution", a top-down modernisation programme. Ayatollah Ruhollah Khomeini's opposition and personal attacks on the Shah lead to his exile.

1971: The Shah presides over a grandiose and extravagant celebration of 2,500 years of the Persian Empire. The "Nixon Doctrine" of relying on regional sub-imperialisms to protect US interests had already assigned the Shah a special importance given Britain's withdrawal from the Gulf.

1973-77: The oil crisis that breaks out with the Yom Kippur war launched by Egypt and Syria against Israel boosts the regime's revenues. The Shah is courted by Western governments eager to sell him arms.

1978: A cycle of protests is started by seminary students in Qom on 9 January. Every 40 days those killed by the security forces in the last protest are publicly mourned, leading to more massacres and marches. By the autumn the movement is hugely boosted by mass strikes by oil workers. Workers' shoras (councils) begin to emerge to organise the strikes. Khomeini establishes himself as the most powerful opponent of the Shah. The scale of the protests grows. The Shah vacillates between repression and concessions, but appoints a military government.

1979: On 16 January the Shah appoints Shapour Bakhtiar of the National Front Prime Minister and flees the country. 1 February: Khomeini returns from exile to a gigantic reception and appoints Mehdi Bazargan, another National Front politician, as the head of a rival government. 9-11 February: a coalition of leftists and Islamists mounts an armed insurrection that breaks the power of the military and ends the Iranian monarchy. 30-1 March: a referendum votes overwhelmingly to replace the monarchy with an Islamic Republic. 4 November: Islamists seize the US embassy in Tehran in protest against the Shah's being allowed to visit the United States for medical treatment. The diplomatic staff are held hostage till 20 January 1981, the day Ronald Reagan is sworn in as US President.

1980: In September, encouraged by the US administration of Jimmy Carter, and the Gulf states, Iraq under Saddam Hussein attacks Iran. The eight-year war greatly facilitates the consolidation of the Islamic Republican regime.

1980-1: Growing repression of the left, show trials, and mass executions, is accelerated after the violent break between Khomeini and the secular President, Abolhassan Bani Sadr, in June 1981.

INTERVIEWEES IRAN

"Bijan"

"Bijan" is a pseudonym for a former school student and youth leader of the Fadaiyan, the former urban guerrilla group, which emerged as the largest secular left organisation after the revolution. Bijan was a 16-year-old schoolboy in North Tehran when he first witnessed the eruption of revolutionary mass demonstrations. He joined in and would quite quickly become a member of the Fadaiyan. He has the dubious honour of twice confronting repressive armed forces at the gates of one of Tehran's universities—first, the Shah's army, when the revolution began, second, three years later, when Khomeini's Islamic army dislodged the revolutionary student university occupation as part of its campaign to destroy leftist influence. On the second occasion he was shot and hospitalised.

Farrokh Negahdar

A leader of the Fadaiyan, Organisation of Iranian People's Fada'i Guerrillas. OIPFG, *sazman-e cherikha-ye fada'i-ye khalq-e Iran* (Behrooz, 2000:51) According to Maziar Behrooz, Farrokh Negahdar led the pro-Tudeh Majority split in 1980, which supported a conciliatory position towards the new regime, regarded as "progressive" (Behrooz, 2000: 106, 109, 116).

Mansor Parhizgar

Mansor was an activist with the main Maoist group, Paykar. This was a Marxist (Maoist) breakaway from the Mujahedin in 1975. "(It) seems they managed to gain control of the bulk of the organisation" (Behrooz, 2000: 71-2). Behrooz also argues that Paykar "looked to Albania for inspiration". (Behrooz, 2000: 121-2) This was not Mansor's view, who based his Marxism on the Russian Revolution, especially the period before Stalin.

Ali Pichgah

Ali was an oil refinery workers' shora leader in the repairs section in the Tehran oil refinery during the Iranian Revolution.

Kobra Qasemi

Kobra was a women's representative on the oil workers' shora committee, Ahwaz, Khuzestan province, in 1979-80, and a member of the Fadaiyan.

Torab Saleth

National secretary (*dabir-e sarasari*) of the largest Trotskyist organisation in Iran, the Iranian section of the Fourth International, 1979-82.

I. The Iranian Revolution 1979

The Iranian Revolution in 1979 involved almost the entire population in the active overthrow of the Shah, the dictatorial self-proclaimed monarch. Ayatollah Khomeini, who came to be recognised as its principal leader, was determined to install what he and his followers described as an "Islamic" Republic. In his authoritative studies of modern Iran, Ervand Abrahamian highlights the military coup against Mohammad Mossadeq, Iran's democratically elected nationalist leader in 1953, and its aftermath, as an essential guide both to the overthrow of the Shah and to the consolidation of Khomeini's regime. Mossadeq also serves as a reminder that the struggle for popular democracy in Iran had a long pedigree, symbolised by the Constitutional Revolution of 1906 and the civil war that followed it (Abrahamian, 2008: 45-54).

Mossadeq, who had nationalised the oil industry, to wide and enthusiastic public acclaim, can be compared to other great contemporary 20th century nationalist leaders, Gandhi and Nasser, resisting colonial and imperialist domination. The Shah, on the other hand, was seen as a puppet placed in power by the British and its Anglo-Iranian Oil Company (now BP) with CIA complicity, following the coup (Abrahamian, 2008: 122). These murky origins would contaminate his rule for the next 25 years: savage repression of opposition, imposed by SAVAK, the Shah's secret police torture and murder squad. Mass arrests, execution and forced exile of their leaders effectively destroyed Mossadeq's nationalist party, the National Front, and Iran's Communist Party, the Tudeh Party. But the ideas of republicanism and nationalism associated with the former and the "Marxism" of the latter, however much tainted by Stalinism, could not be so easily eliminated.

In the 1960s, using Iran's vast oil revenues, the Shah embarked on an ambitious modernisation programme dubbed the "White Revolution". Industrialisation, Western technology, minimal health, educational and other public reforms were all part of the package. But, as the Shah readily admitted, his "White Revolution" was designed "to pre-empt 'Red Revolution' from below" (Abrahamian, 2008: 131). Expectations were raised but few Iranians enjoyed substantial benefits, sowing the seeds of unrest. Frustrations were exacerbated by the Shah's association with the so-called Nixon Doctrine, the Shah protecting US oil and supply interests in the Persian Gulf for US President Nixon (Behrooz, 2000: 49). In his posture as "moderniser", the Shah also antagonised two of the pillars of historic Iranian society. His supporters burst "into the bazaars and the clerical establishment ... undercutting the few frail bridges that had existed in the past between itself and traditional society. It not only threatened the ulama,[212] but also aroused the wrath of thousands of shopkeepers, workshop owners, and small businessmen" (Abrahamian 2008: 153-4). Not least, here was religious leader Khomeini's base.

Khomeini was exiled in 1964 after attacking the Shah for granting the Americans "capitulations", favours (Abrahamian, 2008: 143). The favours were diplomatic immunity for the Shah's US military advisors. The religious leader had been jailed for two months, in June the year before, and was accused of turning a religious procession into a violent street protest. These events transformed Khomeini into the leading anti-regime ayatollah. June 1963 may be interpreted as a precursor for the 1979 revolution (Abrahamian, 1993: 10-11, 41). Khomeini's developing mix of unprecedented political and religious radicalism has been linked to his adaptation to some of the views of the progressive Islamist scholar, Ali Shariati. Shariati was typical of a new generation of college educated professionals coming from traditional rural middle class religious backgrounds. The young Shariati won a state scholarship to the Sorbonne in Paris in the early years of the turbulent 1960s. He attended demonstrations for Algerian and Congolese independence. He wrote articles for the journal of the Confederation of Iranian Students, an organisation founded by younger members of the Tudeh Party and the National Front. Shariati translated some writings by Sartre and Fanon and Che Guevara's *Guerrilla Warfare*.

He praised Amar Ouzegane, the author of a book on the Algerian war, *Le Meilleur Combat*, as a *Musulmani-e Marksisti*, Muslim Marxist. Both the secular Marxist Fadaiyan and the left wing Islamic Mojahedin guerrilla organisations would later recruit in the Confederation.[213]

Shariati returned to Iran in 1965. His lectures were circulated widely in booklets and recorded tapes. He was eventually arrested and forced into exile. Aged only 44, he died suddenly in England in 1977, SAVAK accused of his murder. By then Shariati was a household name. His prolific works had one dominant theme: that "the true essence of Shi-ism is revolution against all forms of oppression ... feudalism, capitalism, imperialism ... the Prophet Muhammad had been sent not just to establish a new religion but ... a classless utopia" (Abrahamian, 2008: 144).

Khomeini built his base primarily amongst the ulama. He developed a distinct interpretation of Shia Islam, a form of "clerical populism", or "Islamic populism". He articulated his ideas first in a series of lectures to seminary students in 1970, and then published them anonymously under the title *Velayat-e Faqeh: Hokumat-e Islami* (The Jurist's Guardianship: Islamic Government). The concept traditionally meant the legal guardianship by senior clerics over those deemed incapable of looking after their own interests; minors, widows, the mentally disabled. Khomeini, however, expanded the term to encompass the whole population. This was because monarchies had betrayed the people's trust. This broke with 12 centuries of traditional Islamic teaching which "deemed one day of anarchy to be worse than ten years of autocracy" (Abrahamian, 2008: 147). Now Khomeini argued that Muslims had a sacred duty to destroy the monarchy. Khomeini's version of Islam, fused, consciously or otherwise, with Shariati's, would help provide the ideological glue for what became a political Islamic revolutionary mass movement, dramatically illustrated by its street slogans:

> Islam belongs to the oppressed, *mostazafen*, not to the oppressors *mostakbaren*

Islam represents the slum-dwellers, *zaghehneshin*, not the palace-dwellers *kakhneshin*

Islam is not the opiate of the masses

The oppressed, *mostazafen*, of the world, unite

Neither East nor West, but Islam

We are for Islam, not for capitalism and feudalism

Islam will eliminate class differences

In Islam there will be no landless peasant

(Abrahamian, 2008: 148).[214]

The first stirrings of revolution began in late 1977 with professional middle class protests against the Shah's autocracy in the form of public statements and poetry readings with audiences that would flow into the streets looking very much like political demonstrations. Violent, sometimes fatal, clashes with the police were inevitable. Students joined in—including the seminary students from Iran's main religious city, Qom, who persuaded local bazaars to close down, initiating waves of street demonstrations that would grow ever larger, involving fresh layers of the public. Two extremely violent though separate incidents drove forward the movement. A large cinema in the working class district of Abadan, in the oil rich Khuzestan southern province, went up in flames in mid-August, incinerating over 400, including women and children. SAVAK was blamed. Then just weeks later, on Friday 8 September, after the Shah had declared martial law, a crowd in Jaleh Square in Tehran was ordered to disband. When they refused, they were shot at indiscriminately, killing nearly a hundred people: The 8 September became known as Black Friday.

In the following weeks and months, strikes spread from colleges and high schools to the oil industry, bazaars, state and private factories, banks, railways, port facilities, and government offices. The whole country, including strategic parts of the government apparatus, went on strike. On 11 December 1978, during Ashura, the climactic day of Muharram, a vital date in the Islamic Shia calendar, Khomeini's representatives reached an understanding with the government. The military would be kept out of sight. The opposition would march along prescribed routes and not raise slogans directly attacking the Shah. On the climactic day, four orderly processions converged on the expansive Shahyad Square in western Tehran. Foreign correspondents estimated the crowd to be in excess of 2 million. The rally ratified by acclamation resolutions calling for the establishment of an Islamic Republic, the return of Khomeini, the expulsion of the imperial powers, and the implementation of social justice for the "deprived" masses. *The New York Times* reported the street presence of an alternative government. One of its most important leaders was Ayatollah Mahmoud Taleghani, jailed by the Shah. Taleghani, whose religious politics were similar to Shariati's, had been specifically selected by Khomeini as one of the leaders of the street movement (Parsa, 1989: 212). He would become the cleric most associated with the independent workers' movement.

Khomeini returned from exile on 1 February 1979. The Shah had already fled two weeks earlier. The crowds that greeted Khomeini totalled more than 3 million (Abrahamian, 2008: 161). When it came to improvised tactics, Khomeini had proved to be the undisputed master. During the Shah's last desperate street curfew, millions of Khomeini's supporters took to their roof tops, nightly, shouting *Allah-o Akbar*, "God is Great!" (Moaddel, 1993: 162). Yet at a critical juncture, it was the intervention by striking workers, and oil workers in particular, that became decisive. By late October 1978, oil workers' strikes were closing down oil production on the oil fields and in the oil refineries, raising openly political demands: end martial law, release political prisoners, Iranianise the oil industry, dissolve SAVAK, end discrimination against women employees. The *Washington Post* reported the oil strikes as the greatest single threat to the Shah's survival. "Oil became a key transmitter of revolutionary consciousness" (Jafari, 2018a: 74-5).

Khomeini had intervened from Paris, where he was then living, to take control of the oil strikes. His political alliance, the Oil Strikes Co-ordinating Committee, OSCC, depended on some of the key cadre from the Mossadeq era. Mehdi Bazargan would lead it, a deputy minister under Mossadeq. He would become Khomeini's first prime minister. The OSCC used the strikes to obtain direct negotiations with the government-backed National Iranian Oil Company. All of its key demands—withdrawal of the military from the oilfields, reinstatement of sacked strikers and the right of return for striking workers who had been forced to leave company accommodation, release of all arrested oil workers, back payment of wages owing—were conceded. The OSCC felt increasingly strong enough to persuade oil strikers to return to work (Jafari, 2018a: 78). Many of the oil strikers' original demands had not been met. But there was a strong sense that the Shah's authority had been damaged beyond repair and outstanding demands would be conceded. In any case, the oil workers lacked their own independent national organisation to sustain the strikes. This would have required a political orientation that was missing. The remnants of the Tudeh Party amongst older workers in the oil fields and refineries tended to adapt to the OSCC. Younger workers attracted to the "new left" organisations like the Fadaiyan and Mojahedin were mesmerised by their urban guerrilla strategy. These organisations would make a political turn, and attempt to build a mass base amongst workers, but arguably it came too late. The secular left's influence certainly had limited impact on the highly successful launch of the OSCC.[215]

The OSCC spawned two further organisations which together with itself would help form the infrastructure underpinning Khomeini's post-revolutionary political authority. The two new organisations, unlike the OSCC, would explicitly identify themselves as Islamic. In January 1979, the Council of the Islamic Revolution was formed "to study and explore conditions for a transitional government", and "to prepare for a constitutive assembly and hold elections". Finally, neighbourhood committees, encouraged by OSCC members, later transformed into Committees of the Islamic Revolution, were formed to distribute heating and cooking oil, to overcome shortages that had mounted as a result of the strikes. Though these committees often sprang up from local initiatives, the mosques were obvious organising centres and used very effectively by the political Islamists. Saeed Jalili, today a political Islamist hardliner, recalls: "At the height of the revolution ... neighbourhood committees played an important role serving people's needs ... At the time Marxism had many followers ... The slogan of Marxism was based on the shoras. This slogan was everywhere ... In this situation, the neighbourhood committee with its centre in the mosque was a 'slap in the face' (*tudahani*) and a harsh reply to them [the Marxists]" (Jafari, 2018a: 84).

Workers' shoras, independent democratically elected workers' councils, which were beginning to develop out of the strike movements, had the potential to focus on an alternative political pole of attraction. The detailed investigation of these shoras, section IV below, will also examine the reasons for their limited influence in the neighbourhoods and localities. Oil workers' strike organisation had been decisively outmanoeuvred but it was by no means broken. A group of oil workers, for example, called for a workers' representative on the Council of the Islamic Revolution (Jafari, 2018a: 85). In Ahwaz, clerics challenged left leaders of the oil workers, prompting the resignation of one of them, Mohammad Javad Khatami. He accused "reactionary" clerics of making death threats against him. American journalist, and future Pulitzer Prize winner Kai Bird, who interviewed oil workers wrote:

> The oil industry is virtually controlled by dozens of inde-

> pendent workers' komitehs, committees, which, though loyal to the central government, are nevertheless participating in all of the decisions related to production and marketing ... the komitehs have unquestionably demonstrated that they can run the oilfields and the refineries without the top rank Iranian managers and without the expertise of some 800 foreign technicians (Jafari, 2018a: 85-6).

A Tehran striking workers' slogan, from industries other than oil, contained a potential warning for the new revolutionary government: "Our oil worker, our determined leader!" (Jafari, 2018a: 87).

Khomeini's first task following his sensational arrival and mass greeting in Tehran was to secure the position of the armed forces, already overwhelmed by the sheer scale of public loathing of the Shah. The Shah's last bastion of armed support was his elite Imperial Guard. In a remarkable battle, cadets and technicians, supported by armed guerrillas from the Fadaiyan, and the Islamic Mojahedin, took them on at the main air force base near Jaleh Square. The chiefs of staff declared their neutrality and confined troops to barracks. Astonished Western journalists reported the readily available distribution of weapons to any civilians ready to join in: "Two days of street fighting completed the destruction of the 53-year-old dynasty" (Abrahamian, 2008: 162).

Former Fadaiyan school student and youth leader Bijan recalls how the newly radicalised youth joined in:

> We all made Molotov cocktails and that was where the fight gradually started. The Shah's guards came but people with guns stopped them. But then we heard that they were sending the tanks, we were all asked by the more experienced around ... to go on top of the buildings and attack the tanks with the Molotov cocktails. That's what we did that night. At least 10 tanks tried to

come through, we set them on fire ... we stopped all the tanks (A-B: 373).

Immediately after the revolution Khomeini and his supporters were determined to institutionalise their concept of *velayat-e faqeh* within a new Islamic constitution. This was opposed by Bazargan, the official prime minister, and his liberal lay Muslim supporters and fellow veterans from Mossadeq's nationalist movement, "eager to draw up a constitution modelled on Charles de Gaulle's [French] Fifth Republic". They wanted a republic, Islamic in name but liberal-democratic in content. Khomeini had set up Bazargan's Provisional Government to reassure the government bureaucracy—the ministries as well as the armed forces. He wanted to remove the Shah, not dismantle the whole state. But Bazargan was undermined by the far more formidable shadow clerical government (Abrahamian, 2008: 162).

This incorporated Khomeini's Council of the Islamic Revolution and the Committees of the Islamic Revolution. This group would become known as the *Maktabis* (committed and doctrinaire). It was unambiguously "anti-imperialist", especially when compared to Bazargan's liberals. It stressed the independence of the new Islamic Republic, "neither East nor West". They would form the core of the IRP, the Islamic Republic Party (Behrooz, 2000: 102). Khomeini now insisted on an immediate "yes or no" referendum for an Islamic Republic, observing, "We don't use the Western term 'democratic'. Those who call for such a thing don't know anything about Islam" (Abrahamian, 2008: 163). The referendum, held on 1 April 1979, produced a 99 percent yes vote for the Islamic Republic. Twenty million—out of an electorate of 21 million—participated (Abrahamian, 2008: 163). Yet Fadaiyan school student and youth leader Bijan strongly denied this was a vote for a totalitarian Islamic state: "It was seen as a vote against the Shah's regime ... Before the revolution he [Khomeini] gave lots of interviews where he said it's going to be a democratic country, everyone is free to do what they want. So we had no issue with this" (A-B: 376).[216]

Indeed Khomeini, sensing this ambiguity, made concessions. Abrahamian describes the new Islamic constitution, published later in the year, as a "hybrid", albeit one weighted in favour of *velayat-e faqeh* as against Bazargan's French Republic, "between divine rights and the rights of man, between theocracy and democracy" (Abrahamian, 2008: 163). It acknowledged Khomeini as "Supreme Leader" and "most potent of all, 'Imam of the Muslim Umma'—Shi-ism had never before bestowed on a living person this sacred title with its connotations of Infallibility" (Abrahamian, 2008: 164). At the same time the new constitution did make concessions to democracy. The general electorate, defined as all adults, including women, would be able to vote in a secret ballot for the president, highest official authority after the Supreme Leader, the Majles (parliament), provincial and local councils as well as the Assembly of (religious) Experts. There had already been public elections for the Assembly.

According to one historian who is a constitutional expert (Randjbar-Daemi, 2013) these elections, especially in Tehran, where the balloting process "was shielded from significant manipulation", provided "unique empirical information" about the popularity of competing political forces. Although candidates loyal to Khomeini, especially members of the IRP, swept the field, one political Islamist leader's outstanding victory deserves notice: "Ayatollah Taleqhani led the ranking with approximately 2 million preferences."

As already noted, Taleqhani was the most left wing cleric openly sympathetic to Marxist ideas and a staunch defender of the shoras, and had clashed with Khomeini over their significance (Bayat, 1987: 156). Meanwhile the secular left failed to win any seats. Whatever complications it raised, the result emphasised the popularity of political Islamism and the necessity for the secular left to find principled means of relating to it. The result however was immediately marred by the banning of the liberal and leftist independent press, especially the newspaper *Ayandegan*, following their investigations of voting irregularities in other parts of the country. Unfortunately, Taleqhani died one month later. The "Assembly" had produced the draft of the constitution. Assembly candidates had been vetted by Khomeini and his advisors. In principle, most of the democratic values, taken for granted in parliamentary democracies, were at least rhetorically enshrined in the constitution, even the right, with a two thirds majority, for the Majles to call for a new referendum to amend it. In practice the theocracy had the upper hand, though the strictly limited "democratic" space for political manoeuvre could and would later be tested by the "reform" movement.

The constitution also promised economic and political reforms on pensions, unemployment benefits, disability pay, decent housing, medical care, free secondary as well as primary education, home ownership and to eliminate poverty and inequality. Public ownership of large industries would co-exist with private ownership of light industry, agriculture and services. As we shall see shortly, some of these promises were far from rhetorical. They would help stabilise the regime, secure genuine improvements for the poor and divide the left, seemingly fulfilling the constitution's requirement to help the "*mostazafen* [downtrodden] ... struggle against their *mostakaben* [oppressors]."[217] Bazargan and seven members of the provisional government attempted rearguard opposition to the new constitution. They called for the Assembly of Experts to be dissolved on the grounds that the proposed constitution violated popular sovereignty and elevated the ulama to a ruling class. They threatened to make their opposition public.

Before he died, Taleqhani also criticised the Assembly of Experts, despite being its most electorally successful candidate. He made the provocative statement that the new constitution might be inferior to the famous previous version which had precipitated civil war following the Constitutional Revolution of 1906: "In his last public speech, Taleqhani reiterated that the only solution to Iran's problems was to give people responsibility for governing themselves through councils." He suggested that those in power opposed the formation of councils because they feared losing their position. He criticised sectarianism, opportunism and ideological domination (Parsa, 1989: 294). Abrahamian argues that Taleghani, had he lived, would have posed a serious challenge to Khomeini (Abrahamian, 2008: xxiv). Similarly, given the choice, and an open debate, Bazargan might now have won in a new public referendum on the constitution.

But it was at this critical moment that the infamous anti-imperialist occupation of the US embassy, and the ensuing 444-day US hostage crisis, began. We will have occasion to re-visit this moment several times in this chapter. The occupation was popular throughout the country, the embassy understandably viewed as a focus for counter-revolution. Bazargan, opposed to the occupation, resigned. And Khomeini "under the cover of this new crisis ... submitted the constitution to a referendum ... on December 2nd 1979" (Abrahamian, 2008: 168), and easily won. Khomeini took advantage of a left deeply divided, the Fadaiyan and the Mojahedin abstained in the referendum on the grounds that it wasn't democratic. The Iran-Iraq war, which broke out in September 1980, would consolidate Khomeini's control.

Islamisation of the new revolutionary state proceeded apace but once again posed a dilemma for the left. Was the new regime pro-capitalist or anti-capitalist? On the one hand public control was preached and practised. The assets of millionaires and high profile Western companies were confiscated, Coca Cola became Zam Zam Cola. The Hilton Hotel found its name and ownership changed. Semi religious public foundations controlled commercial operations, including former private companies, agri-businesses worth over $20bn. On the other hand, the new regime cultivated the bazaars. The Chamber of Commerce was packed with importers and exporters with impeccable records of giving alms. One of the most famous was Rafsanjani, millionaire pistachio nut grower and future president of the republic. Khomeini was unambiguous. Free enterprise "turns the wheels of the economy ... Islam differs from communism ... we respect private property" (Abrahamian, 2008:

179). At the same time, whilst it placed no ceiling on private land ownership, it distributed confiscated agri-business land to 220,000 peasant families. It raised agricultural prices, helping the country to become self-sufficient in cereal production. A Reconstruction Crusade launched an ambitious literacy campaign amongst the peasantry, and extended roads, electricity, piped water, health clinics to the villages. The strategy "transformed the countryside, turning peasants into farmers". One key indicator of progress is: "on the eve of the revolution, life expectancy at birth had been less than 56, by the end of the century it was near 70" (Abrahamian, 2008: 180).

The regime also brought direct benefits to the working class. It spent a quarter of the annual budget in subsidies to the poorer population, for bread, rice, sugar, cheese, fuel, cooking oil, as well as indirect subsidies for electricity, sanitation and piped water. Its Labour Law, whilst banning strikes and independent trade unions, conceded six-day 48-hour working weeks, paid (religious day) Fridays, a minimum wage, 12-day annual holidays and some job security. The percentage of children in school rose from 60 to 90; infant mortality per 1,000 dropped from 104 to 25. Most important for all, the literacy rate doubled, "almost eradicating literacy among the age group six to twenty nine" (Abrahamian, 2008: 180). For the first time, the very poor, both urban and rural, could access further and higher education. By the early part of this century, 65 percent of university students were women (Rostami-Povey, 2010: 48). Yet the reform programme co-existed with the bloody oppression of the left and other opponents. This was massively intensified when the Mojahedin—supported by President Bani Sadr—tried to overthrow the government in June 1981 and instead ended up assassinating numerous prominent figures.[218]

Between February 1979 and June 1981, revolutionary courts had executed 497 political opponents as "counter-revolutionaries" and "sowers of corruption on earth". In the next four years, from June 1981 until June 1985, revolutionary courts executed more than 8,000 opponents. Although they targeted mainly the Mojahedin, victims included the Fadaiyan and Kurds as well as Tudeh, National Front, and (Grand Ayatollah) Shariatmadari supporters. Many—including Shariatmadari and Bazargan supporters, and Tudeh leaders—were forced to appear on television and recant their previous views (Abrahamian, 2008: 181):

> One final bloodletting came in 1988, immediately after Khomeini ended the [Iran-Iraq] war by accepting a UN-mediated ceasefire. In four short weeks ... prisons hanged more than 2,800 prisoners ... former Mojahedin for ... secret sympathies for the organisation. Leftists ... for "apostasy" ... This extraordinary bloodbath has one plausible explanation. Khomeini, in his dying years, was eager to leave behind disciples baptised in a common bloodbath. The killing would test their mettle, weeding out the half-hearted from the true believers. It would sever ties between religious populists ... and secular radicals outside. Some of his followers had toyed with the dangerous notion of working with the Tudeh Party to incorporate more radical clauses into the Labour Law as well as into the Land Reform Law (Abrahamian, 2008: 181-2).

II. An Islamic Revolution?

Haideh Moghissi and Saeed Rahnema have provided a graphic account of the formation of the infrastructure of the Islamic Republic of Iran. They describe the central role of the mosques as a base for the regime in every neighbourhood.[219] In addition, the Islamic Revolutionary Committees were "one of the most feared and repressive institutions of the regime, formed by the lumpen proletariat and bullies of the neighbourhoods (these committees were later incorporated into the regular 'law-enforcing' bodies)" (Moghissi and Rahnema, 2004: 292):[220]

> In addition to massive propaganda and ideological

> indoctrination, the clerics maintain control over their followers through economic means and the provision of social welfare. The largest fund of this type belongs to the late Ayatollah Khomeini, known as "Imam Khomeini's Aid Committee". Established in 1979 and now secured through more than 1,130 branches throughout Iran, it provides a vast array of social and financial services to needy followers. Over 1.7 million people are "permanent" beneficiaries of this fund, mostly the working poor and the unemployed. The Aid Committee also provides health services through clinics, covering over 4.3 million people. It provides educational grants to over 769,000 students and has created over 850 youth centres in urban and rural areas to provide "education, ideological guidance, and physical education". It also gives allowances for the construction and repair of dwellings, marriage allowances, and interest-free loans ... there are also several extremely powerful religious/para-statal organisations, including the Mostaz'afan and Janbazan Foundation, the Martyrs Foundation, and the Fifteenth Khordad Foundation, which run the lucrative confiscated properties of the last shah's Pahlavi Foundation and those of the richest families of the previous regime. The Mostaz'afan Foundation, one of the largest corporations in Iran, is the richest cash cow of the clerical establishment outside the oil-rich government itself. With links to the powerful bazaar, the traditional economic base of the clerics, this foundation has helped create a new bourgeoisie out of the Islamic elite ... [which has] amassed enormous wealth in their religious funds, endowments and foundations (Moghissi and Rahnema, 2004: 293-94).

Jafari has also proposed an analytical framework compatible with this view describing the formation of a new Islamic state ruling class or bourgeoisie (Jafari, 2018b: ch8). He focuses on three of Khomeini's Islamic concepts, *Velayat-e Faqeh,* providing a fusion of religious and political legitimacy, the *Maktabi,* ideologically committed Islamists, the new cadre, who wanted to further their own cause, enhancing their status, but also the cause of the *mostazafin* (downtrodden), the powerful social justice motif in traditional Islam but also an ideological and when necessary physical battering ram against the left. Jafari argues that *Maktabi* discourse facilitated the formation of a new Islamic bureaucratic social class. Born into traditional petty bourgeois families, they were often the first generation to access universities: lawyers, engineers, doctors, journalists, writers, jobless graduates and teachers who staffed the expanding bureaucracy of the new state. Three processes enabled this process of upward mobility. First, the purges opened up positions at the top of companies, the oil industry, ministries, the army and other public institutions like universities and hospitals. Second, the expansion of the state bureaucracy with a plethora of new semi-religious public foundations created new employment opportunities. Third, ideological loyalty could open promotion routes from humble beginnings to senior executive posts both in business and politics. For example, *Maktabi* supporting oil workers displaying initiative and flair could rise to and up through management and then be considered for local or regional governmental posts (Jafari, 2018b: 497-8).

The ideological cement is provided by *Islamic populism.* Elsewhere Jafari has cited Abrahamian's definition of populism:

> A [political] movement of the propertied middle class mobilising the urban poor with radical rhetoric directed against imperialism, foreign capitalism, and the political establishment. Populist movements promise to drastically raise the standard of living and make the country fully independent of outside powers ... they intentionally stop short of threatening the petty bourgeoisie and the whole principle of private property. Populist movements, thus, inevitably emphasise the importance, not

> of economic-social revolution, but of cultural, national and political reconstruction (Abrahamian, 1993: 17, Jafari, 2009: 106-7).

Writing in the aftermath of the Islamic reform movement in Iran in the 1990s and 2000s, and the open struggle between the Islamic conservatives and liberals, Elaheh Rostami-Povey observed, "the reality is that the process of Islamisation in Iran has mass support ... the religious middle class, the urban poor and the working class who supported the Islamic state were given priority in employment and education" (Rostami-Povey 2010: 44-5).

But was Islamisation an inevitable outcome of the Iranian Revolution of 1979? Certainly, the Islamic movement was the major player but a particular form of improvisation—borrowing from the left whilst excluding the left—formed part of its strategic and tactical foresight, alongside creative adaptation of the religious traditions.[221] This should have provided the left with its own strategic and tactical opportunities. After all, they were supposed to mean it. The left really was in favour of the strategic objective of a classless society with the strategic means to achieve it, collective workers' action. Yet the left itself, as we shall see, was overwhelmed by the Islamic movement—was it friend or foe? Two very different left political leaders testify to the challenge posed. Here is Farrokh Negahdar, one of the Fadaiyan leaders who helped turn the former guerrilla organisation toward the emerging revolutionary mass movement in the late 1970s:[222]

> If you have a positive mind set, you can interpret these upcoming [Islamic] elements as revolutionaries, anti-imperialists. It was a real mass movement with their own psychology, their own culture, their own tactics. If you are negative to them, you would probably call them a fascist movement, an oppressive movement, reactionary forces against the people. I do not agree

> with this second ... interpretation. All major changes, not only in Iran, but within MENA, Middle East and North Africa, were influenced by the outcome of the 1967 war between Israel and the Arab world.[223] From that point onwards we are witnessing the growth of the influence of the Islamist element—everywhere. Islamism gets momentum, strength and status. Secular elements in these societies needed to think about it. How do we deal with these rising Islamic movements, with their growing power ... When the Shah's regime collapsed ... there was no political or legal structure of power to control the people. But the balance of power between the Islamists and non-Islamists was ten to one. Millions of people followed the Ayatollahs ... We realised before the revolution that the Islamists had a far greater opportunity to win hegemony over the people than the left. Jazani had predicted this prospect in the early 1970s (A-FN: 385, 384).

Bizhan Jazani was the best known of the Fadaiyan leaders, and, arguably, their most talented theorist, a philosophy graduate student arrested in 1968. He was one of the very few leftists to understand Khomeini's appeal. He wrote: "With this background, Khomeini has unprecedented popularity among the masses, especially petty bourgeois businesses, and with his opportunities for relatively free political activity has an unprecedented chance of success" (Behrooz, 2000: 53). Workers in tiny traditional workshops far outnumbered workers in modern industry and were influenced by their employers, sometimes relatives or part of a cultural network reflecting prevailing ideas in the bazaars and the mosques. This discussion is developed in section IV below on the shoras. Jazani, in other words, was sensitive to the popular mood and recognised the need for political propaganda to relate to it. He called explicitly for proletarian leadership of any coalition emerging to lead mass mobilisation. Behrooz implies that Jazani's murder in jail in 1975, along with other Fadaiyan founders, was linked to this potential shift of political perspective (Behrooz, 2000: 53, 54, 56).

Farrokh Negahdar continued:

> During the first year of the revolution we never believed that we could gain the upper hand in relation to Khomeini. A few months before the fall of the Shah, specifically 8 September 1978, we realised that Khomeini had hegemony over the liberals ... One of the clerics gave a good example using the children's story of the cat and the mouse cartoon, "Tom and Jerry". We had to play with that cat, not fighting face to face with them (A-FN: 384, 386).

Torab Saleth was leader of the tiny Trotskyist Fourth International group in Tehran in 1979:[224]

> In the beginning ... these shoras ... most of them were actually calling themselves Islamic. This was not accidental. Most of the young workers were organised, radicalised by the general movement which was dominated by the religious leadership. They got most of their information when they were on general strike through the mosques, so these strike committees after the revolution called themselves Islamic shoras ... [But it is essential to make a distinction in the workplaces between] two different organisations which appeared immediately after the revolution, Islamic shoras and Islamic Associations. The Islamic Associations began as little support groups ... directly linked to the regime and the forces of the repression of the regime right from day one[225] ... But alongside this the general mass of workers in the factory which [had followed] the strike committees, now obviously... followed the shora ... But the workers were organised in these Islamic shoras ... [which] included

everybody, including whoever was part of the left at the time ...Yet the actually existing shoras were completely open, all sorts of radical workers were in these shoras. There was a fight over who can appoint managers. These workers who were thinking of calling themselves Islamic councils immediately confronted the Islamic government—driven by the logic of class struggle itself, demonstrating to everybody the lines of cleavage in these shoras, in these councils—between the capitalists and the workers, forget the Islamic bit (A-TS: 405).

The Islamic movement had become increasingly hegemonic as the revolution unfolded. But was the left confronting the inevitability of a totalitarian Islamic state-in-the-making or an Islamic state where the political meaning of "Islamic" had yet to be determined, or rather would be determined by the balance of social class forces? Both versions are capitalist class societies, but in the latter the left and the workers' movement might have fought and achieved maximum capacity for independent democratic organisation and action.

III. The Left in the Iranian Revolution, 1979

The Shah of Iran's close ties to US interests in the Middle East didn't prevent his powerful northern neighbour, then the Soviet Union, also benefitting from his exploitation of the country's oil and gas wealth. In 1966 the two countries signed a pact under which Iran provided natural gas, the Soviet Union made limited military sales and assisted the Shah with his new steel complex in Isfahan (Behrooz, 2000: 50). It wasn't difficult for Khomeini to denounce the Soviet Union and Soviet "Communism" as the lesser Satan. The new Soviet pact did little to restore the fortunes of Iran's main Communist Party, the Tudeh Party, effectively neutered by SAVAK, with many of its surviving leading members exiled in the Soviet Union. New left political formations were gathering momentum, the most important of which was the Fadaiyan. All of them were inspired, directly or indirectly, by Che Guevara's *Guerrilla Warfare* and "Régis Debray's metaphor of the 'little motor' and 'big motor' to describe the relation between the guerrilla force and the revolutionary classes" (Behrooz, 2000: 53).

The battle with police at Syahkal, a village in northern Iran in 1971, referred to earlier, launched the Fadaiyan's armed campaign. Whilst, undeniably, it carried out waves of courageous military-style operations often with surprising success—military chiefs, SAVAK torturers, particularly repressive employers were assassinated, and strategically important centres, like American oil companies, were bombed—this was an urban war the Fadaiyan could not possibly win. Inevitably, it would prove far more costly to the Fadaiyan than to the Shah's state in terms of loss of life and repeated arrests (Behrooz, 2000: 62). It also meant that when the mass movement began to stir in the late 1970s, Khomeini's clerical cadre was far more effectively positioned than the cadre of the Fadaiyan.

Though very weak inside Iran, the remnants of the old Tudeh Party had an impact that must also be taken into account. It retained a grudging respect from some older, surviving middle class intellectuals and working class political activists. It was the strongest of the exile organisations outside Iran, backed by financial and logistical support from the Soviet bloc. It smuggled publications into Iran as well as using radio broadcasts (Behrooz, 2000: 76-7). It welcomed and encouraged the Soviet Union's relations with the Shah. This generated an almost permanent internal argument about the prospects of genuine reforms by the Shah and even Tudeh participation in them. This helped the Shah peel away some senior Tudeh party leaders, in the hope that they would make his "modernisation" programme more credible. Though its intervention in the revolution was minimal, the Tudeh Party's influence, many would argue a malign influence, on events as they unfolded afterwards would be highly significant.

The Fadaiyan was the secular Marxist organisation best placed to take advantage of the revolutionary opportunities that opened up immediately after the fall of the Shah. It faced three major questions: how to relate the workers' shoras which were springing up everywhere (see section IV below), to the women's question, which the new regime quickly forced onto the political agenda, and to the struggle of the national minorities. The struggle of the national minorities, especially the Turkmen and the Kurds, against the new regime was very important and some Fadaiyan fighters took up arms alongside them (Behrooz, 2000: 105-7).[226] But it was the women's question, above all, which almost immediately exposed the limitations of the Fadaiyan's theoretical and practical grasp of Marxist politics.

Bijan recalls:

> Tension with Khomeini started over hejab [the headscarf] and the International Women's Day demonstration just one month after the fall of the Shah [8 March 1979]. I went there and actually got hit with a stone in my face. They had highly systematically organised thugs—not very big[227]...Fadaiyan did not support demonstration. They didn't take a view. We all went because of a sense of justice. We didn't go as an organisation formally supporting it. If I remember correctly, there was an article against forcing hejab on women in the Fadaiyan's newspaper. My sense, looking back at it now, I think there was confusion. Years later we discussed it. What was important at that time—were we distracting the movement by focusing on hejab, rather than focusing on workers' rights? (A-B: 374-5).

The Fadaiyan position caricatured the classical Marxist position on women's oppression, which was made very clear at the 1921 Third Congress of the Communist International.[228] Whilst the Fadaiyan argued that women's oppression would be overcome by the elimination of the class system in the future, that did not justify abstaining from resistance to a regime that was intensifying women's oppression in the present. But that, in effect, became their position. An independent women's movement was condemned as "false agitation" (Behrooz, 2000: 108).[229] The Fadaiyan had failed to see that the International Women's Day demonstration had the potential to disrupt the consolidation of the new regime and build a broadly based left opposition. The new regime had immediately politicised the role of women in society by attempting to impose its own particular interpretation of Islam on gender relations. A liberated woman was declared to be one who followed the path of Fatimah, daughter of the prophet Muhammad, and Zaynab, her daughter. Fatimah symbolised motherhood and womanhood. A woman's place was in the home. Even Shariati had projected Fatimah as the ideal role model. Many women were sacked because they did not comply with Islamic dress and behaviour codes.

On 26 February 1979, in the same month of the revolution and just a few days before the International Women's Day demonstration, the Family Protection Act, the Shah's minimal reform of women's rights, was suspended. Men were given the exclusive right to divorce and permitted to take four permanent and an unlimited number of temporary wives (*sighe*). On 3 March 1979, just five days before the International Women's Day demonstration, a decree forbade women judges to work, because women were deemed not fit to judge. Just three days later women were told they would no longer be drafted into the army, all women serving their conscription terms were dismissed (Poya, 1999: 64-68). Then just before the demonstration Khomeini announced the hejab, the headscarf, must now be worn by women (Poya, 1999: 130).

Thus the International Women's Day demonstration became a major test of strength between the regime and its left wing opponents. It was a resounding success, involving hundreds of thousands of women throughout the country. In Tehran the demonstration was attacked, as reported earlier, by stone throwers linked to the IRP; one of their slogans was "Either hejab or tisab [acid]" (Poya, 1999: 131). The new regime was shaken by the level of support. Khomeini's prime minister,

Bazargan, hurriedly announced that there had been a misunderstanding, that women activists had been manipulated by left wing trouble-makers. Women should be "guided", not forced to wear the hejab (Tabari, 1982: 14).

This was the moment for the left to act quickly in defence of women's rights. Suspension of compulsory headwear was obviously only temporary. Demands needed to be raised uniting the (often poorer working class) religious women, the majority, for whom wearing the hejab was taken for granted, with the (often middle class) secular women—for example, setting up workplace nurseries and organising for women's participation in the election of workers' shoras. The Women's Solidarity Council, *Shoraye Hambastegie Zanan*, was formed for precisely this purpose. Alas, the Fadaiyan would withdraw its support at a crucial moment (Poya 1999: 132-3).[230]

In November 1979 the regime rallied support for the anti-imperialist occupation of the US Embassy. Most of the left seemed unable to combine support for the occupation with an independent stance on other issues—not least the women's question. A government sponsored demonstration in support of the Embassy occupation coincided with a Women's Solidarity Council Day of Action. The Fadaiyan, originally a sponsor, now proposed it be cancelled. It wasn't and the Fadaiyan did not support it (Poya, 1999: 133). Tehran oil refinery workers' leader, Ali Pichgah, has confirmed this standpoint:

> One day we were meeting with Yazdi, Minister of Foreign Affairs, at a meeting of Tehran refinery representatives. He'd just heard about the occupation of the American embassy, he ... told us it was a bad idea. We disagreed and the next day we had a demonstration in support, outside the embassy. We believed that it was the Fadaiyan who had occupied the embassy and that's why we were so keen to support them. I read a document outside the embassy in support. But that day it meant that we didn't support the women's demonstra-

tion that was taking place on the other side, which was a mistake (A-AP: 397).[231]

Another prominent communist oil workers' leader, Yadollah Khosroshahi, has also reflected, "We were very weak in supporting the women's movement and we didn't do anything about it" (Khosroshahi, 2013: 4).[232]

The ambiguity over the women's question reflected deeper confusion about how to relate to Khomeini's regime. His general popularity in the country made forms of adaptation to his regime tempting—particularly to the *Maktabi* (IRP), the regime's "anti-imperialist" wing.[233] This adaptation would have a catastrophic debilitating impact on the Fadaiyan at the very moment when it should have been concentrating its efforts on the workers' shora movement, already withering because of political disorientation. The Fadaiyan began to split more openly into two factions, the "Majority" (*aksariyyat*) and the "Minority" (*aqaliyyat*). When war broke out between the regime and the Kurdish national movement in August 1979, the two factions clashed head on. A re-surfacing Tudeh Party gleefully circulated a version of the internal dispute between the factions. Tudeh "had strong supporters ... among the Majority faction" (Behrooz, 2000: 110). The occupation of the US Embassy helped crystallise the split, reinforcing the Fadaiyan Majority view of the progressive role of the IRP, whilst the Minority faction regarded the occupation with suspicion. The Tudeh Party welcomed the split, viewing the Fadaiyan Majority as a source for replenishing a younger cadre of its own. Indeed, the Tudeh Party would become the Majority's "mentor and ideological guide" (Behrooz, 2000: 126). Tudeh's own adaptation to the IRP deepened even to the extent of collaboration to suppress the opposition, including the independent Marxist groups, a fact recorded in the Soviet Embassy's KGB files (Behrooz, 2000: 126). Tudeh gained no benefits from this collaboration. Not only was it eventually caught up in the total onslaught on the left by the regime, many of its imprisoned members became the subject of extraordinary Stalin-like show trials, replete with "confessions" from recanting "former" Communists.[234]

The 1979 revolutionary May Day rallies also exposed the failures of the left in relation to Khomeini and the IRP. Khomeini moved swiftly when he realised, apparently belatedly, that the left were not only planning workers' rallies on May Day but that they were likely to prove immensely popular. In response, the government raised the minimum wage and declared May Day a public holiday. Khomeini broadcast a resounding May Day speech, warning workers to be aware of non-believers. "Every day should be considered Workers' Day, for labour is the source of all things, even of heaven and hell as well as of the atom particle." As Abrahamian noted, this theory of value sounded more radical than that of Marx (Abrahamian, 1993: 71).

When May Day arrived, no less than four separate rallies assembled in Tehran, three left wing and one Islamist led by the IRP. Reports hostile to the IRP conceded that its march was three kilometres long. Its placards proclaimed Every Day a Workers' Day. Speakers at its rally included a Palestine Liberation Organisation activist. A coalition of leftist groups led by the Fadaiyan and the Maoist Paykar group also staged an enormous march and rally—claiming half a million, though this is almost certainly an exaggeration. Tudeh also had a demonstration, one sympathetic foreign observer claiming it had more trade union support than the other leftist demonstrations.[235] Finally, the Islamist left Mojahedin also staged a demonstration and rally. The left, then, clearly failed to achieve unity. Similar demonstrations were held in towns and cities throughout the country. The struggle for the hearts and minds of workers was well underway.

A little noticed turning point came in August 1979 with the escalation of the war between the Kurds and the new regime: "Massive bloodshed resulted" (Parsa, 1989: 260). Armed Fadaiyan support for the Kurds was used as a trigger by the regime not just for an attack on the Fadaiyan but against all left and liberal democratic forces. Not only were Fadaiyan members and other leftists arrested, a total crackdown on the freedom of the press was imposed.[236]

Kobra Qasemi was one of the hundreds of Fadaiyan members arrested at this time. She was also one of the three women activists amongst the 60 representatives elected to the leading committee of the General Shora Oil Employees of Ahwaz (the capital of Khuzestan). They represented shoras in the oil fields, the production units, maintenance departments, and administrative offices in and around the city. "I was in prison for 3 or 4 months.[237] I was able to return to work after I was released, but the shora organisation had been dismantled" (A-KQ: 401). As we shall see Kobra's description fits with the generally agreed periodisation for the rise and fall of the shora movement. August 1979 represents the peak of their independence. In fact, formal shora organisation was not so much dismantled but institutionalised—fully Islamised, leftist influence eliminated, under government control. In fact, some Islamic Association oil worker leaders were ready to defend Kobra.[238]

But the Fadaiyan itself must take some responsibility for what happened next. The organisation was split, with the 'Majority' group ready to find accommodation with the *Maktabi* (IRP) "anti-imperialist" wing of the regime. How to support the regime's "anti-imperialism", without surrendering your independence in the wider political context was indeed the challenge. One test was the Fadaiyan's approach to democracy both within its own internal structure but also in the Islamic Republic. A test it failed, as Kobra Qasemi explains:

> But there was a paradox. We raised the women's question with the Fadaiyan "Majority". We couldn't accept our leaders' response. They said the revolution was the priority. Anti-imperialism was the priority. The demand for democracy was not given equal priority. Nor was there internal democracy in the Fadaiyan. I felt personally free in the Fadaiyan but I knew that it wasn't really democratic. Personally, I did not accept their

> ideas and I was considered a "problematic" member, a "troublemaker".[239] I was one of the most experienced members of the Fadaiyan cell in Ahwaz. Most of the other members were students. I told them you haven't had to fight for the bread. So you don't know what it is. You have read only the books and you are repeating what you have read.[240] When the revolution started I had been working for seven years. I was trusted in the cell, a friend, a comrade[241] (A-KQ: 403).

At the end of 1979 the question of democracy flared in the most dramatic way. In section I above, reference was made to the prospects of Khomeini losing the vote in the referendum for his theocratic, hence undemocratic, Islamic constitution. Ayatollah Shariatmadari, a highly respected leading cleric, the association of human rights lawyers, the Mojahedin, the Fadaiyan and the Kurds called for postponement of the referendum, though the Tudeh Party did not and supported Khomeini. Shariatmadari made it clear that there was a serious conflict between the article of the constitution vesting sovereignty in the people and the articles on *velayat-e faqeh* (guardianship of the jurist). This was an unambiguous public attack on Khomeini's authority.

Demonstrations and fighting broke out on 5 December. In Qom, Iran's most religious city, Shariatmadari's house was attacked by Khomeini supporters. In Tabriz, in Azerbaijan, where a majority refused to vote, Shariatmadari supporters seized the radio station and chased the pro-Khomeini governor from his office. A panicking Khomeini met Shariatmadari two days later and agreed that Shariatmadari was to be consulted on changes in the constitution and on all matters dealing with Azerbaijan. But the agreement broke down. The struggle in Tabriz escalated, planes carrying revolutionary guards were denied permission to land by pro-Shariatmadari armed supporters (Fischer, 2003: 236-8). A general strike was organised in Tabriz (Poya, 1987: 159) raising the possibility of the Tabriz shoras uniting with progressive Islamists demanding a genuine democratic constituent assembly, with guarantees protecting workers' rights to organise independently—a vital opportunity ignored by the Fadaiyan and the other leftist organisations.

Meanwhile Khomeini supporters in Qom and Tehran demanded that Shariatmadari disband his Muslim People's Republican Party, charging that it was divisive. The IRP was clearly threatened by the existence of a second more liberal Islamic political party. Khomeini claimed that the troubles in Tabriz were American-inspired. Shariatmadari responded sharply that to connect all events to American imperialism would not solve any problems. He warned Khomeini that he was in danger of provoking civil war.[242] Shariatmadari's followers in Tabriz took nine revolutionary guards hostage with supporters demanding the release of 200 persons arrested by the revolutionary guards in the previous weeks. Shariatmadari, demonstrating that his leadership was different from Khomeini's, ordered the release of the hostages. The conciliatory gesture was to no avail. The Khomeini regime asserted itself and subsequently executed eleven members of Shariatmadari's party in retaliation for this resistance (Fischer, 2003: 236-8).

IV. Shoras

Assef Bayat's *Workers' Revolution in Iran* (Bayat, 1987) remains the most authoritative study of the shoras. Its great strength, based as it is on extensive interviews with shora activist workers as the revolution unfolded, is that it captures both the mood and experience at a critical moment in the revolution, illustrating the potential for a politically independent workers' movement. A weakness, however, is that it is mainly based on 14 manufacturing plants in Tehran (Rahnema 1992: 70), so prone to over-generalisation, and there are only cursory references to the oil worker shoras, arguably the best organised and most radical shoras (Jafari, 2018b: 437).

Jafari's investigation of the oil worker shoras has attempted to fill this gap. Shoras were workplace organisations (blue-collar and white-collar) which elected committees representing all employees, irrespective of trade, skill or sex. They demanded "workers' control and the transformation of power relations" in the workplace (Bayat, 1987: 100). At the point of production, "workers developed a strong sense of possession of the factory ... a commitment to responsibility for it as part of the people's wealth". During this period workers sometimes "managed and ran the factories themselves" (Bayat, 1987: 101). Typically, at the Yamaha Motor Cycle company in Ghazvin, Bayat interviewed workers who had not only dismissed managers but had travelled to the central office and physically ejected the director and major shareholder from their desks (Bayat, 1987: 118): "Nowadays you don't need to tell a worker to go to work. He works for himself; why? The reason that he didn't work [under the Shah] was because he was under the boss's thumb. He couldn't speak out. Now he'll say, 'the work is my own, I'll work'" (Melli Shoe workers, in Ghotbi, 1980; Bayat, 1987: 111).

Jafari cites a later study by Bayat detailing the immense significance of the shoras:

> The councils by their nature were democratic, grassroots organs. Their executive committees were directly elected and were subject to recall, at any time, by the members. The committees were accountable to general assemblies, and their members were not paid any extra salary for their positions on the committee. Almost all workers in a unit would attend meetings in which heated debates would take place on issues concerning the running of the workplace. At crucial meetings, such as the ones concerning the conduct of management, a few officials from the Ministry of Labour or the "Imam's representatives" would also attend. The day-to-day activities of the shoras, including elections, debates in general meetings and operations of the affairs of the enterprise, had a dramatic effect on the way workers conceptualised society, authority, and their social position in the society at large ... the workers were involved

in a learning process. To understand the significance of this change, the reader should recall that, during the last thirty years, democratic institutions, (whether state or non-state), have been almost totally non-existent in Iran. In family, in school, in workplace and political organisations, both open and clandestine, decision making has been basically authoritarian. It was against such a background of a political culture that the councils established nascent democratic tradition and culture (Jafari, 2018b: 443; Bayat, 1988: 48).

Bayat identifies four periods which describe the rise and fall of shoras in the first two years, following the fall of the Shah. Bayat's periodisation has not been challenged by his critics. The first period begins with the revolution in February 1979 and ends with the first signs of repression in August 1979, signalled by armed resistance by some of the national minorities, especially the Kurds. Some of the former guerrilla groups like the Fadaiyan supported the Kurds, so it became a trigger for a generalised crackdown against them, especially in the shoras. Left wing papers were banned, individual worker activists were arrested, as we saw, for example, in the case of Kobra Qasemi. The second period from September 1979 to June-July 1981 was marked by the systematic return of management from above coupled to the gradual demise of workers' control.

Two events marked the determination of the government first to isolate and then eliminate leftist influence in the shoras, as well as neutering the independence of the shoras. The first one was the US embassy occupation which began in November 1979, the second was the Iran-Iraq war which began in September 1980. Both events strengthened the influence of the government linked Islamic organisations inside the shoras like the IRP and the Islamic Associations (IAs). Bayat argues that the IRP and the IAs strengthened their grip on the shoras at both rank and file and management level, leftists were effectively banned amongst workers, and liberal managers replaced by *maktabi*

(Islamic) managers under much tighter government control. This reflected an internal power struggle within the regime between the remnants of the liberal nationalists led by President Bani Sadr and the hard-line Islamists loyal to Khomeini.

The third period began with the sacking of Bani Sadr as President and the executions that followed the failed bid at armed overthrow of the government by the Mojahedin, supported by Bani Sadr, in June 1981. Khomeini and his supporters now had total state power, and the Islamists, the *maktabi* managements and the IAs total control in the factories which led to their militarisation and a lowering of wages. The shoras were now dominated by these Islamic organisations and in some cases ceased to exist altogether. The fourth period reflected splits in the IRP and the IAs as they found themselves pressurised to reflect workers' interests against management and government. Despite full Islamisation, shora influence and recent memories of what had been possible, were still struggling to find expression, ready to use the government's own agencies if necessary (Bayat 1987: 100-2).

The study here focuses exclusively on 1979, the high point of shora activity. It will look in more detail at the formation of shoras and their successes, as well as the weaknesses. It will discuss the viability of a comparison with the soviets which developed during the Russian Revolution in 1917. It will consider the role of key professionals in the shoras, technicians, engineers, managers. And it will examine shora relationships with the urban poor. The shoras had grown out of the strike movements and their strike committees which had played such a strategic part in the overthrow of the Shah. Some Islamist progressive clerics like Ayatollah Taleqhani were influential from the very beginning.[243] Bayat reports that Taleqhani "instructed" that each industry should have "only one single central nucleus to carry out decision making". But no steps were taken to co-ordinate strike committees across industry. Bayat identifies this "lack of a co-ordinating organ" as one the key strategic weaknesses of the shoras' movement (Bayat, 1987: 94).

Ali Pichgah was an oil workers' leader in the repairs section of the Tehran oil refinery during the revolution. Here he describes the fascinating way the repair workers made contact with the wider workforce which would help lay the basis for the Tehran refinery shora:

> We decided to enter the [refinery] employees' restaurant, our restaurant was separate from the employees' restaurant, we started shouting slogans celebrating [repair] workers' and [oil refinery] employees' unity. I took the microphone and recited the famous poetry of Khosrow Golesorkhi, and other workers made some very useful speeches. We set up a secret unity committee in the restaurant's kitchen, calling it a strike committee (A-AP: 394).

Khosrow Golesorkhi was a well-known poet, writer, communist and part of a "famous cell, some of whose members had sympathy for the Fadaiyan," arrested in 1972 (Behrooz, 2000: 69). The Shah and SAVAK attempted to use their trial to celebrate success against the guerrilla movement, and its proceedings were broadcast on national television. There were forced "confessions" but five including Golesorkhi, "refused to confess, even after extensive torture. Golesorkhi and Daneshian used the fact that the proceedings were televised to put the regime on trial, defend revolution and Marxism and refute the charges. They refused to ask for the Shah's pardon and were executed" (Behrooz, 2000: 70).

In other words, Ali Pichgah's workers' unity plea drew upon Iran's secular revolutionary political and cultural tradition rather than its Islamic tradition. Yadollah Khosroshahi, another Tehran oil refinery workers' leader, and a prominent communist amongst the oil workers,[244] also recalls this moment and a particular slogan that was shouted: "Who robbed the oil? America. Who robbed the gas? Soviet Russia. Death to the Pahlavi regime!" (Khosroshahi, 2013: 2). But the slogan would also give advantage to the hard-line political Islamists and their denunciation of imperialisms, East and West. The main secular left organisations, Tudeh and the Fadaiyan, were directly or indirectly associated with the former Soviet Union.

Nevertheless, the Fadaiyan, the largest left organisation, made a promising beginning amongst workers. They had made a turn away from armed struggle to the workers' movement—expressed with the launch of their new journal *Kar*, Labour. Its first editorial, 10 March 1979, stated:

> Workers' collective struggles are organised through labour unions around economic demands ... but in order to be finally free, the working class has no other choice but to take political power, abolish private property of the means of production and destroy capitalism ... If the shoras act correctly and organise those who are capable and knowledgeable, and actively interfere with political affairs, they can develop into people's organisations for running the politics of the country (Jafari, 2018b: 445-6).[245]

However, as reported in section III, the Fadaiyan was quickly distracted from this perspective, disoriented by the complex and contradictory politics of the new regime. Whilst it cracked down ruthlessly with assaults, arrests and even executions of women's rights and democratic rights activists more generally, it also made its own enticing overtures to the workers' movement, as well as parading its virulent brand of anti-imperialism. The Fadaiyan would quickly split with its Majority wing (critically) supporting the regime. Just one month after the revolution, in March 1979, Khomeini had launched his Islamic Republican Party, IRP, opposed to "liberals", meaning Bazargan's government, "communists" and *monafeqin* "hypocrites" (a term used for the Mojahedin). The aim of the IRP was to smash the left, sometimes literally with their *chomaqdars* (club wielders)—we saw in section III above their use against the March women's demonstration, but also as competitors in the shoras, its newspaper *Jomhuri-ye Islami* proclaiming "the importance ... of shoras" (Jafari, 2018b: 448). And the IRP had of course organised its own May Day march. *Jomhuri-ye Islami* intervened in shora elections to isolate known communists and support candidates "who are struggling against Western and Eastern imperialism" (Jafari, 2018b: 459).

According to *Time* Magazine in April 1979 "the world's largest oil refinery" in Abadan, Khuzestan, was controlled by revolutionary workers dissatisfied with their own revolutionary government. Given the centrality of oil supply to the global economy, the more serious sections of the Western press were almost obsessively chasing these developments. A fascinating Associated Press (AP) report from the Abadan refinery reflects both the strength of revolutionary sentiments amongst workers as well as the tensions and overlap between political Islam and the left. The oil workers demanded "redistribution of income, an end to foreign control of industry and the right to reject management appointees", with a new strike threatened if their demands were ignored. "Although most workers claim to be devout Muslim followers of ... Khomeini and disavow atheistic communism, they espouse political views very close to Marxism." Oil committee member, Habib Khabiri, told AP that only the elementary stages of the revolution had been completed.

The report continued:

> Managers left over from the previous regime ... avoid any decisions that might conflict ... with the committee, *who also have the power of arrest* [my emphasis]. It is unclear how many workers belong secretly to the illegal pro-Moscow Tudeh Communist Party or to the People's Fadaiyan ... "Out of a section of 8 people, maybe 2 or 3 are communists," said one worker. "No one pays them any attention." Others estimate as many as 25 per cent of some departments may be Marxists or sympathisers

> ... Marxist pamphlets ... appear regularly on company billboards and on walls in working class districts (Jafari 2018b: 456-7).

At the Tabriz and Pars Oil Company refineries, shoras took almost total control of administration and production. The latter, near the city of Karaj, was Iran's only privately owned refinery (25 percent by Shell). The shora there put demands for nationalisation to the Labour Ministry and Ayatollah Taleqhani. With no response, the shora took over the refinery itself, selling its products to pay wages and salaries. It co-ordinated the takeover with the production managers, establishing a "committee for the provisional administration of the refinery" consisting of shora members and two technicians. The "National Oil Company of Iran: Karaj Refinery" was publicly declared. A reluctant government would quickly accede to the nationalisation demand (Jafari, 2018b: 458).[246]

Nor was this an isolated example of workers directly taking over their own means of production and distribution. Torab Saleh explains:

> another example—(it) must have been repeated a hundred times in Tehran alone. It was a factory connected to Rayovac battery factory in Japan. Like many industries in Tehran, these were joint venture companies. A foreign producer provided the technology, the means of production—with some Iranian capitalists producing these under licence for the internal market. This was the biggest battery factory in Iran. It had 500-600 workers. The executive committee of the shora had been radicalised by the mosques. They had learned how to organise strikes from people they had met in the mosques. The left had no influence on them before the revolution. They had not even met leftists. After the revolution the city is open. In front of Tehran University is the main centre for gatherings, discussion. Everybody comes

there. Newspaper sellers, book sellers, everybody. Some even became Trotskyists simply by reading our newspapers. They would say ah this is all very good, we agree so let's contact these people, they came and they joined us. It shows how fluid the situation was in terms of the consciousness of the working class.

Anyway, Rayovac battery factory they had participated in the last three months of the general strike. The owners had escaped ... the country but their manager was still there. Most of the leading members of the shora were also members of the local neighbourhood committee. During the insurrection 50 or 60 of the workers from Rayovac actually participated in the fighting. The people who resisted the shah's guards, coming to the airforce base in Tehran to suppress the technicians. In this fight a lot of workers from Tehran participated, organised by the neighbourhood committees. They became armed after the insurrection. In Rayovac factory 30, 35 workers actually carried guns. Immediately after the insurrection, they go to the manager's house, the manager had also escaped. They confiscate his assets and they discover 50 million toumans—equivalent in those days of £5m, which they give to the local mosque.

So these were the type of workers who took part in the insurrection...and they were now managing the factory. They elected one of their own as the manager. And they had worked out through the books of the company that the quality control is based in Japan. They send samples to Japan for them to be given quality control as a condition for producing goods. In their fight with the government over who can manage this factory, they win the competition with the government by proving they are producing batteries of the same quality as before. So the government could not use the excuse that the fac-

> tory is not working so we have to appoint a new manager ... These workers are now fighting the Iranian government which has become the Islamic government. The workers have become so radicalised they say these bastards are all linked to the bazaar merchants, to the same guys who used to screw us before the revolution, so why should we sell our goods through the same distribution network. We can sell batteries ourselves. So they set up tents to sell the batteries outside the factory on the main road between Tehran and Karaj, the main industrial centre ... they [had] accepted our suggestion to set up tents outside Tehran University. We said nobody would dare to touch you. This was three months into the revolution (A-TS: 407-8).

Chris Goodey[247] visited several Tehran factories in August and September 1979 where he obtained access to some of the worker activists. He provides a useful snapshot both of the shoras and their diversity at this critical moment (Goodey, 1980). The Chit-e-Jahan textile factory lies just outside the industrial town of Karaj near Tehran. The owner of the company did not flee the country after the revolution, but the workers elected a seven-man committee to represent them, a majority sympathetic to the Mojahedin. The owner accused it of wanting "to expropriate property by armed struggle". But the government seems to have ignored his pleas and allowed the situation to develop, at least in the short term, whilst the committee occupied the office of the former SAVAK agent. Critically, it reached agreement with the qualified technical management and therefore was able to carry on production. Goodey reports that council claims to have increased production by half were justified, the minimum wage had been doubled, while top salaries reduced to one third their former level. Every worker received a litre of milk a day. Mojahedin propaganda tended to dominate. Goodey also noted that although general assemblies are called once a month for all workers, there was no constitution or system of recall. In Goodey's view, the general assembly did not provide an adequate forum or mechanisms for self-management.

Goodey found the opposite extreme at Iran National, formerly associated with Chrysler UK, employing 12,000 workers used to reasonable housing and health care. It continued to receive kits from Britain even though it had been nationalised. The head of the workers' council there was a member of the factory administration during the Shah's time. A council spokesperson told Goodey that they were 100 percent religious, 100 percent in support of Imam Khomeini. Goodey points out that this was as unique in its own way as the situation in the textile factory, but he reasonably surmises that this was the kind of rubber stamp council the regime envisaged for the nationalised sector.

At General Motors, also nationalised, Goodey found another fully "Islamic" worker council executive committee, supporters of the Islamic Republican Party. It had 21 members, 15 manual workers and 6 office staff. Although unconvinced about its democratic shop floor credentials, Goodey was impressed by their degree of autonomy, their involvement in management, the fact that only one of its members worked full time, the rest put in all the extra hours without pay. Top management salaries had been reduced to 40 percent of what they had been. The committee's main aim was now to divert production away from cars to public service vehicles such as buses.

The Caterpillar factory was similarly nationalised after the owner, who had leased it from the US parent company, had fled. Here the workers' council committee, ten manual workers and two office staff, was evenly divided between leftists and Islamists. Women workers organised separately, having rejected what they regarded as a "token" offer of one place on the committee. Weekly committee meetings took place in the office of the one remaining director who, Goodey writes, was "ejected" for the purpose whenever necessary. The factory was under full control of the council who signed cheques, controlled accounts, fixed wage levels. Goody was allowed unchaperoned access to the shopfloor. In his view democratic control from below was not fully functional, nevertheless he concluded: "It was clear that the council and the self-management of the factory were supported with enthusiasm and pride by the workers, whatever their political colouring."

Khomeini's new regime viewed these developments with increasing alarm. A twofold strategy developed to minimise and ultimately eliminate leftist influence, using government structures outside the workplaces and quasi government agencies inside the workplace. For example, one of the most important Committees of the Islamic Revolution would increasingly police the main road between Tehran and Karaj, the main industrial centre, according to Torab Saleth, with the explicit aim of identifying leftists (Jafari, 2018b: 462). Elsewhere in his interview Torab Saleth describes the precautions he had to take to attend a shora meeting in order to avoid arrest (A-TS: 409). In Abadan the Committee of the Islamic Revolution was established by pro-Khomeini oil employees. It was a city-wide Committee but it was located in the compound of the oil refinery's security organisation and was funded by local rich bazaar merchants. Farivah Batmanghelich, Abadan's main government representative, made clear the priorities—to curb the activities of "the left and the Mojahedin" (Jafari, 2018b: 463).

The struggle, and its complexity, between the Islamists and the left in the shoras is particularly well illustrated by the General Shora of Ahwaz [capital of Khuzestan] Oil Employees. It had 60 representatives from the oil fields, the production units, maintenance departments, and administrative offices in and around the city. It elected a chair and deputies, oil workers who were leaders of the Islamic Association (IA), and oil workers who were devoted Muslims, supporters of Khomeini. Their contacts with leading clerics added to their credibility. In its first few months it managed to force the authorities to lessen the inequalities between the blue-collar and white-collar workers. The blue-collar workers received air conditioners, which most of them weren't able to buy, unlike their white-collar colleagues. The shora also gave support to workers of the drilling companies who were demanding their nationalisation (Jafari, 2018b: 461).

Kobra Qasemi was one of three women on the shora committee. She worked in the administration at the head office. The demands of these women focused on childcare provision and they managed to increase pregnancy leave. Kobra was, of course, also a member of the Fadaiyan. Kobra was very cynical about some but by no means all of the IA leadership. Some had opposed the earlier oil strikes as supporters of the monarchy. Kobra describes a "Shah loving man" who switched to "zealous Islamist" telling us, "ladies, the revolution is over, go sit behind your desks" (Jafar, 2018b: 463).

At the same time Kobra describes members of the Islamic Association in the shora collaborating well with secular members and defending the shora from attacks from the government. Later when leftist members were purged, the IA was protective and tried to give them a way out. She recounts the period after she had been in prison and returned to work: "When the purge committee investigated me, they [IA members] told them: 'She is good. She is Islamic like us, but we don't understand why she doesn't believe in God.' We didn't have any problems with those religious colleagues around us" (Jafari 2018b: 464).

Kobra Qasemi's arrest along with other Fadaiyan members in the summer of 1979 would however signal the peak of independent shora organisation and influence. In the oil industry this coincided with the dismissal of Hassan Nazih, chair of the nationalised oil industry. He had provoked Khomeini with his public scepticism about the "Islamisation" of politics, economics, and the law. The IRP and the Islamic associations began a campaign against him, spicing their hostility with polemics against Nazih's proclaimed pro-capitalist sympathies. This posed a dilemma for oil shora activists, especially the leftists. It was again the dilemma that would haunt the left throughout this first decisive phase of the Iranian revolution and one which it failed to resolve. When do you support the Islamic liberal opposition to Khomeini, when do you oppose them? When do you support the IRP with its pro-worker, anti-capitalist, anti-imperialist rhetoric, when do you oppose them?[248] On the one hand, Nazih was hostile to the shoras, on the other hand there was a sense that his removal would intensify the crackdown on shora activists. Despite their reservations, many different groups of oil workers petitioned on his behalf. But it was a lost cause. Nazih himself feared for his life and fled to France (Jafari, 2018b: 473-5).

Khomeini now intensified his two-fold strategy towards oil workers—repression and incorporation—in recognition of their centrality to the economics underpinning the new revolutionary state. The independence of the oil workers' shoras was gradually eliminated but many of their gains were at first maintained and repackaged as Islamic state policy, the five-day working week, building new houses, reducing pay and conditions inequalities between blue-collar and white-collar workers, nationalisation of foreign drilling companies. In addition, resignations and the purging of senior managers opened up routes for upward social mobility for workers expressing loyalty to the regime. But this balancing act would come to an abrupt end with the declaration of war on Iran by Iraq in June 1980. Repression gained the upper hand, and many of the gains mentioned above were rolled back. Ideologically Khomeini was able legitimately to present the war as an all-out assault on the revolution, demand unconditional loyalty, and thus consolidate the state's total control over the oil workers (Jafari, 2018b: 554-5).

How did the Fadaiyan, the largest secular leftist organisation with growing roots in the shoras, understand the complexities thrown up by what appeared to be the rapid Islamisation of the revolution? Farrokh Negahdar, Fadaiyan leader, argues that their organisation at first based their intervention in the shoras on the model of the Bolsheviks providing leadership in the soviets which played such a decisive role in the 1917 Russian Revolution: "We were copying the same model. And our understanding is that the process that happened to Bolshevik Revolution from February to October is happening in Iran. We have to prepare ourselves for a socialist revolution based on the transfer of power to the shoras. And this idea was widely accepted by members of our organisation" (A-FN: 383).

But they were quickly disillusioned:

> In the workplaces, particularly in the oil industry, the steel corporation in Ahwaz, universities, civil service, municipalities and other government organisations, people themselves formed shoras. They started to decide who should be head of the departments, who should deliver the demands of the employees, the workers. The shoras survived until the summer of 1979, perhaps until the autumn. They lasted about 6 months maximum. After that Khomeini and the government started to maintain their control in workplaces (A-FN: 384).

The Fadaiyan and the left in general confronted a reality completely different to that of the Bolsheviks in Russia in 1917. Lenin's famous demand "All Power to the Soviets" assumed a workers' state based on workers' soviets rooted in the workplaces and the localities was a plausible outcome of the 1917 Russian revolutionary upheavals and process. But it was far more problematic for the left in the Iranian shoras to raise a similar demand. First, organisations like the Fadaiyan, unlike the Bolsheviks in 1917, had no developed worker cadre when the Iranian revolution erupted in 1978-9, partly as a result of their preoccupation with the armed struggle. Secondly, as discussed in section I above, Khomeini and his nationalist allies were at pains not to overthrow the Shah's state but to insert themselves inside it and transform it from within. The revolutionary crisis in the Iranian armed forces was different to the political and psychic collapse of the Russian Tsar's army, exhausted and demoralised by the First World War.

Although his brief summary risks oversimplification, Farrokh Negahdar expresses it as follows: "There was an agreement between the clerical religious elements of the revolution and the army generals to surrender the army to the ayatollahs, to Khomeini" (A-FN: 383). Khomeini and his supporters "had carefully adopted the deliberate tactic of trying to win over the army ... issuing appeals to officers as well as to the ordinary soldiers to join the revolution". Even so by July 1979, "over 60 percent of the army had simply disappeared, most simply going home". To secure his control of the army, Khomeini conducted limited purges as well as creating the Revolutionary Guards, the *Pasdaran*, and a militia tied to them, the *Basiij-I Musta 'zafan* [mobilisation of the dispossessed] (Cronin 2014: 200-1). But there were no soldiers' shoras, and certainly no workers' and soldiers' shoras constituting the embryo of an alternative state power. This meant that the demand on the state for nationalisation under workers' control was a contradiction in terms. As Moghadam noted, this demand when it was raised in the Tabriz shoras "ironically ... allowed the government to undermine activist councils" (Moghadam, 1985: 169). The Islamic state as it consolidated, emerged unambiguously as a capitalist state, as discussed in section II, even if the state itself was a major employer.

Thirdly, the soviets were seen as "tribunes of the people", the political and democratic expression not just for organised workers but for all the exploited and oppressed peoples. The constituency of the soviet was rooted in the locality, the neighbourhood, even if the strategic leadership was at the point of production in the workplace in the towns and cities. This is in sharp contrast to the shoras which were exclusively workplace based. As Bayat pointed out, the Iranian councils were similar to factory committees that temporarily took over and ran factories during the Russian Revolution. One difference was that in Iran there were no city level type organs to which the shoras could relate (Rahnema, 1992: 85). Most of the large firms were government owned or controlled, relying, indirectly or directly, on subsidies and often involved in foreign licensing agreements with multinational corporations. Most of the shoras were located on these sites. Rahnema says this undermined the most basic principle of the shoras, "worker control and management from below" (Rahnema,1992: 74), because shoras could not resist government-imposed managers for firms dependent upon government finance.

But Rahnema's conclusion is not so obvious. The demand for "worker control and pressure on management from below" did not cease when the government imposed managers. We have already reported examples, particularly from the oil industry which Rahnema here ignores, which did not receive government subsidises because it was itself the source of the subsidy. There were many months of battles in the oil industry between oil workers and government-imposed managers. Also, as reported earlier, the Islamists themselves were compelled to find ways of accommodating pressures for workers' control.

However, Rahnema raises a further argument about the role of white-collar specialists, engineers and other professionals in the leaderships of the shora movements, including the oil and steel industries. This is, perhaps, the one area where the shoras had an advantage over the soviets. Lenin knew that the revolution in Russia could not survive without the white-collar specialists, but he took for granted they were "bourgeois specialists" and had to be paid "bourgeois salaries" (Lenin, 1965g). In the Iranian revolution at least a section of the "bourgeois specialists" were committed socialists ready to put their skills at the service of the revolution.[249] Rahnema argues their impact was double-edged. On the hand, it meant that the shoras had at their disposal technical and managerial skills to support their claims for self-management and workers' control. On the other hand, their role in the shoras also depended on their political outlook: "Some with left wing orientations struggled in the interests of workers ... others ... pursued their own interests" (Rahnema, 1992: 82).[250] Rahnema argues that Bayat misunderstood this point, first, by not acknowledging their role in the shoras' leadership and secondly assuming they were a homogeneous pro-management and pro-capitalist social layer (Bayat, 1987: 164).[251]

However, Rahnema and Bayat both agree that the left in the shoras "were confused about what to do and ... what ... role the shoras could play politically" (Bayat, 1987: 146; Rahnema, 1992: 84). Rahnema cites the split in the Fadaiyan, the largest left presence amongst the organised workers, into its "Majority" and "Minority" sections, as having a "devastating effect" on the shoras. He also argues that the left was compromised by the IRP in the shoras and its "anti-imperialist and pro-dispossessed rhetoric", which "disguised the anti-democratic and anti-working class nature of the Islamic clerics" (Rahnema, 1992: 85).

Rahnema has also emphasised the challenge the shoras faced in relating to the majority of workers and the urban poor outside the shora movement—reinforcing the distinction between the shoras and the soviets. Rahnema was politically active in one of the strongest networks of shora organisations: the Union of the Workers' and Employees' Councils Development and Renovation Organisation of Iran, IDRO. IDRO was the largest industrial conglomerate in the country, comprising 110 establishments of heavy and light industry with over 40,000 workers and employees. In 1980, Rahnema carried out an extensive survey of workers' attitudes with the support of the IDRO.[252]

Rahnema is today highly critical of the left's "illusions" in the shoras, which he says, at the time, he shared (Rahnema, 1992: 70). He points to the limited number of firms hiring a large number of workers, the potential "proletarian fortress" was very small (Rahnema, 1992: 74). Similarly, Moaddel cites "a well-known saying amongst Iran's labour activists—'in the vast ocean of the petty bourgeoisie, the industrial concentrations represent only small islands'. In Tehran alone there were about 750,000 merchants, middlemen and retail traders ... on the other hand ... in large industrial enterprises (with ten or more employees) ... there were 426,000 blue-collar workers and 60,000 white-collar workers." And only one fifth of these had more than a hundred employees (Moaddel, 1992: 239).

Iranian sociologist Val Moghadam discussed this question with "Javad" in 1985, a former shora workers' leader in Tabriz, a major industrial city in the north western "Azari Turkish" province of Eastern Azarbaijan.[253] Javad was on the run following the Islamic state's murderous crackdown on leftists. A former member of Paykar, he had started working in menial jobs like office sweeper, tea boy, even preparing the *aftabeh* (toilet bucket) for the workshop owner, in Tabriz's myriad of tiny workshops before obtaining skilled employment in a new motor assembly factory, typical of Iran's industrialisation surge in the 1970s. He was trained for this type of work at the Institute of Technology in Tabriz where he first encountered both leftist students as well as the "showdowns", often physical, between leftist and religious students.

Javad told Moghadam that it was his parents who had pushed him to attend both school and then the Institute, otherwise, he said, he would have started work as a rug weaver at the age of seven. Child labour was still taken for granted. The story illustrates well the co-existence of pre-industrial and industrial forms of work in 1970s Iran. Moghadam shows that despite the Shah's economic reforms, the informal, rural and urban workshop and handicraft sector remained the dominant form of employment. Javad described workers in the informal sector. For example, a Tabriz construction worker still had very strong ties to the countryside. He aspired to become a *bana*, an independent self-employed builder, while many of those labouring in the workshops longed to have their own shops.

Apologising in advance for the following statement, Javad said:

> They want to move from being "Hassan khar" (Hassan the donkey) to "Hassan agha" (Mr Hassan). These workers want to become owners. Ideologically, the workers in the informal sector, for the most part, can identify more easily with traditional religious values and practices than with any secular or socialist ideas. Having come from rural areas and facing the complex realities of Iranian urban life, they can expect to be susceptible

> to recruitment by a religious populist movement. On the other hand, workers with urban backgrounds are more likely to be interested in secular ideas and modes of life (Moghadam, 1985: 161).

This raised the critical question confronting the shoras' movement. Could they give a lead to the weaker, poorer sections, the urban workshop and rural sectors? In Tabriz the shoras were organised by mainly skilled workers including some foremen and technicians (Moghadam, 1985: 167). A sophisticated politics was required to reach out to the unskilled workers in the factories and the mass of poorer workers in the informal workshop sectors in the rest of the city. Javad describes how in Tabriz shora politics were dominated by the Fadaiyan, Paykar and the Mojahedin. These organisations were unable to respond to this challenge. In fairness, they had little time; they quickly came under attack when the left in all the shoras found that their defence of the Kurdish revolt against Khomeini's regime, especially in August 1979, made them also a target of the regime.

Nevertheless, the Tabriz shoras survived, at least briefly and even developed, in the winter of 1979-80, a co-ordinating committee uniting eight factory councils, initiated by supporters of Fadaiyan and Paykar. The workers' council at the machine-tool factory, representing 3,000 workers, was the leader; other councils were at the lift-truck, motor assembly plants and several others. Altogether, the co-ordinating council represented 5,000 workers (Moghadam, 1985: 168). At the same time the Islamic Associations organised by the Islamic Republican Party intervened. Unfortunately, Moghadam gives only a very brief description of how they took control of the shoras.

Assef Bayat in a separate investigation of the urban poor, has challenged the view that they were so obviously a vanguard base for Khomeini and the political Islamists.[254] He agrees that "the portrayal of the revolution by new Islamic leaders as the *inqilab-I mustaz'afin*, the revolution of the downtrodden, signified the so called centrality of the underclass to the revolutionary process" (Bayat, 1997: 37). But Bayat, using empirical data, shows the poor, squatters' illegal settlements, for example, battling the Shah's paramilitaries, organised separately, independently of the religious leaders (Bayat, 1997: 46). He notes that the term *mustaz'afin* entered Khomeini's discourse only during the height of the revolution. But he argues that it was used "merely to repudiate the Communists and attempted to offer an alternative [Islamic] conceptualisation of the poor" (Bayat, 1997: 43).

Immediately after the revolution, Bayat charts in detail an escalating kaleidoscope of numerous, scattered actions by the poor, squatters seizing unused land, the homeless occupying empty homes and even hotels after their owners had fled, unemployed actions, including sit-downs, occupations and hunger strikes, and the growth of unemployed action committees. Sometimes there was explicit Islamic intervention, such as the hotel occupations (Bayat 1997: 63), but as often it was the leftist groups giving a lead or simply talented, courageous individuals with no prior political or organisational history. At the same time, employed workers were resisting "lock-outs and lay-offs", in other words unemployment. Immediately after the revolution this was the cause of 20 percent of "worker collective actions ... the largest proportion of industrial action" (Bayat, 1997: 119).

Yet Bayat is unable to report any worker shora policy or campaign strategies connecting to the unemployed activists' movement. In fact, the unemployed activists' movement was momentarily very impressive. In April 1979, delegates from 20 cities and towns met for three days in the House of Labour in Tehran with the aim of creating a national unemployed organisation. It called on all the unemployed to join the May Day demonstration. It warned the government of "harsher and more resolute measures" if no action was taken to alleviate their plight (Bayat 1997: 125-6). Sadly, the May Day demonstration was to be the high point of the movement. One reason for its demise was the failure to consolidate links with the organised workers' contingents on May Day. Bayat in his earlier study of workplace shoras did point to the disconnect with "the mass movement outside the points of production" (Bayat, 1987: 96). Yet we see glimpses of the way successful shora campaigns might have raised similar demands for the urban poor.

Ali Pichgah described the Tehran oil refinery shora campaign for its own housing demands: "We did manage to get the land and divide it amongst workers. It meant each worker received 200 square metres of land and some of them started building their houses on that" (A-AP: 397). The oil workers' shora might have taken up the housing crisis in the city more generally. In Abadan, oil workers obtained land to build 3,000 houses, developing "housing cooperatives, the first of their kind in Iran" (Jafari, 2018b: 538). Oil women workers' committee member Kobra Qasemi implies that shora sentiment existed to become "tribunes of the people": "You know oil workers have a high position, economically, compared to other workers. There were not really many things we wanted for ourselves. We wanted to interfere in political issues, for others" (A-KQ: 402).

There was even support amongst the most enlightened of the clergy for a debate about the democratisation of political power. Ayatollah Taleqhani envisioned a socialistic Islam with emphasis on popular democracy and community control over politics. City and regional councils should run the country (Parsa, 1989: 293-4). However, the reality is that the shoras had minimal impact on the politics of the urban poor, prior to the undermining of their independence and formal "Islamisation".[255]

V. Conclusion: The struggle for popular democracy, the struggle for a workers' democracy

In the early 1990s, Saeed Rahnema interviewed several leading former cadres of the Fadaiyan. They were, anyway, participating in a series of discussions which Rahnema describes as "reformist debates which came to be known as 'the New Insight'" (Rahnema: 2004). In every interview the former Fadaiyan leaders reject the Stalinism or Soviet-style Communism that had dominated their thinking and political action in the Iranian Revolution and instead appear to be embracing variants of liberal democracy. Here are five brief extracts (Rahnema 2004: 257-8):

Ali Keshtgar, a former member of the Central Committee and Political Bureau:

> The Iranian left arrives at the conclusion that, without wide-ranging political and individual freedoms, [social] justice is unattainable ... The new left puts aside the Bolshevik-style party ... [and along with it] the notion of "professional revolutionaries".

Nasser Kakh-saz, a celebrated Iranian left political figure:

> As for the "Workers" question ... the theory of class struggle that [believes] workers' [should become] masters of society is not valid. The left, while defending the rights of workers, should make the workers conscious that no class should be superior among different social classes.

Nasser Rahim-khani, a former member of the Central Committee and its Political Bureau, and long-time political prisoner:

> The most important aspect of the new perspective is that it distances from its past dogmas ... The left comes to the conclusion that it cannot explain and analyse the world ... on the basis of a once-and-for-all pre-determined paradigm and ideological framework ... The main elements of this development relate to a revisiting and rethinking of ideology ... and the question of democracy, be it political democracy ... in-party organisational democracy ... or democracy between parties or within a front ... Each ideology turns its believers to a cult ... For its believers, ideology becomes an obstructive element in thought, in method and in behaviour ...

> each ideology develops its own set of internal rules and criteria, a set of behavioural patterns, customs, rituals, ceremonies and manners.

Heybat Ghafari, another former Central Committee and Political Bureau member and a long-time political prisoner:

> To understand the new perspectives, you need to consider what were the main features of the old perspective. We had a simple unidimensional perception of the world ... Our perspectives ... similar on many accounts with those of the Islamic Republic ... had the following features ... We thought if a regime nationalises the economy and brings it under state control, all problems will be solved ...We were advocates of a single party system ... and an ideological state ... We talked a lot about human rights but in reality we did not believe in these rights ... and left them to the bourgeoisie to defend ... Our theory of imperialism ... and the notion that whoever is against imperialism is our ally ... put Khomeini on our side.

Bijan Rezai (pseudonym), another Central Committee and Political Bureau member and long-time political prisoner:

> We believed that socialism and communism ... could be attained through force and dictatorship. The new perspective is the revision of this way of thinking. Of course, Marx himself did not believe in progress through dictatorship and through leadership ... he rejected the notion that society should be divided into a minority of decision makers and administrators, and a majority who follow their orders. Politically [the old perspective] ... focused on the role of vanguards ... those isolated from the society, yet the ones who should lead the masses. Organisationally ... it focused on the role of a minority

of active revolutionaries in an elitist organisation with sharp boundaries dividing them from the masses …The new developments question all these perceptions.

Similarly, Farrokh Negahdar told me:

not only Fadaiyan but every left oriented movement around the world was affected by Stalinism … [But] the reason why the shoras crashed has nothing to do with Islamism or Marxism. Shoras have no place in a modern organised society. Nowhere has that experience been implemented so far. We do not have any reliable background history of shoras' governance. We start with the Paris Commune and the soviets in the Bolshevik Revolution—but it's always a very short lived phenomena.You can't say Islamists destroyed the shoras. Shoras would have ended with normal governance, which is not shora based. Shora is a dream, a myth for self-governance of the masses … I abandoned many of the unrealistic elements in our ideology and world outlook. First, I believed that the world was divided by two parts, the West is evil and the East is good. I realised when the Soviet Union collapsed that the world is not divided like that. Both these elements exist, mixed with each other, everywhere in our world. The second is about how to rule these societies. What is the best way of organising life? The consent of the people is the most important, the core element of governance is that consent. If you can't deliver that consent you have to go. You have to get rid of mental or practical elements or your policy should be abandoned if the consent of the people is missing (A-FN: 388).

Rahnema concluded that in his opinion:

None succeeded in clarifying the ambiguities and contradictions of their arguments, and they failed to develop a theoretical framework for the new perspective. It was obvious from the start that they had totally broken with past paradigms and dogmas, but they could not develop new theories and perspectives. Their failure to theorise was a reminder of what Kautsky had said about some European revisionists: "they have nothing to revise, as they have no theory" (Rahnema, 2004: 259-60).[256]

However, a non-Stalinist, yet Marxist, even pro-Leninist democratically-based theoretical and historical model was available during the Iranian revolution. In November and December 1918, at the end of the First World War, workers' and soldiers' councils briefly flourished across Germany. This appeared to be the much-anticipated internationalisation of the 1917 Russian socialist revolution. Certainly, that's how they were greeted by Russia's revolutionary leaders, Lenin and Trotsky, and by Germany's revolutionary socialist leaders-in-waiting, Rosa Luxemburg and Karl Liebknecht.[257] Alas, it was not to be. Hostile ideological and organisational political forces opposed to the revolutionary overthrow of capitalism but committed instead to its reform through parliament were overwhelming. This found expression in the German socialist party, the SPD. The SPD had a majority amongst the workers and especially the soldiers in the workers' and soldiers' councils. Despite the councils momentarily holding political power during those two months (Hoffrogge, 2014: 6), and to that extent they were far more advanced than the workers' shoras in Iran, the pressure to capitulate to parliament proved irresistible.

Two developments are particularly relevant: First, Luxemburg and Lenin's appeal that circumstances now dictated that communists should participate in parliamentary politics. Second, the fight for workers' rights in parliamentary democracies, especially organisational independence in the workplace, should be guaranteed in capitalism's legally binding constitutions. The German Communist Party had just been formed and

Luxemburg was to lose this argument, despite the authority Lenin was giving it. Indeed, Lenin wrote one of his most famous pamphlets, *"Left wing" Communism, an Infantile Disorder*, insisting that it was "obligatory" for communists to use parliament as a platform to argue for an alternative politics. It "is not possible to bring about the soviets' victory over parliament without getting pro-soviet politicians into parliament, without disintegrating parliamentarianism from within" (Lenin, 1965i).[258]

In Iran, the workers' shoras were similarly overwhelmed by hostile ideological and organisational political forces, the Islamic movement. However, the Islamic movement, unlike the SPD, had no a priori commitment to parliamentary democracy. The Islamic movement was an all-class movement, very dependent upon its base in the mosques and the bazaars. The German SPD was *the* major working class party, its base was Germany's long established trade unions, and it had a strong rhetorical commitment to achieving socialism through parliament. This allowed it to survive its surrender to Germany's nationalist rulers during the First World War and successfully present itself and its democratic credentials to a working class electorate after the war.

In Iran, when it became clear that the workers' shoras could not offer an alternative route for the revolution, a route where the workers' democracy of the shoras would have laid the foundations for the new revolutionary state, an immediate switch in strategy became essential. The Islamic movement was openly split over popular democracy, parliamentary democracy, theocracy versus democracy. The shoras could have intervened in the debate over the Islamic constitution, calling for maximum democratic freedoms. The shora left needed a voice in the planned new constituent assembly explaining the enormous potential political significance of the workers' shoras. It was surely "obligatory" to fight for that outcome.

In Germany, the prestige of the workers' and soldiers' councils extracted an ambiguous double-edged but nevertheless legally binding guarantee of workers' rights in the new post-war

Weimar constitution. The constitution's Article 65 sought:

> to integrate the working class ... organisations into appendages of the employers' authority through the *Mitbestimmungsrecht*, the right to participation and to consultation. The workers' organisations had rights in questions of administration and general policy of the firm's working conditions, hiring and firing, and, in addition, they formed the electoral basis for the "workers' section" of the membership of the Economic Council ... the fact that they were elected by all the working people in the firm ... meant that revolutionaries could make use of them (Broué, 2006: 608).

Of course, the objective was to consolidate the employer's authority with institutions which were designed to enhance working class collaboration. But to be credible they had to concede a degree of independence to workplace organisation. This meant independently elected factory councils. The employers expected the full-time trade union officials to help maintain orderly industrial relations and "integrate" these factory committees. Nevertheless Heinrich Brandler, the German Communist Party leader, argued that the factory councils could strive for independence even from the trade union officials. During the Communist Party Congress in November 1920, Brandler gave a very upbeat account of the prospects for the factory councils: that they had the potential for workers to assert some "control of production, stocktaking, accounting and records, which would help the workers to learn that the rule of the bourgeoisie had to be overthrown" (Broué, 2006: 609).[259]

The German communists in 1919 had one tremendous advantage over their Iranian counterparts in 1979. Both shared the experience of taking part in revolutionary upheavals, toppling tyrannies, as a result of decisive collective workers' action. Both shared the experience of witnessing and participating in very advanced experimental forms, though at different stages of development, of organised workers attempting to establish democratic forms of workers' control of production. Both shared the experience of hostile political and organisational forces undermining and ultimately eliminating these experiments.[260] But the German left had at least secured elementary democratic and constitutional rights, which allowed the German Communists and the independent workers' movement time to recover from the defeat.

The tragedy of the Iranian left is that not only was this decisive advantage denied to them; the Iranian left itself has to share some of the responsibility for this failure. The struggle for popular democracy, including the defence of women's rights, and an independent press, in 1979 was just as important as defending the workers' shoras and the new regime's anti-imperialist stance. This meant different tactical and strategic alliances with different groups of Islamists at different times and on different occasions. It meant elevating the importance of the struggle over the democratic content of the new Islamic Republican constitution to a fundamental priority, including, where necessary, temporary tactical alliances with Islamic liberals.[261] But as Rahnema's interviews illustrate, the Stalinist mind-set not only ruled out such essential tactical and strategic flexibility, it altogether downplayed the importance of the struggle for popular democracy for the simple reason that those who shared the mentality didn't believe in this struggle.

In conclusion, let's echo the words spoken to Saeed Rahnema by former Fadaiyan leader, Bijan Rezai. Marx did not believe that socialism and communism should be based on force and dictatorship. A socialist society would not be divided into a minority of decision makers and administrators, elitist organisation with sharp boundaries dividing them from the masses. Soviet "communism" wasn't communism at all but a masquerade. Little wonder that Iran's political Islamists could so successfully borrow its costumes.

CHAPTER 5

Year Zero 1989: Two Trotskyisms and the workers' movement of Brazil

Introduction

In 1989 Brazil was emerging from 25 years of military dictatorship. In ways that paralleled developments in South Africa and also in South Korea in the same years, rapid industrialisation based on a high level of repression created the conditions for the emergence of a militant workers' movement that played a decisive role in helping to force a transition to liberal democracy where earlier guerrilla struggles had failed. A civilian presidency replaced the generals in 1985—though chosen on the basis of an electoral college set up under the junta. A new, relatively progressive constitution was adopted in 1988, under which the president was directly elected by popular vote.

Could the workers' movement of Brazil have become a global epicentre for resistance to the intensification of the neoliberal onslaught on trade unions, pay, jobs and hard-won welfare, pensions and health rights in the 1990s? [262] Neoliberalism thrived on the back of the implosion of Soviet Communism and its satellite state system in 1989. "The revolutions which transformed Eastern Europe in the last three months of 1989 were that rare thing, genuinely world-shaking events" (Callinicos, 1991: 1). The destruction of the Berlin Wall was perhaps the year's most important symbol. Not just "Communist" state interventionism, but the Western capitalist version too, was, allegedly, now destined for history's dustbin. International market forces, multinational corporations and highly mobile international finance, criss-crossing national-state borders in nanoseconds, courtesy of the internet, was to shape our futures.

Meanwhile, Brazil was marshalling the forces of resistance with "unprecedented levels of direct worker engagement ...

strike militancy highest in the world over the latter half of the 1980s ... backbone of what came to be called 'organised Brazil'," according to Jeff Sluyter-Beltrao (Sluyter-Beltrao, 2010:10-11, 178-9). 25 million workers took part in a two-day general strike in March 1989 (Sluyter-Beltrao, 2010: 270). Sluyter-Beltrao is a Weberian sociologist, who has carried out a remarkable investigation of Brazil's very much rank and file focused trade union confederation in the period of its formation, the CUT, the Central Unica dos Trabalhadores.

BRAZIL TIMELINE

1888-9: Brazil abolishes slavery and becomes a federal republic.

1924-7: The Prestes column, a leftist military revolt, is led by the future leader of the Brazilian Communist Party.

1930-45: A military coup brings to power Getúlio Vargas, who presides over an authoritarian statist regime.

1945: After Vargas is undermined by the defeat of fascism in the Second World War, liberal democracy is restored.

1961: João Goulart, a protégé of Vargas, and leader of the PTB (Brazilian Labour Party) becomes President.

1964: In March a military coup supported by the United States overthrows Goulart.

1966-72: Various armed leftist groups, notably National Liberation Action (*Ação Libertadora Nacional*, ALN), a breakaway from the Brazilian Communist Party, wage urban guerrilla struggle against the military junta, for example, kidnapping ambassadors to free political prisoners. They are crushed by massive repression.

1978-80: Mass strikes centred on the metal industry in the ABC (São Andre, São Bernardo, São Caetano) region of São Paulo represent a challenge that the military cannot crush. Luis Inácio Lula da Silva emerges as the key leader.

1980: Foundation of the PT, Partido dos Trabalhadores, the Workers' Party of Brazil, with Lula as the dominant figure.

1983: The Central Unica dos Trabalhadores (CUT) is founded.

1984: 16 April over a million people march in São Paulo to demand direct elections to the presidency.

1985: Tancredo Neves is elected president by the Congress, the first civilian president since 1964, but falls ill and dies. His vice-president, José Sarney, replaces him.

1988: A new Constitution is adopted, providing for direct elections to the presidency.

1989: Fernando Collor de Mello defeats Lula in the presidential election. The adoption of neoliberal policies accelerates.

1992: Collor is impeached and removed for corruption.

1995: Fernando Henrique Cardoso, who as Finance Minister pioneered Brazil's neoliberal turn, is elected President.

2002: Lula is elected President, promising to respect the neoliberal economic policy regime.

INTERVIEWEES BRAZIL

Valério Arcary
Valério was radicalised as a school student while living in Portugal during the Revolution of 1974-5. He became a leading militant of Convergência Socialista (Socialist Convergence, SC) after returning to Brazil in 1978. He helped to found both the PT and the CUT in the early 1980s and after SC was expelled from the PT became a leading figure in the Partido Socialista dos Trabalhadores Unificado (PSTU) until, with others, he broke away in 2016 to form a current in PSOL (Partido Socialismo e Liberdade). Now retired from university teaching, he is a prolific writer.

Renato Bento Ruiz, Antonio Donizete Ferreira (Toninho), and **José (Zé) Maria de Almeida,** worker militants in SC.

The CUT was closely tied to PT, Partido dos Trabalhadores, the Workers' Party of Brazil, and Luiz Inácio Lula da Silva, better known as "Lula", former metal worker trade union militant, the internationally recognised leader of PT, and once again Brazilian President. PT was and remains the world's first and only post-Communist mass-based workers' party: moreover, one that openly welcomed revolutionary socialists into its ranks. The CUT Left was dominated by two highly influential Trotskyist factions, both providing a challenge to Lula and the "Articulation" leadership.[263]

The workers' movement of Brazil, and its repeated waves of aggressive strikes, had finally broken one of the world's most vicious military dictatorships. The new Constitution, enshrining many important workers' rights, would be tested in the 1989 presidential elections, bringing Lula and PT tantalisingly close to government.[264] David Beecham and Ann Eidenham wrote an outstanding article in the journal *International Socialism* in 1987 that captured the spirit of those earlier workers' battles and especially the revolutionary potential of the rank and file metal workers' movement, spearheading the mass strike resistance, known as the Metalworkers Opposition, MO. MO resolved to build factory committees as part of the trade unions but also, if necessary, independent of them. MO stated that factory committees fought for the economic struggle—"sectional issues, control over the work process, wage questions ... and also for the political struggle, the class struggle, when they advance beyond trade unionism, with potential for becoming instruments for the revolutionary transformation of society" (Beecham and Eidenham, 1987: 35-6).

According to labour historian Marieke Riethof:

> The strike cycle began in May 1978 when 1800 workers stopped work in the Saab-Scania truck factory in São Bernardo de Campo in Greater São Paulo ...[265] The workers in this factory circumvented the military's limitations on strikes by entering the workplace but

refusing to switch on their machines. The local press reported the "paralysing of the company's entire production process within minutes ..." Because it was not a normal strike in accordance with the 1964 strike law, with picket lines that the police could forcibly remove, the authorities were unable to repress this "cross-armed" protest (Riethof, 2018: 90).

Strike leader Gilson Menezes and his comrades understood this as a political as well as an economic strike: "I knew the strike had a political nature, but the workforce as a whole did not...They participated in a wage dispute. If we had said that the strike was against the dictatorship then they would not have gone on strike."[266] Nevertheless that perception soon changed and the strike became "a symbol of labour opposition, sparking similar actions in other factories, marking the beginning of a major strike wave which simultaneously challenged authoritarian politics and reshaped the union movement's political strategies" (Riethof, 2018: 90). Within two months of the Saab-Scania strike, a quarter of a million workers were on strike in companies such as Ford, Mercedes-Benz and Volkswagen (Riethof, 2018: 91). In 1979 almost a million workers had been on strike involving wider groups in education and urban transport.

The emerging workers' movement at this time developed two critical characteristics: the rank and file elected factory committees or factory commissions and the giant assemblies of striking workers, voting on strike developments and employer and government proposals for concluding strikes. Over a hundred wage agreements were negotiated in the São Paulo region in 1979 by factory commissions and not the official *pelego* union leaders.[267] Many commissions were then recognised by the companies (Riethof, 2018: 92). However, many commission leaders were later fired with the tacit support of the *pelego* union leaders. MO, the potentially revolutionary Metalworkers Opposition referred to earlier, was broken in this way (Sluyter-Beltrao, 2010: 90, fn13).

However, the lingering impact of the Metalworkers Opposition was profound. Its dedication to rank and file activity, and the sense that a new form of politics was implicit in that approach, would help shape both PT and the CUT, the Central Unica dos Trabalhadores, when it emerged. MO had its own distinctive leader, rank and file metal worker Waldemar Rossi. The politics are complicated by Rossi's commitment to the militant Catholic liberation theology grouping, Pastoral Operária, Workers' Pastoral, which was very influential amongst rank and file workers in the early days. Rossi mixed Marxism with his radical Catholicism with the resulting perspective tilting to the secular left:

> people who entered into the movement, who had a clear class vision of the struggle, and an expectation, in terms of the movement, of creating a class-based movement and not one of Catholic orientation ... the question of liberty, the question of equality, the question of democracy, the democratic process, the sticking to the decisions of the majority, the going forward together, the work of the base ... of a process that goes from below to above and not from top to bottom.[268]

Giant open-air assemblies of striking workers voting on the progress of their strikes were also a major challenge to the faltering military dictatorship. Yet the assemblies combined genuine democratic aspirations with unintended invitations for union leader demagogy, not least from the most important of the new union leaders, Lula. On the plus-side, "workers' wives were encouraged to attend the assemblies, in part as a strategic response to distorted media coverage. Union leaders wanted to keep workers and wives away from their television sets in order to mitigate the conservative broadcast media's stream of 'demoralising' information" (Sluyter-Beltrao, 2010: 94, fn18). On the minus-side, "Lula's charismatic authority ... undermined the democratic potential of mass participation, with leaders settling into a pattern of carefully choreographed, univocal plebiscitarian events" (Sluyter-Beltrao, 2010: 94).

"Lula occasionally spoke openly of the difficulties of living up to the expectations of people who viewed him as a god that would solve all their problems. Workers placed his likeness next to that of Jesus on assembly banners and wrote public prayers" (Sluyter-Beltrao, 2010: 94, fn20). Lula's capacity for honing ambiguities defined his emergence as both union and political leader from the beginning. On the one hand he was associated with the "new unionism", rank and file orientation and participation. On the other hand, he had been deliberately chosen by one of the old guard, retiring president Paul Vidal in the officially sanctioned metal workers' union, as a trustworthy successor (Sluyter-Beltrao, 2010: 88, fn11).

Riethof cites a 1985 union report showing how the repression of factory commissions created a "dynamic" that shifted strikes from the shop floor to the streets. Community organising, as a broadening of solidarity with the strike movements, also becomes an end in itself. This coincides with the foundation of PT, Partido dos Trabalhadores, the Workers' Party of Brazil in 1980 (Riethof, 2018: 94-6). Whilst fighting to preserve and revive factory commissions as a vehicle for rank and file trade union organising, they were not seen as a decisive *political* organising base unit of the new party.

In 1983 workers had elected factory commissions in 20 companies in Greater São Paulo, rising to 101 in 1986 and peaking at 211 in 1993 (Riethof, 2018: 101). 1983 also saw a resurgence in workers' militancy resulting from an IMF-backed government austerity package aimed at both sacking workers in state-owned companies and reducing the wages of those who kept their jobs. The government declared the resulting strikes illegal, using the 1964 strike law. 60,000 metal workers came out in solidarity, uniting private and public sectors. Pressure mounted for a general strike with clear political overtones—threatening the very existence of the military government. Though this failed to materialise, rank and file union leaders had a strong sense that they had established "the protests as proof that they were capable of organising a political strike" (Riethof, 2018: 101). The CUT was founded in August of that year.

The CUT's founding conference took for granted that combat with the government was its top priority. But, again, a planned general strike failed to materialise, partly as a result of divisions emerging between left and right. This is despite the fact that the CUT conference "identified the general strike as the most important political instrument in the hands of the union movement" (Riethof, 2018, p103). At the same time, however, the military government's authority was collapsing: "Reflecting Brazilians' generalised discontent with repression and economic crisis, the strike movement (had) helped create conditions for the growing pro-democracy coalition ... by mobilising large protests, *largely through the unions' own networks* with social movements" (Riethof, 2018: 107; my emphasis). Thus the 1983-85 campaign for direct presidential elections, *Diretas Já!* (Direct Elections Now!), put both PT and the CUT centre stage for the democratic transition but simultaneously created circumstances for it to overwhelm their political and trade activities and perspectives.

As it developed in the 1980s, alongside the CUT, PT at first, encouraged a:

> commitment to internal democracy... [and]...rank-and-file participation—which works to maintain movement solidarity by involving and empowering members. Militancy and mobilisation are embraced not only as tools of movement empowerment and expansion, but also because they are the primary producers of activists and sympathisers. Pluralist inclusion and toleration of competing viewpoints within consensus-oriented decision-making processes are geared to keeping component groups on board by according minority voices real say in internal debate (Sluyter-Beltrao, 2010: 7).[269]

Lula and the wider PT and CUT leadership were not only relaxed about the intervention of the revolutionary left, they positively welcomed what Sluyter-Beltrao calls "factional pluralism and bottom-up participation" (Sluyter-Beltrao, 2010:12). Lula readily conceded that he had enjoyed "fruitful co-operation" with independent leftist shop floor groups during strike mobilisations. He argued that "divergences" should be "resolved through the most democratic discussion possible", then "making a decision which will be carried out by all" (Sluyter-Beltrao, 2010: 105). He added: "The way to confront these extremist groups is to place them amongst the working class, and the working class will take it upon themselves to make these groups stop being radical ... It's all very simple, you just have to remove them from the theoretical world and put them in the real world" (Sluyter-Beltrao, 2010: 105-6, fn40).

This would prove to be an extremely effective challenge to Brazil's revolutionary left, part of the well-rooted wider Latin American Trotskyist tradition which, to its credit, grew to dominate the CUT Left opposition at the height of worker militancy in the late 1980s.

I. Two Trotskyisms

In 1979 the Ligue Communiste Révolutionnaire, LCR, the French section of the Fourth International (FI), seconded one of its leaders, Daniel Bensaïd, to intervene in the rising workers' strike movement of Brazil. He recalled the emphasis FI leader Ernest Mandel had laid on how Brazil's growth in the 1970s had generated a massive and concentrated industrial proletariat:

> The "ABC" industrial triangle [São Andre, São Bernardo, São Caetano] alone counted more workers than the legendary Ruhr ... Ernest saw Brazil as a kind of tropical equivalent to Bismarckian Germany, the cradle of the modern European workers' movement. He was convinced that we could rapidly develop there a

> revolutionary organisation of several thousand militants (Bensaïd, 2013: 214-5).[270]

It would not be Daniel's first visit to Latin America. He had been sent to Argentina after the 10th Congress of the Fourth International in January 1974: "Controversy raged over the outcome of the armed struggle in Latin America, over the imminence of revolution in Europe, and over a Basque commando's execution of Carrero Blanco," appointed successor to Spain's fascist dictator, Franco, then still in power (Bensaïd, 2013: 127).

Two blocs had formed at the Congress. The tangled politics, caught up in how revolutionary socialists should respond to armed struggle, especially in Latin America at this time, and very much still in the shadow of the death of Che Guevara, need not concern us here. What matters is how the two blocs would evolve and impact on Brazil's left wing politics a decade later.[271] They would emerge as the leaderships of the two Trotskyist factions dominating the left wing of the CUT, Socialist Democracy, led by Mandel's FI, with Daniel as its visiting representative, and Convergéncia Socialista, Socialist Convergence, part of a Latin American network of Trotskyists, based in Argentina and led by Hugo Brassano, also known as Nahuel Moreno. Moreno had swung from a Guevara-ist "armed struggle" position to an orientation on "strikes and urban uprising, against a fetishism of the rural guerrilla inspired by the Cuban revolution" (Bensaïd, 2013: 128). Nevertheless, reconciliation between Moreno and the European-based FI proved impossible.[272]

Unfortunately, Daniel doesn't mention this competition with the Moreno tendency in his account of the impact of the Trotskyist left in Brazil in the 1980s and 1990s.[273] This is a serious omission in an otherwise indispensable description of many of the key developments. As we saw earlier, Lula and his closest allies welcomed the participation of the Trotskyists in building PT, believing, with some justification, that their organisational skills could be harnessed to PT's growth whilst, as they saw it, the harmful side of their politics could be kept under control. As soon as he arrived in Brazil, Daniel immediately began working with potentially sophisticated political leaders, who regarded themselves as revolutionary socialists. Political activists like João Machado, simultaneously, a co-founder of PT, member of the International Committee of the FI, and 20 years later, a leading member of the breakaway PSOL, Party for Socialism and Liberty, following the final marginalisation of the Trotskyists when PT formed the government in the early 2000s.

Daniel has left us some stunning early impressions:

> In autumn 1980, the great strike of engineering workers in the ABC region industrial zone tolled the bell for the dictatorship ... Sunday morning assembly of 80,000 workers, gathered in the São Bernado do Campo stadium. Lula's talent as a popular agitator amazed me. The archbishop of São Paulo, Dom Evaristo Arns, came to support the strikers, opening the churches for them to organise solidarity and food distribution. He asked the crowd to pray for the success of the struggle. In the absence of indigenous traditions of the workers' movement, this collective communion had the value of a solemn oath. There were few who abstained, as we did, from this act of faith. The red flags and the "Internationale" appeared much later, in the later 1980s (Bensaïd, 2013: 218).

The FI's perspective was to link its growth in Brazil to that of the Workers' Party, "conceived not as a mere tactical opportunity but rather as strategic orientation ... to give the Brazilian working class ... a major class party, pluralist and democratic. Programmatic and ideological definitions would follow in the due course of collective experience" (Bensaïd, 2013: 220).[274] João Machado was Daniel's key link in PT. Machado's paper, "The experience of building the DS and the PT, from 1979 to the first Lula government", published in 2012, is an indispensable source for understanding the FI and Socialist Democracy's role, and its subsequent demise, in the PT (Machado 2012.):[275]

> The idea of forming the Partido dos Trabalhadores (PT, Workers' Party) in Brazil was launched at the end of 1978, and it began to be organised in 1979. The original party texts spoke of socialism and denounced capitalism, their central idea was that of building an independent workers' party, without bosses, which could express their interests and not manipulate them. Its Charter of Principles used—without explaining its origin—the famous formula of Marx of the time of the First International ("the emancipation of the workers will be the work of the workers themselves").[276]
>
> To a large extent, the formation of the PT mirrored the strike movement that began in Brazil during the final phase of the dictatorship and was driven by a trade union movement called "genuine trade unionism" (which essentially meant "classist"). Besides these trade unionists, however, various revolutionary political organisations were already participating in the initial process of forming the party; some had an influence in its initial conformation—particularly two organisations of Trotskyist tradition, Convergência Socialista and Fração Operária Trotskista.[277]

To fully understand the FI position, the following passage from Machado's paper needs to be carefully studied, particularly the last sentence:

> The defeat of the Lula [presidential] candidacy in 1989, at the start of a great international crisis of the left, represented a turning point in the trajectory of the PT. Lula and his political relatives gradually began to develop the idea that it was possible for him and the PT to win

> through moderation of the programme and broadening of alliances. Indeed, over time, and more clearly after Lula's second defeat in a presidential election in 1994, what became the core of electoral strategies was the disregard of the inevitability of class antagonisms in capitalist society. *The left orientation to win elections—the bet on a greater popular mobilisation, likely to expand on what we had known in 1989, by understanding that a national election constitutes a moment when class alternatives clash—was rejected* (Machado, 2012; my emphasis).

We shall explore further the 1989 election defeat and its coincidence with the "great international crisis of the left" in a moment, but here we need to clarify what Machado means in that last sentence. Later Machado explains how he and his comrades understood PT as a "revolutionary party under construction". Even though Bensaïd criticised this formulation, he accepted the underlying implication that if such a party succeeded in winning the elections it would trigger the "moment when class alternatives clash": in other words, a revolutionary showdown with the bourgeoisie.

The dangers implicit in this approach are obvious. Whatever the intentions, the key perspective, "the emancipation of the workers will be the work of the workers themselves", hinges on initial success in the electoral process. Nevertheless, we need to recall that Marx and Engels had kept open just such a possibility of using the British parliament in this way (see Callinicos, 1983: 160-62). Perhaps more important, the question of electing a "workers' government" in a parliamentary system was raised in the early congresses of the Communist International and, as Daniel Bensaïd concluded, they revealed an "unresolved ambiguity" in "the range of interpretations which they could give rise to in practice".[278] In addition, again as we shall see in a moment, Lula himself was signalling parliamentary scenarios before 1989. A further factor reinforcing what would become an electoral trap for the FI was that they were far stronger and influential inside the PT than outside.

Machado describes their position at that time as follows:

> At the end of the 1980s, immediately before the turning point in the evolution of the PT began in 1989, the DS had around a thousand activists who were a benchmark for a larger number of party activists; in general, it had almost 10% of the delegates in the national Encontros [congresses] of the PT. It had great importance within the left of the PT and in the party itself ... a remarkable presence in the CUT ... a sustained force within the student movement, its original main base. It was beginning to have elected representatives (with in particular the election of Raul Pont as state deputy for Rio Grande do Sul in 1986, and federal deputy in 1990) ... the PT during this period was moving towards the left, and the DS certainly had a role in this process.

Valério Arcary was a key leader of Socialist Convergence in Brazil.[279] Here he describes relations between the small group of recently recruited youngsters and the Moreno tendency in Latin America:[280]

> Moreno was not very pre-occupied with Brazil. He only came twice. Argentina was a big mess, he was very concentrated on it. He used to say I'm not a specialist on Brazil, Brazil is a very different country, a very complicated country. But one thing he told us in 1983: "Now you are 25 years old or older. There is a problem. You left your parents' house. You went to college. And you became immediately full timers in your revolutionary nucleus. You built it so you are probably very proud of it but there is a problem, you have to join the working class. You have to go to work, all of you!" So we had a meeting. We were 21 members of the national leader-

> ship. He said: "One of you, only one of you, will stay a full timer. And it has to be the youngest. Who is the leader of the youth? The one who is still a student, never was a full timer ... And all of you have to do two things: find a job in the working class and split yourselves because you are starting to fight each other because you all live in Rio and São Paulo ... you have to work as a team, but you can't do it if you don't split. You have to prove yourselves. Two or three go to the north east, two or three go to the south and a few stay in Rio and São Paulo, which are major cities. But you have to go to work! You can choose different sectors of the working class but which is concentrated and there is a high level of fighting ... You are joining the working class to prove that you can lead fights. So don't go to retarded sectors of the working class, sectors still sleeping, not awake. Go to sectors already awoken, metal workers, oil workers, teachers, bank workers and split yourselves." And that's what we did. It was difficult. Some did not survive this period. There was a natural selection. We made this experience for several years. And a new generation of younger people became full timers. When you have 1,000 people, you need 20 to 30 full timers, otherwise you don't organise a Leninist organisation.

Paradoxically, Socialist Convergence had an unanticipated breakthrough by intervening successfully, not at first with workers, but in a major school student rebellion in the early 1980s. They were able to form the Foundation of Socialist Youth which became their main base (Almeida Ribeiro de Miranda 2014: 160-61). Former school student leader Henrique Carneiro has provided a unique insight into this period:

> I was elected as the first president of UMES (Metropolitan Union of Secondary Students) in São Paulo, in 1980, and then president of UPES (Paulista Union of Sec-

ondary Students) in 1981. There were a few hundred schools participating across the state and polls reached about 50,000 voting students.

I took part, both personally and as representing UMES and UPES in various social struggles in the period. In 1978, before joining the organisations, I had participated in a hunger strike in support of the political prisoners of Socialist Convergence ... I also supported the MNU (Unified Black Movement) demonstrations and the first demonstrations for LGBT rights. When Lula and others were arrested in 1979, we went on a one-day strike at Equipe school, where I was studying. Since 1979, I participated in the formation of the PT, of which I signed the list of the first members. In 1982, I was a candidate for federal deputy for the PT, obtaining 21,000 votes. In 1983, I was arrested during the wave of looting in S[ão] P[aulo], for distributing leaflets for the general strike. I was detained for about two weeks and was prosecuted under national security law, and then amnestied.[281]

Socialist Convergence was involved in discussions about the formation of a workers' party from the beginning and emerged as one of the strongest leftist factions (Keck, 1992:79-80, 120). It developed a reputation for causing problems for the Lula leadership by its advocacy of factory occupations,[282] and its resistance to the multiple compromises that PT administrations made when they participated in local and regional governments. Yet its militant worker members had to be taken seriously. As Valério Arcary puts it:

Firstly, we were very honest people. Where we worked we were not seen as... extravagant, but normal persons. When you are inside a workplace and you are a Trotskyist you get respect because you are a very honest person. And that counts a lot to build confidence. Secondly, we could explain to workers complex ideas that gave us an advantage over the Lula current because workers prefer leaders who understand things better than they do. They don't want leaders who are not smart. They want smart leaders. We had more educated people who were able to explain what was happening in national politics inside the workplaces. And also explain tactical differences between the left and right inside the CUT.[283]

At the peak of their influence Socialist Convergence had about 1,500 members, with a wide periphery, at the time of their expulsion in 1992, well rooted in the workplaces and well respected, selling about 10,000 papers mainly to PT activists.[284]

The 1980s had witnessed a series of factory occupations, the most famous one being the workers' occupation of the US-based multinational General Motors plant in the Brazilian city of São José dos Campos, demanding a 40-hour week in 1984. Although the occupation was broken by a thousand-strong police raid, the occupation has assumed almost legendary status in the Brazilian workers' movement for challenging a unique almost apartheid-like internal structure which pitted monthly salaried "superior" employees against the rest of the workforce: and where violence and intimidation were an integral part of managerial "strategy". There was a very high level of rank and file worker involvement in the occupation. "Total from beginning to end", according to Moacyr Pinto da Silva, white-collar worker in the occupation and author of a book about it.[285]

Renato Bento Ruiz and Antonio Donizete Ferreira, known as Toninho, were young workers during the General Motors occupation, where they first came across Socialist Convergence. Later they would develop as political cadres for the organisation.[286] Both were caught up in the struggle in the early 1990s to resist the neoliberal privatisation onslaught as well as to defend Socialist Convergence from pressure from the PT leadership calling for the organisation's expulsion. Both experienced the intense political confusion and disorientation of the time. As Renato puts it, world capitalism and its ideologues told workers that all communists "thought like Stalin and that the communist or socialist system was not a democratic system…not for expanding democracy. It is in this sense…there was confusion and that we lost, and we lost a lot. The left did not explain the difference between anti-democratic communism and democratic communism."[287]

José Maria de Almeida, also known as Zé Maria, a leading worker activist in Socialist Convergence, was one of the leaders of the occupation of Mannesmann, manufacturer of telecommunications equipment, at Belo Horizonte, capital city of Minas Gerais state in Brazil. The occupation grew out of the strike—part of the two-day 25 million-worker strong general strike in March 1989: "At the beginning of the process, approximately 2,500 workers remained within the company per shift (the factory had around nine thousand employees at that time). The occupation lasted 10 days." There were several other occupations of companies during the same strike. "In all of these occupations, an agreement was reached along similar lines to the agreement made to end the strike at Mannesmann." Confrontations with the police were avoided, despite the company obtaining a court order for police to vacate the factory, because the state governor intervened. The agreement included a 26 percent increase in wages and no retaliation: "The workers were quite radicalised, expressing the same feeling of discontent and revolt that was growing throughout the country with the situation."[288]

Nevertheless, according to a National History Symposium in 2017 which discussed workplace occupations in Brazil in the 1980s, the occupation movement also endured a massive, indeed murderous, defeat at the end of the 1980s. A strike at CSN, Companhia Siderurgica Nacional, a massive steel producer in the city of Volta Redonda in the state of Rio de Janeiro, was deliberately targeted by the government when it turned into an occupation:

> Defeating the occupation of CSN ... would serve as a government message to an entire battalion of strikers. The strike at the steel mill lasted 17 days, but the occupation only three. This is because, after cutting off the supply of water, electricity and food to the plant, on 9 November 1988, army troops invaded CSN to expel the strikers, resorting to the use of lethal ammunition. The action ended with the deaths of three workers: Carlos Augusto Barroso, who had his skull crushed with blows, Walmir Freitas Monteiro and William Fernandes Leite, hit by rifle bullets. After the evacuation was over, the troops did not withdraw, remaining inside the plant for several days... murders of factory workers had not occurred even during the period of the civil-military dictatorship (De Oliveira Martins, 2017).[289]

The former military dictatorship, overseeing a carefully orchestrated unfolding of a parliamentary democratic process, wasn't about to tolerate the challenge of a potentially insurrectionary general strike, stimulating workplace occupations, or for that matter, an insurgent land-grab campaign. One month after the murder of the three occupying workers at CSN, Chico Mendes, the leader of the rubber tappers, part of the *Movimento Sem Terra*, MST, the Landless Workers Movement, was assassinated.[290]

II. Lula, PT and the 1989 presidential election

Lula had made an extremely important speech in 1985 reflecting on the possibility of a Chile-style military intervention in the event of a PT electoral victory.[291] The speech illustrated the revolutionary potential implicit in the Brazilian workers' movement as well as the confusion Stalinism had created about workers' power and democracy. It also reflected pressure from competing parts of the left, the Trotskyists, but also some of the former urban guerrilla fighters, now part of the Articulation leadership, who, at that stage, looked to Castro's Cuba for inspiration. Lula balanced between them without definite commitments to any of them:

> I have doubts that the economic power and the ruling classes will allow the PT to come to power through elections. That is why, anticipating an armed reaction from preventing the PT from taking over the government, I accept the use of weapons by the population to guarantee respect for the results of the ballot boxes; in practice PT is a Marxist party, although it would prefer to be a PT party; I do not accept the use of the expression dictatorship of the proletariat, because when the proletariat reaches power, democracy is being brought to its ultimate consequences; I will not accept it if the right tries to retain power through the use of weapons, so I am in favour of armed resistance (Arcary, 2014).[292]

Soviet Communism, Stalinism, had so contaminated the idea of "dictatorship of the proletariat" in the last century as to drain it completely of its democratic content. Lula understandably associated it with the totalitarianism implicit in Stalinism. Lula here exposes the major fault line which would help derail left advance for PT. It is worth restating here how Lenin understood it as a mass-based democratic dictatorship over the rump of the capitalist class that would inevitably play some part in the early transition phases to socialism:

> Simultaneously with an immense expansion of democracy, which for the first time becomes democracy for the poor, democracy for the people, and not democracy for the money-bags, the dictatorship of the proletariat imposes a series of restrictions on the freedom of the oppressors, the exploiters, the capitalists. We must suppress them in order to free humanity from wage slavery (Lenin, 1965e, ch2).

Lenin's perspective presupposed workers' control of production in a workers' state, as we saw in chapter 1 above. PT's electoral programme for the presidential election in 1989 had no such perspective, though it was sufficiently radical to terrify the employers, "reflected in a famous public warning by Mario Amato, head of the country's leading industrial association, that if Lula won, 800,000 Brazilian entrepreneurs would abandon the country":

> the party's programme ... called for a "rupture" with free-market capitalism and the construction of a democratic-socialist welfare state geared to redressing Brazil's unsurpassed social inequalities ... PT called for an immediate suspension of payments on the foreign debt, radical land reform "under workers' control", nationalisation of the financial and transport systems, and ambitious state-led overhauls of the housing, healthcare and education systems (Sluyter-Beltrao, 2010: 12, 13-14).

Lula was defeated by Fernando Collor, who became the first elected President in almost three decades (Saad-Filho, Morais, 2018: 36). That defeat accelerated the shift of the Lula leadership to the right, especially under the impact of Collor's neoliberal agenda. But it needn't and shouldn't have done. Lula had every reason to be extremely proud of that election. The PT leftist-led "Brazilian Popular Front" coalition received 47 percent of the 23 million valid votes cast. There was a widespread view that the extreme bias of the Brazilian conservative mainstream media had undermined the democratic process (Sluyter-Beltrao, 2010: 13).

PT historian Lincoln Secco documented some of the abuses, in particular how Collor won support from some of the "shirtless", the very poor, unemployed, crowding into the slums, the *favelas*, from the countryside (Secco, 2018: 137).[293] Here was an already expanding base for the evangelical Protestants, the media highlighting religious warnings that Lula would close all churches (Secco, 2018: 137). There was a claim that he had forced a woman to abort her child, following a relationship with her: a media "exposé" directed by Collor's brother, almost immediately proved to be false (Secco, 2018: 139). The kidnapping of a businessman, sensationally exposed in the media, was attributed to PT.

Ann Eidenham, one of the authors of the *International Socialism* article referred to earlier, witnessed the election. Her reporting captured the two sides of Lula's campaign, tilting left, pulled along by the movement he himself had helped to unleash:

> Though Lula often tried to appear moderate and appeal to the middle classes, especially after the first round of the election, in other ways his style and message were anything but moderate ... He insisted that strikes should not be called off, even if they might damage his electoral chances. Workers' share of the national income could only come by reducing profits. Political discussion involved huge numbers of people that no previous electoral campaign had reached. By the second round of the election, it was the ruling class versus the workers (Socialist Review, February 1990, No. 128).

In other words, at this stage Lula maintained an opening to the left, sustaining a view that his election victory could indeed be a springboard for a far more radical action. In fact, Lula had an unambiguous mandate to fight the incoming Collor government with its neoliberal policies. A clear majority of workers, especially organised workers, had supported him.

III. PT's regional and local electoral perspectives

But before turning to the collapse of PT and the workers' movement in the face of the neoliberal onslaught, it is important to stress how deeply PT was already committed to electoral politics through some significant successes in regional and local politics. Of course, the grinding poverty in urban areas helped propel this perspective. One third of the population in Brazil's major city, São Paulo, for example, lived in *favelas*, lacking even minimal urban infrastructure. Infant mortality at just under 83 per thousand live births contrasted with an average of just over 50 for the state as a whole. Because children began working very young to contribute to family support, in 1980 less than 40 percent finished four years of schooling, and only 8 percent finished eight years. Few central roads were paved and public transport was inadequate. Add chronic flooding, mudslides, the lack of sewage and regular garbage collection (Keck, 1992: 201), it is not difficult to see why the *favela* became the focus of attention.

PT developed a model of what this might mean when it contested and won the mayoralty at Diadema in 1982, part of the industrial belt of Greater São Paulo. Former metal workers' leader Gilson Menezes, one of the organisers of the strike at the Swedish-based multinational Saab-Scania that had triggered a strike wave in 1978 (Keck, 1992: 202), became PT's first democratically-elected mayor: "The PT focus on democratisation from below led to the call for the formation of popular councils and the development of mechanisms of direct democracy" (Keck, 1992: 198).

Margaret Keck has provided a comprehensive account of Mayor Gilson's efforts to stimulate popular participation in genuinely progressive projects. In one of many examples, Gilson's team opposed attempts by the bus company for a fare hike. It created a Transit Users' Commission and then negotiated with the bus company at public hearings. It made an overwhelming case that what was needed was a fare reduction not an increase, "leaving Diadema with the lowest bus fare in the region", and later, "free passes outside of rush hour for senior citizens and the unemployed" (Keck, 1992: 200). Open neighbourhood budget hearings were encouraged with the idea that grassroots popular councils control local spending decisions. This would become a hallmark and flag bearer of PT local and regional government. But paradoxically, once the PT had finally formed a nation-wide government at the start of the new century, especially in the context of neoliberal economics, the flaws in this approach quickly became apparent. In a seminal essay about PT's city government at Porto Alegre in Brazil, the British writer and socialist Hilary Wainwright summed it up with the sub-heading "Under siege": "Unrestrained ... global deregulation ... pressures to privatise and run down the state's social capacities ... federal government has strengthened central control over public spending and cut the funds going to cities" (Wainwright, 2003: 124).

In fact, in 1990, a São Paulo public transport strike had already brought to a head the contradiction between PT's electoral strategy and the continuing militancy and high level of expectation of its organised worker-base. 60,000 bus workers went on strike for nine days, halting 90 percent of public transport: "The strike ... pitched the union against the PT-led municipal government ... over proposed wage increases ...The city government under budgetary pressure...resulting in the PT mayor firing 475 public transport workers" (Riethof, 2018: 133).

João Machado, the Fourth International and Socialist Democracy leader cited earlier has provided a startling account of the experiences of PT in local and regional government:

> We never made a joint assessment of all the experiences of our participation in municipal ... or state ... administrations ... we never seriously confronted [the problem] of campaign finance ... The election campaigns of the PT benefited from the contributions of companies very early on. In addition, from the second half of the 1990s and more clearly after 2001 and 2002 (when two mayors who were members of the PT were assassinated in circumstances which remained unclear) we had some information indicating that the way of fundraising in the linked town halls in the PT were far from "orthodox".

The most plausible hypothesis to explain the assassinations of the mayors of Campinas and Santo André, two important towns, is that these mayors tried to stop or limit fundraising from companies working for the local governments. These hypotheses were formulated by relatives of the murdered mayors and denied by the PT leadership.[294]

IV. Two Trotskyisms and PT's surrender to the neoliberal offensive

The Brazilian Marxist economists Alfredo Saad-Filho and Lecio Morais define neoliberalism, applied to Latin America and in particular Brazil, as a system of accumulation of capital designed to raise the exploitation of labour by using a global base rather than a national one. This created "a dependence on foreign suppliers, markets and technologies, the subordination of strategic planning to the global interest of transnational corporations", combined with local labour "flexibility" which minimises legal protections for workers, creating mass unemployment and a huge "informal" labour sector with few if any trade union rights (Saad-Filho and Morais, 2018: 74, 56, 76).

Sue Branford, a writer who specialised in the growth of PT in the early years, has identified one particular and decisive way neoliberalism simultaneously broke and then transformed PT in the 1990s *before* it became a national government in the 2000s:

> Trade barriers were smashed and the market flooded with cheap imported manufactured goods. One-third of manufacturing jobs were lost. State companies were privatised, and thousands of public sector jobs were wiped out. *The social base of PT was shattered* [my emphasis]. The party responded by moving to the centre ... In what many see as a betrayal of PT's original vision, power became concentrated in the hands of professional politicians, and the earlier practice of consulting the base on important decisions ... abandoned (Branford, 2009: 155).

And Mike Gonzalez has placed these events on a broader canvass:

> Export agriculture and the extractive industries were the areas that attracted new external investment throughout the 1990s, from China in particular at the expense of manufacturing and services ... direct foreign investment in agriculture grew exponentially ... Soybean cultivation and cattle-raising spread across the region at an accelerated pace, together with maize production—not for consumption but to produce ethanol as fuel. The devastation this expansion caused was and is most visible in Brazil, where vast swathes of the Amazon rain forest were cut down to permit the conversion of the land to arable and cattle-raising use ... their populations were driven off the land to add to the swelling populations of the marginal communities around the exploding cities of the region. The numbers involved are astonishing. It was often impossible to imagine where these people were in the overcrowded barrios of Latin America ... It seemed inconceivable that so many human beings should be crammed into such restricted space and continue to function (Gonzalez, 2019: 13).[295]

Here was a huge boost in numbers of the "shirtless" crowding into the shanty towns and favelas, completely disoriented, a target for the "US based Protestant evangelical groups with their vast wealth...establishing links...with those sectors of the population who had been abandoned by the state" (Gonzalez, 2019: 15). At least 15 percent of Brazilian voters would identify as evangelicals, "expanding rapidly in the working class" and voting "massively against Lula and for Collor" (Hunter, 2010: 115, fn10).

But was this victory for neoliberalism inevitable? In fact, the attempt by the incoming newly-elected Collor administration to impose neoliberalism was a complete disaster. It ripped up some of the most progressive parts of the 1988 constitution, itself a provocation that demanded an immediate response, arguably de-legitimising the 1989 election result, which had been based on the new constitution. Foreign companies would be allowed to explore the subsoil,[296] the state monopoly on shipping on coastal routes was removed, as was the state monopoly on telecommunications. The monopoly on oil exploration was watered down. Financial institutions could obtain a stake in the social security system. Privatisation and labour "flexibility" would now be underpinned constitutionally (Saad-Filho and Morais, 2018: 59). But the plans failed in their own terms, resulting in hyper-inflation with Collor forced out in 1992 amidst "a mind-boggling array of scandals involving thievery, drugs, sex and the misappropriation of public funds" (Saad-Filho and Morais, 2018: 59).

But, according to Valério Arcary, the PT leadership vehemently opposed what was to become the main issue at PT's National Congress in 1991: the proposal for mass mobilisation to challenge and, if possible, bring down the Collor government.[297] The Lula leadership were certain they would win elections planned for 1994. They were obsessed with demonstrating that they respected the recently installed electoral processes. They were convinced that if they mobilised to bring down Collor, a Lula government in 1994 would face a "revenge" disruption and ultimately destruction from a similar type of mass mobilisation.[298]

The Lula leadership were also determined at that Congress to shatter illusions that socialism was possible. José Dirceu, PT President and one of Lula's closest associates asserted PT must abandon any identity with socialism, adding bluntly that it was an "unburied corpse" (Secco, 2018: 145). As PT historian Secco put it:. "The Berlin Wall fell on the party" (Secco, 2018: 145, 146). The PT Congress formally adopted a position that "we have to recognise that we are witnessing the end of the cycle of socialist revolutions begun with the Russian Revolution in 1917 and the model of society that they inspired" (Branford and Kucinski, 2003: 47). Florestan Fernandes, Brazil's most highly respected radical sociologist, exposed the debilitating flaw in the evolving PT strategy:

> The workers, unionised or not, taken as a class, support predominantly explosive offensive positions, given the degree of resentment they show towards the existing order ... The party does not try to take political advantage of the potential of this collective behaviour and allows it to dissipate in directions that are institutionalised and regulated by the system, in terms of representation and ritualized elections. Nor does it infuse it with a permanent duration and with ideological content against the system.[299]

In other words, the PT leadership has to take a major share of responsibility for the de-mobilisation of the workers' movement, in the face of the neoliberal onslaught, resulting from the combination of ideological disintegration and strategic surrender to the electoral process. Could the Trotskyist organisations have stopped the rot? There is some confusion about their strength. In combination, they numbered no more than a few thousand. But in PT their influence was much greater than their numbers would suggest, as the following fascinating anecdote from Valério Arcary about the 1991 National Congress illustrates:

> There were more than 1,500 delegates in the gigantic shed of the disabled Vera Cruz studios in São Bernado do Campo. The Trotskyist delegations and supporters were about one third of the Workers' Party. We received information that the US embassy was to be represented by the Consul. We demanded that the Congress of the Workers' Party refuse official representation of the government of the Unites States. Congress was halted whilst the Lula majority tendency called a parallel assembly

> lasting for four to five hours whilst they discussed what to do with this. They decided that the diplomatic representative of the US government should stay at the Congress. The Stalinists split and voted with us. At that point there was a dramatic intervention by the official diplomatic representative of Cuba, Marta Harnecker, wife of Manual Pineiro, also known as Barba Roja, "Red Beard", the Cuban leader, close to Castro, responsible for liaison with armed guerrilla groups during the '70s in Latin America. She broke with the Lula tendency majority and came to sit with us, side by side with the Trotskyists, as a public signal of Cuba's displeasure. The delegation of all the left-wing currents stood up and shouted for about five minutes at the top of their lungs: "Cuba! Cuba! Cuba!" She was touched.[300]

The PT leadership were sufficiently concerned about Trotskyist opposition to their embrace of electoralism that they embarked on a sustained campaign to expel Socialist Convergence, regarded as the most serious potential threat to their plans—a drive that would succeed in 1992. The attack on Socialist Convergence began almost the moment the 1989 election was over (Sluyter-Beltrao, 2010: 317). The pages of *Teoria e Debate* were thrown open for a full-scale assault on SC led by Apolonio de Carvalho, an ageing former Stalinist, a combat veteran of the Spanish Civil War, and guerrilla leader during the military dictatorship, widely respected amongst PT activists. The campaign also reflected the PT leadership view that left party factions had contributed to the party's failure to secure the 1989 election (Sluyter-Beltrao, 2010: 317).

The argument was unambiguous. De Carvalho argued that moderates and radicals were incompatible in a liberal democracy. PT's electoral success would depend upon "consolidation of its position at the centre of a broad party alliance" (Sluyter-Beltrao, 2010: 318). The attack was followed by a *Teoria e Debate* interview with SC leader Valério Arcary, an "ostensibly 'balancing' exploration of the hard left perspective" (Sluyter-Beltrao, 2010: 319). But Sluyter-Beltrao, reporting the exchange, was unimpressed. No friend of the hard left, he nevertheless spots a deliberately "aggressive" interview, designed to put the interviewer's argument more "coherently and elegantly" (Sluyter-Beltrao, 2010: 319, fn71).

Behind this rhetoric lurked the far more important argument that had dogged the PT leadership for several years, following the victory of democracy over the military dictatorship—SC's promotion of factory occupations as a strategic weapon in the class struggle. As we saw earlier, this provoked accusations about SC using "workers as pawns in ugly spectacles of factory occupations" from PT and CUT leaders. These remarks were made by mainstream Articulation union leaders during a crucial election in February 1990 for control of Brazil's fourth largest metal workers' union, MWU-São Jose dos Campos.[301] "Stunning then was the [SC-led] left slate subsequent victory by a substantial margin (5,785 to 4,760) despite active public support for Articulation from both Lula and—for the first time—CUT president Jair Meneguelli" (Sluyter-Beltrao, 2010: 291-2).

"For Meneguelli, who had consistently demonstrated genuine commitment to being the leader of *all* CUT factions, this was a jarring shift. Widely criticised ... Meneguelli admitted he had erred and promised that it would not happen again but the aura of his neutrality had been broken." The Articulation leadership were losing support at a critical moment. The new Collor administration was digging in, its neoliberal "reforms", were kicking in with the beginnings of relentless job losses. In 1990 the number of industrial workers in the state of São Paulo fell by 10 percent (Sluyter-Beltrao, 2010: 292 fn16, 18).

"The left minority factions had established themselves as the CUT's advancing camp, often taking advantage of Articulation's strategic waffling" (Sluyter-Beltrao, 2010: 292). Strikes by electrical workers, social security workers and bank workers were led by SC and CUT *pela base,* CUT from below. The part played by CUT *pela base* was potentially very important. Here was an opportunity to unite the most militant and advanced sections of the Trotskyist Left with others who shared some of their views. Valério Arcary, Socialist Convergence leader, explains:

> This third current, bigger than us but smaller than Articulation, was very plural, very diversified. You have the very left wing of Catholic unionism, some anarcho-syndicalist tendencies but they came from the left wing of the Catholic Church of Brazil ... Pastoral Operária, Waldemar Rossi, their main leader... the Trotskyists with roots in Europe, associated with the tendency of Ernest Mandel, and smaller groups. This sector was a fighting sector, although politically they were inclined to accept the political leadership of the majority of the WP [ie the PT]. So you had this ambivalence, fighters in the unions, but their political references inside the WP were ... in tension but collaborative ... for the Lula leadership.[302]

However, this important opening for the far left proved to be only momentary. The Articulation CUT leadership was consolidating its grip and in a particularly ominous way. It was increasingly involved with the ICFTU, the International Confederation of Free Trade Unions, and its strong ties to the conservative trade union AFL-CIO leaderships in the US, the TUC in the UK, and their equivalents in the rest of Western Europe. By 1989 two major training schools and associated projects, organised by the Articulation leadership in Brazil, had been funded to the tune of $10m with assistance from the ICFTU. Affiliation to the ICFTU was perceived by the majority leadership as critical to gaining hegemony over the CUT and "a unionism that accepts much of business competitiveness agenda" (Sluyter-Beltrao, 2010: 410-11).

It is not surprising then that alongside the demand for occupations to resist the impending factory closures associated with Collor's anticipated acceleration of the neoliberal programme, the idea of democratically elected factory committees or factory commissions revived as a means for re-asserting rank and file trade unionism. CUT president Jair Meneguelli had been quite open about why they had been abandoned. They "don't exist, in truth, because they would share power with union leaders ... The more people you organise, the more people you have stepping on your toes and giving you a hard time in the union" (Sluyter-Beltrao, 2010: 283, fn5).

This position would be sealed with the expulsion of SC from the PT in 1992 for campaigning publicly for an immediate presidential election after Collor's impeachment, contrary to the leadership's policy. Two years later this current launched an independent revolutionary organisation, the Partido Socialista dos Trabalhadores Unificado, United Socialist Workers Party (PSTU), which remains a powerful force on the Brazilian radical left. But with their expulsion, any prospect vanished of the PT developing into a political combat organisation based at the point of production through factory commissions.

Meanwhile the FI and Socialist Democracy continued to believe that their electoral participation leading to a Lula presidential victory in 1994 would provoke a class confrontation with revolutionary implications. However, João Machado reports disagreements opening up within the FI leadership with both Mandel and Bensaïd voicing doubts about this perspective. And certainly by 2002, when Lula actually won the presidential election, Machado reports telling Bensaïd that the Lula government "would be even worse than he thought" (Machado, 2012).

Daniel went back to Brazil in 2002 and although he could write, with some justification, that Lula's victory "was also to a degree our victory", he was under no illusions about the implications. "Politically ... the country had changed. Lula sat in the Planalto [Palace] where the generals had been enthroned. Since 1994, his PR advisers had set out to fashion him a respectable image. No more wrinkled suits and tousled hair ... ironically termed 'genetically modified' by the leaders of the landless peasant movement ... The ex-Trotskyists in his entourage, who had rallied to the neoliberal model, were also dressed up to the nines."

In December 2003, Daniel would witness the beginning of the expulsions of the FI-linked Trotskyists in Socialist Democracy. Some were now prominent and very popular PT politicians like Heloisa Helena, who had struggled to maintain basic principles, now excluded officially for opposing the party's plans for pension "reform" (Bensaïd, 2013: 227, 228).[303]

Later Daniel would reflect on the strategy of viewing a potential PT Lula government as a "workers' government":

> It would be irresponsible to provide a solution that is universally valid; nevertheless, three criteria can be variously combined for assessing participation in a government coalition with a transition perspective:
>
> The question of participation arises in a situation of crisis or at least of a significant upsurge in social mobilisation ...
>
> The government in question is committed to initiating a dynamic of rupture with the established order. For example ... radical agrarian reform, "despotic incursions" into the domain of private property, the abolition of tax privileges, a break with institutions...treaties, military pacts, etc.
>
> Finally, the balance of forces allows revolutionaries to ensure that even if they cannot guarantee that the non-revolutionaries in the government keep to their commitments, they have to pay a high price for failure to do so.

In this light participation in the Lula government in Brazil appears to have been mistaken:

> For ten years or so, with the exception of the landless movement, the mass movement has been on the retreat.
>
> the colour of Lula's social-neoliberal politics was clearly shown in his electoral campaign and in his Letter to the Brazilians (promising to keep to the previous government's financial commitments). The financing of his agrarian reform and "zero-hunger" programme was mortgaged in advance.
>
> Finally, the social balance of forces within both the party and the government was such that to be a half-minister in agriculture [referring to a DS member] was not to support the government "like a rope supports a hanged man"[304] but rather like a hair that could not. That said, and taking into account the history of the country, its social structure and the formation of the PT, we chose not to make this a matter of principle (though we expressed our reservations orally to the comrades about participation and alerted them to the dangers). We preferred to go along with the experiment so as to draw up the balance sheet alongside the comrades, rather than give lessons "from a distance" (Bensaïd, 2007).

Conclusion

The two very different Trotskyist interventions or experiments with PT, the Workers' Party in Brazil, failed. The political argument developed in this book suggests the following thought experiment as an alternative. It requires a "what if" and "what ifs" are pure speculation, "counterfactuals" so much disliked in the academy. Nevertheless, what if the Trotskyist organisations had combined around a perspective of building revolutionary socialist organisation in the factory commissions? It would have meant immediate expulsion. But what kind of organisation would have emerged? Crucially, would it have carried a significant sector of PT's worker-base?

First, by the early 1990s we have seen that the PT/CUT leaderships wanted to close down factory commissions, precisely because of the threat they posed to PT/CUT political authority. Secondly, on the most optimistic forecasts, the Trotskyists had some level of support from about a third of PT activists; SC selling 10,000 papers to PT activists hints at the possibility of the beginnings of a mass base. But, of course, this does not translate into the same level of support outside PT. Perhaps thousands of workers may have been ready to endorse a revolutionary socialist perspective from individual PT leaders. It does not follow that they would support the same leaders outside PT. When SC were expelled, they left with just 1,500 members. PT was greater than the sum of its parts. The strength of its parts depended to a significant extent on the mass-based credibility of the society-wide organisation. Thirdly, the Trotskyists themselves could not escape the mind-numbing impact of the implosion of Soviet Communism. Orthodox Trotskyism itself retained illusions in Soviet Communism as in some sense an advance on capitalism.[305] But most important of all, the public mood was deeply affected by a "common-sense" acceptance that Communism had been tried and failed. As Renato, the SC worker-militant, was quoted earlier in this chapter, world capitalism's ideologues told workers that all communists "thought like Stalin and that the communist or socialist system was not a democratic system".

PT and the revolutionary left were caught up in an international crisis for socialism and communism confronting a neoliberal onslaught which they were ideologically ill-equipped to resist. The pattern was everywhere and exactly at the same time, the early 1990s, particularly acute with the outcome of three very different major struggles that helped shape politics and history at the close of the last century that we have studied in earlier chapters. In South Africa the successful overthrow of apartheid gave way to the ANC, the African National Congress and the SACP, the South African Communist Party, as they formed the first post-apartheid government, capitulating to the neoliberal demands of the IMF, the International Monetary Fund and the World Bank and foregoing any attempts at serious wealth re-distribution. In Poland at the so-called "Round Table" negotiations, the former Solidarity leaders, who had so courageously confronted the military dictatorship that had masqueraded as "Communism", gave way to a Western banks' imposed privatisation agenda that immediately created mass unemployment and a destruction of the equality and self-management ideals of the original Solidarity workers' movement.

In Iran, the "Green" street protest movement, trying to complete the democratic revolution of 1979, which had stalled as a theocracy rather than a democracy, undermined itself by accepting a Western democratic model tainted by neoliberal principles (Rostami-Povey, 2010: 48). This was a particular tragedy because the original 1979 Iranian Revolution, one of the most significant events of the last century, had briefly witnessed the appearance of "shoras", democratically-elected workers' councils. The shoras challenged the right of both employer and government to manage at the point of production, anticipating a practical return of the beginnings of a real communism where workers, and the mass of the population, control both economics and politics based on a democratic mandate. But this debate had disappeared in the 1990s, leaving only Margaret Thatcher's acronym, TINA, There Is No Alternative to free market capitalism, and the catastrophic consequences that are enveloping the third decade of the new century.

CONCLUSION

Sparks for the Future

The independent workers' movements in Poland, South Africa, Iran, and Brazil have sometimes been compared to the revolutionary syndicalist workers' movements in the early part of the last century.[306] There is little agreement on a precise definition of revolutionary syndicalism (van der Linden 2003: 49-84).[307] Here I concentrate on what syndicalism seems to have in common with the workers' movements in Poland, South Africa, Iran, and Brazil, adapting a definition used by the Iranian scholar Assef Bayat. He described syndicalism, in the case of Iran, as workers' action confined to the industrial workplace, assuming in principle that social relations at the point of production were the determining factor in the social structure (Bayat, 1987: 146).[308] It will be argued that this focus, or partial definition, also fits the other case studies rather well. It raises the crucial question: can workers seize control of the means of production without confronting the state?

The question had been raised particularly dramatically during the mass strike and wave of factory occupations that swept Italy in September 1920, as 1 million workers took over the running of the factories, with factory councils springing up across the country. As Ralph Darlington has observed, "even though workers took control of production, the capitalist class still maintained a firm grip on the institutions of political state power, including the army and police...two irreconcilable forces found themselves locked in mortal combat" (Darlington 2008: 250). Darlington cites Gramsci's damning assessment: "It is essential that workers should not believe for one instant that the communist revolution is as easy to accomplish as the occupation of an undefended factory. These events, on the contrary ... show up with blinding clarity the ... anarcho-syndicalist utopia" (Darlington, 2008: 251). Gramsci goes on to insist that a political-economic centre, the workers' state, is essential to unite one factory to another and to take over the banks to support workers' self-management. In April of the same year, 50,000 troops had been in the city of Turin, the main organising centre for the factory occupations, with armed reinforcements on the city's outskirts. Gramsci had similarly warned not to limit "insurrectional action to a factory or a town". The factory occupation is "just one element in relation to state power" (Darlington 2008: 251).[309]

In the end the Italian Socialist Party and the trade union leaders defused the situation which ended the factory occupations, despite their rhetorical enthusiasm for them. But the employers were severely shaken by the experience. Socialist revolution may have been put on hold but counter revolution now stalked in the shadows. Mussolini and Italian fascism began their march to power. Of course, this in no way dampened Gramsci's awe and respect for the workers' creativity in the factory occupations. They had indeed confirmed Marx's and Engels's 1848 *Communist Manifesto* prediction that workers could seize control and reorganise production in their own interests. But the question of who controlled the state was left fatally unanswered, which is why Lenin's *The State and Revolution* is the 20th century complement of the *Communist Manifesto*.

This perspective provides the framework for the rest of this conclusion, comparing and contrasting the case studies at different levels: first (I), the limitations on even very advanced forms of workers' control imposed both by pre-revolutionary and post-revolutionary national-state structures; second (II), the relations between organised workers at the point of production and the urban poor, the argument hinging on the former winning the support of the latter for a successful confrontation with the state; third (III), the relations between organised workers at the point of production and the professional technocrats, engineers and managers, again, the argument hinging on the former winning at least some support from the latter: fourth, (IV), the role of rank and file workers' leaders and worker intellectuals at the point of production and their need for a revitalised non-Stalinist communist party or revolutionary socialist party to maximise their effectiveness; fifth, (V) the conservative role of the Communist state in Poland and the Communist parties in South Africa and Iran: how they undermined the independent workers' movements in the three countries and their implicit aspirations for a genuine communism based upon workers' control of production. This made it very difficult to develop new independent communist or revolutionary socialist parties to articulate a revitalised communist narrative which could both compete with the dominant ideologies in the resistance movements and minimise the negative legacy of Soviet Communism, which also played an important role in Brazil at the end of the 1980s.

I. The limits of workers' control

In Poland, Jacek Kuroń and the KOR leadership that transferred to Solidarity brought with them the "Anti-Politics" perspective of the so-called *self-limiting* revolution. Workers' self-management was to be extracted from the Soviet Communist satellite state of Poland through negotiations, without provoking Moscow's intervention with Soviet tanks. But this perspective was shattered at Bydgoszcz, March 1981. The call for an all-out general strike—in response to the police assault on Solidarity leaders—would have brought Poland to a halt (as it had done in the earlier four-hour general strike). The loyalty of the Communist Party membership and the morale of Poland's police and army were disintegrating by the hour. But just the threat of Moscow's intervention forced a retreat, and the general strike was abandoned. Martial law was imposed at the end of the year. At least, however, Poland's independent Solidarity workers' movement had reached its full potential—it had demonstrated a fundamental Marxist principle that an organised workers' movement can provide political leadership for all the oppressed and all others across society, the vast majority.

In South Africa the "workerist"-led independent workers' movement did not reach its full potential. It became instead a very junior, indeed, arguably, subservient, partner of the ANC, the African National Congress. It had failed to stand by one of the very principles it, itself, had enunciated. As reported in Chapter 3, in 1982, a white trade union organiser had been tortured to death in a police station. FOSATU, the recently formed Federation of South African Trade Unions, which preceded COSATU, called strikes on the day of his funeral. More than 100,000 workers responded. The solidarity strike helped inspire the legendary speech by FOSATU general secretary, Joe Foster, at the Federation's 1982 April conference. The Foster speech came to be seen as a "manifesto" for the "workerist" movement, with its very advanced and unambiguous aspirations for workers' control of production.

But did those aspirations go beyond the workplace? A recently published paper, defending "workerism" and FOSATU, insists that they did: "Nor did workerism reject struggles beyond the workplace. FOSATU stated it would 'support any democratic organisation involved in struggles in the community'" (Byrne, Ulrich, and van der Walt, 2017: 263).[310] But the test of this principle—solidarity—had presented itself very dramatically with the miners' strike of August 1987. "Workerism" failed the test. An ANC-induced strategy of "ungovernability" had come to the townships. After the launch of COSATU in 1985, it spread to the workplaces with a strike wave, successful because of solidarity action. With the miners' strike, the largest strike in South African history bringing paralysis to the coal, gold and all the precious metals mines, the heartbeat of the apartheid economy, ungovernability threatened the apartheid state itself. But the miners could not win without solidarity. James Motlatsi, former working migrant miner and National Union of Mineworkers' president at the time of the 1987 strike, and the strike's principal leader, alongside general secretary Cyril Ramaphosa, accepted this position in my interview with him. Similarly, Bethuel Maserumule, one of the most militant "workerist" leaders in the metal workers' union, NUMSA, deplored the failure of metal workers' solidarity with the 1987 miners' strike.

The reality was that "workerism" did tend to trap itself

within the confines of the workplace. This was illustrated very vividly in Karl von Holdt's study of the "workerist" stronghold at Highveld steelworks, one of South Africa's biggest industrial companies, producer of precious metals, also owned by Anglo American, the main mining company. The Witbank region also produced most of the country's coal, in turn producing half of South Africa's electricity. The Witbank mines were also amongst the most militant in the country. But there was no steel worker solidarity with the miners. von Holdt noted a failure at the steel-works to discuss socialist politics. This was historically a classic criticism of syndicalism (Darlington, 2008: 233-45).

Maserumule also observed that "workerism" repeatedly underestimated the impact and ideological influence of the ANC and the national liberation movement outside the workplaces. There is an interesting comparison here with the independent workers' movement in the Iranian revolution. The workers' councils' or shoras' influence was also restricted to the work-places. Impressive though the shoras were, they were unable to withstand either the ideological or organisational onslaught of political Islam. Here the question of who controlled the state was crucial. Workers' control of production and even distribution was often very advanced. But in the oil industry, in particular, which was the leader both in terms of the economy as well as in terms of workers' resistance, both before and after the fall of the Shah, the question of state control was never in doubt. Oil workers' shoras might impose far-reaching demands on local management but ultimately, they had to contend with national state management. This raised the question of what kind of post-revolutionary "Islamic" state, democratic or theocratic? At least in a democratic state, the Marxist left might have had a voice.

But it was never going to be a workers' state. This would have meant the transformation of the shoras into the equivalents of the early soviets in the Russian Revolution. But this necessitated a Marxist left that properly understood the complexity of the situation, itself dependent upon open political discussion—anathema to the Stalinist tradition which dominated the Iranian Marxist left—having far greater roots both in the shoras as well as amongst the urban poor, a decisive base for political Islam. The question of the urban poor will be considered shortly but before this part of the discussion closes, the comparative strengths, as well as the weaknesses, of these independent workers' movements must also be briefly acknowledged.

Karol Modzelewski remains Poland's principal witness to the strength of feeling generated by the aspiration to workers' self-management, the defining characteristic of the Solidarity movement. He might have broken with the Marxism of the *Open Letter* he had co-written with Jacek Kuroń, but he remained committed to the Marxist principle of workers taking control of their own lives by taking control of the means of production. He looked on with mounting incredulity as the "reformed" Solidarity leaders, many personal friends now converted to a neo-liberal agenda, trampled all over this principle at the so-called Round Table negotiations in 1989 which dismantled the Soviet Communist-style Polish state.

Modzelewski took this shock and despair to his grave in 2019. It is also appropriate to recall that Jan Rulewski, one of the Solidarity leaders badly beaten by the police at the height of the Bydgoszcz revolutionary crisis in March 1981, was a bicycle design engineer who relished the prospect of workers' involvement in the design of exciting new bicycle products appropriate for the 21st century. In Rulewski's view, here was a source of innovation far more dynamic and potentially productive than reliance on the crisis-prone driver of capitalist competition. Black workers at the South African East London plant of Mercedes-Benz in the early 1990s also proved self-managed workers to be far more productive than workers managed by capitalists. They built a special bullet-proof luxury model as a gift for Nelson Mandela. Union power in the plant was such that management had rapidly agreed. Mandela's car came off the production line so quickly and with so few faults that it provoked outrage and astonishment from the company chairman.

As noted, this was a tribute indeed from one of international capital's most prestigious corporations.

In the Iranian Revolution, Torab Saleh gave the example of the largest battery factory in Iran, employing 500-600 workers, a joint venture company with its base in Japan providing the technology. After the revolution, the Iranian management fled and the workers' shora took over. Quality control was based in Japan, so they sent samples to Japan to prove they could maintain technological standards. They attempted to establish their own distribution networks, even setting up tents to sell the batteries outside the factory which was part of the country's main industrial centre. Of course, this could only be a temporary arrangement. It was almost political and economic theatre but that made it no less significant. Inevitably, the Japanese parent company and the Iranian state would undermine their efforts. Yet workers' self-management had been proved possible. But it was sustainable only if it had been part of a far wider political movement, rising to the challenge of both a hostile national state and, in this case, an ultimate dependency on international capitalism.

II. Workers and the rest of the poor

In Poland, the Solidarity workers' movement commanded the support of the vast majority in society. This was confirmed when Rural Solidarity was formed, the countryside backing the towns and cities, the Bydgoszcz crisis perceived correctly as existentially threatening to the Soviet-backed Polish state. In South Africa and Iran, the organised workers' movements alone could never claim majority support. This hinged on the role of the urban poor. In South Africa, this had expressed itself in the tension between "populists" in the townships and the "workerists" in the workplaces. The exiled ANC and the SACP leaderships saw the township rather than the shopfloor worker as the primary agency of liberation from apartheid. In 1985, this was by no means secure. Indeed, the launch of COSATU triggered a strike wave which might have shifted that balance, if the miners' strike had been successful. The apartheid state itself expressed this fear by putting on trial for treason in 1986 metalworkers' leader and leading "workerist", Moses Mayekiso, the prosecution papers making it clear that they wanted to break the link between workplace and community-based politics.

SACP leader Jo Slovo had described the UDF (the ANC-backed United Democratic Front in the townships) as the umbrella of the broad legal liberation front. Slovo's 1988 paper, *The South African Working Class and the National Democratic Revolution*, explicitly ruled out a political role for COSATU. The exiled liberation movement led by the ANC and the SACP had a growing and strong internal base in the townships, including the township majority, the urban poor. "Workerist" politics, by contrast, were frail and could not compete, even though Mayekiso was right, shop floor power at the point of production was potentially the decisive ingredient for a successful revolution against the apartheid state. This conundrum can only be unravelled by exploring the politics of the SACP, to which we will return.

In Iran, the Islamic movement, with its base in the mosques, was the loudest voice amongst the urban poor, in the cities' slums, shanty towns, and especially the tiny traditional workshops in the bazaars. The mosques were also a decisive influence even in the more modern industrial sector, including the oil industry. And this was not just because most workers were religious. The traditional left, led by the old Communist Tudeh Party, was in forced exile. The New Left, in the form of urban guerrilla organisations, mainly the Fadaiyan and the Islamic leftist Mojahedin, with their preoccupation with the armed struggle, were slow in realising the potential of the revolutionary mass movement gathering both on the streets and in the workplaces. Street demonstrations and later industrial strike plans were often made in the mosques. The leftist groups were late in rooting themselves in the workplaces.

Bayat makes a spirited defence of some leftist and independent organisation amongst the urban poor but concedes a vital point of the Islamists' strategy and ideology: "The portrayal of the revolution by new Islamic leaders as the *inqilab-I mustaz'afin*, the revolution of the downtrodden, signified the so-called centrality of the underclass to the revolutionary process" (Bayat, 1997: 37). In my interview with him, former Fadaiyan leader, Farrokh Negahdar, explained well the overwhelming pressure exerted by the Islamists. The bazaars, as much as the mosques and the factories, were major organising units of the revolution. The innovative interventions of the workers' shoras in the modern workplaces had the potential to assert overall political leadership, to become the "tribune of the people". That was the challenge for the independent leftist groups, belatedly rooting themselves in the shoras. But they could not meet it, unable to abandon the legacy-as-burden of failed official Communist politics both at national state and political party levels. In Brazil the gap between the organised workers in the big workplaces and the "shirtless" poor dominating the *favelas* was an important limitation on the influence of the far left within the Workers' Party (PT).

III. Workers and "technocrats"

In their *Open Letter* to the Polish Communist Party, Kuroń and Modzelewski, anticipating a revolutionary workers' movement against Poland's Soviet-satellite state, had warned against what they described as the "technocratic current" undermining the resistance. This was the social layer of professional technocrats, engineers and managers, traditionally politically conservative but capable of asserting their own independent political demands in times of economic, social and political crisis. This social layer is indispensable to any system of workers' control or self-management. Even the demand for workers' self-management betrays a potential ambiguity in relation to these professional experts. For some, but by no means all, Polish managers who supported Solidarity, "self-management" offered the prospect of breaking away from the Polish Communist state system in favour of the "free market". An independent workers' co-operative might be proposed which would then seek foreign private investment, some members of the "technocratic current" re-inventing themselves as entrepreneurial capitalists. This was a perspective very much favoured by the purveyors of neoliberalism who stalked Solidarity during the martial law period in the mid to late 1980s and who were so brilliantly exposed in those autobiographical extracts of Karol Modzelewski cited in Chapter 2 above.

However, Saeed Rahnema, the Iranian scholar cited in Chapter 4, demonstrated that this was a contested pathway for the "technocratic current" in the Iranian Revolution. Some of the white-collar specialists, engineers, and other professionals in the leaderships of the shora movements, including the oil and steel industries, were committed socialists ready to put their skills at the service of a revolution which they saw as potentially socialist. It was argued that this reinforced the view of the sociologist Erik Olin Wright who proposed that this social layer was ambiguously placed in the class structure, in "contradictory class locations" and susceptible to the pressures of rank and file organised workers if it proved possible to align their mutual interests. In Poland too there were outstanding examples of white-collar specialists, Solidarity leaders, committed to the workers' cause—for example, Jan Rulewski, the bicycle design engineer committed to workers' control and at the centre of the Bydgoszcz revolutionary crisis in March 1981, also Andrzej Gwiazda, professional engineer, one of Solidarity's most outstanding leaders. It is worth recalling the report of the journalist and academic Tim Garton Ash who travelled with Gwiazda in the early months of the Solidarity upheavals. He described "Gwiazda as a fighter for fundamental principles, with more than a streak of intransigence ... more closely in tune with the mood of the workers than the counsellors of caution."

As I pointed out in Chapter 2, I interviewed Andrzej Gwiazda and his wife Joanna Duda-Gwiazda, also a founder of the Free Trade Unions which preceded Solidarity, in November 2017 at their flat overlooking the port at Gdańsk, Solidarity's birthplace. The Gwiazdas were middle class professionals who had effectively "proletarianised" themselves. Irrespective of their political outlook today, they proved to be hardened fighters throughout the 1980s, sharing the contempt expressed by Modzelewski for the Solidarity leadership that collapsed into neoliberalism. The experience of the workers' movements both in Iran and Poland proved it was possible to win some significant support from this vital layer of middle class professionals. In South Africa, the apartheid structure made this almost impossible. The "technocratic current" was almost exclusively white and pro-regime.

IV. Workers and intellectuals

Worker-intellectuals, who emerge as leaders in independent workers' struggles, are not simply discovering suppressed personal natural talents. They are the most articulate exponents of a fascinating trend in revolutionary periods, the opening up to knowledge, previously understood to be beyond the reach of the ordinary man or woman. Solidarity workers' leader Władysław Frasyniuk expressed this extremely well. But Wladysław Frasyniuk's educational programme politically was, perhaps understandably, limited to extolling the virtues of the freedoms available in liberal democracies. Marxist classics were ruled out, assumed to be tainted by, and even responsible for, the totalitarian practice of the Soviet Union and its satellite state system. This denied Polish workers the ultimate intellectual challenge: how to grasp Marxist ideas untainted by Stalinism. Kuroń and Modzelewski's *Open Letter* might have been a start-point. But as we saw in Chapter 2, Kuroń was by now aggressively denouncing the pamphlet. This also meant that Polish workers had no idea how similar the Solidarity revolution was, in its early phases, to the Russian Revolution, in *its* early phases—not least the enthusiasm for workers to widen their intellectual horizons.[311]

By contrast, Bethuel Maserumule, the South African black "workerist" leader, had no such problem with the Marxist classics. He had read Marx, Lenin, Trotsky, Luxemburg, and also Mao, Che (A-BM: 333). However, I was surprised when he told me that he found Maoism and guerrilla-ist concepts and approaches to struggle more useful. I believe this helped inform his, in my opinion, mistaken judgement in supporting the division between the shop stewards and the strike committee at the strategically important Highveld steelworks that I analysed in Chapter 3 above. But my opinion is not the point here. The point is the political and intellectual argument itself as illustration of how Bethuel developed as a worker intellectual. And I was delighted when Bethuel attended my presentation of a summarised version of the South African chapter of my thesis at a conference in Johannesburg in June 2019, and participated fully in the discussion afterwards.[312] It is perhaps worth emphasising that Bethuel has enthusiastically endorsed the interview I did with him.

There can be no question that many workers' leaders in the Iranian Revolution were worker intellectuals. Ali Pichgah, oil workers' leader in the repairs section of the Tehran oil refinery during the revolution, described the unexpected way the repair workers made contact with the wider workforce which would help lay the basis for the Tehran oil refinery shora. Recited poetry helped cement workers' unity. There were women worker intellectuals in the leadership of the Iranian oil workers' shoras. Kobra Qasemi was one of the three women activists amongst the 60 representatives elected to the leading committee of the General Shora Oil Employees of Ahwaz, capital of Khuzestan capital, Iran's southern oil field regional state. They represented shoras in the oil fields, the production units, maintenance departments, and administrative offices in and around the city. She was also one of hundreds of Fadaiyan members arrested in the summer of 1979 as a prelude to the Islamic regime breaking the independent left in the oil industry. A former sociology graduate, she had a low-level administrative office job but this in no way inhibited her provoking arguments amongst her comrades. It is worth recalling what she told me in Chapter 4 above about the debates she provoked. Unfortunately, Kobra's political organisation blocked rather than facilitated her intellectual and political potential.

The most prominent worker leaders, those the regimes most feared because of their widespread influence, were the ones they singled out and tried to silence. They were all developing as worker-intellectuals. South Africa's Moses Mayekiso, the "workerist" metal workers' leader, put on trial for treason in 1986. Andrej Słowik, former bus driver, Poland Solidarity's Łódź regional leader who promoted "Active Strikes", the euphemism for workers trying to take control of production and distribution, and which helped precipitate the imposition of martial law in December 1982. Słowik, jailed and tortured in the 1980s, became Deputy Minister of Labour under Kuroń in the "Solidarity" government in the early 1990s. Słowik vehemently denied he was a worker-intellectual. Yet look again at the extracts from his interview in Chapter 2. Despite himself, he is not only a would-be intellectual but one grappling with the legacy of Karl Marx.

Yadollah Khosroshahi, who helped create the Iranian Syndicate of Oil Workers in the 1970s and was jailed by the Shah, released, along with others, in 1978 when demonstrations against the Shah began. Khomeini's regime would arrest him again in early 1982, along with other leaders of the Shora of Oil Industry Employees (*Showra-ye Sarasari-ye Karkonan-e san 'at-e Naft*), following its suppression. A number of them were executed and others sentenced to long imprisonments. Khosroshahi was released in March 1983 and fled the country. He later died in London. A critical concern for Khosroshahi was that the workers' movement had "no vision of socialism", hence the need for a new socialist party (Khosroshahi: 2013). The problem of how to revitalise that vision in the shadow of Soviet Communism and its Iranian apologists was never resolved. The same applied in Poland, South Africa, and Brazil. It also meant that the nascent worker intellectuals were unable fully to develop their political abilities.

V. The legacy of Stalinism

The historic role of the Solidarity-led workers' movement in

Poland, in the period 1980-82, before the imposition of martial law, has yet to be properly acknowledged. Ten million strong, it was arguably the largest, most democratic mass revolutionary workers' movement ever witnessed: its domineering demand for workers' self-management echoing one of the most powerful sentiments of the earlier 1968 global upheavals. Without doubt, it was the most important independent mass workers' movement to confront the Soviet Russian satellite state system of Communist dictatorships in the 20th century. It played a unique part in destroying those dictatorships, helping precipitate the implosion of Soviet Communism in 1989. And it has left us a web of unresolved paradoxes.

It was a revolutionary workers' movement that wanted to avoid a revolution, in its own words, wanting instead a self-limiting revolution demanding reform of the Polish Communist state, yet helped to overturn the 20th century's largest and most important Communist inter-state system. At the same time, it itself displayed all of the characteristics of a genuine mass democratic communist workers' movement, except for one major and decisive impediment, the absence of a communist theory underpinned by a communist organisation which could have helped develop that theory, test it and revise it as circumstances dictated, generating appropriate strategies and tactics amongst workers and intellectuals. Zbigniew Kowalewski, a Solidarity leader in Łódź, addressed these concerns in considerable detail in Chapter 2, where he outlined the extraordinary difficulties of posing a genuine communist or revolutionary socialist alternative in the oppressive context of confronting a state system acting both in the name of communism and using, or rather misusing, its political language and concepts. The absence of communist theory and organisation, or perhaps it is preferable to write the absence of a non-Stalinist Marxist theory and organisation, created a political vacuum at the heart of the Solidarity movement.

That vacuum was filled at first by Solidarity's theory of a self-limiting revolution which proved to be such a disaster, ill equipping it to confront the aggressive posture of the Moscow-backed Polish state which ultimately made it plain it would not tolerate a self-limiting revolution. After martial law, neoliberalism ideologically cemented the defeat that martial law came to represent for Solidarity. It is worth noting the irony that both victor and vanquished, the Communist authorities and the cowed Solidarity leadership, had both succumbed to neoliberalism when the Communist system imploded in 1989. Chapter 2 argued that this was not an inevitable process. The left had failed to theorise effectively Poland's crisis in the 1970s, seeing it only through the lens of the stagnation of Soviet Communism rather than the additionally wider stagnation of the global economy which was increasingly dominating both East and West. Poland's politics might have been ultimately controlled from Moscow, but its economics was increasingly dependent on the goodwill of the Western banks, their loans increasingly linked to determining Poland's economic policies.

On the basis of this, Chapter 2 posed the possibility of Kuroń and Modzelewski responding differently to the weaknesses of their original *Open Letter*. Rather than abandoning it, they might have revised it, re-presenting it as an updated *Communist Manifesto* for our times, developing their original critical analysis of Soviet Communism but linking it to the wider crisis of the global capitalist economy. This might have helped Solidarity leaders see their struggle as being both against Soviet Communism and the global capitalist economy, rather than seeing the latter as saviour. Of course, this argument merits nothing more than a political thought-experiment but it is posed to underline the possibility of an alternative approach. At the same time, it acknowledges the enormity of the negative influence of Soviet Communism, even at, and perhaps because of, the very moment of its historic disintegration, and its capacity to eliminate the possibility of an alternative communism.

Again, in Iran, the potential of the workers' shora movement in the Iranian Revolution of 1979 to have resisted the consolidation of a semi-totalitarian theocratic Islamic state has yet to be properly acknowledged. Here again the absence of a non-Stalinist Marxist theory and organisation proved decisive. The independent leftist groups that belatedly rooted themselves in the shoras, especially the secular leftist Fadaiyan, carried too much Stalinist baggage. This prevented them developing the strategies and tactics required to respond to the remarkably innovative phenomenon that was the political Islamic mass movement. This is particularly true of its very effective leftist posture which included class struggle rhetoric mimicking the Marxist left as well as legitimate hostility to Eastern or Soviet imperialism, an argument which the major leftist groups simply could not answer. United front strategy and tactics were required that were not available in the Stalinist repertoire. Again, these arguments were addressed in Chapter 4 through the interviews with former Fadaiyan leaders and will not be repeated here.

Similarly, the united front strategy, discussed in the chapter, which the Fadaiyan and other leftist groups might have pursued with the left Islamic leaders, critical of Khomeini's plans for a theocratic dictatorship, a mass campaign for a properly democratic Islamic state, will not be repeated here. The workers' shora movement demonstrated beyond doubt the capacity for workers to control production in many different workplaces. It also demonstrated that these could only be short-lived experiments if the national state was hostile. But if that national state, the Iranian Islamic state, had been forced to concede democratic space, the significance of the shora experiment might have found a public voice to remember and articulate it. That could have become a rallying point for the later democracy movements from below and a focus for far-reaching left renewal.

In South Africa the argument is rather different. The "workerist"-led independent workers' movement must accept some responsibility for failing to make the apartheid state ungovernable by the mid-1980s—the stated aim of the ANC and SACP in exile—when it failed to rally around, and provide solidarity for, the great miners' strike in 1987. It is not at all surprising that many of the best "workerist" leaders went on to join the SACP when it was unbanned at the end of the decade. The argument used by SACP leader Joe Slovo aimed at "workerist" leaders was explored in detail in Chapter 3. Plausible though it was, its key weakness was its rhetorical claim about the centrality of the working class to the political process both in terms of the struggle to overthrow apartheid and then the struggle for socialism that would follow. This appeared to cut through the traditional criticism of the SACP that it separated the two struggles into distinct stages. If the working class was central to both struggles then, Slovo insisted, this was a false argument, working class struggle would bridge the two stages. But Slovo undermined his own argument, first, by placing the leadership of the internal struggle against apartheid with the townships and not the workplaces, secondly, by asserting, quite mistakenly, a fundamental misreading of Lenin, that trade union federations like COSATU had no claim to leadership in the political struggle.

The logic of this position led to the Triple Alliance, of the ANC, SACP and COSATU in the early 1990s, which would lead the struggle to end apartheid. But this was not an alliance of equal partners, as Chapter 3 illustrated with several graphic examples. And it paved the way, rather like in Poland, for the almost immediate capitulation by the newly elected ANC government to neoliberal policies with the SACP and COSATU meekly subordinated. Policies like reducing economic inequality, wealth taxes, nationalisation of the mining industry were dumped.

In reality the SACP was completely disoriented by the implosion of Soviet Communism in 1989, posing a unique challenge to Chris Hani, the highly talented and courageous former MK Chief of Staff. Chris Hani was making the transition to become general secretary of the SACP, after its unbanning. Former "workerist" leaders testified to the efforts he made on their behalf: not least in promoting "workers' democracy at plant level". Was there a momentary window when the SACP might have transformed itself into a democratic communist party acknowledging a leading *and independent* role for the working class? This would have meant warning ANC leaders that it would not be dragged along with its capitulation to neoliberal polices. It would have meant a fight with the ANC to win COSATU, organised workers, to openly resist neoliberal policies. Of course, this is pure speculation but it is not without plausible foundations.

At the same time this scenario underestimates the impact of the collapse of Soviet Communism and the growing doubts about its viability that preceded it. Criticisms of the Soviet Union, its lack of democracy, let alone workers' democracy, rejection of Stalin's genocidal polices in the 1930s as detrimental to the communist cause, even dismissed as counter-revolutionary, easily flowed over into a demoralising sense that the original socialist revolution in Russia 1917 was itself flawed. It is noticeable that the independent workers' movements in the four countries, Poland, South Africa, Iran, and Brazil were, admittedly in very different ways, both dogged by the experience of Soviet Communism and lacked confidence to develop sustainable ideological responses which would revitalise a communist project centred on their own self-activity. In each case instead they settled for the limited political objectives flagged up by others, to be sure allies in the original cause in bringing down their oppressors, but wedded ultimately to a new status quo which protected class divisions in a capitalist society.

In Poland, it was the model of Western liberal democracy even as it morphed into its increasingly illiberal nemesis of neoliberalism. In South Africa it was the national liberation promise of the ANC as it also collapsed into neoliberalism, abandoning even its quite mild reforming proposals for at least reducing social and economic inequalities in a post-apartheid capitalist society. In Iran, political Islam, at first with a leftist tinge, simply proved far more popular than the political organisations promising communist alternatives, haunted by the experiences of their northern neighbour over the border, the Soviet Union. The Brazilian Communist Party, while an important historic force, had become relatively marginal by the 1980s, but the collapse of the Stalinist system at the end of that decade played an important role in the efforts by Lula and his allies to drive the PT rightwards.

And yet something did stir in these independent workers' movements which kept alive a spark for the future. Demands for workers' control of production surfaced in all four cases. Implementation was attempted, even if only temporarily, with varying degrees of success. Workers' leaders, potential worker-intellectuals, with deep roots in the mass movements, emerged, perfectly capable of becoming political leaders. One of 1968's greatest slogans, "self-management", resounded across four continents. Alas, they were ideologically and organisationally disarmed and blocked at critical moments when circumstances created openings that might have thrust them forward.

APPENDIX
KEY TO INTERVIEWS

A-AP: Ali Pichgah (Ch4)
A-AG: Andrzej Gwiazda (Ch2)
A-AS: Andrzej Słowik (Ch2)
A-B: "Bijan" (Ch4)
A-BM: Bet
#huel Maserumule (Ch3)
A-DM: Darlene Miller (Ch3)
A-FN: Farrokh Negahdar (Ch4)
A-JM: James Motlatsi (Ch3)
A-JP: Józef Pinior (Ch2)
A-JR: Jan Rulewski (Ch2)
A-KM: Karol Modzelewski (Ch2).
A-ML: Makoma Lekalakala. (Ch3)[313]
A-MM: Moses Mayekiso (Ch3)
A-KQ: Kobra Qasemi (Ch4)
A-MP: Mansor Parhizgar (Ch4)
A-RK: Ronne Kasrils (Ch3)
A-RP: Rob Petersen (Ch3)
A-TS: Torab Saleth (Ch4)
A-WF: Wladysław Frasyniuk (Ch2)
A-ZK: Zbigniew Kowalewski (Ch2)

The text of all the interviews above can be found in the Appendix to John Rose, 2020, "Workers' Power and the Failure of Communism" (PhD Thesis, King's College London), pp 230-409, available at https://kclpure.kcl.ac.uk/ws/files/129644633/2020_Rose_John_1641033_ethesis_version_for_Pure_upload.pdf

The editors have been unable to find any recordings or transcripts of the interviews with Brazilian activists.

Acronyms

ABC Santo Andre, São Bernardo de Campo, and São Caetano do Sul industrial region of São Paulo conurbation (Brazil)

ALN National Liberation Action (Brazil)

ANC African National Congress (South Africa)

ARCFC All-Russia Council of Factory Committees

AZACTU Azanian Confederation of Trade Unions (South Africa)

BC Black Consciousness (South Africa)

CCAWUSA Commercial, Catering, and Allied Workers Union of South Africa

COSATU Congress of South African Trade Unions

CUSA Council of Unions of South Africa

CUT Unified Workers' Central (Brazil)

FCWU Food and Canning Workers Union (South Africa)

FI Fourth International

FOSATU Federation of South African Trade Unions

IMWA International Working Men's Association

IFP Inkatha Freedom Party (South Africa)

IRP Islamic Republican Party (Iran)

IS International Socialists (Britain)

KOR Workers Defence Committee (Poland)

LCR Revolutionary Communist League (France)

MAWU Metal and Allied Workers Union (South Africa)

MK Umkhonto weSizwe (South Africa)

MO Metalworkers Opposition (Brazil)

MWT Marxist Workers Tendency (South Africa)

NP National Party (South Africa)

NRZ Neue Rheinische Zeitung

NUM National Union of Mineworkers (South Africa)

NUMSA National Union of Metalworkers of South Africa (NUMSA)

OSCC Oil-Strikes Coordinating Committee (Iran)

PAC Pan-Africanist Congress (South Africa)

PSOL Party of Socialism and Liberty (Brazil)

PT Workers' Party (Brazil)

PZPR Polish United Workers Party

SACCAWU South African Commercial, Catering, and Allied Workers Union

SACP South African Communist Party

SADF South African Defence Force

SASM South African Student Movement

SAVAK Organisation of National Security and Information (Iran)

SPD Social Democratic Party Germany

SWP Socialist Workers Party (Britain)

TsIK All-Russian Central Executive Committee of Soviets of Workers' and Soldiers' Deputies

UDF United Democratic Front (South Africa)

UNITA National Union for the Total Independence of Angola

BIBLIOGRAPHY

Abel, Richard, 1995, *Politics By Other Means, Law in the Struggle Against Apartheid 1980-94* (New York: Routledge).

Abrahamian, Ervand, *1993, Khomeinism: Essays on the Islamic Republic* (Berkeley: University of California Press).

Abrahamian, Ervand, 1999, *Tortured Confessions: Prisons and Public Recantations on Modern Iran* (Berkeley: University of California Press).

Abrahamian, Ervand, 2008, *A History of Modern Iran* (Cambridge: Cambridge University Press).

Alexander, Anne, and Mostafa Bassiouny, 2014, *Bread, Freedom, Social Justice, Workers and the Egyptian Revolution*, (London: Zed Books).

Ali, Tariq, 2017, *The Dilemmas of Lenin: Terrorism, War, Empire, Love, Revolution* (London: Verso).

Allen, Barbara C, 2016, *Alexander Shlyapnikov 1885-1937 Life of an Old Bolshevik* (Chicago: Haymarket).

Allen, V.L., 2005, *The History of the Black Mineworkers of South Africa: Organise or Die 1982-1994* (London: Moor Press and Merlin).

Almeida Ribeiro de Miranda, Vinicius, 2014, "Dois trotskismos num partido de massas : as trajetórias das organizações Democracia Socialista e Convergência Socialista no PT de 1978 a 1992 (PhD Thesis, State University of Campinas).

Arcary, Valério, 2014, "Os trotskistas e o PT, 35 anos atrás" (4 August), https://esquerdaonline.com.br/2014/08/04/os-trotskistas-e-o-pt-35-anos-atras/

Arcary, Valério, 2019, "Brazil: How Big a Defeat?", *International Socialism 161* (winter),

http://isj.org.uk/brazil-how-big-a-defeat/

Arendt, Hannah, 2006, *Between Past and Future: Eight Exercises in Political Thought* (London: Penguin).

Arthur, CJ, 1996, Introduction, Karl Marx and Friedrick Engels, *The German Ideology* (London: Lawrence & Wishart).

Ascherson, Neal, 2005, "The Victory and Defeat of Solidarnosc", *Open Democracy* (5 September), https://www.opendemocracy.net/en/solidarity_2806jsp/

Ash, Timothy Garton, 1983, *The Polish Revolution 1980-82* (London: Jonathan Cape).

Auer, Stefan, 2006, "The Lost Treasure of the Revolution", *Osteuropa* (25 October), http://www.eurozine.com/the-lost-treasure-of-the-revolution/

Azzellini, Dario, and Immanuel Ness, 2011, eds, *Ours to Master and to Own: Workers' Control from the Commune to the Present* (Chicago: Haymarket)

Barker, Colin, 1986, *Festival of the Oppressed Solidarity: Reform and Revolution in Poland 1980-81* (London: Bookmarks).

Baskin, Jeremy, 1991, *Striking Back: A History of COSATU* (London Verso).

Bayat, Assef, 1987, *Workers' Revolution in Iran: A Third World Experience of Worker's Control* (London: Zed).

Bayat, Assef, 1988, "Labour and Democracy: The Case of Post-Revolutionary Iran", in Amirahmadi, Hooshang, and Maniucher Parvin, eds, *Post Revolutionary Iran* (Westview Press, Boulder).

Bayat, Assef, 1997, *Street Politics: Poor People's Movements in Iran* (New York, Columbia University Press).

Beecham, David, and Ann Eidenham, 1987, "Beyond the Mass strike: Class, Party and Trade Union Struggle in Brazil", *International Socialism 36* (autumn).

Behrooz, Maziar, 2000, *Rebels with a Cause: The Failure of the Left in Iran* (Oxford: I.B. Taurus).

Bell, Terry, 2009, *Comrade Moss, A Political Journey* (Johannesburg: Terry Bell).

Bensaïd, Daniel, 2007, "The Return of Strategy", *International Socialism 113* (winter), http://isj.org.uk/the-return-of-strategy/

Bensaïd, Daniel, 2013, *An Impatient Life, A Memoir* (London: Verso).

Bensimon, Fabrice, Quentin Deluermoz, and Jeanne Moisand, (eds), 2018, *"Arise Ye Wretched of the Earth": The First International in a Global Perspective* (Leiden: Brill).

Birchall, Ian, 2011, *Tony Cliff: A Marxist for His Times* (London: Bookmarks).

Blackledge, Paul, 2014, "The great schism: socialism and war in 1914", *International Socialism 143* (summer), http://isj.org.uk/the-great-schism-socialism-and-war-in-1914/

Bloom, Jack, 2015, *Seeing Through the Eyes of the Polish Revolution: Solidarity and the Struggle against Communism in Poland,* (Chicago: Haymarket).

Botiveau, Raphael, 2017, *Organise or Die: Democracy and Leadership in South Africa's National Union of Mineworkers* (Johannesburg: Wits University Press).

Branford, Sue, and Bernardo Kucinski, 2003, *Politics Transformed: Lula and the Workers' Party of Brazil* (London: Latin American Bureau).

Branford, Sue, 2009, "Brazil: Has the Dream Ended? in Geraldine Lievesley and Steve Ludlam, eds, *Reclaiming Latin America: Experiments in Radical Social Democracy* (London: Zed Books).

Broué, Pierre, 2006, *The German Revolution 1917-23* (Chicago: Haymarket).

Butler, Anthony, 2007, *Cyril Ramaphosa* (Johannesburg: Jacana).

Brzechcyzn, Krzysztof, ed, 2022, *New Developments in the Theory of the Historical Process: Polish Contributions to Non-Marxian Historical Materialism* (Leiden: Brill).

Byrne, Sian, Nicole Ulrich, and Lucien van der Walt, 2017, "Red, Black and Gold: FOSATU, South African 'Workerism', 'Syndicalism' and the Nation", in Edward Webster and Karin Pampallis, eds, *The Unresolved National Question: Left Thought Under Apartheid* (Johannesburg: Wits University Press, 2017).

Callinicos, Alex, 1983, *The Revolutionary Ideas of Karl Marx* (London: Bookmarks).

Callinicos, Alex, 1988, *South Africa between Reform and Revolution* (London: Bookmarks).

Callinicos, Alex, 1990, *Trotskyism* (Milton Keynes: Open University Press).

Callinicos, Alex, 1991, *The Revenge of History, Marxism and the East European Revolutions* (Cambridge: Polity).

Callinicos, Alex, 2004, *Making History, Agency, Structure and Change in Social Theory* (Leiden: Brill).

Callinicos, Alex, 2012, "Daniel Bensaïd and the Broken Time of Politics", *International Socialism 135* (summer), https://isj.org.uk/daniel-Bensaïd-and-the-broken-time-of-politics/#135callinicos4

Callinicos, Alex, 2014, *Deciphering Capital* (London: Bookmarks).

Callinicos, Luli, 1993, "Interview with Comrade Chris Hani" (23 and 31 March), https://www.sahistory.org.za/sites/default/files/archive-files/chris_hani_interviewed_by_luli_callinicos.pdf

Ceruti, Claire, 2021, "The End of Apartheid in South Africa", in Colin Barker, Gareth Dale, and Neil Davidson, *Revolutionary Rehearsals in the Neoliberal Age* (Chicago Haymarket).

Charlton, John, 1997, *The Chartists* (London: Pluto Press).

Chase, Malcolm, 2007, *Chartism: A New History* (Manchester University Press).

Cieochinska, M, 1992, "The Development of the Private Sector in Poland, 1989-1990", *Communist Economies in Transition,* 4.2:2-3-239.

Cliff, Tony, 1978, *Lenin*, Volume 3, *Revolution Besieged* (London: Pluto).

Cliff, Tony, 1988, *State Capitalism in Russia* (London: Bookmarks).

Cohn-Bendit, Daniel, 1968, *Obsolete Communism: The Left-Wing Alternative* (London: Andre Deutsch).

Copelyn, Johnny, 2016, *Maverick Insider, A Struggle for Union Independence in a Time of National Liberation* (Johannesburg: Picador Africa; Kindle edition).

Collins, Henry, and Chimen Abramsky, 1965, *Karl Marx and the British Labour Movement, Years of the First International* (London: Macmillan).

Cronin, Stephanie, 2000, "The Left in Iran: Illusion and Disillusion", *Middle East Studies*, 36.3: 231-43.

Cronin, Stephanie, 2014, *Armies and State Building in the Modern Middle East, Politics, Nationalism and Military Reform* (Oxford: I.B.Tauris).

Darlington, Ralph, 2008, *Syndicalism and the Transition to Communism, An International Comparative Analysis* (Aldershot: Ashgate).

De Oliveira Martins, Richard, 2017,"A tática das ocupações de fábrica na década de 1980: greves do setor metalúrgico em São José dos Campos (SP) e Volta Redonda (RJ)", *XIX História Nacional Simpósio*, https://anpuh.org.br/uploads/anais-simposios/pdf/2019-01/1548953096_7c8534770723bcaec02830ba7eff9aec.pdf

Deutscher, Isaac, 1970a, *The Prophet Armed, Trotsky: 1879-1921* (Oxford: Oxford University Press).

Deutscher, Isaac, 1970b, *The Prophet Unarmed, Trotsky 1921-1929* (Oxford: Oxford University Press).

Draper, Hal, 1977, *Karl Marx's Theory of Revolution*, Volume 1, *State and Bureaucracy* (Monthly Review Press: New York).

Draper, Hal, 1986, *Karl Marx's Theory of Revolution*, Volume 3, *The "Dictatorship of the Proletariat"* (Monthly Review Press, New York).

Dunayevskaya, Raya, 1981, *Women's Liberation and Marx's Philosophy of Revolution,* (Atlantic Highlands NJ: Humanities Press).

Enckell, Marianne, 2018, "Bakunin and the Jura Federation", in Fabrice Bensimon, Quentin Deluermoz, and Jeanne Moisand, eds, *"Arise Ye Wretched of the Earth": The First International in a Global Perspective* (Leiden: Brill).

Engels, Frederick, 1979, *The Condition of the Working Class in England* (London: Panther).

Engels, Frederick, 1993, *Socialism, Utopian and Scientific* (London: Bookmarks).

Erwin, Alec, 2017, "Workerists and the National Question", in Edward Webster and Karin Pampallis, eds, *The Unresolved National Question: Left Thought Under Apartheid*, (Johannesburg: Wits University Press).

Fernbach, David, 1973, Introduction, *The Revolutions of 1848: Marx's Political Writings*, Volume 1 (Harmondsworth: Penguin Books/New Left Review).

Fernbach, David, 1974, Introduction, *The First International and After: Marx's Political Writings*, Volume 3 (Harmondsworth: Penguin Books/ New Left Review).

Fernandes, Florestan, 1991, *O PT em movimento - contribuição ao I Congresso do Partido dos Trabalhadores.* (São Paulo: Ed. Cortez).

Figes, Orlando, 1997, *A People's Tragedy: The Russian Revolution 1891-1924* (London: Pimlico).

Fine, Alan, and Eddie Webster, 1989, "Transcending Traditions: Trade Unions and Political Unity", in *South African Review*, Vol 5 (Johannesburg: Ravan Press).

Fitzpatrick, Sheila, 2017, "What's Left?", *London Review of Books*, 30 March 2017.

Fiori, Giuseppe, 1990, *Antonio Gramsci: Life of a Revolutionary* (London: Verso).

Fischer, Michael M.J., 2003, *Iran: From Religious Dispute to Revolution* (Ann Arbor: University of Wisconsin Press).

Foot, Paul, 2005, *The Vote How it was Won and how it was Undermined* (London: Viking).

Forrest, Kally, 2005, *Asijiki: A History of the South African Commercial, Catering and Allied Workers Union, SACCAWU* (Johannesburg, STE Publishers and Picturenet Africa).

Forrest, Kally, 2011, *Metal That Will Not Bend, National Union of Metal Workers of South Africa* (Johannesburg: Wits University Press).

Foster, Joe, 1987, "The Workers' Struggle—Where Does FOSATU Stand?" in Johan Maree, ed, *The Independent Trade Unions 1974-84, Ten Years of the South African Labour Bulletin* (Johannesburg, Ravan Press).

Friszke, Andrzej, 2010, *Anatomia buntu—Kuroń, Modzelewski I komandosi* [*Anatomy of a Rebellion—Kuroń, Modzelewski and the Commandos*] (Kraków: Wydawnictwo Znak).

Friszke, Andrzej, 2014, *Rewolucja Solidarności 1980-1981* [*Solidarity Revolution 1980-1981*], (Kraków: Społeczny Instutut Wydawniczy Znak).

Friske, Andrzej, and Tadeusz Koczanowicz, 2018, "Leszek Kołakowski's Political Path", *Eurozine* (23 April), https://www.eurozine.com/leszek-kolakowskis-political-path/

Gilbert, Alan, 1981, *Marx's Politics: Communists and Citizens* (Oxford: Robertson).

Gluckstein, Donny, 2011, *The Paris Commune A Revolution in Democracy* (Chicago: Haymarket).

Goodey, Chris, 1980, "Workers' Councils in Iranian Factories", *MERIP Reports* (June): 5-9.

Gonzalez, Mike, 2019, *The Ebb of the Pink Tide: The Decline of the Left in Latin America* (London: Pluto).

Gramsci, Antonio, 1971, *Selections from the Prison Notebooks* (London: Lawrence & Wishart).

Gramsci, Antonio, 1977, *Selections from the Political Writings 1910-20* (London: Lawrence & Wishart).

Gramsci, Antonio, 1995, *Further Selections from the Prison Notebooks,* edited and translated Derek Boothman (London: Lawrence and Wishart).

Gramsci, Antonio, 2016, *The Modern Prince and other writings* (New York: International Publishers).

Gwiazda, Andrzej, and Joanna Duda-Gwiazda, Joanna, 2008, *Poza układem* [collection of articles and speeches delivered by the Gwiazdas published in their *Poza układem* paper] (Łódź: Obywatel).

Hardy, Jane, 2009, *Poland's New Capitalism* (London: Pluto).

Harding, Neil, 1981, *Lenin's Political Thought*, Volume 2 (London: Macmillan).

Harman, Chris, 1976, "Poland: Crisis of State Capitalism" (Part 1), *International Socialism* 93 (first series), https://www.marxists.org/archive/harman/1976/11/poland.htm

Harman, Chris, 1983 *The Lost Revolution: Germany 1918-1923* (London: Bookmarks)

Harman, Chris, 1988, *Class Struggles in Eastern Europe 1945-83*, third edition, (London Bookmarks)

Harman, Chris, 1990, "The Storm Breaks: The Crisis in the Eastern Bloc", *International Socialism 46* (spring), https://www.marxists.org/archive/harman/1990/xx/stormbreaks.html

Harman, Chris, 1996, *Party and Class* (London: Bookmarks), also available at https://www.marxists.org/archive/harman/1968/xx/partyclass.htm

Harman, Chris, 1988, *The Fire Last Time, 1968 And After* (London: Bookmarks).

Harman, Chris, 2009, *Zombie Capitalism, Global Crisis and the Relevance of Marx* (London: Bookmarks).

Harman, Chris, and Tim Potter, 1977, "The workers government", *SWP International Discussion Bulletin*, no 4, http://isj.org.uk/the-workers-government/

Hinton, James, 1973, *The First Shop-Steward Movement* (London, Allen Lane).

Hunter, Wendy, 2010, *The Transformation of the Workers' Party in Brazil, 1989-2009* (Cambridge: Cambridge University Press).

Jafari, Peyman, 2009, "Rupture and Revolt in Iran", *International Socialism 124* (autumn), http://isj.org.uk/rupture-and-revolt-in-iran/

Jafari, Peyman, 2018a, "Fluid History: Oil Workers and the Iranian Revolution", in Touraj Atabaki, Elizabetta Bini, and and Kaveha Ehsani, eds, *Working for Oil: Comparative Social Histories of Labor in the Global Oil Industry* (Cham, Switzerland: Palgrave MacMillan), pp. 69-98.

Jafari, Peyman, 2018b, "A Social History of Oil in the Iranian Oil Industry, 1973-83" (PhD thesis, Leiden University).

James, C.L.R., Raya Dunayevskaya, and Grace Lee, 1986, *State Capitalism and World Revolution* (Chicago: Charles H. Kerr Publishing).

Johns, Sheridan, and Hunt Davis Jr, 1991, R. *Mandela, Tambo and the African National Congress, The Struggle Against Apartheid 1948-1990 A Documentary Survey* (New York: Oxford University Press).

Johnstone, Monty, 1967, "Marx and Engels and the Concept of the Party", in Ralph Miliband and John Saville, eds. *Socialist Register 1967* (London: Merlin), pp121-58, also available at https://www.marxists.org/archive/johnstone/1967/xx/me-party.htm

Kapuściński, Ryszard, 1982, "Notatki z Wybrzeza [Notes from the Coast]", *Kultura* (Warsaw, September 14, 1980), reprinted in *Grazyna Pomian, Polska Solidarnosci [Solidarity's Poland]* (Paris: Instytut Literacki).

Kasrils, Ronnie, 2008, *Historic Turning Point at Cuito Cuanavale* (Grahamstown: University of Rhodes),

http://www.ssa.gov.za/Portals/0/SSA%20docs/Speeches/2008/Minister%20Kasrils%20Cuito%20Cuanavale%20Rhodes%20University%2027%20May%202008.pdf

Kasrils, Ronnie, 2017, *A Simple Man, Kasrils and the Zuma Enigma* (Johannesburg: Jacana).

Keable, Ken, ed, 2022, *London Recruits: The Secret War Against Apartheid* (London: Merlin Press).

Keck, Margaret E, 1992, *The Workers' Party and Democratization in Brazil* (New Haven: Yale University Press).

Khosroshahi, Yadollah, 2013, *Oral History of Oil Workers' Shora, a dialogue between Mohamad Fattahi (Partoo TV broadcast) and oil workers' leader, Yadollah Khosroshahi* (Committee of Research Institute—Workers Education, PAK) (in Farsi),

http://b-pak.org/files/books/unwritten-history-of-oil-labours.pdf

Kirk, Neville, 1985, *The Growth of Working Class Reformism in Mid-Victorian England* (London: Croom Helm).

Kołakowski, Leszek, 1964 "In Praise of Inconsistency", *Dissent* (spring): 201-9

Kouvelakis, Stathis, 2003, *Philosophy and Revolution From Kant to Marx* (London: Verso).

Kouvelakis, Stathis, 2007a, "Lenin as a Reader of Hegel", in Sebastian Budgen, Stathis Kouvelakis, and Slavoj Žižek, Eds *Lenin Reloaded: Towards a Politics of Truth* (Durham NC: Duke University Press)

Kouvelakis, Stathis, 2007b, "Marx's Critique of the Political: From the 1848 Revolutions to the Paris Commune", *Situations*, 2.2: 81-93.

Kouvelakis, Stathis, 2016, "The Time of History, the Time of Politics, the Time of Strategy", *Historical Materialism*, 24.4: 150-69.

Kowalewski, Zbigniew, 1982, "Solidarnosc on the Eve", *Labour Focus on Eastern Europe* (Spring).

Kowalewski, Zbigniew, 2011, "Give Us Back Our Factories! Between Resisting Exploitation and the Struggle for Workers' Power in Poland, 1944-1981", in Dario Azzellini and Immanuel Ness, eds, *Ours to Master and to Own: Workers' Control from the Commune to the Present* (Chicago: Haymarket)

Kucinski, Bernardo, 2004, "'The Rise of the Workers' Party", in Sue Branford and Bernardo Kucinski, eds, *Politics Transformed: Lula and the Workers' Party of Brazil* (London: Latin America Bureau).

Kuroń, Jacek, and Karol Modzelewski, 1966, "An Open Letter to the Party", *New Politics*, (spring) http://www.unz.org/Pub/NewPolitics-1966q2-00005

Kurzman, 2004, Charles, *The Unthinkable Revolution in Iran* (Cambridge MA: Harvard University Press).

Kwiatkowska, Wiesława, 1990, *Gwiazda, miałeś rację [Gwiazda, you were right)* (Sopot: ZP).

Le Blanc, Paul, 1993, *Lenin and the Revolutionary Party* (Atlantic Highlands NJ: Humanities Press).

Le Blanc, Paul, ed, 1999, *Rosa Luxemburg, Reflections and Writings* (Atlantic Highlands NJ: Humanities Press).

Legassick, Martin, 2007, *Towards Socialist Democracy* (Pietermaritzburg: University of KwaZulu-Natal Press).

Lenin, V.I., 1919, "'The Soviets at Work: The Problems of the Soviet Government" (https://www.marxists.org/archive/lenin/works/1918/mar/soviets.htm

Lenin, V.I, 1965a, "Our Tasks and the Soviet of Workers' Deputies", *Collected Works* (Moscow: Progress), Volume 10, https://www.marxists.org/archive/lenin/works/1905/nov/04b.htm

Lenin V.I., 1965b, "The Tasks of the Proletariat in the Present Revolution", *Pravda*, April 7 1917, *Collected Works* (Moscow: Progress), Volume 24, https://www.marxists.org/archive/lenin/works/1917/apr/04.htm

Lenin V.I., 1965c, "All Power to the Soviets!", *Pravda*, July 18, 1917, *Collected Works* (Moscow: Progress), Volume 25, https://www.marxists.org/archive/lenin/works/1917/jul/18.htm

Lenin V.I., 1965d, *The Impending Catastrophe and How to Combat It, Collected Works* (Moscow: Progress), Volume 25, https://www.marxists.org/archive/lenin/works/1917/ichtci/index.htm

Lenin V.I., 1965e, *The State and Revolution Collected Works* (Moscow: Progress), Volume 25, https://www.marxists.org/archive/lenin/works/1917/staterev/index.htm

Lenin V.I. 1965f, *Draft Regulations on Workers Control*, October 26 or 27, 1917, *Collected Works* (Moscow Progress), Volume 26, https://www.marxists.org/archive/lenin/works/1917/oct/26.htm

Lenin V.I. 1965g, "The Immediate Tasks of the Soviet Government", April 1918, *Collected Works* (Moscow Progress), Volume 27 https://www.marxists.org/archive/lenin/works/1918/mar/28.htm

Lenin V.I., 1965h, "Report on the Immediate Tasks of the Soviet Government", to All Russia CEC April 29 1918", *Collected Works* ((Moscow: Progress), Volume 27, https://www.marxists.org/archive/lenin/works/1918/apr/29.htm

Lenin, V I, 1965i, *"Left-Wing" Communism: An Infantile Disorder, Collected Works* (Moscow: Progress), Volume 31, www.marxists.org/archive/lenin/works/1920/lwc/ch09.htm

Lenin V.I. 1965j, "New Times and Old Mistakes in a New Guise" *Collected Works* (Moscow: Progress), Volume 33, https://www.marxists.org/archive/lenin/works/1921/aug/20.htm

Lih, Lars T, 2008, *Lenin Rediscovered: What Is To Be Done? in Context* (Chicago: Haymarket).

Lipski, Jan Józef, 1985, *KOR: A History of the Workers Defence Committee in Poland, 1976-1981* (Berkeley: University of California Press).

Lissagaray, Hyppolite-Prosper-Oliver, 1971, *History of the Paris Commune of 1871* (London: New Park).

Luxemburg, Rosa, 2009, "Lassalle's Legacy" (first published *Die Gleichheit*, No.18 1913), *Weekly Worker* (15 January), https://www.marxists.org/archive/luxemburg/1913/xx/lassalle.html

Machado, João, 2012, "L'expérience de construction de la DS et du PT, de 1979 au premier gouvernement Lula", in *Europe Solidaire Sans Frontières*, http://www.europe-solidaire.org/spip.php?article25856

Mandel, David, 2018, *The Petrograd Workers in the Russian Revolution, February 1917-June 1918* (Chicago: Haymarket).

Marx, Karl, 1973a, *The Revolutions of 1848: Political Writings*, Volume 1 (ed David Fernbach; Harmondsworth: Penguin).

Karl Marx, 1973b, *Surveys from Exile: Political Writings*, Volume 2 (ed David Fernbach; Harmondsworth: Penguin).

Marx, Karl, 1974c, *The First International and After: Political Writings*, Volume 3 (ed David Fernbach; Penguin).

Marx, Karl, 1975 *Early Writings* (Harmondsworth: Penguin).

Marx, Karl, 1990, *Capital* Volume 1 (London: Penguin Classics).

Marx, Karl, 1996, *Wages, Price and Profit* (London: Bookmarks).

Marx, Karl, and Frederick Engels, 1975-2005, *Collected Works* (50 vols; Moscow: Progress).

Marx, Karl, and Frederick Engels 1998, *The Communist Manifesto* (London: Verso).

Mayekiso, Moses, 1985, "South Africa: Towards a workers' party?", *Socialist Worker Review*, 80 (October).

Mayekiso Moses, 1986, Interview, *Socialist Worker* (5 April).

Mayekiso, Mzwanele, 1996, *Township Politics: Civic Struggle for a New South Africa* (New York: Monthly Review Press).

Mestre, Abel, 2021, "Le lambertisme, une histoire clandestine de la gauche française", *Le Monde* (14 August).

Meszäros, George, 1991, "The Catholic Church and Trade Unions in Brazil: A Case Study of the Relationship Between the Dioceses of São Paulo and Santo Andre and the Metalworkers of Greater São Paulo, 1970-1986" (PhD Thesis, London School of Economics). http://etheses.lse.ac.uk/20/

Michnik, Adam, 1987, *Letters from Prison and Other Essays* (Berkeley: University of California Press).

Moaddel, M 1992, *Class, Politics and Ideology in the Iranian Revolution* (New York: Columbia University Press).

Modzelewski, Karol, 2013, *Zajeździmy Kobyłę Historii - wyznania poobijanego jeźdźca* (Warsaw: Wydawnictwo Iskry).

Modzelewski, Karol, 2021, *Riding History to Death: Confessions of a Battered Rider* (Lanham: Rowman and Littlefield; Apple Books edn).

Moghadam, Valentine M, 1987, "Industrial Development, Culture and Working-Class Politics: A Case Study of Tabriz Industrial Workers in the Iranian Revolution", *International Sociology*, 2.2:151-75.

Moghissi, Haideh, and Saeed Rahnema, 2004, "The Working Class and the Islamic State in Iran" in Stephanie Cronin, ed., *Reformers and Revolutionaries in Modern Iran: New Perspectives on the Iranian Left* (London Routledge Curzon).

Moisés, José Alvaro,1982, "What is the Strategy of the 'New Syndicalism'?", *Latin American Perspectives*, 9.4: 55-73.

Molyneux, John, 2003, *Marxism and the Party* (Chicago: Haymarket).

Monbiot, George, 2019, "Dare to Declare Capitalism Dead—Before It Takes Us All Down With It", *Guardian* (25 April), https://www.theguardian.com/commentisfree/2019/apr/25/capitalism-economic-system-survival-earth

Murphy, Kevin, 2007, *Revolution and Counter-Revolution in a Moscow Metal Factory* (Chicago: Haymarket).

Nettl, JP, 1966, *Rosa Luxemburg* Volume I (Oxford: Oxford University Press)

Nimtz, Jnr, August H, 2000, *Marx and Engels: Their Contribution to the Democratic Breakthrough* (New York: State University of New York Press).

Nowak, Leszek, 1983, *Property and Power: Towards a Non-Marxian Historical Materialism* (Dordrecht: Reidel).

Okraska, Remigiuszem ("Remik"), 2009) *Gwiazdozbior "Solidarnosci" ('Constellation in Solidarity'), Joanna i Andrzej Gwiazdowie w rozmowie* (Łódź: Stowarzyszenie "Obywatele Obywatelom"). Electronic edition.

Ost, David, 1990, *Solidarity and the Politics of Anti Politics, Opposition and Reform in Poland since 1968* (Philadelphia: Temple University Press).

Ost, David, 1993, Introduction, *The Church and the Left* by Adam Michnik (Chicago: University of Chicago Press).

Ost, David, 2005, *The Defeat of Solidarity: Anger and Politics in Post Communist Europe* (Ithaca NY: Cornell University Press).

Panitch, Leo, Colin Leys, Greg Albo, and David Coates, eds, 2001, *Socialist Register: Working Classes Global Realities* (London: Merlin)

Parsa, Misagh, 1989, *Social Origins of the Iranian Revolution* (New Jersey: Rutgers University Press)

Persky, Stan, and Henry Flam, eds, 1982, *The Solidarity Sourcebook* (Vancouver: New Star Books)

Piper, Laurence, 2002, "Nationalism without a nation: the rise and fall of Zulu nationalism in South Africa's transition to democracy, 1975–99", *Nations and Nationalism*, 8.1, https://doi.org/10.1111/1469-8219.00039

Poya, Maryam, 1999, *Women, Work & Islamism, ideology and resistance in Iran* (London: Zed).

Rabinowitch, Alexander, 2007, *The Bolsheviks in Power: The First Year of Soviet Rule in Petrograd* (Bloomington: Indiana University Press).

Randjbar-Daemi, Siavush, 2013, "Building the Islamic State: The Draft Constitution of 1979 Reconsidered", *Iranian Studies*, 26.4: 641-63.

Rahnema, Ali, ed, 2005, *Pioneers of Islamic Revival* (London: Zed).

Rahnema, Saeed, 1992, "Works Councils in Iran: The Illusion of Workers Control", *Economic and Industrial Democracy*, 13.1: 69-94.

Rahnema, Saeed, 2004, "The Left and the Struggle for Democracy in Iran", in Stephanie Cronin, Ed, *Reformers and Revolutionaries in Modern Iran: New Perspectives on the Iranian Left* (London: Routledge Curzon).

Riddell, John, *2015, To the Masses, Proceedings of the Third Congress of the Communist International, 1921 (Lieden Boston: Brill).*

Riethof, Marieke, 2018, *Labour Mobilisation, Politics and Globalisation in Brazil—Between Militancy and Moderation* (Crum: Springer).

Rose, John, 2004, *The Myths of Zionism* (London, Pluto)

Rose, John, 2005b, "We Need a Post-Zionist Leap of Faith", *Guardian* (3 April).

Rose, John, 2007, "Debate Sparked by Six Day War 1967 Transformed a Generation", *Socialist Worker* (5 June), https://socialistworker.co.uk/features/debate-sparked-by-six-day-war-1967-transformed-a-generation/

Rose, John, 2012, "Memories of Ronnie Kasrils at LSE", in Ken Keable, ed, *London Recruits: The Secret War Against Apartheid* (London: Merlin Press)

Rose, John, 2013, "Lenin's *'Left Wing' Communism, an Infantile Disorder* revisited", *International Socialism 138* (spring) http://isj.org.uk/lenins-left-wing-communism-an-infantile-disorder-revisited/

Rose, John, 2015, "Luxemburg, Richard Müller and the Berlin Workers' and Soldiers' Councils", *International Socialism 147* (summer)

http://isj.org.uk/luxemburg-muller-and-the-berlin-councils/

Rose, John, 2016, "Revolutionary Workers' Movements and Parliaments in Germany, 1918-1923", *International Socialism 150* (spring) http://isj.org.uk/revolutionary-workers-movements-and-parliaments-in-germany-1918-23-a-reply-to-tony-phillips/

Rose, John, 2017a, "All Power to the Factory Councils?" *International Socialism 153* (winter)

http://isj.org.uk/all-power-to-the-factory-councils/

Rose, John, 2017b, "Rescuing Lenin", *International Socialism 155* (summer)

Rose, John, 2018, "Chris Harman, 1968, and the historic *Open Letter* to the Polish Communist Party", *International Socialism 158* (spring), http://isj.org.uk/chris-harman-1968-and-the-historic-open-letter-to-the-polish-communist-party/

Rose, John, 2020, "Workers' Power and the Failure of Communism" (PhD Thesis, King's College London), https://kclpure.kcl.ac.uk/ws/files/129644633/2020_Rose_John_1641033_ethesis_version_for_Pure_upload.pdf

Rosen, Michael, 2009, "Chris Harman Obituary", *Guardian* (9 November).

Ross, Kristin, 2015, *Communal Luxury: The political imaginary of the Paris Commune* (London: Verso).

Rostami-Povey, Elaheh, 2010, *Iran's Influence, A Religious-Political State and Society in its Region* (London: Zed).

Saad-Filho, Alfredo, and Lecio Morais, 2018, *Brazil Neoliberalism versus Democracy* (London: Pluto).

Sanford, George, 1990, *The Solidarity Congress 1981* (London: Macmillan).

SAHO:1 http://www.sahistory.org.za/article/rivonia-trial-1963-1964

SAHO:2 http://www.sahistory.org.za/article/people-armed-1984-1990

SAHO:3 http://www.sahistory.org.za/topic/inkatha-freedom-party-ifp

Saville, John, 1987, *1848: The British State and the Chartist Movement* (Cambridge: Cambridge University Press).

Schmidt, Jürgen, 2009, *August Bebel, Social Democracy and the Founding of the Labour Movement* (London: I.B.Taurus).

Secco, Lincoln, 2018, *Historia do PT*, (São Paulo: Atelie Editorial).

Seekings, Jeremy, 2000, *The UDF, A History of the United Democratic Front in South Africa, 1983-1991* (Athens OH: Ohio University Press).

Serbin, Kenneth, 2019, *From Revolution to Power in Brazil: How Radical Leftists Embraced Capitalism and Struggled with Leadership* (Notre Dame: University of Notre Dame Press).

Slovo, Joe, 1988, *The South African Working Class and the National Democratic Revolution*,

https://www.marxists.org/subject/africa/slovo/1988/national-democratic-revolution.htm

Sluyter-Beltrao, Jeffrey, 2010, *Rise and Decline of Brazil's New Unionism, The Politics of the Central Unica dos Trabalhadores* (Lausanne: Peter Lang).

Smith, S A, 1983, *Red Petrograd: Revolution in the Factories 1917-18* (Cambridge: Cambridge University Press).

Smith, S A, 2017, *Russia in Revolution: An Empire in Crisis, 1890 to 1928* (Oxford: Oxford University Press;).

Smith, Janet, and Beauregard Tromp, 2009, *Hani A Life Too Short*, (Johannesburg: Jonathan Ball).

Sperber, Jonathan, 2013, *Karl Marx* (London: Liveright).

Schorske, Carl, 1983, *German Social Democracy 1905-1917* (Cambridge MA: Harvard University Press).

South African Communist Party, 1988, "Leading Role of the Working Class in the Present Situation", *African Communist*, 113: 5-15.

Stedman Jones, Gareth, 1977, "Engels and the Genesis of Marxism", *New Left Review*, I/106: 79-104.

Stedman Jones, Gareth, 1985, "Karl Marx and the English Labour Movement", in Bernard Chavance, ed, *Marx en perspective* (Paris: EHESS).

Stedman Jones, Gareth, 2016, *Karl Marx: Greatness and Illusion* (London: Allen Lane).

Tabari, Azar, 1982, "Islam and the Struggle for the Emancipation of Iranian Women", in Azar Tabari and Nahid Yeganeh, eds, *In the Shadow of Islam: The Women's Movement in Iran* (London: Zed).

Thomas, Peter D, 2010, *The Gramscian Moment: Philosophy, Hegemony and Marxism* (Chicago: Haymarket).

Thompson, Edward, 1968, *The Making of the English Working Class* (London: Pelican).

Touraine, Alain, 1983, *Solidarity: The Analysis of a Social Movement: Poland 1980-81* (Cambridge: Cambridge University Press).

Trotsky, Leon, 1967, *The History of the Russian Revolution* (three vols, London: Sphere Books).

Trotsky, Leon, 1972, *1905* (New York: Vintage Books).

Upchurch, Martin, 2020, "Is There a New Extractive Capitalism?", *International Socialism No 168* (autumn), http://isj.org.uk/extractive-capitalism/

Van der Linden, Marcel, 2003, *Transnational Labour History: Explorations* (Aldershot: Ashgate).

Van der Linden, Marcel, 2008, *Workers of the World: Essays toward a Global Labour History* (Leiden: Brill).

Van der Linden, Marcel, 2009, *Western Marxism and the Soviet Union* (Chicago: Haymarket).

Van Kessel, Ineke, 2000, *Beyond Our Wildest Dreams: the United Democratic Front and the Transformation of South Africa* (Charlottesville VA: University of Virginia Press).

Von Holdt, Karl, 2003, *Transition from Below Forging Trade Unionism and Workplace Change in South Africa* (Pietermaritzburg: University of KwaZulu-Natal Press).

Wainwright, Hilary, 2003, "Porto Alegre: Public Power beyond the State", in Sue Branford and Bernardo Kucinski, eds, *Politics Transformed: Lula and the Workers' Party of Brazil* (London: Latin America Bureau).

Warzecha, Jaroslaw, 2014, *Nie Kracz Słowik, Nie Kracz* (Warsaw: Narodowe Centrum Kultury).

Waters, Mary-Alice, ed, 1970, *Rosa Luxemburg Speaks* (New York: Pathfinder).

Webster, Eddie, 1981, "Stay-aways and the Black Working Class: Evaluating a Strategy", *Labour Capital and Society*, 14.1: 10-38.

Webster, Eddie, 1985, *Cast in a Racial Mould Labour Process and Trade Unionism in the Foundries* (Johannesburg: Ravan Press).

Žižek, Slavoj, 2002, *Revolution at the Gates: Selected Writings of Lenin from 1917* (London: Verso).

Endnotes

Introduction

1. Unedited transcripts of all interviews are reproduced in the Appendix to my original PhD thesis, Rose 2020, which is available online here https://kclpure.kcl.ac.uk/ws/files/129644633/2020_Rose_John_1641033_ethesis_version_for_Pure_upload.pdf. Biographies of the interviewees are included in the chapters. Each one is referenced by the letter 'A' for Appendix, immediately followed by the initials of the interviewee's name. **Editors' note**: Unfortunately, we have not been able to trace the transcripts of the interviews for the Brazil chapter, the research for and writing of which was completed after John's thesis had been submitted and examined.

2. Daniel Bensaïd, *Qui est le Juge? Pour en finir avec le tribunal de l'Histoire* (Paris, Fayard, 1999).

3. Louis Althusser, "The Crisis of Marxism" (1977), available on viewpointmag.com.

4. Hamba Kahle means 'go well' in Zulu.

5. Fitzpatrick, 2017, reviewing *October: The Story of the Russian Revolution* by China Miéville (Verso, 2017), *The Russian Revolution 1905-1921* by Mark D. Steinberg (Oxford, 2017), *Russia in Revolution: An Empire in Crisis, 1890 to 1928* by S.A. Smith (Oxford 2017), *The Russian Revolution: A New History* by Sean McMeekin (Basic 2017), *Historically Inevitable?: Turning Points of the Russian Revolution* by Tony Brenton Profile 2016.

6. His biographer, Ian Birchall tells it extremely well and thoroughly: Birchall, 2011.

7. I first told this story in some detail in the *Socialist Worker*, weekly newspaper of the SWP, on the fortieth anniversary of the June 1967 war (Rose 2007). Birchall republished it in his biography of Cliff (Birchall, 2011: 279-80). I developed it further in Rose, 2012: 45-7. When I left LSE in 1969, I briefly worked for Ronnie Kasrils, who had recruited several LSE students for secret underground work in South Africa. In the *London Recruits* book we tell the full story (Keable, 2020), which is now also the subject of a film. Ronnie and I have remained friendly over the years, despite his membership for most of that time of the Central Committee of the SACP, South African Communist Party, and indeed the post-apartheid neoliberal ANC Government where he held several governmental ministerial posts. Ronnie is a key interviewee for the South Africa chapter of my thesis where his more recent rejection of both the SACP and the ANC, and his subsequent reflections on his past political role are particularly relevant.

8. This raises the wider question of the role of the professional managers and the technicians and other professionals essential to organising production as well as the capitalists themselves. The thesis attempts to explore thoroughly all of these aspects.

9. See my discussion of the failed German Revolution in Rose, 2015, 2016, and 2017a.

10. I return to this question in the Conclusion, following Gramsci and his response to the wave of factory occupations in Italy in the early 1920s, proposing that the idea of syndicalism and its limitations is an extremely helpful guide not just to the French 1968 events but also to understanding the weaknesses of the four workers' movements in Poland, South Africa, Iran, and Brazil studied in this book. My PhD supervisor Stathis Kouvelakis repeatedly suggested that I take the syndicalist tradition more seriously. Belatedly, I came to the conclusion that he was right.

11. As van der Linden has noted, Harman was one of the first former revolutionary socialist students to notice the collapse of 1968 activism by the mid-1970s, citing Harman's book on 1968, *The Fire Last Time*. Non-stop activism "was fine when the movement was going from strength to strength. When the forward march was checked, much of the activity seemed to lose its point" (Harman 1998: 346, van der Linden 2003: 133).

12. I use one of these Gramsci passages introducing the idea of worker intellectuals in Chapter 1. Gramsci scholar Peter Thomas (Thomas, 2010), recognised Chris's contribution to the development and promotion of Gramsci's thought, post 1968. In a note to me Thomas wrote, "Point out that I reference one of Chris's texts on Gramsci...as an antidote to post-Marxist readings... Chris and I also spoke together at an *International Socialism* Dayschool on Gramsci in 2007, and I was pleased to see that we were in agreement on central issues" (Rose 2013: 137, fn33).

13. For how Cliff developed his theory of state capitalism, which involved a break with Leon Trotsky's view that, however bureaucratically distorted, Russia was still some kind of workers' state, see Birchall, 2011:88-127; Callinicos, 1990: 73-79. Van der Linden describes how Cliff dealt with his "dilemma" over Trotsky. He quotes Cliff, "I had to choose between what Trotsky said...(about)...the self-activity of workers or the form of property...". Workers' self-activity took precedence, workers did not control the state (van der Linden 2009: 119). In 1956 the KGB, Russia's secret police, commissioned a special translation of Cliff's book (Birchall, 2011:117). See also Chapter 2 below, referencing Stalin's favourite British banker who also argued that Stalin was building a state capitalist economy.

14. Titled a *Revolutionary Socialist Manifesto: written in a Polish prison*. In fact, the title made an error. Kuroń and Modzelewski were sent to prison for writing it. It wasn't written in prison. I recently wrote about Chris, 1968 and the *Open Letter* for the '1968' fiftieth anniversary edition of *International Socialism* (Rose, 2018). Chris's "1968" book is also an essential text for understanding the period (Harman, 1998). A thorough discussion of the *Open Letter* and the subsequent political evolution of Kuroń and Modzelewski as leaders of Solidarity, Poland's ten million strong mass workers' movement, is central to Chapter 2 below. In 2017, I had the good fortune to interview Karol Modzelewski, as part of my research, at the University of Warsaw. He was delighted to see, for the first time, the English language edition of the *Open Letter*. Sadly, he died in early 2019.

15. I was by no means expert, but I thought I had better try and become one by enrolling for a Master's Degree in Jewish Studies. It was an appropriate decision, resulting in my book *The Myths of Zionism* (Rose: 2004). See also

Rose, 2005. I also wrote the Introduction to *The Ghetto Fights* (London: Bookmarks, 2nd edition, 2014) by Marek Edelman, one of the leaders of the Jewish socialist workers' Anti-Zionist Bund in pre-war Poland as well as the Jewish Warsaw Ghetto resistance to the Nazi Holocaust, Poland 1943. I had interviewed Marek Edelman in 1989 in Lodz, Poland where he gave permission for the memoir's first-time publication in the UK. See my two-page article in the *Weekend Guardian*, 17 November 1990. I became a Visiting Lecturer, Israel Palestine conflict, BA/MA module, Middle East Studies, International Dept, Rhodes University, Eastern Cape, South Africa, 2011 and 2012 and a contributor to *Holy Land Studies*, edited by Palestinian Professor Nur Mashala (Edinburgh University Press).

16. See n9 above.

17. The focus on the moment when these workers' movements lost the political initiative—and in each case I identify the month and the year, Iran—August 1979, Poland—March 1981, South Africa—August 1987, Brazil—December 1989, concentrates much of the historical and political discussion around these periods. Whilst this weakens both medium and long term historical and political contextualisation, I don't believe that the core argument is undermined.

18. Unedited transcripts of all interviews are reproduced in the Appendix to my original PhD thesis, Rose 2020, which is available online here: https://kclpure.kcl.ac.uk/ws/files/129644633/2020_Rose_John_1641033_ethesis_version_for_Pure_upload.pdf . Biographies of the interviewees are included in the chapters. Each one is referenced by the letter 'A' for Appendix, immediately followed by the initials of the interviewee's name. **Editors' note**: Unfortunately, we have not been able to trace the transcripts of the interviews for the Brazil chapter, the research for and writing of which was completed after John's thesis had been submitted and examined.

Chapter 1

19. https://www.encyclopedia.com/social-sciences/dictionaries-thesauruses-pictures-and-press-releases/ideographic-versus-nomothetic-approaches

20. Throughout this book, 'communism' and 'communist' appear in lower case to refer respectively to the political idea of a classless society and to its adherents, and are capitalised when referring to official organisations and their members.

21. August Nimtz (2000: 155) cites the example of Marx and Engels's departure from the Communist League in 1848 to edit the "bourgeois" liberal democratic newspaper, *Neue Rheinische Zeitung (NRZ)*, in Cologne. They believed this was the best method of advancing the workers' cause in Germany in 1848, to prioritise the "bourgeois" democratic revolution, modelled on the French Revolution of 1789. They would later, as we shall see, strongly repudiate this position, but the point here is they saw themselves acting on behalf of the "party", as the most advanced theoretical section of the organised working class.

22. See section II below. The Chartists demanded universal manhood suffrage, which they hoped would result in a workers' parliament.

23. As we have already noted it was the Chartists that informed the phrase in *The Communist Manifesto* "This organisation of proletarians into a class, and consequently into a *political party*" (Marx and Engels, 1998: 46; see Johnstone, 1967: 124 and Gilbert, 1981: 53). The intriguing failure of Marx and Engels explicitly to acknowledge the Chartists cannot be addressed here. There may have been some unstated or unresolved ambiguity about them. Marx was very dependent on Engels's knowledge of the Chartist movement. At the same time, Engels's pre-Marxist "Utopian socialist" theoretical approach to the Chartists had ill-equipped him to fully comprehend it (Kouvelakis, 2003: 222-29). The Utopian socialists will be discussed shortly. Hal Draper argues Marx had previously misunderstood the Chartists' movement and the defeat of their general strike in 1842 (Draper, 1977: 176).

24. See also John Charlton on the prospects in the 1840s for a workers' parliament (Charlton, 1997: 86).

25. Posted on the internet by a modern Chartist enthusiast http://www.archive.org/stream/trialfeargusoco00ocogoog/trialfeargusoco00ocogoog_djvu.txt

26. Robert Owen, Utopian socialist, see next section.

27. This reinforces Kouvelakis's view of the nascent reformism of the 1789 French communist and Utopian socialist tradition and its impact on Chartism (Kouvelakis, 2003: 222-29).

28. With hindsight we can speculate that it needed a communist leadership, training and debating with its cadres, coherent strategies, tactics and objectives, responsive to fast moving and changing economic, social and political circumstances, but it is utopian to impose that retrospectively on Chartist history.

29. The pamphlet was part of a wider critique, *Anti-Dühring*. Dühring was a Berlin academic influential in the German socialist party in the mid-1870s. Marx and Engels dismissed what they regarded as his crude claims about science and society. Their criticism of him was an opportunity to reinforce their own theories of socialism and communism as having firm scientific foundations.

30. Some of the most powerful ideas in the *Communist Manifesto* and later Marxist text were first developed by the Utopian socialists. It was Louis Blanc who first coined the egalitarian slogan, "from each according to his capacities, to each according to his needs." The Enlightenment and the French Revolution and its extreme left wing of radical republicans both contributed to demands for communist interpretations of Equality, Liberty, Fraternity. But the revolutionary communism of Blanqui, arguably the most important of the inheritors of the French Revolutionary tradition, would be imposed from above thus sharing the elitism of the Owenites (Callinicos, 1983: 47-51).

31. "Legislative recognition" carried with it unanticipated and far-reaching political implications and risks which have dominated the movement from then until now—capitalism could absorb working class protest and split the movement between reform and revolution.

32. Fernbach argues convincingly that this is unstated self-criticism (1973: 53).

33. See the later sections on the Paris Commune and the *Critique of the Gotha Programme* for a discussion about how Marx and Engels used this concept.

34. As mentioned in the Introduction, Chris Harman, one of the most theoretically gifted of the leaders of the revolutionary student movement in 1968 in the UK, developed this argument, using Gramsci's insights, and others in combination with Lenin, to argue how students could unite with workers in a revolutionary socialist party (Harman, 1996: 28).

35. Collins and Abramsky, 1965: 84.

36. It meant admitting to the International Liberal sympathising leaders of the British trade unions, French, Italian and Spanish Proudhonists and the German Lassalleans (see section VII below) as well as Bakunin's (anarchist) International Alliance of Socialist Democracy (Johnstone, 1967: 131). Whilst proper exploration of these trends is not possible here, Marx and Engels's analysis of Proudhonism in *The Communist Manifesto* as "Bourgeois Socialism" (Marx and Engels, 1998: 70) or "the Socialism of the small peasant and master craftsman" (Engels, 1968: 14) requires further comment because of Proudhonist influence on the Paris Commune. Proudhon accepted the market exchange of commodities as essentially fair, including labour-power as a commodity, because of a focus on small scale individual property owners. Large scale industrial capitalism distorted market relations and either deskilled the artisan and/or forced his integration into a productive process where he lost individual control of his work. Proudhon's "market anarchism" could appear extremely attractive to the traditional craftsman (Gluckstein, 2011: 61-2; Gilbert, 1981: 88).

37. The earlier victory he refers to is the carrying of the Ten Hours Bill, the basis for one of his most famous chapters in *Capital*, Volume 1, Chapter 10: "The Working Day".

38. Also in *Capital* Volume 1: "On 26 May 1866, a philistine English periodical, the Spectator reported after the introduction of a sort of partnership between the capitalist and the workers in the 'Wirework Company of Manchester', the first result was a sudden decrease in waste, the men not seeing why they should waste their own property any more than any other master's, and waste is, perhaps, next to bad debts, the greatest source of manufacturing loss. The same paper finds that the main defect in the Rochdale co-operative experiments is this: 'They showed that associations of workmen could manage shops, mills, and almost all forms of industry with success, and they immediately improved the condition of the men, but they did not leave a clear place for the masters." Marx adds an ironic exclamatory, *"Quelle Horreur!"* (Marx, 1990: 449, n15).

39. At the core of the IWMA was the co-existence of competing working class political tendencies but with no satisfactory means of resolving the differences. In this very important sense, it cannot be considered as an international political party. This had made the International in the Commune important symbolically but unable to move beyond the particular influence of its very different component parts, Blanquism, Proudhonism, Jacobinism etc. In addition, the English trade union centre of the IWMA acted as a conservative brake.

40. Hyppolite-Prosper-Oliver Lissagaray, journalist, editor of *Le Tribun du*

Peuple, author of the best known contemporary history, *The History of the Paris Commune*, exiled to London where he knew Marx. His book was translated into English by Marx's daughter, Eleanor (Gluckstein, 2011: 228).

41. This meant they were subject to immediate recall.

42. "Marx did not recognise the ... weakness. The exclusion of women ... is especially striking in the light of the magnificent role played by the working women ... in the Commune" (Callinicos, 1983: 159). See the discussion later of the Commune's Women's Union.

43. Nimtz questions the validity of this interpretation because it is based on a report of the speech—the only record we have—in a New York newspaper which had misquoted Marx in the past (Nimtz, 2000: 218-19). Nevertheless, Engels forcefully used the term to describe the Commune (Callinicos, 1983: 156-7). There is, however, a further difficulty—interpreting the remarkable letter Marx sent to Domela Nieuwenhuis, an anarchist in the Hague, on 22 February 1881. Here he seemed to repudiate at least parts of his earlier analysis on the Paris Commune. He writes that "the majority of the Commune was in no sense socialist, nor could it have been. With a modicum of common sense, it could, however, have obtained the utmost that was then obtainable—a compromise with Versailles beneficial to the people as a whole. The appropriation of the Bank of France alone would have been rapidly put an end to the vainglory of the Versailles people, etc, etc" (Marx and Engels, 1975-2005, vol. 46: 66). Stathis Kouvelakis alerted me to this letter. Engels also discusses this—see later in this section.

44. "The founding documents of the International—Marx's *Provisional Rules and Inaugural Address*—transcended the limitations of Proudhonism and Blanquism ... The *Rules's* famous first statement, 'That the emancipation of the working classes must be conquered by the working class themselves' was acceptable to Proudhon but anathema to Blanqui." Whereas "the Address calls for the working class 'to conquer political power' "Proudhon rejected this ... whilst Blanquists applauded it" (Gluckstein, 2011: 72). But it must be emphasised that this interpretation of the founding documents did not translate into decisive political influence in the Commune.

45. Unfortunately, we cannot explore here the role of Louise Michel who "embodied the proletarian character of the Commune" (Lissagaray, 1971: 169), who had the potential to organise a communist women's cadre alongside Elizabeth Dmitrieff (see below).

46. See Ross's commentary on the implications of Dmitrieff's discussions with Marx about the Russian peasantry (Ross 2015: 76-89). According to him, the Commune rightly told the French peasants that "its victory was their only hope" (Marx and Engels, 1975-2005, vol. 22: 337).

47. Also, Gluckstein, 2011: 23-24; Lissagaray, 1971: 239.

48. Ross's enigmatic book is particularly strong on the Commune as a "Universal Republic", also giving Dmitrieff pride of place. Dmitrieff's support for the International partly grew from her disgust at the Russian suppression of the Polish rebellion in 1863 (Ross, 2015: 25). Marx may have been exaggerating when he wrote: "The Commune honoured the heroic

sons of Poland by placing them at the head of the defenders of Paris", Marx and Engels, 1975-2005, vol. 22: 339, but the statement was firmly rooted in Commune principles. Incidentally, Frankel, also a "Marxist", the Commune's "Minister of Labour", was Hungarian.

49. Recent scholarship suggests a more nuanced approach. Marianne Enckell argues that the "federalist" anarchist wing of the International associated with Bakunin lasted longer than the "centralist" wing associated with Marx and Engels, that it was "genuinely proletarian and internationalist", and that it marked the moment of anarchism's breakthrough into modern politics (Enckell, 2018: 364).

50. Often mistakenly described as a woodworker, Bebel was in fact an "artisan and entrepreneur", "manufacturing doors and window knobs out of buffalo horn" (Schmidt, 2019: 17-28).

51. Marx described the *Critique* as "critical marginal notes" (Marx 1974c: 341) and they were not published at the time.

52. *Norddeutsche Allgemeine Zeitung,* editorial mouthpiece for Bismarck.

53. She adds that Lenin's *The State and Revolution* was based on these two principles.

54. *Anti-Dühring* would become the "bible" of the Second International: Kouvelakis, personal communication.

55. Sperber reports an extraordinary episode when the party leadership, in order to avoid Bismarck's partial ban on the party, proposed starting a daily newspaper in Switzerland. Marx and Engels were furious to discover that the editors intended to renounce violent revolution, advocate reforming capitalism, rather than introducing socialism, class cooperation instead of class struggle. Eduard Bernstein, who would become the principal architect of reformism in the German party, was on the editorial board (Sperber, 2013: 528-31).

56. There is however, arguably, ambiguity in this statement by Engels. Coming to power in a democratic republic is, presumably, through parliamentary elections. See also Engels's 1895 Introduction to the French edition of Marx's *The Class Struggles in France.* Discussion of whether, and if so how, both Marx and Engels viewed the prospects of workers taking power via parliamentary elections will not be possible here.

57. See also the problem as John Molyneux poses it: Should the revolutionary party of the working class seek to represent the working class-as a-whole or just that minority, in non-revolutionary situations, open to revolutionary socialist ideas, prioritising its growth in gains made through its intervention in the class struggle, in particular strikes, against the employers, and other grassroots mass-based social movements against different forms of oppression, over electoral gains? (Molyneux, 2003: 33-35).

58. As Trotsky put it in his discussion of *The State and Revolution* in his own *History of the Russian Revolution,* "Lenin ... regarded the very conquest of power in Russia primarily as the impetus for a European Revolution ... incomparably more important for the fate of humanity than the revolution in backward Russia" (Trotsky 1967, III: 124).

59. There is in addition a complex and implicitly critical clarification of how Engels understood and interpreted these two writings of Marx which cannot concern us here.

60. Proposed by Tony Cliff: Cliff, 1978:62. *The Impending Catastrophe and How to Combat It* is one of the key documents in the 1917 collection of Lenin's writings put together by Slavoj Žižek—Žižek, 2002.

61. Lenin's article headline in the Bolsheviks' paper Pravda July 18, 1917 (Lenin, 1965c), the Bolshevik's main slogan following Lenin's *April Theses*, "the necessity of transferring state power to the Soviets of Workers' Deputies" (Lenin 1965b).

62. Hobsbawm had a simple solution to Figes's peculiar and contradictory blend of genuine innovative scholarship, creative invention and peculiar version of the facts, which recognises the brief flowering of the soviets and workers' power whilst at the same time monstering Lenin and the Bolsheviks. He ignored it. Hobsbawm endorses Figes's view that this was essentially a peasant revolution, whilst sliding over Figes's views on its roots in the intensity of backwardness. Figes borders on what some would say is racism in his contempt for *Russian* backwardness—with its medieval aristocracy incapable of reform, its reformers gross in their incompetence, its revolution, led by leather jacketed thugs and fanatics, turning in on itself and drowning in blood, terror and cannibalism.

63. Discussion of the Kornilov crisis—the failed military coup against the Provisional Government of Aleksandr Kerensky in August 1917—is not possible here. But the significance of this point is that the crisis decisively weakened Kerensky's authority thus strengthening the demand for soviet power.

64. That is of the main reformist socialist party.

65. As Figes observes, "this was roughly the import of the Bolshevik Decree on Workers' Control passed on November 14" 1917, almost immediately after the October Revolution (Figes, 1997: 461n). A more detailed discussion of this decree will follow shortly.

66. Figes also has here a lengthy description of the intensification of the peasant war against the landed estates.

67. The similarity here between Figes's description and many passages from Trotsky's *History of the Russian Revolution*, Volume Three, "The Triumph of the Soviets", is quite remarkable (Trotsky, 1967, III).

68. This passage, without making it explicit, concedes Trotsky's perspective of "Permanent Revolution", by-passing the need for a "bourgeois" or capitalist revolutionary stage, and adopted by Lenin in his famous *April Theses* (Lenin, 1965b). There is, though, an important qualification. Figes appears to believe that the reformist socialist parties could have exercised Soviet power to isolate the Bolsheviks whilst adopting their initial programme of Land, Peace and Bread. This would have opened the possibility for Russia to become "a socialist democracy rather than a Communist dictatorship; and as a result, the bloody civil war ... might have lasted weeks rather than years" (Figes, 1997: 464). The rest of this chapter in his book is a condemnation of the "political bankruptcy" of the non-Bolshevik socialist parties for failing to pursue this path (Figes, 1997: 464-473).

69. See also Mandel, 2018.

70. Figes explicitly endorses and references Smith's argument that the factory committees simultaneously wanted workers' control and nationalisation (Figes, 1997: 369).

71. In his most recent book, Smith reinforces his argument about the way both "class" and "socialism" became mass-based inspirational ideas driving the revolution, however vaguely defined (Smith, 2017: 133-38).

72. Smith later comments on the workers' militias: "a major achievement of the February Revolution, which guaranteed workers' power in the factories and in society at large. Workers, in general, never accepted that there were 'bourgeois' limitations on the February Revolution ... it was a 'popular-democratic' revolution, which was potentially threatened by the bourgeoisie. It was crucial that workers organise independently to defend the democratic gains of the revolution, and it was thus inconceivable that the workers' militias should be absorbed into a civil militia under the control of the middle classes ... The militias were closely linked to the factory committees and underpinned workers' power in production. Later, the campaign to establish Red Guards became intimately bound with the campaign to establish workers' control of production" (Smith, 1983: 102). Here is the root of Lenin's confidence in a "state power of the armed workers".

73. Larin is a particularly interesting observer, a former Left Menshevik who joined the Bolsheviks in the summer 1917 and became known as one of a group of "moderate Bolsheviks", openly critical of many of Lenin's perspectives (Rabinowitch, 2007: 3, 45-49, 89-90).

74. The problem was often finding intellectuals to assist. Intellectuals generally were moving to the right, hostile to the Bolsheviks and their perspective of all power to the workers' soviets (Mandel, 2018: 243-49).

75. Shlyapnikov was a particularly impressive example of a workers' cadre, learning his Marxism from books and pamphlets as a fourteen-year-old metal workers' apprentice. He was also steeped in Russian classical literature and, because he worked in factories in different parts of Western Europe before the revolution, was fluent in several European languages. As we shall see shortly, he was less of an enthusiast than Lenin for workers' control (Allen, 2016).

76. An attempt to involve the critically important layer of professionally trained, scientific industrial personnel.

77. "Shlyapnikov later recalled that he worked closely with Lenin on the first decree on workers' control and that it reflected Lenin's aim that as many workers as possible participate in economic management. Nevertheless, there were crucial differences in their views on workers' control, which were reflected in the two different draft decrees. Radical Bolsheviks aligned with the factory committees and moderate socialists in the trade unions disagreed on workers' control. Lenin perceived the danger that the moderate Bolsheviks would join forces with moderate socialists in the trade unions. He tried to undermine them by throwing his support to the radicals, so his draft decree on workers' control reflected the wishes of factory-committee activists" (Allen, 2016: 111).

78. "The conditions of absolute scarcity and of political-military emergency made it very difficult, probably impossible, to find a suitable compromise between centralism and workers' self-management, both of which are necessary elements of socialism" (Mandel, 2018: 421).

79. "Scholars disagree as to when the civil war began, but it seems sensible to see it building up gradually from Kornilov's rebellion and intensifying after what many saw as the illegal seizure of power by the Bolsheviks" (Smith, 2017: 154). "The exalted hopes unleashed by the October insurrection lasted until the beginning of 1918" (Smith, 1983: 246).

80. Many went "to their native villages, in the hope of qualifying for some of the land that was being distributed" (Smith, 1983: 243).

81. That some of these detachments would become notorious for their violent methods of requisitioning food from the peasantry deepened the sense of catastrophe. Its consequences, leading eventually the NEP, New Economic Policy for the peasantry, cannot concern us here.

82. "Beginning in late November ... thousands of Petrograd Bolsheviks, Red Guards, Baltic Fleet sailors, and ordinary workers ... joined the rag-tag Soviet forces bound for the south," where the threat of "this first episode of the Russian civil war" was deemed most threatening (Rabinowitch, 2007: 59).

83. Shlyapnikov was by now a member of the banned faction the "Workers' Opposition". Trotsky, at the time approving of the ban, would later regard it as the moment that "brought the heroic history of Bolshevism to an end and made way for its bureaucratic degeneration" (Le Blanc, 1993:307).

Chapter 2

84. This was a particular definition of "state capitalism" Lenin was using at the time to emphasise the workers' state's necessary partnership with some capitalists.

85. See n58 below.

86. For example, Raya Dunayevskaya and C.L.R. James (James, Dunayevskaya, Lee, 1986) who worked with Trotsky during his final exile in Mexico as well as Tony Cliff also developed the theory of state capitalism (Cliff, 1988). Ivan Maisky, the Soviet Ambassador to Britain during the war recorded in his diaries Stalin's enthusiasm for a leading British Conservative banker, J. Gibson Jarvie, who praised Stalin's Five-Year Plan. But Maisky writes that Stalin always ignored Jarvie's insistence that Russia was practising state capitalism (Gorodetsky, 2015: 37). See also n58 below on Trotskyism. In his book comparing and contrasting how Western Marxists have attempted to analyse the Soviet Union and its satellite countries, van der Linden prefers to associate Kuroń and Modzelewski's analysis with the "New Class" theory of Yugoslav dissident Milovan Djilas rather than with the state capitalist approach (van der Linden 2007: 164-71). A thorough comparison of the similarities and differences between the "New Class" theory and the state capitalist analysis is not possible here.

87. Chris Harman applied Cliff's theory of state capitalism to Poland in the mid-

1970s. He identified the competitive military pressures between the two Cold War power blocs as the key mechanism driving accumulation: "accumulation soon exhausted the raw materials to hand ... Imports were necessary to sustain it. But imports could only be obtained if exports were increased ... a situation not appreciably different to that of any western capitalist ... To survive they have ... to subordinate the internal development of their economies to the needs of external competition" (Harman, 1976: 26).

88. In 1956 there was a popular uprising in Hungary, following a speech by Soviet leader Nikita Khrushchev in which he attacked the period of Joseph Stalin's rule. Workers occupied their factories and established a society-wide network of independent workplace organisations with the capacity both to halt production and then re-start it under their own terms and conditions. Although Soviet military intervention finally broke the resistance, a precedent had been established of organised workers challenging Soviet Communism.

89. This statement is also extremely relevant to both the "workerist" view of workers' control in the struggle against apartheid in South Africa and the workers' shoras (councils) in the immediate aftermath of the revolution in Iran 1979. The *Open Letter* develops a detailed programme for implementation in its concluding pages (Kuroń and Modzelewski, 1966: 59-66).

90. This is also extremely relevant to the conclusions in the South Africa and Iran case studies, chapters 3 and 4 below.

91. Adam Michnik would become the best known of the student activists in Poland in 1968.

92. The widely recognised leader of the student revolt in France, 1968, but did Cohn Bendit properly read the *Open Letter*? It is not addressed in his 1968 book (Cohn-Bendit: 1968). This was a wider problem. It became a flag, a "red rag" to the Stalinist bull, of symbolic protest. Its sharp incisive analysis was too easily glossed over. Modzelewski would interpret this response as the *Open Letter*'s moral appeal. Cohn-Bendit's response and his anarcho-libertarianism helped spawn "Anti-Politics", arguably a very unhelpful part of the 1968 legacy (Ost: 1990).

93. Student leader Adam Michnik, son of Jewish Communist parents, was a deliberately singled out target. For reflections on his "shock" at this development see Michnik, 1987: 203-5. Attempts to link students and workers in Poland in 1968 are described by Andrzej Gwiazda and Joanna Duda-Gwiazda. (Supplementary interview Appendix to my PhD thesis, available at https://kclpure.kcl.ac.uk/ws/files/129644633/2020_Rose_John_1641033_ethesis_version_for_Pure_upload.pdf). The Gwiazdas discuss their opposition to antisemitism in Gwiazdas, 2008: 50-56). Andrzej Gwiazda as a Solidarity leader is discussed later in this chapter.

94. "It is said that an eventual revolution in Poland would inevitably lead to Soviet armed intervention, the result of which, from the military point of view, is not open to doubt. Those who advance this view assume that everything takes place in 'one country in isolation' which, by way of exception is torn by class struggles while in neighbouring countries there are no classes but only regular armies...planes and tanks" (Kuroń and Modzelewski, 1966:55-6).

95. What was needed was an updated *Open Letter* after 1968. What that might have looked like is the subject of the concluding sections.

96. Zbigniew Kowalewski email communication 10/9/2017: Kowalewski, a Lodz Solidarity regional leader and the movement's most prominent revolutionary socialist: "I told the story of Kuroń mocking me and dismissing the *Open Letter* in the journal, *Nowy Robotnik*, no. 7 (22), July-August 2005. He said I am 'a shnook (frajer) that still believes in the follies/foolishnesses/ stupidities/idiocies (głupstwa) we wrote, Karol and me, in the *Open Letter*.'" Kowalewski's interview with me is based on informal conversations then followed by email exchanges (A-ZK: 258-269). He is fluent in English.

97. This gave it a scientific as well as a moral foundation. See section V for how this might have been developed. The assertion of a Christian context for Marxism has its roots in the intellectual journey from Marxism to Christianity of Poland's most famous dissident, the former Communist, Leszek Kołakowski. For a very useful discussion about Kołakowski and his influence, see the interview with Andrzej Friszke, arguably Poland's foremost historian of the Solidarity movement: Friske and Koczanowicz, 2018. Jacek Kuroń and Adam Michnik would attempt a similar journey in the 1980s.

98. This Polish dissident magazine was produced in Paris. The article was republished by the French dissident Communist journal *Politique aujourd'hui*. Stathis Kouvelakis kindly provided me with an English language extract from the article.

99. The source here Jan Józef Lipski, one of KOR's founders, a dissident with roots going back to the Polish Socialist Party before World War Two. His book is the most comprehensive history of KOR.

100. Another KOR founder, Antonio Macierewicz, cannot be given the attention here he deserves. He represented the Polish scouting tradition which had a unique political role in Poland's long and troubled history of national resistance to foreign occupation. Macierewicz's scout movement, the wonderfully named *Band of Vagabonds*, would play a progressive role in KOR at the beginning (Lipski, 1985: 18, 48) but its nationalist roots would eventually precipitate a hardening of attitudes to the left (Lipski, 1985: 202-3).

101. Michnik here references a Kołakowski essay, "In Praise of Inconsistency" (Kołakowski, 1964).

102. Lipski testifies to the relentless daily persecution of KOR activists in every way possible. Constant police beatings, as well as "anonymous" beatings, arbitrary arrests over fictitious crimes, reckless and wrecking house searches, occasional unexplained murders, harassment and victimisation at work, harassment of KOR family members. Regardless of the politics, the immense courage of KOR activists is beyond dispute.

103. Michnik and Kuroń's journey towards Catholicism would end in unmitigated disaster. See Michnik's "Introduction" in *The Church and the Left* in Ost: 1993.

104. See the discussion in Chapter 1, section III.

105. "And this was more broadly the banner under which a lot of 'dissidents'

from the Eastern bloc fought. It can also be seen as a reaction to the top-down 'politicisation' of all social spheres imposed by the ruling bureaucracy. The literary texts of the period also bear testimony to this trend (withdrawal into the 'private sphere', importance of individual and moral issues etc)", Stathis Kouvelakis, email communication (19/04/19).

106. And the women were in advance of the men. Solidarity was born in Gdańsk in part due to the solidarity strikes from non-shipyard workers. A tiny minority of Gdańsk women workers in solidarity with other women strike leaders like bus and tram drivers' leader, Henryka Kryzwonos, halted an exclusive agreement for the Gdańsk shipyard workers only. "Wałęsa ... smelt the anger and swiftly changed his mind" (Ash, 1983: 41). The full story is told in Polish writer and director, Marta Dzido's magnificent film about the Women of Solidarity, *Kobiety Solidarności.* https://www.youtube.com/watch?v=tAmcnAw4Cu0 (English language subtitles). The film includes fascinating interviews with Henryka Kryzwonos as well as Andrzej Gwiazda and Joanna Duda-Gwiazda.

107. I interviewed Andrzej Gwiazda and his wife Joanna Duda-Gwiazda, also a founder of the Free Trade Unions which preceded Solidarity, in November 2017 at their home, a tiny flat in a tower block, still overlooking the remnant of the port at Gdańsk, Solidarity's birthplace—seen clearly in Marta Dzido's film.

108. He means when I interviewed him in 2017. See my additional note, "Andrzej Gwiazda and Joanna Duda-Gwiazda, tragic symbols of Solidarity's crisis and defeat," Rose, 2020: Appendix: 253.

109. See also "Gwiazda, the toughest Solidarity negotiator with the government, Gdańsk 1980", Rose, 2020: Appendix: 256, on forcing the release of Kuroń from prison.

110. "Activists at all levels ... and rank-and-file members wanted self-governance above all" (Modzelewski, 2021: 425).

111. Kapuściński, 1982: 76, cited in Ost, 1990: 9.

112. I interviewed Józef Pinior in the Polish city of Wroclaw in November 2017. Pinior, well known throughout Poland, famously concealed the union's funds, 80 million zlotys, just before martial law was declared in December 1981. It is the subject of a book in Poland, *80 Milionów: Historia Prawdziwa*, by Katarzyna Kaczorowska, Wroclaw journalist with the city's newspaper, *Gazeta Wrocławska*. I would like to thank Matthew La Fontaine for obtaining this electronic document for me. Matthew was my indispensable Polish language translator in Poland. Józef Pinior told me that the film of *80 Milionów: Historia Prawdziwa*, credited the book. This Hollywood-style film was a Polish candidate for the Oscars. Pinior became a leader of the underground resistance to martial law before his eventual arrest (Bloom 2015: 405).

113. Modzelewski confirms Pinior's legendary status in the movement. See (A-JP: 287) and Modzelewski, 2021: 354.

114. See Stefan Auer, 2006, on Hannah Arendt and the 50th anniversary of the 1956 Hungarian Revolution and its workers' councils. Auer concluded: "It is useful to remind oneself of the open-ended nature of all genuinely political projects, including our attempts at understanding revolutions. 'The lost

treasure of revolution', to use Arendt's unforgettable phrase, may never be found, but this should not prevent us from trying." See Arendt 2006: 5.

115. See comments about him today in Rose, 2020, Appendix: 232.

116. See also his interview with Bloom, 2015: 195.

117. I interviewed Jan Rulewski in Bydgoszcz in November 2017.

118. 1979-81, see Chapter 4.

119. The Shah of Iran, deserted not just by the people, but by the police and army too. Finally, he fled the country in 1979; see Chapter 4.

120. To be found in the full interview in Rose, 2020: Appendix (A-JR: 289-97).

121. See the comment in biographical notes about his Senator's role today (A-JR: 297).

122. I met Andrzej Słowik at Solidarity's Lodz office in November 2017. The planned interview didn't take place because of a misunderstanding over the strength of Andrzej Słowik's spoken English language. Nevertheless, we agreed to email exchanges with a Polish translator: and later a face-to-face interview in Warsaw.

123. Słowik's personal memoir, *Nie Kracz Słowik, Nie Kracz* (Narodowe Centrum Kultury, National Centre of Culture, 2014), based on interviews with Polish journalist, Jaroslaw Warzecha. I would like to thank Jacek Szymanski for translating excerpts from this book. The title "Nie kracz Słowik, nie kracz" means "Do not caw, Słowik, do not caw." It's a little ironic because "słowik" means nightingale. These are the last words recorded when the last meeting of the Solidarity National Commission (KK) was closed, late at night on 12 December 1981. Soon afterward the majority of the National Commission was detained by police as martial law was imposed. Słowik explains: "When the meeting of the KK was already closed the chairman Mirek Krupiński said: 'See you at the next meeting.' 'We'll see each other if we make it—I replied—because the next meeting would not come.' 'Don't caw, Słowik, don't caw', said Krupiński and these were the last words recorded on a reel from the KK meeting before martial law" (Warzecha 2014: 135-136). See also Barker, 1986: 92-93.

124. This echoes Władysław Frasyniuk's view of the revolution as "moral renewal".

125. Andrzej Friszke, Poland's most authoritative historian of Solidarity 1980-81, cites US Intelligence sources on how seriously the US government was taking the threat of Soviet intervention in Poland and the dangers thereby posed to "Cold War stability" (Friszke, 2014: 487).

126. The interview almost descended into farce. Frasyniuk seems to chastise Rulewski for not hitting the policeman back after the first police assault at Bydgoszcz, unready for the rough and tumble of working class life. Unlike street fighting boy Frasyniuk, who declares himself "lumpen-proletarian", a self-portrait which I challenged. See the full interview in (A-WF:232-41).

127. The division between minority "Fundamentalists" and majority "Pragmatists" in Solidarity is usefully discussed in Barker,1986: 118-19.

The Fundamentalists included independent Marxists who analysed Polish "Communist" society along the lines of the original *Open Letter* of Kuroń and Modzelewski.

128. The Fundamentalists' most important strand, the one demanding *active strikes*, is discussed in detail in the next section.

129. Josef Pinior and Zbigniew Kowalewski took the Congress programme very seriously and its demand for workers self- management (A-JP: 286-7), (A-ZK: 267-68).

130. Nowak, who was detained under martial law, sought to develop a "non-Marxian historical materialism": see Nowak, 1983, and Brzechcyzn, 2022.

131. Email communication 15 February 2018, A-ZK.

132. The description of the hunger march is from Kowalewski's book *Rendez-nous nos usines!* (Give Us Back Our Factories!). English language translations and extracts, authorised by Kowalewski, were reproduced in pamphlet form by the group *Socialist Action* in the US in 1988, referenced here. (Kowalewski, 1988).

133. There was a widespread belief in Solidarity that food shortages, at least in part, were the result of secret food exports to Russia. Jan Rulewski discusses this in A-JR: 289-97, where he also discusses his role in Solidarity's own Food Commission.

134. The first paragraph here is taken from Andrej Słowik's interview–memoir (Warzecha 2014), the rest is from my email interview (A-AS: 298-309). Many thanks to Jacek Szymanski for translating extracts of Słowik's memoir as well as the email interview-conversations with Słowik.

135. "But not the formation, the idea was mine, and was elaborated entirely by me in the booklet signed by me individually, *On the Tactics of the Active Strike. [O taktyce strajku czynnego,* Zaklad Malej Poligrafii ZR Ziemi Lodzkiej NSZZ "Solidarność", Lodz, 1981]. The idea—the text of the booklet—was approved by the Lodz regional executive. Both Słowik and Palka supported it firmly." Zbigniew Kowalewski, email communication, 16 February 2018.

136. Słowik also briefly discusses the role of women—a majority of the workers (A-AS: 300). It is clear that the pressure for active strikes was coming directly from the women, who were bearing the brunt of the food and other shortages.

137. The discussion here is based on translated extracts from Friszke, 2014.

138. Bogdan Lis was a comrade of Wałęsa and Gwiazda from the Committee for Free Trade Unions in Gdańsk that preceded Solidarity, also a Communist Party member (Bloom, 2015: 403).

139. Słowik was hounded by the authorities. In our conversation in the Solidarity Łódź office in November 2017, despite the language difficulties, he told me how he has discovered, following the opening of the archives at the Institute of National Memory, the extraordinary level of surveillance (24/7) he was under in 1981. He also seems to have been deliberately singled out for punishment when he was jailed after martial law. He gives a chilling

description of what amounts to the torture he was subjected to—and his resulting hunger strike in Warzecha 2014: 173. He has been pursuing a court case against a particularly brutal prison officer for the past fourteen years. (Details in email communication, 30 January 2018, A-AS) The first neoliberal Solidarity government also recognised his immense prestige in the movement when they offered him a post as Deputy Minister of Labour to Jacek Kuroń. Wisely, or otherwise, he accepted. He told me how his worst moment came when he faced a riot of the unemployed ...

140. This is an edited version of my email conversations with Zbigniew Kowalewski, (A-ZK: 257-268), reproduced here as a continuous narrative.

141. KOR filled this vacuum with disastrous results.

142. The two "Trotskyist" traditions dominant in the early 1980s were the Fourth International led by Ernest Mandel and the *International Socialism* tendency led by Tony Cliff. For a thorough discussion of both see Callinicos, 1990.

143. Ost is here summarising Michnik, *Takie Czasy* (Warsaw: Nowa 1986: 26-32); Ost, 2005: 41, n11.

144. See *Andrzej Gwiazda and Joanna Duda-Gwiazda, tragic symbols of Solidarity's crisis and defeat* in (Rose, 2020, Appendix: 253) Joanna Duda-Gwiazda explained in the film *Women of Solidarity, Kobiety Solidarności,* "The Round Table [negotiations between the former Communist government and some of the former Solidarity leaders] was a huge success for the Solidarity elite who sorted out something for themselves, and sorted out something for the country. Free elections, freedom of the press etc. But if you look at it from the labour union's point of view, the Round Table was catastrophe." Ascherson describes the "Gwiazda group" drifting towards the Polish nationalist right in the 1990s (Ascherson, 2005).

145. Callinicos relies on Harman, 1990 as the main source of his analysis here.

146. Or to be exact: he described his analysis as a "fusion of the analyses of Tony Cliff and Kuroń and Modzelewski" (Harman, 2009: 375).

147. See Lipski's fascinating account of the *Black Book of Censorship in the Polish People's Republic* (Lipski, 1985: 212-217).

148. In the most recently translated edition of Lenin's What Is To Be Done, "Workers as the advanced fighter for democracy" (Lih, 2008: 744-759).

Chapter 3

149. "Legally classified by the government of being of mixed descent" (Johns and Davis, 1991: xi).

150. http://www.anc.org.za/content/does-freedom-charter-mean-socialism (**Editors' note:** at the time of publication, this link no longer appears to work, but a photograph of the document can be found at http://historicalpapers-atom.wits.ac.za/uploads/r/historical-papers-research-archive-library-university-of-witwatersrand/1/7/7/177970152efd7f62cc4b1aad111f21cedff a5503cd9193cdc5720d6212713a4e/AG2887-A2-47-003-jpeg.pdf)

151. The pass law protest had been initiated by the ANC's less influential rival, the PAC, the Pan-Africanist Congress. Unfortunately, it is not possible here to discuss the significance of the PAC.

152. Strictly speaking "re-introduced": the "stay-away" had a long and distinguished history in worker and community struggles with communities giving the lead (Webster, 1981).

153. "Ramaphosa began work as legal adviser at ... CUSA at the beginning of 1982 ... Unlike its competitor FOSATU, it reserved leadership positions for black activists" (Butler, 2007: 130-1). For this reason CUSA has been linked to the black consciousness movement. However, it was broadly based and included underground ANC supporters.

154. The display of Ramaphosa's statement at the Workers' Museum in Johannesburg illustrates its emblematic significance.

155. COSATU and the UDF called it jointly. I described it as a "hybrid" between a stay-away and a strike in an email discussion with Eddie Webster (9 August 2018). Webster was a pivotal figure in the studies of the black workers' movement.

156. The authors issued a warning: "In a post-apartheid society these class contradictions are likely to come sharply to the fore ... Trade unions which emphasise their representative role ... could easily be seen as opponents of the new state's attempt at national development" (Fine and Webster, 1989: 272-3). They didn't anticipate the incorporation of the trade unions into the state.

157. The 20th anniversary of the Battle at Cuito Cuanavale was the subject of a commemoration lecture by ANC government minister, SACP Central Committee member and former MK commander, Ronnie Kasrils, at the University of Rhodes in 2008 (Kasrils, 2008). Ronnie Kasrils is also an interviewee with this project.

158. COSATU would be incorporated into the political process that would now unfold as part of the Triple Alliance, T/A, of ANC/SACP/COSATU. The period 1989-1994 was also subject to a rising tide of strikes and stay-aways justifiably compared with 1985-89, but with the difference that the T/A was firmly in control and was able to use the volatile mass movement to further its negotiating strategy: Ceruti, 2021—a point also discussed by the Trotskyist interviewee Darlene Miller.

159. Alec Erwin, leading "workerist" intellectual, also a former General Secretary of FOSATU, predecessor to COSATU, where he became its Education Officer. Erwin also held various ministerial appointments in the post-apartheid governments of Mandela and others.

160. My emphasis in italics and it worth noting that Foster's original speech is far more powerful than Alec Erwin's recent summary of it (Erwin: 2017). See also Webster, 1985: 253: "The growth of an organised challenge from the shop floor ... pushed forward the invisible frontier of control of the workplace. The reduction of the formal powers of the employer ... threatened management's traditional presumption that workers have no right to participate in the ... planning of production." Webster, 1985 is regarded as "a landmark study" in the field (Botiveau, 2017: 284, n12).

161. However, Foster also made a comparison which will later require further thorough analysis: "The most appropriate comparison is with that of the guerrilla fighter who has to develop the strength to resist daily, the knowledge of his terrain that will give him every tactical advantage and the support for those for whom he is struggling. Probably of most importance, because both the worker leaders and the guerrilla are fighting a powerful enemy, is the development of a sense of when to advance and when to retreat" (Foster, 1987: 232).

162. Bethuel Maserumule, former "workerist" leader, metal workers' union shop steward and organiser is scathing about Erwin. He told Kally Forrest, historian of the union, that Erwin's politics were reformist, "broadly social democratic and he had abandoned even the two-stage philosophy but was loathe to admit it" (Forrest, 2011: 428)—an assessment of Erwin shared by a former apartheid minister, see n48 below. In his conclusion Erwin complains that after the fall of apartheid, "the workerist leadership missed a major opportunity to build working class power" (Erwin, 2017: 251), without making any attempt to assess his own role in the failure. Maserumule's many insights into "workerism" are illustrated during my own interview with him, discussed later in this section.

163. Nevertheless, Erwin concedes, however vaguely, something was going wrong by this stage. By joining the SACP, former "workerist" leaders "increased access ... to the top decision makers [ie the ANC high command]. Given the exigencies of the time, this had many parallels with a 'war cabinet' type situation. In hindsight, though, this situation laid the basis for later inadequacies in building ... working class organisation ... the relationship with the SACP, as a purportedly class-based party, should have been thought through. Key COSATU leaders such as Jay Naidoo stated time and again that the unions were not a conveyor belt for the ANC" (Erwin, 2017: 250-51).

164. Exactly as predicted by Fine and Webster, 1989.

165. Inkatha very nearly succeeded in splitting the resistance movement and plunging the country into a racial civil war even after Mandela had been released and the ANC and SACP had been unbanned. Inkatha battalions were used regularly as strike breakers and as murderous paramilitaries to crush township unrest. Unfortunately, this critical part of the struggle against apartheid cannot be discussed here, but see Piper, 2002.

166. "The tendency to mechanically apply the principles of trade union politics and organisation to the broader political struggle ... using the trade union movement as a model, critics of the UDF allege a lack of democratic control from below" (Slovo: 1988). Slovo's position is even more exposed because we know that the SACP leadership in exile were extremely well informed about COSATU—as is clear from Ronnie Kasrils's interview.

167. Lenin defended at the 3rd Congress of the Communist International, the Comintern in 1921, the highly contested and innovative united front initiative launched by some German communists, the *Open Letter to German Workers' Organisations* (Riddell 2015: 1061-1069). This was an intervention with economic and political demands in the reformist trade union federation, as well as the wider labour movement. The attempt to politicise the federation was quite explicit.

168. By 1991 Slovo was distancing himself from *What Is To Be Done?* admitting it had been "our organisational bible" (Legassick, 2007: 549).

169. That this coincides with a Stalinist conception of party organisation with a professional full time leadership giving instructions to the party members, described by Moses Mayekiso as "commandist" (A-MM), must be noted here, but a wider discussion is not possible. Slovo, in any case, here avoids any serious assessment of the Russian Revolution, Lenin and the Bolsheviks.

170. Kally Forrest's discussion of the "workerists", Gramsci and the party is summarised in my conclusion.

171. Metal workers' union historian Kally Forrest recommended Maserumule to me as one of the most militant and left wing of the former rank and file "workerist" leaders.

172. This argument would particularly apply to the growth of the UDF, heavily influenced by the ANC, in the townships.

173. Maserumule, like Moses Mayekiso, makes a special mention of Chris Hani, former MK chief of staff and general secretary of the SACP at time of his assassination in 1993. See concluding section.

174. There were 5.8 million strike days in 1987 in contrast to nearly 1.5 million strike days in 1986, 1 million in 1988 and falling; nevertheless, Claire Ceruti cautions: "Government statistics excluded 'political' strikes: the graph's decline in 1988 disguises 9-million person-days lost that year to massive stay-aways, including the first successful three-day stay-away in 27 years, called by COSATU against the new Labour Relations Act (LRA)" (Ceruti 2021: 105). However, as we saw earlier, the government still felt confident enough to impose the LRA.

175. This was despite a 90 percent ballot in favour. There was fury at rank and file level—including illegal unofficial strikes, for example the Witbank Ferrometals smelter (see section IV below). The NUMSA leadership's retreat is likely to have influenced its passive attitude to the miners' strike the following month.

176. Butler, Ramaphosa's biographer, provides vivid descriptions of this relationship including how Anglo saw the potential of a black NUM undermining the strength of the white mineworkers' union and how they preferred Ramaphosa to the "workerist" leader, Moses Mayekiso, and the metal workers' union which was also seeking to establish a base in the mines (Butler 2007: 137-9). On Mayekiso, see section III.

177. See *Inqaba Ya Basebenzi*, 24-25, October 1987 available at https://rob-petersen.info/looking-back/1981-1990-inqaba-ya-basebenzi/ The MWT had been expelled from the ANC in 1985 and Slovo attacked them in his document quoted earlier. In the early to mid-1990s, they had good relations with many leading worker and trade union activists not least James Motlatsi and Cyril Ramaphosa. Rob Petersen, editor of *Inqaba Ya Basebenzi* at the time, discusses this in his interview with me, as does James Motlatsi. The MWT had helped arrange a visit to Britain for Motlatsi during the 1984-5 British miners' strike, via the South Wales miners and the Militant Tendency, their sister organisation in Britain. Rob Petersen, then in Britain, was involved in detailed political

discussions with him and describes the close relations at the time, which Motlatsi qualified, but nevertheless confirmed to me. The MWT were a factor, as, of course, were the "workerists", in forcing a shift in position by sections of the ANC and SACP in exile with the launch of a secret project Operation Vulindela ("open the way"), more commonly known as just Operation Vula, involving Ronnie Kasrils amongst others. This was unambiguous recognition that the internal struggle was outstripping the external struggle. "South Africa faced nothing less than an internal revolution", and the ANC and the SACP were not there to take full advantage of it (Butler, 2007: 230-31). Martin Legassick, MWT leader and its chief historian, cites a leading source claiming that Operation Vula by-passed those on the ANC National Executive Committee "wedded to crass militarism" (Legassick, 2007: 427).

178. Abraham Agulhas, former president of the CWIU, Chemical Workers Industrial Union, and COSATU executive member at time of the miners' strike says that, in his opinion, COSATU made no effort to organise solidarity in his industry (personal conversation, Cape Town, 21 May 2018).

179. There is a useful summary of what happened here: http://news.bbc.co.uk/today/hi/today/newsid_9694000/9694645.stm

180. I'm excluding a possible third strand, the Marxist Workers Tendency, which, by this time, had been successfully marginalised following their expulsion from the ANC. Their propaganda continued to be taken seriously by other socialists and communists but they lacked a strong enough base in the workers' movement to influence events. This point is discussed in my interviews with both Rob Petersen and James Motlatsi. Again, see both interviews for Motlatsi's own relations with the MWT.

181. This contrasts starkly with Jo Slovo's failure to mention COSATU's "extraordinary growth and achievements" and hence political potential in his 1988 paper cited earlier.

182. https://www.sahistory.org.za/archive/sechaba-october-1987

183. "What did emerge was active assistance provided to SACTU leaders John Gaetsewe in London and Archie Sebeko based in Manchester, by a group of Martin Legassick, Paula Ensor, Rob Petersen and Dave Hemson. The group assembled a range of experience with Legassick an internationally acknowledged historian, Ensor and Petersen who had experience in the formation of independent workers' organisations in the Western Cape, and Hemson who had been a participant in the 1973 mass strikes which spurred the revival of trade unions and political resistance. The group advocated the development of workers' leadership and socialist policies in the struggle against national oppression. In a short time this became highly contentious owing to what was regarded as presenting a 'independent perspective', factionalism and a workerist (rather than national liberation) agenda. A pity because they had a lot to offer" (A-RK: 318). SACTU, South African Congress of Trade Unions, was the SACP dominated trade union federation that had preceded FOSATU and COSATU a generation earlier but still had a presence in the new trade unions.

184. "At the same time, it should not be denied that focus on MK, and its rising military activity, was a major preoccupation of the Party along with

the ANC and created a militarist deviation at the expense of political work in both cases. Even prior to the influx of the 1976 generation the liberation movement's focus was on armed struggle and this undoubtedly affected even the Party's response to its condition of isolation. This meant that the concentration of effort and resources went into armed responses to the violence and brutality of the regime. Undoubtedly if this had not been the case the Party might have been in a better position to influence the rising tide of working-class struggle. I use the word 'might' since how sure can anyone be that a different outcome could have taken place specifically regarding the strike movement of that time?" (A-RK: 319).

185. Seekings, 2000, and Van Kessel, 2000, are two of the most important studies analysing the UDF and the township uprisings, including Alexandra.

186. This was also the SACP position: see Slovo discussion earlier.

187. Bell's reference is an interview Mayekiso gave to *Socialist Worker Review* magazine in 1985—Mayekiso, 1985. Using a pseudonym at the time, it was Peter (today Kate) Alexander who conducted that interview with Mayekiso. Kate Alexander recalls Moses Mayekiso, worker intellectual: "He knew that capitalists exploited workers and probably had an understanding of the labour theory of value; he had decided that white workers were not the enemy; he knew that workers (implicitly black workers) had the power to smash apartheid if they were sufficiently organised; and he had a vision of a socialist society that was based on a different model to that of the Stalinists. He was aware that the struggle would be strengthened through combining workers and youth/community in a common struggle (though I don't know if this was theorised); he was also an internationalist of some sort (though I can't recall details); and he probably rejected sexism. Perhaps, importantly, he linked theory and practice, doing so in an original way through the workers' charter, and he challenged the unions' acknowledged 'intellectuals'" (Email communication 30/8/2019).

188. This point in particular pre-occupied the judge at the treason trial. He pressed Mayekiso repeatedly on it. Mayekiso gave several alternative explanations, including an explicit denial that he was encouraging people to defy the Alexandra legal court system (Abel, 1995: 354). I would like to thank Charlie Kimber, current editor of *Socialist Worker* (who worked underground in South Africa for the Mayekiso solidarity campaign), for locating and producing photocopies of this vital evidence in a historic trial.

189. Here is an extract from my full interview about Moses's treatment whilst he was in prison during the trial: **"How long were you in prison?** Almost two years. 12 months in solitary confinement. **How did you withstand pressure of solitary confinement, mentally?** Mentally, sometime you feel you [are] cracking. **Were you able to read?** Only the Bible: I read the Bible from cover to cover (Bursts out laughing). **Were you able to exercise?** An hour of exercise. The only people to talk to were the prison guard and the police who were investigating the case. **Were you beaten?** Not physically beaten but tortured. Sometimes they make you stand for whole day whilst they are cross-questioning you. Sometimes you say you want to go to the ... they say, no we are too busy. They are testing your capacity to resist. They want you to say what they want you to say. There was no torture like electrocution, beatings no, no. I

think what helped [were] the protests mounted by the workers" (A-MM: 347).

190. Sipho Kubeka, a trade union organiser with PPWAWU, Paper, Printing, Wood and Allied Workers Union, constantly harassed by the apartheid authorities.

191. **Editors' note**: on 16 August 2012, South Africa police shot dead 12 striking miners at the platinum mine at Marikana, a massacre that recalled some of the worst state violence of the former apartheid era.

192. See the discussion about Chris Hani in the concluding section of this chapter.

193. "Social movement unionism" has become a widely accepted concept applied to black trade unionism's involvement in local community struggles. Raphael Botiveau reviews some of the relevant scholarship, with claims that it also "aimed at transforming society" (Botiveau, 2017: 10-11, 90). Yet whether it is more useful than the older concept and idea of "solidarity" is debatable, especially when infused with Marxism's taken-for-granted assumption that the workers' movement takes a lead in community struggles. Certainly, social movement unionism's intellectuals and scholars have remained curiously silent about the failure of solidarity between metal workers and miners during the 1987 miner's strike, surely a failure of social movement unionism too. As we shall see, for different reasons, von Holdt also challenges its credibility. Karl von Holdt has confirmed to me by email that he cannot recall any discussion about the August 1987 miners' strike amongst the shop stewards or other workplace activists at Highveld Steel either just before or during the strike.

194. Maserumule noted the absence of political discussion at Highveld but also seemed to welcome the emergence of the strike committee (A-BM: 331). Von Holdt writes that a version of socialist ideas only emerged after 1989 in relation to the "new strategy of reconstruction". In other words, a "socialist" defence of the Triple Alliance government. He quotes shop steward Nhlapo's ferocious attack on what he saw as SACP ideological dishonesty (von Holdt, 2003: 288).

195. See *Inqaba Ya Basebenzi*, 24-25 at https://rob-petersen.info/wp-content/uploads/2018/06/Inqaba-24-25-Oct-1987.pdf

196. World Bank South Africa, April 2018 https://www.worldbank.org/en/country/southafrica/overview

197. South African apartheid's last white president, F W De Klerk, boasted about how successfully Keys "played" the ANC leadership. Kasrils quotes De Klerk praising the "wonderful work" of Keys "winning the confidence of the ANC". Keys apparently said of his ANC deputy minister, "God gave me the gift of this communist." The name of that deputy minister was Alec Erwin, former FOSATU, COSATU and of course "workerist" leader (Kasrils, 2017: 236).

198. At issue was the counterposing of the Manuel's neoliberal perspective, later called GEAR, the Growth, Employment and Redistribution programme, to the ANC's RDP, Reconstruction and Development Programme, as well as policies being developed by the ANC's think tank MERG, the Macroeconomic Research Group, led amongst others by Marxist economics scholar, Ben Fine.

199. Jordan was one of the very few independent Marxists in the ANC leadership.

200. "As for Mandela, it has long been understood that it was his trip to Davos in 1992, for a meeting of the World Economic Forum ... that changed his mind about the ANC's economic principles. Meeting the world's business and political elite, he reported, dissuaded him from pursuing radical economic policies. Unless South Africa joined the global free market economy and avoided the disasters of socialism ... the country would suffer economically, investors would be frightened off, and South Africa would face isolation like Cuba or become a failed state like Zimbabwe. No doubt the collapse of the Soviet Union and, before that, signs of failure in the socialist East European bloc would have raised Mandela's concerns in prison" (Kasrils, 2017: 237).

201. Legassick is quoting Slovo from the SACP magazine *African Communist*. Slovo was criticised in the same magazine by Pallo Jordan, amongst others (Legassick, 2007: 641, n182).

202. Bethuel Maserumule in an email to me clarifying his remarks about Chris Hani wrote: "Regarding the reflection on our discussions with comrade Chris Hani: I thought I was saying that we challenged him around two issues: multiclass alliances, to which he said they experimented with various forms of alliances, to win more forces on to the side of the struggle. We also engaged him around the revolutionary process and its phases. He pointed out that they believed in stages and not revolution as one big step, and was willing to hear about our view. I must have stated that we felt encouraged by his open attitude towards debate, that he was not defensive. I wished under such circumstances to have had more time for dialogue with him" (A-BM: 334-5).

203. Hani was not in Lesotho throughout this period. He left in 1982 as South African state security attempts on his life increased (Smith and Tromp, 2009: 5).

204. Ronnie Kasrils, one of his closest comrades, insists that Chris Hani continued to believe in the leading role of the party "but not in the dogmatic sense that it was a right. It would have to win and prove that it warranted a vanguard role. Moeletsi Mbeki was correct to say that Chris believed that the party did not have a sole right to what was or was not true socialism. Chris was tolerant and flexible of rival views, that differences needed to be debated and the acid test was in the praxis. The fall of the Berlin Wall did have lessons... to be more open, democratic" (Email communication from Ronnie Kasrils, 10/9/2019).

205. Inexplicably, Hani's biographers then quote a British journalist, John Carlin, who wrote: "by the time of his death, [Hani's] political vision had mellowed into something more closely resembling [Labour Party leader] John Smith's than Fidel Castro's" (Smith and Tromp, 2009: 269), the same John Smith who certainly did believe that deals with capital were possible.

206. South African sympathisers of the British SWP—today called Keep Left—joined the SACP during this period. "We joined the Johannesburg Central branch, which was undergoing a revival of its fortunes and some good people were joining. It was an open atmosphere ...We continued to publish our magazine and sell it in the branch ... Problems arose for us however when we challenged the neoliberal management of Johannesburg Council's SACP mayor

... It was not long after this that the heavy weights marched into the branch and set up the expulsion of a leading comrade. The dynamism in the branch soon petered out" (Email communication 16/11/2019). Botiveau's account of the SACP takeover of NUM in the 1990s is all about "discipline...mechanically imposed on the union ... and a critical reduction of internal debate" (Botiveau, 2017: 245-6).

207. Quoted in Callinicos, 1988: 180.

208. Whether Turner, who helped to initiate the independent unions in Durban in the early 1970s, would have become more influential we shall never know—he was assassinated in 1978. For a brief and sympathetic introduction to Turner see Legassick, 2007: 15, 37-38.

209. The discussion that follows takes the prospect of a negotiated settlement as context in the late 1980s. This is an easy "hindsight" perspective but it needs qualifying. The unbanning of the ANC and SACP and the release of Mandela in 1990 took all sides of the resistance movement by surprise. All sides, including "workerists", former "workerists", the MWT and other Trotskyists groups and the UDF, ANC, SACP, COSATU were discussing, at the same time, armed insurrectionary tactics and strategies. All were struggling with the problem summed up by Karl von Holt: "The democratic forces were very weak militarily" (Legassick, 2007: 425). Legassick quotes von Holdt's remark as part of an excellent wider review of the different positions, including the shifting line of the ANC/SACP summed up by Kasrils (Legassick, 2007: 413-428). Of course, it should be added that the negotiated settlement, which led to black majority rule after a democratic one person one vote election, was a tremendous victory, whatever its limitations, which was itself partly a result of the complex and contradictory mass insurrectionary movement which included its military wing—however weak.

210. "Wabenzi" is the nickname given the new African ruling class driving around in Mercedes-Benz limos in postcolonial Kenya.

211. He also called for communities to establish armed militia: "Parliament and Revolutionary Democracy: Debating the Constitution for a New South Africa", *South African Labour Bulletin,* 14, November 1989 (pp37-38), cited in Legassick, 2007: 433.

Chapter 4

212. Muslim scholars and preachers.

213. I have adopted the English spelling of Fadaiyan from Behrooz, 2000. The Fadaiyan launched its guerrilla campaign with an attack on a police station in a village called Syahkal in northern Iran, on the edge of the Caspian Forest, in 1971. It was to be the opening salvo in a low-level military insurgency which would dominate the decade. The Mojahedin felt compelled follow them (Behrooz, 2000: 61).

214. "Unlike the secular forces ... the clergy had the comparative advantage of possessing invaluable institutional capacity ... over ten thousand mosques ... Young Islamists, both boys and girls as well as young clergymen, linked the institution of the ulama to the people ... in the mosques higher level decisions

were disseminated to both the activists and the general public" (Bayat, 1997: 37).

215. To give just one example, the strike committee at the strategically important oil refinery in Abadan, Khuzestan, the oil rich province in the south of the country, there were just five secular leftists on the 40-member strike committee (Jafari, 2018a: 73). Following the OSCC intervention, a communique from "striking employees from the oil industry in the south" called for victory for Khomeini's "holy struggle to overthrow the illegal government" (Jafari, 2018a: 78).

216. For Khomeini's Paris interviews with journalists guaranteeing democratic freedoms, see Rahenma, 2005: 1iv.

217. "This was driven by the social justice motive within Islam ... You had people coming to power ... [with] high ideals about the 'just society'. The challenge for us is that when you talk to uneducated people in the working class, it was difficult to explain clearly the difference between what you want and what the government wants" (Bijan, A-B: 378).

218. The Mojahedin would now begin to turn into a reactionary cult, supporting Saddam Hussein in the Iran-Iraq war, and today a puppet of the US administration.

219. Bayat describes mosques as "institutions of leisure". Those workers in his surveys with leisure time (20 percent) went to the mosques, not least because they were the only places, compared to sporting events or cinemas, which were free. He cites similar surveys making the same point. Bayat concludes that this "reflects the contradictory position of workers towards Islam. They both are and are not religious". Islam is a practical reference point for "their socio-cultural activities". Workers interpreted Islam in their own way "to fit with their own socio-economic and political ends" (Bayat,1987: 50-1).

220. This article was first published in Panitch, Leys, Albo, and Coates, eds, 2001.

221. Rostami-Povey cites an example of the latter in Shariati's riposte to conservative apolitical clerics who believed true justice for the world meant waiting passively for the return of the "Twelfth Imam", a key spiritual figure in Shia Islam. Whereas according to Shariati, Islamic political action now would hasten his return (Rostami-Povey, 2010: 91-2).

222. Organisation of Iranian People's Fada'i Guerrillas, OIPFG, *sazman-e cherikha-ye fada'i-ye khalq-e Iran* (Behrooz, 2000: 51). According to Behrooz, Farrokh Negahdar led the pro-Tudeh Majority split in 1980, which supported a conciliatory position towards the new regime, regarded as "progressive" (Behrooz, 2000: 106, 109, 116). Farrokh Negahdar did not deny this description when I put it to him.

223. This argument that the defeat of Nasser by Israel in 1967 was a defeat for radical secular nationalism and a spur to political Islam throughout the Middle East and North Africa is raised by Anne Alexander and Mostafa Bassiouny, who, in turn, reference the argument in Arabic by the Egyptian revolutionary socialist Sameh Naguib: Alexander and Bassiouny 2014: 19, n38.

224. Torab Saleth was its national secretary *(dabir-e sarasari).* Immediately after the revolution it was campaigning openly. In his interview with me,

he emphasises how small was their group—nearly 100—only 30 he would describe as cadres. But because their ideas, as he saw it, fitted with the most advanced workers' struggles and their mood of the time, they were able to grow to over 600—over 400 were workers. The two key slogans: socialist revolution and united shora organisation (A-TS: 409 n412).

225. They would be nurtured by the regime. One writer has likened them to *Arbeitsfronts* in Nazi Germany, "while creating an atmosphere of terror in the workplace, they moved to ideological indoctrination of the workers" (Rahnema, 1992: 73).

226. Unfortunately, it is not possible here to give this question the attention it deserves.

227. Khomeini had launched the IRP, the Islamic Revolutionary Party: "Tied to the IRP were the bands of *chomaqdars* (club wielders) who called themselves *Hezbullah* (Party of God ... [Later] The bands ... invaded the universities, injured and killed members of political groups who were resisting the cultural revolution [launched in April 1980], and burned books and papers thought to be unIslamic" (Moaddel, 1993: 213).

228. "Theses on Political Work amongst Women" (Riddell, 2015: 1009-1025): a "vigorous struggle" must be "conducted against all prejudices, customs and religious practices that bear down on women. This agitation must also be addressed to men ... apply the principle of women's equal status to the raising of children, family relations and public life ... try to win support of exploited working women engaged in small shops, cottage industries, and rice, cotton and other plantations" (Riddell, 2015: 1026).

229. There was also a problem with a lack of internal democracy within the Fadaiyan. Important questions like the women's question were not properly debated. See the remarks of Kobra Qasemi, women's representative in the Ahwaz oil employees' city wide shora in Khuzestan (A-KQ: 403).

230. Following the Iran-Iraq war, the reform movement would challenge the regressive legislation on women's rights with an equally challenging and progressive re-interpretation of Islam: See "Reversal", Poya, 1999: 94-122.

231. Of course, the Fadaiyan had not organised the occupation, it was Islamist students. But the fact that Ali Pichgah thought it was the Fadaiyan is an interesting measure of their perceived influence, even if illusory. In fact, the occupation helped exacerbate the pro-Tudeh split in the Fadaiyan.

232. On Yadollah Khosroshahi, see n96 below.

233. See section I of this chapter above.

234. "As Abrahamian makes clear ..., public recantation played a key role in the Islamic Republic's search for legitimacy" (Cronin, 2000: 235).

235. Abrahamian (1993: 73) cites Goodey, 1980.

236. I am grateful to former Paykar member Mansor Parhizgar for drawing my attention to this remarkably under-recorded development. Abrahamian, for example, ignores it. In his interview with me, Mansor insists that "Paykar was amongst the first to resist the closure of *Ayandegan*, a daily newspaper dating

back to last period of Shah's period, it was semi-independent, quite radical and critical" (A-MP: 390).

237. https://www.youtube.com/watch?time_continue=3&v=CYvQjCncbrI

This is a video made in November 2018. It shows Rieneke Van Santen, Executive Director of Zamaneh Media in ZamanehGala, a Dutch independent media and human rights NGO. In the video Van Santen provides a horrific account of prison conditions in Iran at this time, late summer 1979, in particular the way prisoners like Kobra could hear the screams of fellow prisoners facing execution.

238. See Kobra's description of this development, in section IV.

239. "As a result of their Stalinist training, not one Marxist group or organisation in Iran in practice respected the right of individual members in internal disputes" (Behrooz, 2000: 160).

240. A damning criticism of the Fadaiyan was its approach to Marxist education: "For example, throughout the period under study, the main reference text on the history of the Russian Revolution was a Persian translation of *History of the Communist Party of the Soviet Union (Bolsheviks)* written in the 1930s. The text offered Iranian Marxists a highly distorted version of Russian history which endorsed the actions of the Bolsheviks, led by Lenin and Stalin, while condemning their opponents ... Very few of Marx's original writings were available and studied" (Behrooz, 2000: 160, 161).

241. Kobra added the following about Stalinism: "I had read many books, many 'romances', novels, from Russia. From my reading I discovered that people are not happy in Russia. They have many questions. They realised they are not really free. I raised these questions in the cell and they said how dare you say these kind of things! Do you know better than our leaders?! I also said that there were differences of opinion about politics within the Soviet Union. They said no, no—there is only the decision of the party. I said that there had been differences of opinion even within the Soviet regime, within the Russian Politbureau at the time of the Shah—about selling weapons to the Shah. Nobody knew about this. When I said it means there is also another voice in the party [the Soviet Communist Party at the time], they didn't know that. They said how dare you say this. So I found the article [from the Soviet press] and I showed them ... I had heard of Trotsky. There had been lots of discussions in the universities and amongst the political groups who for a short period were able to openly promote their ideas in the universities and on the streets. When I asked about him I was told he was against Lenin. I knew two Trotskyists. They were not bad boys but no one liked them, but I was interested in their questions" (AKQ: 403).

242. "Kurdish leader Shaykh Ezzedin Husayn sent Shariatmadari a message of support. In Baluchistan [the Sunni Muslim province bordering Pakistan], the governor was taken hostage and fighting broke out. Baluchis charged that the governor, an outsider, was staffing local offices with his cronies. Far more important, the Baluchi religious leader Mowlavi Abdul-Aziz Mollazadeh accused the revolutionary guards of molesting women during their house-by-house search to disarm the Baluch; guns so seized, it was charged, were being given to local Shi'ites" (Fischer, 2003: 236-8).

243. As we saw earlier, Taleqhani, like Shariati, had openly defended Marxist principles, arguing that "Islamic social justice is consonant with the Marxist position on the distribution of property, wealth and other resources" (Rostami-Povey, 2010: 30).

244. Yadollah Khosroshahi helped create the Syndicate of Oil Workers in the 1970s. He was jailed by the Shah, but released, along with others, in 1978 when demonstrations against the Shah began. Khomeini's regime would arrest him again in early 1982, along with other leaders of the Shora of Oil Industry Employees *(Showra-ye Sarasari-ye Karkonan-e san 'at-e Naft)* following its suppression. A number of them were executed and others sentenced to long imprisonments. Khosroshahi was released in March 1983 and fled the country (Jafari, 2018b: 519). He later died in London. See also Khosroshahi's comments about Taleqhani. Whilst in no way disparaging Taleqhani, Khosroshahi reflects that his influence, which included persuading the bazaaris to raise funds for strikes, made workers too reliant on the bazaaris (Khosroshahi: 2013).

245. Jafari counted five separate Fadaiyan newspapers in Khuzestan aimed at different sections of oil workers both in terms of specialisation as well as different locations, for example refinery, drillers, gas, petrochemicals (Jafari, 2018b: 456).

246. However, this was a double-edged outcome. The workers' victory here was also a victory for the hard-line Islamists in government who backed widening Islamic state control over private industry.

247. An American writer for a highly regarded Middle East research unit, MERIP, Middle East Research and Information Project.

248. The left had failed to unite the shoras, but their increasingly formal Islamisation did provide unity, the US Embassy occupation proving to be the perfect facilitator. "The Islamic Labour Shora representing 128 shoras in Tehran factories organised a demonstration on 23 December 1979 in which tens of thousands of workers participated ... It called for the continuation of the struggle against American imperialism, extradition of the Shah ... the abolition of capitalism and plunder" (Jafari, 2018b: 476-7). In February 1980, the Islamic labour shoras held their first national conference. Many of the main speakers explained that the concept of shora was Islamic not Marxist, and that shoras should strive to achieve harmony between workers and employers. At the same time, though, the demand for workers' control persisted. Legislation would quickly follow turning the Islamic shoras into consultative bodies hence attempting to restrict workers' influence on managements (Jafari, 2018b: 479, 480). However, the formal Islamisation of the shoras, legally sanctioned, proved to be no guarantor of "peaceful" industrial relations. Worker militancy persisted, as did demands for workers' control: the IRP itself developed a left wing to accommodate these developments. For example, see discussion at fifth congress of Islamic shoras, June 1982 (Jafari, 2018b: 501, 502). Meanwhile the national oil workers' shora organisation was officially suppressed in January 1982 with about 140 oil worker activists arrested and, in some cases, executed. Yadollah Khosroshahi was one of the oil workers' leaders arrested.

249. There is the further explanation that in modern capitalism this stratum is more susceptible to working class pressures. They are no longer simply

bourgeois specialists but rather they are ambiguously placed in the class structure, in "contradictory class locations", according to an important theory developed by Erik Olin Wright. For a discussion of this theory and Wright's later rejection of it, see Callinicos, 2004: 219-26.

250. Which meant ultimately the government's interest. As we saw in Chapter 2 above, exactly the same tensions arose in Poland's Solidarity movement.

251. See also Jafari's agreement with Rahnema over the role of the white-collar specialists in the oil industry (Jafari, 2018b: 542).

252. Several thousand questionnaires were filled in by wage workers and over a thousand workers were interviewed. 24 large industries with over 20,000 employees were covered (Rahnema, 1992: 70, fn2).

253. Azari Turks speak Farsi with a Turkish dialect and comprise the largest ethnic community in Iran after the dominant Fars ("Persian") (Moghadam, 1985: 153). Unfortunately, neither Javad nor Moghadam discuss the Tabriz revolt in late 1979 raised in conclusion in section III.

254. Moghadam's comments are also relevant here. She had asked Tabriz worker shora leader Javad about his family life and the importance of religion: "It should be noted that the Khomeini phenomenon notwithstanding, anti-clerical sentiment within large segments of the population, rural and urban, is longstanding, and can be found in the poetry of Hafez and in popular jokes. Javad's response to my query confirmed this view. 'My mother and father didn't like clerics; they didn't like beards,' he laughed. His parents were, however, believers: 'My mother always prayed.' His father became religious, he said, only as he grew old, because 'he was afraid of what might happen after he died.' The family observed religious periods, such as rowzeh, but otherwise they were, in Javad's own words, 'anti-clerical'" (Moghadam, 1987: 154).

255. And even less impact on the much larger rural poor. In a simple but revealing analysis of the class structure of Iran in the 1970s, Abrahamian recorded 32 percent of the population belonging to the urban "lower classes", 45 percent belonging to the rural "lower classes", composing landed peasants, near landless peasants, landless peasants, rural unemployed (Abrahamian, 2008: 140).

256. Lenin would have said the same about Kautsky; nevertheless, the point stands.

257. There is an enormous literature on this subject. I reference some of it in Rose, 2015.

258. See also Rose, 2013.

259. This was not so far-fetched. In 1923 the factory councils, led by the German Communists, would lead a mass revolutionary movement of hundreds of thousands of workers, successfully call a general strike, independent of the trade union leaders, and topple a particularly unpopular government: Rose, 2016.

260. Sections of the SPD leadership were just as bloodthirsty and ruthless as some of their Iranian political Islamist counterparts when it came to

eliminating the Marxist left. In January 1919, SPD right wing Defence Minister Gustav Noske, working closely with the Freikorps, "nationalist death squads with swastikas on their steel helmets", was associated with the murder of Luxemburg and Liebknecht and many more ((Hoffrogge, 2014: 195).

261. The argument here assumes the emergence of a coherent Marxist party during this period that would have campaigned for a united shoras' movement society-wide, which, of course, did not happen. The organisation most likely to form the core of such a party, the Fadaiyan, in fact split. Both the left-wing oil workers' leaders I interviewed, Ali Pichgah and Yadollah Khosroshahi, point to the absence of such a party as a fundamental weakness in the shoras' movement.

Chapter 5

262. I would like to thank Sean Purdy, independent activist in PSOL, Party of Socialism and Liberty, Brazil, since 2004 and David Karvala, leading member of Marx 21, Spain for translation assistance and advice on this chapter. You can read Sean's own account of the history of PT, the Workers' Party of Brazil, in a Jacobin magazine round table discussion with Mike Gonzalez and others at: https://www.jacobinmag.com/2017/05/lessons-earned

263. "Articulacao", Articulation, a group of leaders, close to Lula, who "sought to portray themselves" as defenders of PT against "two extreme wings: right wing moderates ... a liberal opposition...and left-wing radicals", (Sluyter-Beltrao, 2010: 134). "Articulation" included some members of the former urban guerrilla organisation which had fought the military dictatorship in the late 1960s and early 1970s, Acao Libertadora Nacional, ALN, (National Liberating Action). Their story is well told by Kenneth P. Serbin in a book whose title sums up their evolution: *From Revolution to Power in Brazil: How Radical Leftists Embraced Capitalism and Struggled with Leadership*. Nevertheless, their later political collapse should not be used mindlessly to scorn their earlier endeavours. These were part of a world-wide trend partly taking their cue from Che Guevara and the Cuban Revolution which inspired revolutionary movements as diverse as those in South Africa and Iran. However strategically and tactically mistaken, they displayed exemplary courage in the face of ruthless dictators and sadistic torturers who murdered many of their comrades.

264. Saad-Filho and Morais, 2018: 45-6, describe the Constitution's impressive social-democratic content, already a partial victory for PT.

265. The "B" in the ABC region of São Paulo, identified as the newly industrialised militant core base of the workers' movement, A for Santo Andre, B for São Bernardo de Campo, C for São Caetano do Sul.

266. Gilson Menezes, cited by Riethof, 2018: 90.

267. *Pelego*, "literally 'saddle cover', the blanket that is put between the horse's back and the saddle. This was name given to trade union leaders who were often appointed by the minister of labour" in the military government, Bensaïd, 2013: 347, n4.

268. Rossi interview in Mészáros, 1991: 48. Unfortunately, there is no space here to explore this fascinating phenomenon in more detail but an idea of its impact was illustrated during a famous gathering at the Morumbi stadium in 1980, hosting a visit by Pope John Paul II, to be joined by Waldemar Rossi, and with an anticipated TV audience of 120 million people. Given an advance copy of Rossi's proposed speech, the tottering military government and the Pope and his entourage insisted that sections of the speech must be excised. The truncated sections would have spoken of the "fascist, corporative and vertical model", which inspired Brazil's labour codes and which "represses and impedes the independent organisation of the workers". Rossi had also noted how in Brazil, "capitalism imposes violent conditions of work, it subordinates and corrupts, it decides its own laws. It is the savage capitalism of the multinationals", Mészáros, 1991: 200. Riethof also recognises Rossi's influence, "An essential figure of the new unionism movement", Riethof, 2018: 94.

269. Sluyter-Beltrao discusses this as an example of "social movement unionism".

270. See Alex Callinicos on Bensaïd in Callinicos, 2012.

271. For a very useful introduction, see Bensaïd, 2013 chapters 10 and 11: "Crying for Argentina" and "Restrained Violence".

272. The breakdown of relations between Mandel and Moreno is well-captured by Mandel's response to Moreno's book-length rejection of the perspectives proposed for the Eleventh World Congress of the Fourth International in 1979. Amongst the countless accusations and counter-accusations is an argument between them about democracy in the "socialist" countries. This argument would have particular resonance ten years later, highlighted below, when Lula and his allies challenged the idea of the "dictatorship of the proletariat" because of its alleged association with Stalinism. Mandel contemptuously quotes Moreno who had written, "One of the most important tasks of Trotskyism is to educate the world working class in the recognition of the existing proletarian dictatorships ... that they are much more democratic than any imperialist democracy", https://www.marxists.org/archive/mandel/1979/06/moreno.html. It should be noted that Mandel himself also defended China, Cuba, Vietnam and the former Yugoslavia as proletarian dictatorships by claiming they were not Stalinist: Callinicos, 1990: 46.

273. Bensaïd, 2013, Chapter 15, *"E agora, Zé?"*

274. Inexplicably, the Workers' Party sent some of its cadres to East Germany for training courses. This included some of Daniel's comrades from the FI. Some of them were in Berlin when the wall fell in 1989. Daniel's comrades "saw the bureaucracy charged with explaining to them the mysteries of the dialectic fall to pieces, ending up in a flood of tears", Bensaïd: 2013: 21, fn1.

275. I would like to thank George Paizis for assisting with the translation from French to English.

276. It was Francis Weffort, leading political scientist at the time, advisor to PT, who integrated Marx's famous one-liner into PT's perspective and who then linked it to Lula's 1989 presidential campaign in a discussion about PT

for *Teoria e Debate*, PT's theoretical magazine, in September 1988. See also Keck, 1992: 246. "Weffort put into accepted neo-Marxist language what Lula and his fellow workers knew by instinct," Kucinski, 2003: 27. Weffort helped to clarify "the party's political-ideological definition ... complex, not only because of the conditions under which the party was born, but also because of the world-historical moment at which it came to maturity," Keck, 1992: 246.

277. Trotskyite Workers' Fraction (FOT), a small organisation formed out of Lambertist dissent; the FOT was influential mainly because its leader, Paulo Skromov, president of the São Paulo Leather Union. Lambertism is a current of orthodox Trotskyism in France that developed a weird synthesis of theoretical dogmatism (sometimes forcibly imposed), anticlerical republicanism, and deep entry into mainstream social democracy: see Mestre, 2021.

278. Cited in Bensaïd, 2007. See the discussion of this article as well as Bensaïd's evolving disagreements with Ernest Mandel in Kouvelakis, 2016. See also Harman and Potter, 1977, where like Daniel Bensaïd they conclude that the Third International failed to provide clear guidelines on the question but take a position that Lenin had considered before the successful 1917 October revolution in Russia: "recognising that the Bolsheviks were still a minority in the working class, he stated that if the other socialist parties were to form such a government the Bolsheviks would act as a 'loyal opposition' which would continue to criticise its failings in front of the class. The Bolsheviks would take no responsibility for its policies and maintain their independence from it." Hence a clear distinction from the Mandel/Bensaïd/Machado perspective: ruling out participation in such a government.

279. See also Valério Arcary's 2018 interview with Alex Callinicos, Arcary, 2018. I also have had the good fortune to interview him twice (24/07/20, 9/10/20)

280. In 1982 Moreno formed his own "International", the Internationalist Workers' League (LIT), following the split with Mandel's FI: Almeida Ribeiro de Miranda 2014: 151.

281. Email interview 6/12/20.

282. "A band of professional activists who want to use the workers as pawns in ugly spectacles of factory occupations carried out at the cost of destroying machines": PT and CUT leaders quoted in the magazine *Quinzena*, No. 88, March 1990: 7; Sluyter-Beltrao, 2010: 291, fn15.

283. Interview with Valério Arcary (24/07/20).

284. Valerio Arcary's interview *Teoria e Debate*, 1990, No.10.

285. *Ação e Razão dos Trabalhadores da General Motors de São José dos Campos. São José dos Campos (SP) Action and Reason of the Employees of General Motors of São José dos Campos:* Interview Moacyr Pinto Da Silva, 26/9/2020.

286. Today Renato is a member of PSOL, Socialism and Liberty Party, while Toninho is a member of PSTU, United Socialist Workers' Party. Both are derivatives of Socialist Convergence. According to Renato the division between the two organisations resulted from what position to adopt to the impeachment and removal from office of former PT President Dilma Rousseff in 2016.

287. This is an extract from an interview with Renato. Interviews (September 2020) were carried out with Renato, Toninho and other workers politically active in the 1980s and early 1990s in Brazil.

288. Email from Zé Maria 20/10/20. He later became a key leader of the PSTU.

289. See also Secco, 2018: 136.

290. Unfortunately, the phenomenal rise of MST cannot be explored here. For an excellent brief summary see Gonzalez, 2019: 142-7. The assassination did not halt the land occupations which grew from 30 in 1988 to 62 in 1989; Secco, 2018: 136.

291. On 11 September 1973, General Pinochet staged a military coup and forcibly removed the democratically elected socialist President of Chile, Salvador Allende, from government.

292. Sluyter-Beltrao also quotes this speech, in 2010: 186, fn24.

293. A constant warning from Valério Arcary about the dangers of misunderstanding or ignoring the division in the Brazilian working class between registered and non-registered workers cannot be explored here. Nevertheless, his warning must be put on the record. The growth of PT and the left in the working class was based mainly amongst registered workers with contracts with their employers, a minority. The majority worked in small workplaces without contracts, or were self-employed, casually employed and a significant additional number involved in criminal activities. Arcary also stresses a lack of secondary education and literacy amongst a majority of workers who migrated from the countryside in the 1970s and 1980s as an additional contributing factor creating problems for the Left (Interviews 24/07/20, 9/10/20).

294. Machado, 2012 (in the original, the second paragraph is a footnote to the first). Secret campaign slush funds, the *caixa dois*, "were a well-kept secret for many years ... revealed publicly only in 2005 ... an elaborate and centrally organised party financing scheme...in many PT led city halls, who extracted money from firms that bid on municipal contracts", Hunter, 2010: 103.

295. "Neo-liberalism was not simply an economic strategy. The creation of a global system in which no obstacles ... were placed in the way of the movement of capital required both cultural hegemony and political control", Gonzalez, 2019: 12. See also Upchurch, 2020, on "extractive capitalism".

296. The layer of earth immediately below the surface soil consisting predominantly of minerals and other materials such as iron and aluminium compounds.

297. A reluctant Lula leadership did finally put itself at the head of a mass movement to bring down Collor but it would serve as the finale for those type of confrontations.

298. Interview with Valério Arcary, 9/10/20.

299. Fernandes, 1991, analysing the 1991 PT Congress.

300. Interview with Valerio Arcary 9/10/20. Email clarification 26/04/21.

301. São José dos Campos was understood as a conservative city. It was the site of the GM workers' occupation and in his book Moacyr Pinto da Silva reports on the difficulties raising support for the GM workers there.

302. Interview with Valério Arcary (24/07/20).

303. See also Bensaïd, 2013: 226-28, for an excellent discussion of this impressive woman political activist. The deep disillusion of key members of PT's Fourth International cadre is powerfully expressed in the "Letter to the comrades of Democracia socialista (DS PT) Brazil", signed by Michael Löwy, Daniel Bensaïd, Francisco Louçã, https://www.marxists.org/archive/Bensaïd/2005/01/dspt-brazil.htm

304. A famous quote from Lenin about supporting reformist parties or trade union leaderships in united fronts.

305. Orthodox Trotskyism preserved Trotsky's original analysis that the Soviet Union remained a workers' state albeit a "degenerated" one. Hence from this perspective the implosion of the Stalinist system in 1989-91 cleared the way for capitalist restoration, and in that sense, Trotskyism could also perceive it as defeat. At the very least, confusion dominated the ideological fall-out on the Trotskyist left at the very moment when clarity was essential. The inconsistencies of the degenerated workers' state position, of course, formed the basis for Tony Cliff's recasting of Soviet Communism as state capitalism. A useful summary of these arguments and their implications can be found in Callinicos, 1990. Unfortunately, these arguments did not form part of the discourse for Brazilian Trotskyism.

306. Van der Linden on Poland's Solidarity movement (van der Linden, 2003: 66, 79); Byrne, Ulrich, van der Walt, 2017: 254-273 on South Africa's "workerist" movement and syndicalism; Bayat on the Iranian revolution's workers' shora movement discusses comparisons with syndicalism (Bayat, 1987: 146); on the early phase of the Brazilian workers' movement under the dictatorship see Moisés, 1982.

307. The classic view of revolutionary syndicalism is usually associated with Georges Sorel's perspective of the revolutionary general strike: "it counts on expelling the capitalist from the productive domain, and on [workers] taking their place in the workshop". The state is seen as the protector of capitalism hence the objective of the revolutionary general strike is "to suppress the state" (Sorel, 1950: 167). However, in practice syndicalism has taken many forms which does not take confrontation with the state for granted. Van der Linden cites research on the emerging trade union movement in France at the start of the twentieth century where revolutionary syndicalists relied on the "liberal state they despised" intervening on behalf of strikers to help force the employers to make concessions (van der Linden, 2003: 77).

308. Bayat based this explanation on James Hinton's description of syndicalist influence on the revolutionary shop stewards, workers' shop floor representatives, in Britain during the First World War: Hinton, 1973.

309. Darlington quotes Gramsci, 1977: 327, 182-4.

310. I would like to thank Eddie Webster for pointing out to me the importance of this paper.

311. The education programme of the Putilov works committee, a vital base for the Bolsheviks, was discussed briefly in Chapter 1.

312. Colloquium "Social Change from Below", 12-14 June 2019, Centre for Social Change, The Future Reimagined, University of Johannesburg, organised by Kate Alexander, then Research Chair in Social Change and Director of the Centre for Social Change.

313. Interview withheld from publication.

INDEX